HEAVEN AWAITS *the* BRIDE

HEAVEN AWAITS *the* BRIDE

ANNA ROUNTREE

Most Strang Communications/Charisma House/Christian Life/Siloam/FrontLine/Realms/Excel Books products are available at special quantity discounts for bulk purchase for sales promotions, premiums, fund-raising, and educational needs. For details, write Strang Communications/Charisma House/Christian Life/Siloam/FrontLine/Realms/Excel Books, 600 Rinehart Road, Lake Mary, Florida 32746, or telephone (407) 333-0600.

Heaven Awaits the Bride by Anna Rountree
Published by Charisma House
A Strang Company
600 Rinehart Road
Lake Mary, Florida 32746
www.strangdirect.com

Cover design by Rachel Campbell; Executive Design Director: Bill Johnson

Library of Congress Cataloging-in-Publication Data

Rountree, Anna.
Heaven awaits the bride / Anna Rountree.
p. cm.
ISBN 978-1-59979-174-6 (trade paper)
1. Heaven--Christianity. I. Title.
BT846.3.R68 2007
248.2'9--dc22

2007015319

This book was previously published by Charisma House as *The Heavens Opened*, copyright © 1999, ISBN 0-88419-598-8; and *The Priestly Bride*, copyright © 2001, ISBN 0-88419-766-2.

08 09 10 11 12 — 10 9 8 7 6 5 4 3
Printed in the United States of America

To God the Father,
God the Son, and God the Holy Spirit,
who gave the revelation, commissioned the book,
and to whom we offer it in love,
praise, and thanksgiving.

To Jesus, our great High Priest
and our eternal Husband.

Contents

PART I

Revealing a Fresh Vision of God's Love for You

This section is an amazing and beautiful revelation of the place that He has gone to prepare for us and where we will spend eternity. Of the many recent books written about our future home, none reveal so clearly the glory of God that awaits us if we are faithful to Him during the days of testing that many have already begun to experience. You will read it more than once, and you will want to share it with all your friends. You will not be able to put it down!

—Gwen Shaw
End-Time Handmaidens

In this exciting section, Anna Rountree will help to take you beyond the veil into a realm where holiness, obedience, and unconditional surrender are the qualifications that will take you into the very presence of the Lord. She shares the importance of living a life of worship that has caused the heavens to be opened in her own personal life, bringing fresh understanding of the angelic realm that has also taken her into the very throne room of God.

—Suzanne Hinn

Part I

Contents

Revealing a Fresh Vision of God's Love for You

Truly, truly I say to you, you shall see the heavens opened…
—John 1:57

Chapter One
The Attack

The sound was ancient and terrifying.

Startled, I spun around to see a colossal battering ram relentlessly moving under its own power across a desert basin.[1] Its wooden wheels were at least sixty stories high, and they groaned and yawned under the extreme weight they bore. Blasphemies were carved into its black battering arm, the end of which was the iron head of a goat.[2]

God's judgment against sin has begun with His household, the church (1 Pet. 4:17; Rev. 14:7). His purpose is to separate the weeds from the wheat of the living and true church (Matt. 13:40–43; 1 Cor. 11:18–19; Rev. 18:2, 4).

Although it moved slowly, people on the desert floor seemed helpless to avoid its path; they were crushed as it rolled over them.[3] Screams filled the desert valley and ricocheted off distant rock formations, filling the desert basin with terror.

Slowly the battering ram topped a sandy hill and began to pick up speed going down the other side. Breathless from shock, I clawed with my hands and dug with my feet into the deep sand of the hill in order to reach the top and watch its path.

It picked up tremendous speed as it plunged down the other side of the hill into a deep valley. In its path at the bottom of the hill was a walled city. Both city and wall were the color of the sand and seemed to be half sunk into it, almost reclaimed by the sand from which they had come. In faded lettering on the side of the wall I could read: THE CHURCH.[4]

The adobe walls represent that which is constructed by "the flesh" of religious people whom God calls "dust" (Gen. 3:19; Jer. 17:5) and who are powerless against Satan and his hordes (2 Cor. 10:3–4; Isa. 31:1).

The battering ram was massive, and the adobe wall of the city did not look strong. With brutal impact, the goat's head smashed into the wall and continued through it. It plowed through houses and buildings,

1. The battering ram with the iron head of a goat (Lev. 17:7; 2 Chron. 11:15, "satyrs") symbolizes the satanic attack that God permits to come against the false church in the spiritual wilderness (Rev. 17:3–5). He did the same thing to apostate Jerusalem (Ezek. 21:21–27; Rev. 18:8).

The king of Babylon in the Ezekiel passage above represents Satan, who was the power behind the throne of the earthly king of Babylon, even as Satan was in the case of the king of Tyre (Ezek. 28:2, 12).

2. In the last days before the Lord Jesus returns, the false church will be in league with the Antichrist, who is called "a scarlet beast, full of blasphemous names" (Rev. 17:3; 13:1), and who is the personification of Satan, the "great red dragon" (Rev. 12:3). The Antichrist and his armies will turn upon this whorish church and destroy her by fire (Rev. 17:16).

3. The man-controlled organization that calls herself "the church" is centered upon the things of this world and seems oblivious to any impending judgment of God against her. This also was the case with the people in the days of Noah and in the city of Sodom (Luke 17:26–30). This church will not understand what God is doing (Matt. 24:39).

4. The false church is called "Babylon the Great" (Rev. 17:5) because she is the final form of the satanically inspired, religious system that began in the days of the tyrant Nimrod to exalt herself through witchcraft and idolatry (Gen. 10:8–10; 11:1–4). This first Babylonish church used bricks instead of stone to build her city, even as today's Babylonish church builds herself up with man-made materials instead of relying upon Jesus Christ to build her with living stones (Matt. 16:18; 1 Pet. 2:5).

losing little of its speed. When it broke through the wall on the opposite side of the city, it slowed to a stop, settling into the sand.

A strange silence fell.

Occasional screams broke this silence. They came from those who had been mutilated or from those who recognized that a loved one had been killed. But stranger than the silence was the fact that few sought to escape across the rubble of the wall—few.

Then slowly, all by itself, the battering ram turned and began to start up the hill again, moving in my direction. The goat's head on the end of the ram was laughing, exhilarated, as if drunk with blood.

I thought it might see me, so I left the top of the hill and began to run in the opposite direction. As I ran, I frantically scanned the desert basin for a hiding place. I could hear the huge wheels laboring as they carried the battering ram toward the top of the hill again.

Suddenly an angel began to fly beside me.

"Where can I hide from the battering ram?" I shouted as I ran.

"The battering ram rolls relentlessly over all the earth now. Up high," the angel said, "up higher than it can see is the only safe place. Let me show you."

The Escape

Jesus Christ is the ladder or "the way" into heaven, for "no one comes to the Father but through [Him]" (John 14:6).

With a wave of the angel's hand, a stairway appeared, touching the earth and reaching beyond my view into heaven.[5] I moved to the base of the stairs and looked up. I was still heaving from running.

The angel flew beside the stairs, higher than its base on Earth, and waved me upward: "Come on!" the angel shouted. "The ram is coming, and we don't want him to see this stairway. Come on!"

There were no hand rails on the narrow stairs. The stairs were clear like glass, which can be slippery. I could hear the battering ram rolling; although I was still panting, I began to run up the stairs.

"Faster!" the angel called.

The scarlet cord that is secured to the first section of the stairway into heaven represents the first stage of redemption through the cross of Calvary (Josh. 2:18).

I kept my eyes on the stairs. In his hands the angel had a scarlet cord fastened to the stairs at the bottom.[6] I could hear the battering ram getting closer, but the angel pulled the cord and brought up the first section of the stairway, like attic stairs that can be lowered and raised.

"Hurry!" the angel urged.

I continued to run up the steps, breathless. The angel pulled the thin rope, and another section of the stairs rose.

"Keep climbing," the angel said, although now his tone of voice was less urgent.

With a mighty effort, I completed the stairs and turned to make sure I had indeed escaped. The battering ram was directly below, rolling beneath us as the third section of the stairs was pulled up.

The second section of the stairway is the second stage of redemption through the cross of Calvary.

"You were safe after climbing the second set of stairs; but to be *really* safe, you needed to pass the third,"[7–8] he said.

The third section secures one's position in the heavenly realm with Christ "far above all rule and authority and power and dominion" of the enemy (Eph. 1:21).

As the battering ram rolled past, I tried to catch my breath and settle myself. Only then did I look around.

"Where am I?" I asked.

Paradise

"Paradise," the angel smiled, as he tied the cord holding the stairs to a docking post.[9] A sign above the post read STAIRPORT.

The word *Paradise* means "park or garden." The Father designed the true Garden of Eden there especially for the Lord Jesus (Song of Sol. 5:1; 6:2; Ezek. 28:13). In His garden the original tree of life still grows (Rev. 2:7).

I looked out over the most beautiful park I had ever seen. There were gentle rolling hills, beds of subtly colored flowers, and grass as uniform and green as the rolled lawns of English manor houses. A walking path crossed this part of the park. There were also quiet pools, a stream, and luxuriant trees that on Earth would have provided shade, but there was no shade or any shadows here. A soft light emanated from everything growing.

5. In Genesis 28:12–13, Jacob dreamed that "a ladder was set on the earth with its top reaching to heaven" with the angels of God ascending and descending on it. The Lord, in His preincarnate form, was standing above it.

He told the first disciples that they would see the heavens opened and the angels ascending and descending upon Him (John 1:51).

6. This is the shed blood of Christ that releases us from guilt and separation from God that was caused by our sins (Rev. 1:5). The way is now open to the throne of God by faith (Heb. 10:22) through hope (Heb. 7:19) in the Lord Jesus.

7. It is the release from the power of sin by the death of the totally corrupt corporate spiritual heart of the human race. This happened when the old human race died with Christ on Calvary. God gives those who would believe in His Son a new heart that lives by the resurrection life of the Lord (Eph. 2:10; Rom. 6:6–8; 2 Cor. 5:14–17; Col. 3:3; Gal. 2:20).

8. It is to live in God (Col. 3:3) the heavenly life of love, ministering to His needs (Ps. 65:4; Rev. 3:12). It is the place of the disciple who continually bears about in his body the sentence of death from the same inner cross to his own self-expression that Jesus bore daily here on the earth (2 Cor. 4:10; 2 Cor. 1:9; Matt. 16:24; Phil. 2:7). It is the final stage of overcoming the enemies of God, where the soul life (mind, emotions, and will) of Christ Jesus is being imparted to the believer (Matt. 16:25). It is the place of the overcoming Christian in every generation (Rev. 2:7, 11, 17, 26–28; 3:5, 12, 21). The disciple who overcomes the world, the flesh, and the devil as the Lord Jesus overcame them seeks only the living God, in comparison with whom all things are as rubbish (Rev. 3:21; Col. 3:1; Phil. 3:8).

9. The area where one arrives first when entering heaven is called Paradise. One then moves on to the celestial city—the heavenly Jerusalem—and finally to the throne of God the Father (Heb. 12:22–23). Jesus promised the repentant thief whom they crucified with Him at Calvary that He would meet him in Paradise that very day (Luke 23:43).

"Beautiful," I thought.

"Yes, isn't it," the angel answered.

I did not seem surprised that he read my thoughts. I turned to look at him; only then did his appearance register with me. He looked to be six feet two or six feet three inches in height and in his midthirties, if I were gauging by human years. He had brown curly hair and wore a brown, transparent, full-length robe. Underneath the thin brown robe I could see that he had on blue-and-white-striped work overalls, the sort one might obtain in the store of a farming community. The thought struck me that the brown overrobe was so thin that it was probably cool to wear when working.

A coil of rope crossed his shoulder and chest, circled in a wide loop near his waist, and returned across his back to the shoulder again. He wore a white belt, from which hung a white tool pouch. This pouch looked a little like the handtool belt worn by telephone repairers. He was unlacing a pair of silver-tipped, brown, high-top work boots as he spoke to me.

Slaves did not wear shoes in households in biblical days; only the members of the family were shod (Luke 15:22). Hence, removing one's shoes in the presence of God acknowledged that one did not own or control the holy ground on which one stood (Exod. 3:5; Josh. 5:15).

"No shoes up here," he smiled. "This is holy ground." I looked down at my own feet and saw that they too were bare.

He stood up, putting the boots under his arm. "You're safe here," the angel continued. "All of that is down below."

"What was that?" I asked.

"The great enemy of our Lord and of His church."

"But it was *destroying* the church," I exclaimed.

The Two Churches

The living church on Earth is the body of born-again Christians who share a common life of glorifying and obeying the Lord Jesus through keeping His Word and through worship, prayer, and fellowship—all as energized by the Holy Spirit.

"Some of it may be destroyed—that which *calls* itself the church," he continued. "It has a sign saying it is the church, and many live behind that sign. But the church—*the real church*—escaped; the real church is alive and can run faster than any battering ram can roll. It's clumsy, really; but if you are dead stones, if you are not alive, then of course it is more than any man-made structure can resist. However, the real, living church of Jesus Christ can hide in caves, float on the water, or climb into Paradise.[10] A member of the real church will know where the hidden stairs are located. That person can call for help, and we will let down the stairs so that he can escape. The real church is more agile than the battering ram. Living stones have feet."

Then, like someone who had just remembered his manners, he said, "Would you like some refreshments? It would help you."

"All right," I said, trying to get my bearings.

A tray of fruit floated to us.[11] "Here you are," the angel said, gesturing toward the tray, "a choice."

I reached to make a selection of fruit. Some varieties I had seen on Earth, and some I had not. All were without blemish. We both made selections and began to eat.[12]

The heavenly fruit is made of God's light and is eaten by the angels and the redeemed there (Rev. 2:7).

"You need to get acquainted with the locations of the hidden stairs," he continued.

"Is there a map?" I asked.

"No," the angel laughed. "The map is in the Spirit. By your following His leading, He directs you to the hidden stairs."

I glanced toward the stairport. "These stairs look like glass," I said.

"Light," the angel replied.[13] "Nice, aren't they?"

"Do people ever fall off these stairs?"

"Not if they keep their eyes on Jesus," he chuckled, "but I wouldn't advise looking over the side. You might get wobbly doing that."

"This is good fruit," I exclaimed.

"Yup, everything's good up here," the angel said, mimicking a cowhand.

I laughed, bemused. He was not anything like my idea of an angel. "What is your name?" I asked him.

10. The living church is able to climb into Paradise in spirit and to live "hidden with Christ in God" in spirit and heart (1 Pet. 3:4; Col. 3:3) as described in the three sections of the stairway of Christ under notes 6, 7, and 8 (John 3:21; Isa. 26:12; Ps. 31:19–20). His people also are able to: (a) hide in caves in places prepared by God (Rev. 12:14), as did David and his men (1 Sam. 22:1); or (b) float on the water, as did Noah and his household during the flood (Gen. 7:23).

Christians are those who have been born again by the Holy Spirit implanting the Word of Scripture concerning salvation within their new hearts and spirits so that they have begun to experience the life, light, and love of God.

11. In heaven, whatever one asks for immediately appears because the abiding fruit of Christ's character is in everyone; all things are available in Him, as He promised (John 15:16).

12. The garden of God in heaven (Ezek. 28:13), which is the pattern for the Garden of Eden that was on the earth (Gen. 2:8–9), contains fruit trees, too.

13. Every created object and every living creation (angelic, human, animal, plant) in heaven is formed of God's light, which is substantial and can be felt and allows the divine light of the glory of God to shine through everything (Rev. 21:23; 22:5). There are no shadows there, no hint of darkness.

The Angel Azar

The Hebrew word that means "help" is *azar*.

"Azar," the angel said, "I'm the one who answers when you call for help."[14]

"Is there only one of you?" I asked.

"You mean for the whole earth? Oh no, I couldn't take care of the whole earth. We're assigned to a small number to whose call we will respond, more or less according to lifestyle. Sometimes a stunt person will need one of us all by him or herself, but usually we can handle five. The boss chooses who they will be."

"The boss?" I said.

"Well, our immediate boss, not the Lord; no, I mean the angel in charge of helps. While you are living on Earth, I'm the one who will answer your call for help. So don't take up mountain climbing," he laughed.

He amazed me.

"Had enough fruit?" he asked.

"Yes, thank you," I said. The tray of fruit disappeared.

The Suggestion

Angels only know what God the Spirit reveals to them. There are matters that Christians know but that angels do not know (1 Pet. 1:12).

"Now," the angel continued, "you can return the way you came. The present danger is past, but I would suggest that you take the path to the throne room. You must be here for a reason, but that knowledge has not been given to me. Your Father can tell you why you have come."

"My Father?" I said, glancing out into the park, lost in reflection. It seemed inconceivable, not only that I was in Paradise, but also that I could go to see my heavenly Father as a child might go to see an earthly one.

"Certainly," he said, reading my thoughts. "Just take the path."

"Does this path lead to the throne room?"

"All paths here lead to God. They are not like the paths on Earth."

I looked toward the path as if it were a distant horizon too far away to reach.

"Go on," he laughed. "Go see your Daddy. I'll be here when it's time for you to return."

I turned to search his face.

"Don't you want to know why you're here?" he asked.

"Yes," I laughingly exclaimed.

He threw up his hands and shrugged, as if to say, "Well?"

"Thank you," I said earnestly.

He smiled at me and spoke quietly, "The Creator of the universe desires your company. Don't keep Him waiting."

I smiled and showed him that I was stepping onto the path.

He called after me, "I'll be here when it's time to return."

I waved to him, acknowledging that I had heard. Then, somewhat breathlessly, I set my face toward the throne room.

14. The work of certain angels is that of rescuing believers from danger as described in Psalm 91:11–12: God gives "His angels charge concerning you, to guard you in all your ways. They will bear you up in their hands, lest you strike your foot against a stone." An angel of help rescued Daniel from the lions (Dan. 6:22) and Peter from jail (Acts 12:11).

Chapter Two Sandcastles

Much to my amazement, the path on which I had begun to walk seemed to be in motion, like a conveyor belt or a moving sidewalk. I looked down at my bare feet standing on its smooth, advancing surface.[1]

In heaven no one wears shoes, for all the ground there is holy to God (Dan. 10:6; Rev. 1:15).

It was then that I noticed another pair of feet beside mine. I was not traveling alone. I looked up into the face of a large angel.

"Hello," he said formally.

"Hello," I answered. He was about seven feet tall, with blond hair that seemed to have lights in it. Perhaps the light was within him and shone out through his head and then his hair. I could not tell. His face was grave with the demeanor of authority. He wore a long white robe and had large, strong, white wings.

"Who are you?" I continued.

Angel of Promises

"I am a messenger," the angel replied.[2]

The Hebrew and the Greek words usually translated "messenger" are also translated "angel."

I could feel power emanating from him. "What kind of messages do you deliver?" I asked.

"Promises," he said. "I help to bring God's faithful promises to mankind."[3]

God always keeps His promises (Josh. 21:45).

"That's a big job," I quipped. (I was hoping he'd become less formal.)

1. The angel told Moses to take off his sandals because the presence of the angel of the Lord in the burning bush made the soil there holy (Exod. 3:5). The priests who ministered in the tabernacle wore no shoes (Exod. 30:18–20).

Slaves went barefooted (Luke 15:22), but Christians are bondslaves who have freely chosen to serve their Lord and Master forever out of love for Him (Exod. 21:2–6; Rev. 22:3).

2. Angels from heaven not only carry messages, as did Gabriel to the virgin Mary (Luke 1:26ff), but they may also fulfill a special mission or represent God in some manner. All angels who are sent from heaven for a particular task or who are assigned to accompany individual believers on Earth "render service for the sake of those who will inherit salvation" (Heb. 1:14).

3. The first mention of the word *angel* in the Bible is Genesis 16:7, when "the angel of the LORD" brought God's promise concerning His multiplying of Hagar's descendants through Ishmael, her son (Gen. 16:10). This is the first of many recorded promises delivered by angels to people on Earth. "The angel of the LORD" often speaks and acts throughout the Bible for God (Gen. 22:15–18) and at times as God (Exod. 3:2, 4, 6).

When the Bible says that God "remembered His covenant" promises (Exod. 2:24), it does not mean that He had forgotten; it means that He was now going to carry forward their fulfillment in a particular situation.

"Very," he nodded stiffly.

He didn't. "So," I thought, "perhaps all angels are not alike. This spirit is very serious, like an ambassador." Suddenly I remembered that he knew what I was thinking.[4] "Have you been delivering promises on Earth?" I asked aloud.

"Yes," he said, pausing to weigh his words, "yours."

"Mine!" I exclaimed.

"Yours," he reiterated. "When you came into the kingdom, the Lord told you that you would see into heaven, did He not?"

"Yes," I answered vaguely, looking out over the passing landscape. I was searching my memory. "That was years ago."

The Promise

When I came to the Lord twenty years before, it was a time of miracles. At that time He spoke to me several promises that related to my life on Earth. Although I did not keep these pledges in the forefront of my thoughts, I realized that He was fulfilling most of them daily. But this one promise, this amazing promise, had not been fulfilled. At first I looked and longed for its fulfillment; after a time, however, immediate demands crowded out anticipation until truly I had forgotten. "Nothing happened," I continued, "and…" My voice trailed off. I started to say that I had forgotten.

"However, God has not forgotten," he said, "and the fullness of time has come."

I hardly heard him, for I was trying to piece together the past with this present.

"Being ignorant of God's ways does not negate their functioning," he said. "Of course, great unbelief does hinder."[5]

"But what does it mean?" I asked, searching his face.

"I do not have the authority to tell you. Ask your Father. The Revealer of Mysteries will reveal this mystery to you."[6]

I was lost in the wonder of it, so he continued, "Our God is faithful and true, and He loves you."

It seems that at times of great impact or distress, one can think of the most unusual things. Suddenly I wanted to know his name. "What is your name?" I asked.

"Seek for me in Scripture. Your Father wishes you to grow in confirmation from the written Word of all that you see and hear.[7] Seek for my name," he said, and then he was gone.

Jesus said that "the Scriptures . . . bear witness" of Him (John 5:39), for He is the key that opens the Scriptures (Luke 24:32).

The Tour

Before I could adjust to his sudden disappearance, I heard the distinct sound of a voice projected through a megaphone, as on a bus tour: "Pleasant hills, soft turf, cool streams . . ."

I turned to see a winged angel deftly weaving in and out of people farther ahead of me on the moving path, sort of like a ticket collector on a merry-go-round. He too had on a white robe, but on his head was a blue hat on which was embroidered TOUR GUIDE. Around his waist was a silver belt from which hung a silver coin exchanger. However, I never saw him ask anyone for the price of the tour.[8] His voice was high and as loud as a barker at a fair; he was pointing out areas of interest in Paradise. "All streams flow from beneath the throne.[9] All proceed from the same source," he said, weaving through a group of people. "We'll stop here so that you can enjoy this site."

The heavenly river of life is a picture of the flow of unending life by the Holy Spirit to every being and everything there.

The moving path stopped, and people farther up the line got off to look at the view. The tour guide turned to answer someone's question, so I too got off, walked over to a stream, and sat beside it. It was the first time I had been able to look more closely at the flora of Paradise.

4. Angels often know the thoughts of others without them needing to speak (Gen. 21:17). In heaven also one often knows the answer as soon as one asks a question. This is true because there is no sin or "flesh" there to hinder the flow of knowledge to one instantly by the Holy Spirit, for one's spirit is fully open to the Spirit, from whom nothing is hidden (1 Cor. 2:10–11; Heb. 4:13). Paul speaks of this in 1 Corinthians 13:12: "Now I know [on Earth] in part, but then [in heaven] I shall know fully just as I also have been fully known."

5. Jesus did not do many miracles for the people in His hometown of Nazareth "because of their unbelief" (Matt. 13:58). But the promises of God to the Jews will be fulfilled, for the unbelief of some people of that nation "will not nullify the faithfulness of God" (Rom. 3:3; 9:27; 11:23–24).

6. Job, Daniel, and King Nebuchadnezzar all called God the revealer of mysteries (Job 12:22; Dan. 2:28, 47). Mysteries are hidden truths known by God but unknown by others until God reveals them (Matt. 13:11; 1 Cor. 2:9–12).

7. To the two disciples on the road to Emmaus, Jesus "explained . . . the things concerning Himself in all the Scriptures" (Luke 24:27). He also "opened [the] minds [of those gathered in Jerusalem that same day] to understand the Scriptures" by telling them "that all things which are written about [Him] in the law of Moses and the Prophets and the Psalms must be fulfilled" (Luke 24:45, 44). "The Scripture cannot be broken" (John 10:35) and "stands forever" (Isa. 40:8; Ps. 119:89). God has magnified His Word according to all His name (Ps. 138:2).

8. Every firstborn Hebrew male was redeemed in order for him to be allowed to continue living—at the redemption price of five (the number that signifies grace) shekels of silver (Num. 18:15–16; Exod. 13:15). Therefore silver is a type of redemption from death through Jesus Christ. The tour guide made no charge to the people taking the tour, for the full price has been paid by Jesus on the cross. All now is by grace through the blood of the Lamb of God (1 Pet. 1:13, 18–19; 2 Cor. 9:8).

9. In the Garden of Eden on Earth, one river flowed out to water the garden (Gen. 2:10). This river was the physical representation of the one spiritual "river of the water of life, clear as crystal" that waters all of heaven, flowing from the throne of God and of the Lamb (Rev. 22:1).

Even now God grants to His faithful children on Earth to "drink of the river of [His] delights. For with [Him] is the fountain of life" (Ps. 36:8–9) that will flow out through them to others (John 7:37–39).

Because flowers in heaven are made from the light of God, and because they, with all of heaven, obey God fully, they return to their original shape after being trampled (Ps. 103:21–22; 148:1, 5–6).

The grass looked like grass, but its properties were undeniably different. You could walk on it, and it would return to its former position once the pressure had been removed from it.[10] There were several, formal plantings of flower beds near the stream, but again, these were not flowers as we know them on Earth. They were perfect.

I stretched out my whole body at the water's edge and put my hand into the stream. Cool. "But is it water?" I asked myself. "No, " I thought. "I believe it's light." A group of angels passed overhead. They were flying in a wedge formation like a flock of geese. When I returned to look at the water, another face was looking into the stream with me.

The Sandpile

"Hello," a child's voice said.

I turned and sat up to face her.

"Are you on tour?" she asked.

"Yes," I answered, staring at her. She appeared to be a child of about five or six years old, but she was shining. She had no wings, and her eyes looked old beyond the years displayed in her small stature. She wore a pale calico pinafore over a faintly colored, short shift. Her hair was curly and tousled as if from play. She looked like a little girl, but every so often I could see through her arm or leg and knew her to be a spirit. She was intriguing.

"Have you just begun the tour?" she questioned.

"Yes, I think so. Why?" I asked.

"I wanted you to come play with me," she said.

"Play with you?" I said incredulously.

"In my sandpile," she said. "Can you come?"

Just then the tour guide walked over to us, and I stood. I was torn between getting to know this small spirit and continuing my tour.

"May I go with…what is your name?" I asked her, bending over to question her as one might question a child.

The angel Crystal Clear is so named because the Lord teaches the truth through her in very easily perceived and unmistakable terms.

"Crystal Clear."[11]

"May I go with Crystal Clear for a few minutes?" I asked the tour guide.

"Oh, all right," he said. "Meet us at the almond grove when you finish."

"How will I find it?" I asked.

"Crystal Clear will show you the way."

"Yes, I will," she said excitedly. "Come along with me."

The Lesson

Suddenly we were on a vast shore line, but there was no sea.[12] It looked as though the beach was still there, but no ocean. In the sand were all manner of red and blue children's buckets and shovels.

There is no sea in heaven or on the new earth (Rev. 21:1), because the sea represents rebellion that cannot bring life but issues in death.

"Haven't you always wanted to build a sandcastle?" she asked.[13]

Jesus taught the lesson about building on sand in Matthew 7:24–27.

I chuckled, "Well, not really, Crystal Clear."

"Yes, you have," she continued. "Think about it. You've wanted to build on Earth, and all of that is sand.[14] When the tide comes in, it goes away. Even the tools for building remain longer than a sandcastle, for the tools are from God. But if you use them to build on sand instead of in eternity, what do you have? A waste of time," she shrugged. "You have wanted a sandcastle. It's silly really, isn't it?"

"I suppose so," I said quietly. I did not want to admit it, but she was right. I had wanted a home and financial security and to accomplish something—for God, of course—but I had tunnel vision for the life on Earth. I had Christianized the gospel of the world and bought into my own packaging. It was a bitter thing to hear that the focus of my

10. Flowers in heaven and on earth represent revelations of the beauty of God (Song of Sol. 1:14; 2:1; 5:13). But the true flowers in heaven are everlasting and perfect in their form, beauty, and fragrance (Heb. 9:24; James 1:17).

11. Angels who minister to particular believers on Earth (Heb. 1:14) often have names that identify each one's function. All heaven is formed of supernatural light that is substantial and transparent, reflecting the glory of God in everything everywhere (Ps. 8:1; Rev. 5:13).

12. The unbelieving peoples of the earth are often represented by "the tossing sea, for it cannot be quiet, and its waters toss up refuse and mud" (Isa. 57:20–21; Jude 13).

13. His words are "spirit and are life" (John 6:63) to those who act upon them by building upon Christ the Rock as the foundation. But those who put their hope in anything that is built on the sands of Earth will see it all swept away one day (2 Pet. 3:10).

14. "The world" is one meaning of the Greek word *cosmos,* which is used in the New Testament to denote the spiritual kingdom of Satan on the earth that is ruled by aggression, deception, lust, greed, murder, and pride (1 John 2:15–17; John 8:44; Rev. 12:9). All human beings are born into that kingdom with the spirit of evil working in them (Eph. 2:1–3). The only way to leave that kingdom of darkness is to be born again by the Holy Spirit into Jesus Christ (1 Cor. 1:30) and so be transferred out of this "world" and into His kingdom (Col. 1:13).

15. The "flesh" is one meaning of the Greek word *sarx* to denote the independent use of the earthly, outer person of soul and body. The law of sin in the members of the human body (Rom. 7:23) has also corrupted all natural expression of the faculties of the soul (mind, emotions, and will). This expression is called the old self (Eph. 4:22), and "nothing good dwells in . . . my flesh" (Rom. 7:18).

16. The copper in a penny gives it a sour taste in the mouth. Copper in the Scriptures signifies the righteous judgment of God against sin. The altar for animal sacrifice in the courtyard of the wilderness tabernacle was plated with a copper alloy, probably bronze (Exod. 27:1–2; Num. 21:6, 8–9).

The only good we have in us as believers is Christ Jesus (Luke 18:19; John 15:5).

life had been fleshly and worthless to God and that I had not gotten away with it.[15]

"Do you want to play?" she continued cheerily.

I felt a little sick. I thought I would change the subject. "Why such a large sand area?" I asked.

"Many want to build on sand, so we let them. It gets it out of their systems, you know. Maybe if you build on the sand right now, you would feel, 'I've done that.'"

"It seems a silly thing to do," I said stonily.

"Well, yes, it does. However, building on the earth is really the same: silly toys that are long forgotten here, toys that do not even gather dust in the attic but disintegrate and are totally forgotten here—a waste of God's precious time," she said much too breezily.

I had the taste of a copper penny in my mouth.[16] "Is it all right if we do not play today?" I asked.

"Oh, all right," she said. "Do you want to join the tour?"

"I don't know," I said dazed. I felt as though I had been hit by a truck. "I like your name, Crystal Clear," I said acidly. "It's apt."

The angel Crystal Clear imparts a powerful and refreshing blessing because the light from God flows through her hands. The angel Gabriel touched Daniel and revived him (Dan. 8:18), and later another angel came to strengthen him (Dan. 10:10, 16, 18).

"Maybe a little rest," she said, as if she had not heard my remark. "Now, remember to come back to see us. We love you here; do keep in touch." She held up her tiny hands, and I held up mine to reciprocate. Light came from hers into mine and knocked me softly backwards.

I lay on the air, as someone might lie on a gurney while being wheeled through hospital halls. My arms were across my chest, and I floated down the path like a patient returning from surgery.

Chapter Three Angels in Training

An angel began walking beside me as I floated down the path.

"Whom do you seek?" the angel asked.

"I thought I was going to see my Father in the throne room," I answered.

"He is everywhere, but this is not the throne room."

The Terraced Waterfall

I had floated to the edge of a pool; I began descending to rest on the grass. The pool was at the base of a high, terraced waterfall. Lavender flowers and hanging greenery grew on the ledges of the fall. A fine mist hung over the pool, caused by the impact of the falling water.

"What is this place?" I asked.

"One of the gardens," the angel said. "It's peaceful here. Why don't you rest," he suggested, and then he was gone.

There was something soothing in the sound of the waterfall, something restful, but there was also someone humming a lovely melody. The sound vibrated through me, touching every part of my body. Then a high voice began to sing:

> There is a place where travelers rest,
> And lay their heads in peace.
> Returning to the Eagle's nest,

1. For believers to grow up into Christ in the new self (Col. 3:10; 2 Cor. 4:16; Eph. 4:15) and be joined as one spirit to the spirit of Jesus (1 Cor. 6:17), the Holy Spirit must train them to rely upon the Lord's life of complete obedience (Heb. 2:10; 5:8–9) that is available to fill each believer minute by minute (Eph. 5:18; Col. 3:17; 2 Cor. 3:5–6).

2. The angelic host of heaven was created through Christ and for Him, as were all things on the earth (Col. 1:16). Therefore as the redeemed on Earth are to grow up in all aspects into the Lord Jesus, including the experiential knowledge of Him (2 Pet. 3:18; Eph. 4:15), so the heavenly beings are to grow in the knowledge of God both through relationship to Christ Jesus (Col. 2:2–3) and through revelation by the Holy Spirit (Rev. 7:14).

3. God rests in the midst of His working (Heb. 4:10; John 5:17), and so do the heavenly host, because the Father has handed over all things to the Son (Luke 10:22), who gives rest to the angels and to the redeemed as they work with Him in union and trustful obedience (Matt. 11:28–30; Heb. 3:18–19).

It is not their particular duty or gifting that dominates the hearts of the angels but rather their desire to serve and know God more and more (Ps. 103:20–21).

4. When God grants visions of heaven to believers, at times He opens their eyes to see many angels and/or the redeemed gathered together (Rev. 5:11; 7:9). At other times He allows only one or a few to be seen (Rev. 10; 15:5–6).

All war within will cease.
O Lamb of God,
Our heart's desire,
O Truth in Word,
Eternal Fire,
O Lamb of God,
God's chosen Son,
Receive them when
Their race is run.

At the song's end, slowly a figure formed from the mist of the waterfall. I sat up to watch this unusual sight.

Heather of the Mist

"Who are you?" I asked.

"I am Heather," the figure said. "I tend this part of the garden. Sometimes the path leads beside still waters or into perfumed gardens," she smiled.

I lay back on the grass, for I was weary and still recovering from my experience at the sandpile.

She continued after a pause, "Do you wish to grow in spirit or in the natural?"

"In spirit, most of all," I said.

"Then cultivate obedience," she said.[1] "Your Father loves you. I know that, or you would not be here. You would not have access to Him, nor would you be able to enter these perfumed gardens."

"Tell me of these gardens," I said.

"There are many, each filled with untold delights. I suppose, being on the path, you always expect to arrive in the throne room?" she asked.

"Yes, I do."

"But your Father wants you to see more of His beautiful land."

The Question

Suddenly I sat up, looking at her intently. "Heather, what do you do here?"

"We grow in God.[2] Also, I tend this small part of the garden. But we do not toil here.[3] We live for what you would call spiritual growth."

All growth in the natural and in the spiritual is from God (1 Cor. 3:7; Acts 17:25).

Toil in working is the result of sin (Gen. 3:17–19).

Then returning to the subject she was addressing before my question, she swept her hand in a wide semicircle. "The areas to visit are without end and beyond compare."

"I seem to be alone here," I said, "but I know there are others."[4]

"Yes, but your Father is answering your prayers to grow and learn. He decides how each child should be taught," she smiled. "For you there is private tutoring here.[5] One on one. Ask what you will."

"I'm so at peace in this place," I shrugged. "I find it difficult to think of things to ask."

In heaven, in the presence of God, one's heart is satisfied and one's spirit is filled with the light of God. This enables a person to know intuitively in a way similar to how God knows (1 Cor. 13:12), and there is no awareness of the need to ask questions. The disciples had a foretaste of this in John 21:12, after Jesus rose from the dead.

"I've heard that," she mused.

I could think of one question only, for which I felt I already knew the answer, but I asked: "Do you have fellowship here?"

"Yes, we are happy. Actually, there are many of us around, but I alone am sent to you, so you see only me."

"Why are you called Heather?" I asked.

"For the flowers that grow in the midst of the falls," she smiled, looking up at the high, terraced garden.

The Angel Clara

"Hello, Ann," a woman's voice spoke from behind us. "Heather," the voice continued, as we turned our faces toward her.

"Clara," Heather responded; she quickly rose to face her. Heather turned to me. "This is Clara, who is very beloved of us here."

5. There are examples in Scripture of the private tutoring of individuals through visions of God and of heaven: Moses (Exod. 33:11), Ezekiel (Ezek. 1; 2:7–8), and John in the Book of Revelation.

6. The culmination of any vision of heaven would be to hear the Father speak. John in the first twenty chapters of the Book of Revelation saw many things occurring and that were to occur in heaven. It was only in verse 5 of chapter 21 that God the Father spoke to him from the throne.

7. God does not override the measure of free will that He has carefully preserved in each person (Deut. 30:19; Josh. 24:15; Job 34:4). He desires our willing consent; very often Jesus said that if anyone wishes to come... let him (Matt. 16:24; 19:21; 20:26–27; John 7:37).

8. The hand of God caught Ezekiel by a lock of his head, lifted him up between Earth and heaven, and brought him to Jerusalem (Ezek. 8:3). The Holy Spirit also whisked Philip from the wilderness to Azotus (or Ashdod) some twenty miles away (Acts 8:39–40).

9. By the shedding of His precious blood on Calvary, He made atonement for sins and thereby destroyed the power of the works of the devil in causing sickness and death (Matt. 8:16; Acts 10:38; 1 John 3:8; Heb. 2:14).

The Lord continues His ministry of healing from heaven as the Holy Spirit makes effectual Christ's triumph on the cross over the enemies of God (Col. 2:15). Believers are joined to the ascended Lord to share His health from heaven (Rom. 7:4; 8:11; 1 Cor. 6:13–15; 12:27).

10. Angels, assigned to serve a Christian who has been granted the gifts of healings, appear with the facial features and skin color of the nationality of that Christian. Believers are "from every tribe and tongue and people and nation" (Rev. 5:9), for God is not partial to any one nationality (Rom. 2:11).

I rose to my feet also. "Hello, Clara," I said. She was absolutely the most beautiful creature I had ever seen. This angel looked very womanly and had a soft light coming from her head area. The light seemed to gather into streaks of light as it radiated outward from that glow. She parted her botticellian, golden-red hair in the center and caught it in a multiple bun arrangement at the nape of her neck. She wore a white, draped garment similar to the designs adopted by Roman women before the time of Christ. The garment was gathered and belted beneath what would be the bust area in a human. Her eyes were an intense blue.

Clara's Invitation

"I've come to take Ann to a training session," Clara continued.

"What kind of training?" I asked.

"Of the healing angels," she smiled.

"Oh," I said softly, for she amazed me by speaking of an area that was of great interest to me. "I would like that, but...," I grappled for the words as well as for direction, "I'm on my way to the throne room."

"This is on your way," she smiled. "Your heavenly Father is offering you this opportunity."[6]

I looked to Heather for guidance.

"I would go if I were you," she affirmed.

"Would you like to drop by?" Clara asked.[7]

"Yes," I said enthusiastically.

Clara laughed. "Thank you, Heather. She seems wonderfully refreshed."

"Yes, thank you, Heather," I added, turning to her, but already she was fading into the mist of the waterfall, smiling and holding up her hand to acknowledge our departure as she disappeared.

We too left suddenly.

The Annex

Distance in the spiritual realm does not present a problem as it does on the earth. John says that immediately after Jesus spoke to him to come up to heaven, he was there in the throne room of God (Rev. 4:1–2).

Immediately we were outside of a very large building that had a small sign over its double doors: THE ANNEX.[8] It was a short distance from an equally large building that had a sign written in a language that I could not read.

I thought to myself, "I wonder if travel is at the speed of thought here?"

We entered the building.

It was a huge auditorium much the same as the municipal auditoriums in major cities. There were a number of tiers, as well as the main floor. Angels filled the building. They all wore white armbands with a large red cross on each band.[9] They seemed to be attending a lecture.

Their instructor was on an elevated platform before a gigantic, clear board that looked similar to lucid plastic. He held a long pointer with which he would add colored-light illustrations to the board by touching it. He did not draw or write, but pointed only; they appeared on the board complete in their design.

Clara began to make her way to the front of the auditorium. The angels remained attentive, but they moved aside so that we could pass down the aisle. We stood near the raised platform, and I could see the instructor more clearly.

He had a crew cut and wore white armbands with a red cross on each band. He also had stripes on his sleeves.

The red cross worn on the arms of the healing angels signifies the ministry of healing through Jesus Christ that He began on Earth as a foretaste of the coming redemption through His blood sacrifice (Isa. 53:4–5; 1 Pet. 2:24).

11. This will be what the Bible calls the "latter rain" (Joel 2:23), which comes in the spring to water again the fall planting. In Joel 2:30, God says that He will display wonders on the earth at that time.

"For you who fear My name the sun of righteousness will rise with healing in its wings" (Mal. 4:2). In these last days, believers will do greater works of healing than those Jesus did when He was first on the earth (John 14:12). If in the "early rain" following Pentecost, "they were all being healed" (Acts 5:16), how much more will the latter rain bring healings.

12. Two angels were present when Jesus rose from the dead (John 20:12). Angels are able to strengthen and encourage believers in their weakness (Dan. 10:10–11, 15–16, 19), to stand against the enemy (Dan. 10:12–13, 20), to help protect the believers (Dan. 6:22), and to relay instructions from God (Dan. 12:4).

God gives general grace to the church as His healing agent through prayers, promising that "those who have believed . . . will lay hands on the sick, and they will recover" (Mark 16:17–18; James 5:14–15). Jesus sent the twelve out "to heal diseases" (Luke 9:1), and then later He sent the seventy out two by two to "heal those in [the city] who are sick" (Luke 10:9). The use of two believers to pray for the sick is in accordance with His Word: "If two of you agree on earth about anything that they may ask, it shall be done for them by My Father who is in heaven" (Matt. 18:19).

But not all Christians are given the special grace that accompanies "the gifts of healings" (1 Cor. 12:30). This anointing to heal varies among believers. God empowers some believers with these manifestations to be used in the healing of particular kinds of infirmity or illness. The anointing may operate in one or more of the categories of healings such as: physical disease or debility, healing of emotions and the mind, deliverance from curses and the control of evil spirits, and healing of the wounded human spirit.

13. Jesus spoke the phrase "only believe" to the synagogue official when others reported to him that his young daughter had died (Luke 8:49–50). The Lord needed the father to trust Him, and He needed the faith of the three disciples He allowed to enter the room with Him where the child lay.

Each believer needs the revelation of God's will for healing and health for His children, and he needs to receive the measure of Christ's faith allotted to each believer through the Scriptures (Rom. 12:3; Eph. 4:7).

14. There their spirits are clothed with bodies of light similar to those of the angels. Each of the redeemed is recognizable in this spiritual body (Rev. 14:1, 4).

Peter, James, and John on the mount of transfiguration could see, recognize, and hear Moses and Elijah (Luke 9:30, 33). The redeemed in heaven sing and praise God, serving Him (Rev. 14:1, 3; 7:9–10, 15). They await the day when they will receive glorified, resurrected bodies like the present body of the Lord Jesus (Luke 24:39; 1 John 3:2), so that they will be prepared to reign with Him on this present earth for a thousand years (Rev. 20:6).

Angels of Healing

I turned to look at the faces of the angels. They looked like the United Nations of angelhood, representing many nationalities.[10] I supposed that the Lord would send them on assignments all over the world. They were very intent upon the lecture.

The instructor continued, "You realize that you play a very important role in verifying our Lord's victory in the area of health. The enemy will use any wile to attempt to bring into a place of unbelief those to whom our God assigns you. He is a master of unbelief. He has succeeded mightily with humankind in general and with the elect specifically. It is often easier for the redeemed to believe our Lord will provide for them financially than to believe He wants His people well. The healing revival is about to begin.[11] Instead of one, we will be assigning two of you to each person slated for the gift of healing.[12]

In the last days a mighty outpouring of the Holy Spirit on all mankind is prophesied (Joel 2:28–29).

"We want you to learn to work together now. We have some badges for you to fasten to those receiving this gift."

He held up a badge. It was green with red letters: ONLY BELIEVE.[13]

Resurrection is the ultimate healing.

"We have a large number of the redeemed, who will be here later, who will act like believers on Earth.[14] Don't be discouraged by what they say to you. They are here to show you exactly what you might be facing with your charges. Some of the replies they will give you will seem fantastic, but they are usual. You will be able to see how effectively the enemy has eroded belief in the Lord's gracious provision of health. Work through this dismay now. We've given you a 'buddy system' for this revival. There are to be many, many with the gift of healing this time around. Any questions?"

The redeemed go immediately to heaven when their bodies die on Earth (2 Cor. 5:8; Phil. 1:23).

"When will this be?" an angel shouted from far back in the hall.

"The Lord God, the Almighty, knows this. You just get ready!" he called to the angel asking the question. "He did say, 'Soon'; I can tell you that much. That is the reason for this mobilization and intensification of training. Any other questions?"

There was general silence.

"All right, I want you to rally back here after your work with the redeemed. Do not, and let me repeat this, do *not* individually question the redeemed so that you 'bone up' before this workout. We want the full impact of their answers to hit you together. If there are no other questions, you are dismissed."

There was a great deal of movement as the angels rose and began talking to one another while leaving. Clara and I started up some stairs toward the top of the platform. The instructor was clearing the transparent board as we reached the top.

The Angelic Instructor

"Hello, Clara. Who is this with you?" he teased, as an adult might tease about a child whom he knows well.

"I believe you know Ann," Clara said, playing along.

His eyes twinkled. "Yes, I do know her. If I hadn't told the trainees to refrain from cramming for this exam, I could have had Ann give them some of the answers they will hear on Earth."

"Now, Chabburah," Clara smiled, shaking her head as one might when indulging an inveterate jokester. I knew what he meant, however, so I changed the subject.

"What are the stripes on your sleeve?" I asked.

"By His stripes we are healed," he smiled tenderly, looking at the stripes.[15]

Clara continued: "We're taking a tour. Do you have any suggestions?"

"The hanging gardens..." he began.

"No," she laughed, "concerning the healing angels and the revival that is coming in the area of healing."

He looked at a slate in his hand with mock seriousness. "Well, I see here that Ann is slated for a couple of my finest angels."

15. "By His scourging [wounds or stripes] we are healed" (Isa. 53:5; 1 Pet. 2:24). The "we" in this passage includes human and angelic beings. Jesus had to be wounded in order for His atoning blood to be shed (Lev. 17:11; Heb. 9:22).

The sin of the rebellious angels led by Lucifer affected the loyal host remaining in heaven. These good angels needed healing from the deep sorrow over the defection of many of their angelic friends. The peace of heaven was disturbed, and so the Father reconciled heaven also to Himself through His Son, "having made peace through the blood of His cross" (Col. 1:20).

The Hebrew word for "stripes," *chabburah,* is pronounced "khab-boo-raw," the transliterated name of the angel who led the training meetings.

16. Jesus received the anointing of the Holy Spirit with power to minister when He returned from the forty days in the wilderness (Luke 4:14). He could exercise the anointing to heal the sick on certain occasions, as in Luke 5:17 and 6:19.

The anointing of a believer by the Holy Spirit with power to minister a spiritual gift or gifts is not constantly activated but is under the control of the Spirit.

"Me?" I questioned. "Is it possible?" I knew that God gave this giftedness to some of His children. In fact, I had stepped into a stream of such a gift at one time. It was as though God healed everyone for whom I prayed. This amazing and utterly supernatural anointing lasted for several months, and then it was gone.[16] Why He gave it and why the anointing lifted, I never understood. Since that time, there were more questions than answers in my mind.

Classes

The instructor did not respond to my inner dialogue, but continued, "Clara, I would suggest that she begin classes soon. She's almost a classic example of 'gelatin belief'—'touch it and it shakes.' I'm going to teach these classes myself," he continued. "She can study this series at home as a correspondence course, but since she's here right now, she could tour the warehouse."

Clara turned to me. "Would you like that?"

"Yes," I said. "If the Lord is going to use me to pray for healing in others, I...well, I need to learn all that I can."

"All right," he said. "You can get a head start by touring next door; we'll page you when you're to begin your course at home. How's that?"

"That sounds good to us," Clara said. "We'll begin right away. Thank you." She began moving us toward the stairs of the platform.

"Yes, thank you," I said.

The Request

He called after us, "Now don't talk to any of the students on your way out. You might tempt one of them to stumble and ask you questions," he chuckled. Suddenly, as if struck by a thought, he called to us.

"Wait a minute. This is really an excellent opportunity. You're here, and..." I could not understand what he was saying. "Would you be willing for the students to question you in order that they might hear your reasoning?" he asked. "Sometimes it's difficult for the redeemed believers up here to remember why they thought as they thought while on Earth. Would you be willing?"

"Mercy," I laughed lightly. "Am I so tough?"

"No, no, no," he said, putting down his slate and crossing to place his hands on my shoulders. "You're just...typical of the reasoning given on Earth."

"If it would be helpful to you and the others..." I said.

"It would," he replied. "Good! You and Clara tour next door. We'll page you there," he said, going back to the large board. But almost immediately he whipped around again to look at us. "Now, don't ask Clara about healing," he smiled. "We want a raw example for them."

"OK," I laughed.

He went back to his board, and we started down the stairs. Immediately we were at the back of the large auditorium and exiting the double doors.

As we stepped from the building, we could see thousands of angel trainees sitting on the lawn in twos with one or two of the redeemed. They were in deep discussions.

I looked up at the sign over the doorway of the building toward which we were walking. I could not read it before, but now, much to my amazement, it appeared clearly: BODY PARTS.

Clara opened the door, and we stepped inside.

Chapter Four

Healing Angels

The warehouse was large, as large as the auditorium we had just left and as white as a "clean room" at a research facility. It seemed unusually bright in the building, as though the contents were either preserved or incubated in light.

"This building holds an inventory of available parts of the human body," Clara said.[1]

These body parts are not made of earthly flesh, blood, and bones, for nothing of the natural can be a part of heaven (1 Cor. 15:50). They are made of supernatural light (as are all created things in heaven), and they are the true body parts that God knows will be needed in the coming healing revival.

There were bins upon bins of parts of all colors and sizes.

The Warehouse Workers

Angels in white were working inside. These angels were the size of humans and had no wings. Each wore an armband with the same red cross on it. One of these angels walked over to us. "We're pleased that you have come to visit the parts department, Ann."

"How do you know me?" I asked.

"We know everyone slated for the gift of healing," he smiled. "You need to know that these are available."

He walked with us down the wide center aisle. As I looked at the bins, I wondered what it might be like to have the gift of healing for the remainder of my life. Through the written Word, Jesus commands us to heal the sick and raise the dead, but I was not among those through whom He was fulfilling His own command consistently. Healing seemed as general a commission to Christians as "go ye...," but many of us saw little of the early church's power to heal physically. I had always made excuses for others and myself, but secretly, I wondered why.

The angel continued, "We're ready here. The Lord has made ample provision. Please enjoy your tour."

"We will," Clara said.

"Yes," I said, somewhat distractedly.

He bowed slightly from the waist and stepped backward before returning to his work.

The Page

There were so many questions I wanted to ask Clara. Suddenly a piece of paper floated before our eyes and paused in the air. It read, "Please return to the annex." Then it zipped away.

"This is sooner than I thought," Clara said.

We turned and began to walk toward the door of the warehouse. In hushed tones I said, "Oh, Clara, this is getting really exciting. I'm going to be able to help these angels. What an honor…what a gift!"

"Yes," she agreed.

"And just think, I might see some of these angels with other people during the revival," I mused.

We exited the warehouse and began to cross to the annex.

I was reiterating to myself, "…to assist angels." Then I addressed Clara again, "…because you angels are so helpful to us, but rarely do we get the opportunity to help you."

She gave a wise smile that seemed to indicate that this was not true but did not want to dampen my enthusiasm.

Angels Who Have Their Stripes

We entered the annex. Again a crowd of angels filled the room. A group of angels was on the platform. They wore no armbands but had red stripes up and down the sleeves of their garments. We stood in the back of the hall.

"These are angels who have their stripes," Clara said. "The Lord assigned them to believers during the last healing revival."

The last healing revival that occurred in America was in the 1950s, when God granted the "gifts of healings" to only a small number of Christians (1 Cor. 12:30).

"There aren't many of them," I said.

Clara sighed, "No, only a few on Earth were given the gift of healing in great measure. These believers were meant to train the many; instead, most of them erected tents and held the gift for themselves. The gift was used, but since they did not train others, it was corrupted and became a means of enriching themselves personally."

She glanced out over the large auditorium and smiled as she continued, "This roomful is only one group of trainees. Others are at other levels of training; some have their stripes already and are beginning to join those to whom the Lord assigned them. Many of the redeemed on Earth have been taking a correspondence course, most without knowing it.

The believer needs to complete the course before he receives the two assigned angels. So, everyone is in training right now, aren't they?"

"Is this correspondence course the same that I'll take?" I asked.

"Yes," she said. "It is study concerning healing in the Word."[2] She then turned her attention to the angels on the platform.

God extended the promise of healing in body, soul, and spirit to all mankind who would repent of their sins and receive Christ as the new life within them (1 Thess. 5:23; Mark 16:17–18).

There was a great deal of light coming from these angels. One was speaking. "The Lord wishes those of us who were used in the last revival to hold a reunion on Earth before the beginning of this outpouring of the Holy Spirit. You might say that we are bringing closure to that which was. We are being honored by the reunion being the commencement celebration that will usher in the next great move of our God for healing."

Another of the veteran angels interjected, "We know what your next question will be: 'When?'"

There was a chuckle of laughter from the trainees.

"We don't know when, but the Lord has said, 'Soon.'"

I whispered to Clara, "What beautiful angels."

"Yes," she said.

The Former Outpouring

Another angel on the platform spoke. "That which occurred during the last great outpouring of the Spirit for healing was very painful to all of us." They shook their heads, sadly looking at one another.

1. The true and the good of everything on Earth must originate in heaven (James 1:17; John 3:27; 1 Cor. 4:7; Heb. 9:23; 8:5). The God who knows the number of hairs of each head (Matt. 10:30) certainly knows each part of our bodies that will need replacement.

2. The first promise made by God to the Israelites on their journey from bondage in Egypt concerned healing. He spoke it three days after they crossed the Red Sea (Exod. 15:22). He said that if they would heed His voice, do what is right in His sight, and obey His laws, then He would "put none of the diseases on you which I have put on the Egyptians; for I, the LORD, am your healer" (Exod. 15:26).

Through the forty years of their wandering in the wilderness, God was faithful to His word and preserved them from sickness on a diet of bread from heaven and water (Deut. 8:4; Ps. 78:23–25; 105:41; 1 Cor. 10:4).

This health is made possible by faith in His work on the cross of Calvary and in His resurrection and ascension into heaven (Isa. 53:4–5; Matt. 8:16–17). Matthew uses the same words, "healing every kind of disease and every kind of sickness," twice about Jesus and once about His disciples (Matt. 4:23; 9:35; 10:1). At one point in the life of the church in Jerusalem, all the sick and the demonized were being healed (Acts 5:16).

3. Christians through whom the Lord Jesus would exercise His healing ministry in a pure way must hate their natural self life (John 12:25; Luke 14:26) and the things of Satan's kingdom on the earth: "the lust of the flesh and the lust of the eyes and the boastful pride of life" (1 John 2:15–17; James 4:3–4).

"Corruption crept in," another said, "elusive sin by elusive sin. Finally, most had corrupted the gift beyond the recognition of those of us who were serving them."

"Mankind may be deceived by outward show," another angel said, "but we saw all that happened. God is not mocked."

They paused a moment; the gravity of that which had occurred was still painful to them.

The first angel spoke again. "In this coming revival the gift will be so widespread that the corruption due to pride and power is less likely to occur."

To his statement, another angel added, "But watch for these: pride, the lust for power, greed, and sexual lust."[3]

"It will not be the lesser demons you will need to battle, but demons as strong as you and rabidly determined because the time is short," the first angel said.[4] "We'll turn the meeting over to Chabburah again," he concluded.[5]

God the Holy Spirit imparts and sustains all life, whether it be in heaven or on Earth (Acts 17:25; Job 12:10; 1 Tim. 6:13).

The angels seated in the auditorium stood before the angels on the platform and blew toward them.[6] I supposed that this was some form of a standing ovation.

"Thank you," they smiled.

Chabburah spoke to them briefly. Then they left the platform. Chabburah came to the center of the platform. "Remember, these friends will be available to answer questions and assist, not only now, but when the revival begins."

The other angels were touching the angels with stripes as the latter walked through the crowd. As they passed, they saw me and acknowledged Clara. The last angel stopped before me. "Hello, Ann," he said, touching my right shoulder. He looked into my eyes and then looked at Clara, smiled, and left.

"Stretch a bit," Chabburah said, "for Ann has come to be with us."

Preparing to Teach

Clara began to move us to the front of the auditorium. The angels smiled as we passed. They were moving about and talking among themselves.

Chabburah was waiting for us on the platform, smiling, following us with his eyes. "There you are, Ann," he said effusively.

"This was very quick," Clara remarked.

"She was about to ask you questions," he shook his finger at me, as one would to tease a child. "Come over here," he added. "I have seats for you both. Sit down and make yourselves comfortable."

Then he turned to the auditorium. "All right, take your seats," he said to those who were talking. "You can talk later." He gestured toward me. "Ann is with us. She has graciously accepted an invitation to answer any questions you might have concerning her or humans in general."

I tugged at Chabburah's robe. "I don't know everything," I whispered to him.

Everyone laughed.

He smiled, "We know you don't know everything. We don't either, so we're all in good company. I'll just step back over here and let you begin."

Teaching the Angels

I did not know how I expected the meeting to be conducted, but I certainly did not expect to be handed "the floor." I was stiff as I began. "In the first place, it is such a blessing for me to be able to assist you. *Hmmm...*" I did not know where to start, so I just jumped in. "Well, most people on Earth do not believe in divine healing."[7]

Through Christ Jesus, faith in God, as imparted through the Scriptures, is the basis of mankind's relationship with Him (Rom. 10:17; Heb. 11:6).

A mumble ran through the auditorium.

I continued, "Even those who are saved have a difficult time believing."

4. Demons are evil spirits who are part of Satan's forces. Those who work on the earth try to possess or oppress human beings who allow themselves to become vulnerable to their attack because of sin, deception, or ignorance (Deut. 32:16–17; 1 Tim. 4:1; 2 Cor. 2:11).

There is much greater demonic activity recorded in the Gospels and the Book of Acts because of the ministry of Jesus Christ while on Earth and of His disciples in the New Testament church. The Lord cast them out of afflicted people who came to Him, and so did His disciples (Matt. 8:16; Luke 10:17). Known as exorcism, or deliverance, or the casting out of evil spirits, this ministry has always had some part in the work of the church throughout the centuries.

5. The Hebrew word for "scourging" or "stripe," found in the phrase "by His scourging we are healed" (Isa. 53:5), is *chabburah,* the name of the instructor for these training sessions.

6. The angelic beings are spirits (Heb. 1:14) whom God created by two means: (a) "by the word of the LORD" they were made, and (b) "by the breath of His mouth" they began to live (Ps. 33:6). God's breath, the Holy Spirit (Job 33:4), continually sustains the angels in life, and He is able to pass through them purely and powerfully to enliven other angels.

7. When Jesus visited His hometown of Nazareth, "He could do no miracle there except that He laid His hands upon a few sick folk and healed them. And He wondered at their unbelief," or lack of faith (Mark 6:5–6). The people of Nazareth lost their faith in Jesus because "they took offense at Him" (Mark 6:3).

Another time Jesus told the father of a child with severe epilepsy who was brought to Him for healing, "All things are possible to him who believes." The father replied that he believed but that he needed help with his unbelief (Mark 9:23–24). There was a mixture of faith and lack of faith in his heart, as there is with many Christians regarding healing through prayer (Matt. 7:11; James 1:6–8; 5:15).

There was a very loud reaction. The amazement was such that I looked at Chabburah. He urged me to proceed.

"Even those who have seen divine healing have difficulty believing all the time."

There was general, loud alarm throughout the auditorium.

"Hold it down," Chabburah said. Then to me he said, "Why don't you suggest that they ask you questions?"

"Would you like to ask questions?" I asked rather meekly.

Angelic Questions

An angel rose from his seat and spoke loudly, "Don't they believe the Word?"

"The unbelievers don't, of course. Some believers do, but many believers really do not."

There was a stunned silence in the auditorium. I looked at Chabburah. "Give them time, Ann," he said. "They're shocked."

"Some believers, you see, think that parts of the Bible do not apply today, that certain sections were for long ago," I said.

An angel near the platform said in a normal voice that carried because of the silence, "But the Word says that The Eternal is the same yesterday, today, and forever. Why would they consider the Word apart from Him? He is the Word."

There was a great deal of general agreement among the angels.

"Well," I shrugged and laughed, "they do."

"Do you?" another asked.

"I believe in healing, and I believe that the Lord promises health and that He has paid for healing for believers, but I do not understand it."

"It is a covenant promise," another angel said, rising from his seat.[8] "By His stripes He has knit you back or mended or joined you again to Him who is divine health. It is sure."

"But often people are sick," I said.

Another angel rose. "It's a covenant promise, as has been said. One needs to abide in Christ."

"Of course, if a person deliberately abuses his earthly vessel...," another said.

"Forgiveness needs to be absolute," another added without standing. "Break the knitting together with Christ, and some sort of illness will result."[9]

"As night follows day," they all said. You could tell they were members of a class. They all laughed.

I interjected, "But most who will receive this gift will not be abiding by the covenantal agreements won by Jesus. How can this be?"

Grace

Again they all laughed, responding in unison, "Grace."

Chabburah explained, "There is coming an outpouring of grace as the Holy Spirit moves in power in the coming revival." As he spoke to me, he added, "Are you tiring, Ann?"

"Yes, this is all so much," I chuckled wistfully.

"Students," Chabburah said, "that is enough for today. Let's stand and give Ann a big hand." The angels stood and cheered as they clapped.

8. When God covenanted with the Israelites at Mount Sinai (Horeb) to bless and multiply them if they would obey His laws, one of the covenant promises rehearsed by Moses was to "remove from you all sickness...and not put on you any of the harmful diseases of Egypt which you have known" (Deut. 5:2; 7:15).

God made another covenant of blessings and curses with the Israelites in the land of Moab just before they crossed the Jordan into Canaan, again contingent upon their obedience (Deut. 28:1–2, 15). In verses 21–22, 27–28, 35, 58–61, and 65–66, God promised to bring upon them every sickness and plague known to man if they did not obey His commandments.

Under the new covenant of grace through the shed blood of Christ Jesus, God promised that the Holy Spirit would put His laws in the hearts and minds of believers (Heb. 8:10). Their obedience would then originate from within them (even as sin does—Matt. 15:19). The Spirit plants the word of Christ in their hearts and then works to enable them to choose and do the will of God through Christ in them (Phil. 2:12–13; Rom. 6:17; 1 Cor. 12:6; Heb. 13:21). Christians "serve in newness of the [promptings of the] Spirit and not in oldness of the letter [of written rules]" (Rom. 7:6). How much more certain is the promise of healing by grace through faith in Christ (Mark 9:23) than that originally made to the Israelites under a covenant of law through their works (Heb. 8:6–9; Gal. 2:20–21; 3:5).

9. Believers abide in the new covenant of grace through the shed blood of Christ by cooperating with the Holy Spirit in exercising that freedom of their will to choose Christ Jesus as the Lord: in every outer circumstance, in every thought and intention of their heart, and within their whole being. Therefore the members of the body are continually presented to God; the Lord Jesus is honored in their use (Col. 3:5; Rom. 6:12–13; 12:1), the power of the flesh to control the believer having been broken on the cross (Rom. 6:6–7).

Also, the old self is denied and laid aside as worthless (Matt. 16:24; Eph. 4:22; Col. 3:9). Its thoughts are taken captive to obey and to be set upon Christ (2 Cor. 10:5; Col. 3:2), and the whole mind is renewed by the new human spirit imparting the kind of thoughts He has (Eph. 4:23; Rom. 12:2). The natural emotions are not allowed to control the believer (Col. 3:5, 8; Eph. 4:31). By the Spirit he longs for God (Ps. 42:1–2) and the heart feelings of Christ (Eph. 4:23; Col. 3:12–13). The will is continually kept alert and active in siding with God's will and refusing the will of the enemy (Phil. 2:13; Rom. 12:2).

The new spiritual self (Eph. 4:24; Col. 3:10) of heart and human spirit (1 Pet. 3:4) seeks to know and do the will of God by being guided through the peace of Christ acting as umpire and guardian (Phil. 4:7; Col. 3:15); the conscience witnessing as to whether Christ's life is flowing or death (Gen. 2:9, 16–17; Deut. 30:19); and the enlightening of the Word concerning Christ, as quickened by the Holy Spirit, as to whether the faith of Jesus is being exercised or not (Heb. 4:12; Rom. 10:17; 14:23).

"All right, all right," he said, "settle down. You're dismissed." He turned to me, "Thank you, Ann. That was wonderful. These students thought they could not be shocked again."

"Why didn't they blow toward me as they did toward the angels who were here before me?" I asked.

He gave a mighty laugh. "It might have killed you," he said. "They were passing the breath of God to them. That's the highest compliment they could pay the angels who were lecturing. The angels, being spirit as they are, could receive it. They breathed it in. The breath was as food to them. Although you are in spirit here, some experiences would be beyond your capacity at present."

He put one hand behind Clara and one hand behind me as we started down the steps to leave. I could tell that he was strengthening me as we walked. At the bottom of the steps stood two blond, rather nervous-looking angels.

The Twins

"Chabburah," one said, "we'd like to meet Ann."

"Of course," he said with great understanding, almost tenderly. "Ann, these are the angels whom the Lord has assigned to you for the revival."

These angels looked seven feet tall, young, eighteen to twenty years old; they appeared identical. "You look like twins," I said.

"Yes," the other said, "I'm Rapha, and he's Raphashanah."

The name of one of the healing angels is Rapha, the Hebrew word meaning "to heal." The other healing angel is Raphashanah, the addition being the Hebrew word shanah meaning "to repeat or do again." They looked like a matching pair.

Raphashanah said, "Thank you for sharing with us. We need as much understanding as possible before we are on the job."

"Thank you for saying that," I said. "I became tired, and Chabburah felt that was enough."

"It was most helpful," said Rapha.

"I'll be taking classes; maybe we could talk more then," I added.

They looked at Chabburah. He nodded yes. "Yes," they smiled broadly, "we'll talk more then."

"You students are going to miss your next class if you don't hurry," Chabburah said to them.

"Very well," they smiled, "we'll see you later," and ran off.

"I'm staying here, Clara," Chabburah said. "And thank you, Ann. That was most helpful. Now, don't forget, we'll send a page to you when class is to begin."

"I'll be ready," I said as I hugged him. I had never hugged an angel. They do not feel exactly the same as flesh and blood on Earth. Not as solid, I suppose is the best way to express it, but substantial.[10]

"See you later, Clara," he said.

"Yes," she replied.

"Good-bye," we both said, and we started to walk away from the platform. Suddenly we were at the back of the auditorium and exiting the doors. By stepping onto the path, we were quickly quite a distance from the two buildings.

He Comes

Immediately ahead of us on the path was a burning light. Hundreds of spirits surrounded this brilliance, darting in and lifting out like eagles catching heat currents. They were flying with the light as if escorting it. So bright was this great light that it reduced the spirits to silver outlines of themselves in its radiance. It reminded me of figures passing in front of bright headlights on a dark night, although here there was no surrounding darkness. Everything paled that was near this intense brightness.

Clara spoke to me. "He is coming," she said. "He comes for you, Ann."

Both of our faces were catching the glow of His radiance. My heart leaped within me, yet a peace settled over me like warm oil.

Clara continued, "We will be with one another later. All of your attention needs to be given to Him now." She smiled toward the light and vanished.

10. Angels have bodies of light that can be seen and felt. We know this because an angel touched Elijah twice, and the touch awakened him from sleep (1 Kings 19:5, 7). Jacob wrestled all night with an angel and held on to him (Gen. 32:24–26). An angel touched Daniel as he lay on the ground prostrate and set the prophet on his hands and knees (Dan. 10:10, 18).

Chapter Five The Lord Jesus

He was coming—my Beloved, my Friend.

My breath was knocked out of me, and my knees went slack as He came closer. Then, like a tree overtaken by a dust cloud from a wind flurry, the cloud of His glory engulfed me. The spirits still were darting in and lifting out on the periphery, but I could see only Him.

Remembering

I had seen Him standing in the sanctuary of a church several times before over a period of years. The last time was two and a half months earlier. He was standing twenty-four feet high in the sanctuary of a church where the pastors met for citywide prayer meetings. It was Yom Kippur. For four years we had labored in the citywide prayer movement of that metropolitan area, and we had returned to the city for a Bible conference after being gone for a year.

At that time He stood in the sanctuary, a rainbow encircling Him, clothed in a shimmering, multicolored cloak.[1] The light radiating from Him looked alive. Suddenly He telescoped to the size of a man and spoke.

The multicoloring of Jesus's garment signifies the multifaceted aspects of His glorious ministry.

"Look at Me," He said. His eyes, though far away, suddenly were near and riveting, as if aflame.

As I looked into His eyes, the robe of vibrating colors passed through His body, came to me, and encircled my body. I could feel it as well as see it.

Then, without walking, He came forward until He passed right into my body.[2] He was facing the back of my head, and I was facing the back of

1. Jesus is the greater Joseph and wears "the true" of Joseph's varicolored cloak (Gen. 37:3; Heb. 8:2). The Hebrew word for such a garment is *pas,* which means that it was a full-length tunic, reaching to the hands and the feet. The ordinary tunic reached only to the knees and was usually without sleeves.

2. The resurrected body of the Lord Jesus was able to pass through a closed door on Earth (John 20:19, 26). He is "Lord of all" (Acts 10:36), all things having been put in subjection to Him (Eph. 1:22). It is not strange that His resurrection body can assume a form (Mark 16:12) that can enter a human being on Earth who is also "light in the Lord" (Eph. 5:8).

Here is another tactile sign of the Lord opening human eyes to see spiritual realities, in the same way that He offered eye salve to the Laodiceans (Rev. 3:18).

His.[3] He turned around within my body, and we were both facing in the same direction, both wearing the cloak. After this I had the even stranger sensation of having someone look out of my eyes—Jesus, not I, was looking out of my eye sockets.[4]

Suddenly He moved forward out of my body, leaving the cloak on me and returning to the place from which He had come. In an instant He disappeared, and I was left wearing the shimmering, multicolored cloak.[5]

The experience two and a half months before this present moment when He stood before me in heaven seemed wonderfully strange and yet very natural. But I had never understood what it all meant. I expected some change in my life, some increased anointing, but I found myself amazingly the same and stunningly unanointed, which was usual.

The Desire of All Nations

Now He was standing before me in Paradise.

How can one describe "the Desire of All Nations"? Far more than the impact of His physical appearance, He embodies life. His eyes are clear blue but as deep as a bottomless pool. It seems that if you could travel into those eyes, you would understand all mysteries, that in plunging toward the bottom of that deep pool, you would pass the answers to all things.

He embodies love, light, and truth. A kaleidoscope of understandings flooded my spirit, computing faster than lightning, causing me to react as Job reacted when the Lord confronted him—I could only cover my mouth.[6]

He stepped up to me.

He was smiling broadly, as a childhood sweetheart that you knew you would always, always love, but that you had not seen since childhood. The years dropped away as you saw Him, and you were right—you would always, always love Him; no one could ever take His place.

He took my right hand in His left, which strengthened me.

If humans are able to walk on water when the Lord bids them to do so, then they are able to fly when the Lord wills it (Matt. 14:28–29).

"Come," He said. Immediately we were flying.

The Mountains of Spices

Paradise began to pass beneath us. The spirits accompanying Him flew to the side and behind us. We were flying up to an astonishing mountain range. The color of each mountain varied. As we drew closer, I realized that the first mountain emitted an aroma.

"Where are we, Lord?" I asked.

"You have often called Me to the mountains of spices," He said.[7] "We are here."

A description of the spices can be found in Appendix B.

Aromatic spices were growing on these mountains. The colors, as well as the aromas, varied from mountain to mountain.

The Father's Delight

"These are for your Father's delight," Jesus said, "and for the delight of His children. They bring joy." Without turning His head to look at me, He asked, "Do you wish to bring joy?"

"Yes," I answered.

Jesus responded, "Obedience brings joy to My Father, holiness of heart, thankfulness, truth with mercy. Each is like a spice. Each has a fragrance. Collectively the aromas are pleasing to My Father. The aromas speak of Me to Him, not just one spice but the aroma of the blend as one passes from mountain to mountain. Together they witness of Me, and this pleases My Father. Also the aroma of these spices coming from His adopted children speaks of Me, and He is pleased."

As we passed over each mountain, wave upon wave of the most tantalizingly delicious smells washed over me. Then some of the particular spices growing from each flew up into my free arm and hand. As we passed over the twelfth mountain, my arm and hand were full of the complete complement of aromatic spices from the mountain range; the smell was beyond compare. I breathed in deeply and felt permeated with the aroma. I could almost taste the fragrance.

3. Ezekiel saw four cherubim (Ezek. 10:20), each of these heavenly creatures having four faces (Ezek. 1:5–10; 10:20): the face of a man in front, the face of a lion on the right side, the face of a bull on the left side, and the face of an eagle behind. One interpretation of these faces is that they represent the four aspects of the ministry of Christ Jesus: man as priest, lion as king, bull as servant, and eagle as prophet. The Lord Jesus, facing out in the position of the eagle, was a tactile sign that one could feel, as with Ezekiel eating the scroll of God's Word (Ezek. 3:1–3).

5. When the Lord puts His cloak over someone but does not require the other's cloak, it signifies His initiating a unilateral or one-sided covenant. Jesus pledges His love and loyalty, as did Jonathan to David in total commitment by his giving the Lord's anointed his cloak, his armor, and all of his weapons (1 Sam. 18:3–4).

6. To put your hand over your mouth signifies consternation and the inability to speak further. Job did this when God spoke with him (Job 40:4).

7. To call the Lord Jesus to the mountains of spices is to urge Him to manifest the sweet aroma of His perfection through the believer without delay (Song of Sol. 8:14; 2 Cor. 2:14–15).

A dove with an olive leaf in its beak is a symbol of peace. That bird returned to Noah in the ark with this evidence that the waters of judgment had subsided and that God was at peace with the earth (Gen. 8:8–11).

The fire of God, the Holy Spirit, is coming to the church to touch all those who call themselves Christians.

Every believer who is in love with Christ is that garden in the new heart (Song of Sol. 4:12), to be kept locked and sealed for Jesus alone to meet us there.

Suddenly I wanted to give out that which had come to me. I flung the spices up into the air, and they became white doves.

"My covenant of peace," Jesus said.[8]

Before my eyes I could see the whole Earth as if I were the distance of a satellite from it. The doves flew and became flames of fire resting over the whole Earth.[9]

The picture before my eyes so intrigued me that I did not realize that the spirits had disappeared and that Jesus and I were coming down into a walled garden.

The Walled Garden

The enclosure seemed to be a private garden.[10] It was not extremely large, but it was large enough to have a variety of trees as a part of its planting: the pomegranate, myrtle, and cedar; the balsam, cinnamon, frankincense, myrrh, and aloe.

The garden was in the full bloom of spring with narcissus and jonquils in the beds and vines of yellow jasmine and purple wisteria intertwined on the stone wall.

There was a three-tiered fountain in the center of the garden with a bench near it. The bench was under a very large apricot tree, which resembled more an oak than a fruit tree. It was in bloom also and exuded a lovely, invigorating scent.

Our feet came to rest on the ground near the fountain.

"What a lovely garden," I said.

"Yes," He smiled, allowing His eyes to scan the area lightly. "I enjoy walking here."

Suddenly into my mind came a phrase from the Song of Solomon: "Until the cool of the day when the shadows flee away..."[11] It was cool here, and certainly there were no shadows. Did that song speak of Paradise?

We began to walk.

A Garden for Lovers

The path circled the garden, with plantings and beds near the wall as well as on the opposite side of the path in the center of the garden. Camphire (henna) was blooming there, and the star-of-Bethlehem, blue flax, and the scarlet lily were blooming in beds near it.

"Who tends this garden?" I asked.

"You do," He answered.

"I tend this garden?" I exclaimed with astonishment.

"Yes," He replied.

I looked over the garden. I felt that I had been here before, but the feeling was an elusive impression, rather like trying to piece together a dream when you only remember snatches of it. I could not bring it into clear focus.

"Would You tell me of this garden, Lord?" I asked finally.

"Each such garden is different. Each is unique, and I delight in each." He paused before speaking again. "Do you enjoy being here?" He asked.

"Yes, it's..." I could not find the words.

"Yes," He agreed.

We came to a spring that flowed from a rock in the garden. Spanning the water was an arch of a bridge that seemed only wide enough for two people. As I thought about it, the bench near the fountain also seemed only wide enough to seat two. Perhaps this was a garden for lovers. As we crossed the bridge, I could smell the scented calamus that grew on the banks by the water.

8. God gave the levitical priest Phinehas and his descendants "My covenant of peace... because he was jealous for his God and made atonement for the sins of Israel," turning away God's wrath from destroying them (Num. 25:11–13; Mal. 2:4–6).

The Levites camped directly around the tabernacle on all four sides so that, by their position between God and the people, God's wrath for the sins of the Israelites might be averted (Num. 1:53).

Jesus "made peace [with the Father] through the blood of His cross" (Col. 1:20; Rom. 5:1). Under the New Covenant, the holy priesthood of God's people may intercede through Christ our High Priest (Heb. 7:25–26; 1 Pet. 2:5) on behalf of other believers who commit sin; God will, for the intercessor, grant life to the sinner (1 John 5:16).

9. God's fire will burn away all that is not of Christ (Matt. 3:12; 1 Cor. 3:11–13). It is able to set ablaze the sacrificial offering of the new heart with flaming passion for the Lord Jesus (Song of Sol. 8:6; 1 Kings 18:38). We are to learn to love "the spirit of burning" that brings His glory as a canopy over all (Isa. 4:3–5).

10. God created the first human beings to live in a garden with Him (Gen. 2:8; 3:8). His re-creation of the human race also began in a garden where He rose from the dead (John 19:41; Matt. 28:1, 6). Every garden that God plants is to honor His Son: first, the Garden of Eden in heaven (Ezek. 28:13); then the copy of that heavenly garden that was on Earth (Heb. 9:23–24); and finally the individual, private garden in the new heart of every believer (Song of Sol. 4:12–16). In order to tend this interior garden, we are to keep it clean and pure from adulteration by the world, the flesh, and the devil.

It is a garden with a selection of the delicious fruit of His character (Gal. 5:22–23) and an assortment of spice plants and trees to waft the fragrance of His perfections of virtue abroad (2 Cor. 2:14–15); His beauty is represented by a unique planting of flowers (Song of Sol. 6:2–3). The Father selects those aspects of His Son that He delights to have grown and manifested in each, new heart (1 Cor. 12:4–7, 11; Rom. 12:3, 6; Eph. 4:7). This is true, eternal individuality, and it comes from God.

His Burden

"Do You become tired?" I asked.

The Lord promised those who walk in step with Him and share His burden would find rest (Matt. 11:29) instead of the heavy load of trying to obey legalistic rules and rituals by their own efforts (Luke 11:46).

"There is a burden in My heart for mankind," He replied. "I will bear this burden until all is completed, but this is not like the body fatiguing and needing rest.[12] No, I do not tire as those who are housed in the flesh tire."

"Do You get lonely?" I asked.

"I long for completion, but that is not loneliness.[13] Loneliness comes from unfulfilled desires, passions that cause one to seek to live in the future through a desire for fulfillment. I live in the present. I am concerned with that which is now. All things are complete here... although incomplete moment by moment. I long for the completion of this gift to My Father, that He may be glorified as well as pleased.[14] He loves having His children around Him. What satisfaction is greater: a crown upon the head, a smile in the heart, a joy that is beyond compare."

We passed beds of saffron and nard. I remembered that on Earth these were of great worth.

He continued, "The eyes of those in Satan's kingdom are blind to My Father, as well as to Me, but they are open to and aware of their subsistence coming from the evil one. He too has gifts, and he displays them. The harlot stands in the doorway and beckons the naive: 'Come in; my bed is scented with all manner of spices and balms. Your sleep will be sweet.'

God is love (1 John 4:7–8). His children know love by the Father giving Himself to them through His Son (1 John 4:9). The Father's love is incarnate in His Son, and the Holy Spirit makes that love flow in us (John 15:9; 17:26; Rom. 5:5) as we love the brethren (John 15:12; 1 John 4:11–12).

"But it will not be sweet. A thousand torments embrace the one on that bed; a thousand heartaches that can never be satisfied lie with the naive on that bed. True love springs forth from God, a never-ceasing fountain fed by springs of living water within the Godhead. I am that Spring. I am that Fountain. I AM."

By now we had circled half of the garden and were back at the center fountain. We sat on the bench.

"Lord," I said, "show me something precious in Your sight."

He opened His hand, and in it was a tear. "In this tear is a world, a universe, an infinity of love. In this tear is the DNA, as it were, of a loved one's spiritual genes. In this tear are salt and light. I can look into this tear and see the face of God, for it is clear. I can look through it to Him who births the universe. This tear is very precious to Me."[15]

We both looked at the tear, and then He closed His hand and continued, "Close your eyes and hold out your hand."

I closed my eyes, and He placed into my hand something smooth.

"Now open your eyes."

A New Name

I opened my eyes and my right hand to look at a smooth, white stone with the name *Anna* engraved upon it.

"Your new name," He said.[16] "I am adding the breath of life to your name. Here you will be called Anna."

"Anna," I said to myself.

"Now, Anna, My sister and My love, our names have been joined in covenant."

"Thank You," I said, holding the stone to my heart.

"I have been waiting for you, Anna. The loneliness you experienced is nothing compared to the heartache I experienced as I waited for you, seeing you run after all manner of idols to seek satisfaction." He looked out into the garden. "How I called to you."[17] There was pain in His voice. "Year after year you dallied, and I grieved, waiting for you to realize that no one can, or ever will, bring you life itself but Me alone."

The Lord will reign in His thousand-year kingdom on Earth with those white, living stones who through Him have overcome all of their enemies (Rev. 20:4–6) and have learned to live hidden in God (Col. 3:3–4).

11. "Until the cool of the day when the shadows flee away, turn, my beloved, and be like a gazelle or a young stag on the mountains of Bether" (Song of Sol. 2:17).

12. Jesus said in Scripture that His burden or load was light because the yoke of responsibility He carried was easy (Matt. 11:30). This was true because He did nothing on His own initiative (John 5:30). The Father gave Him all those who were to be saved and resurrected (John 6:38–40). Furthermore, He lost none of those given Him by the Father. He relied not on His own strength but by accomplishing all in the power of the Holy Spirit (John 16:14).

13. In eternity all things are complete and present to God, but in time they are not complete (Rev. 21:5–6). The Lord Jesus longs for the completion of the full number of the redeemed, adopted children to stand before the Father and before the Lamb (Rev. 7:9): "a kingdom, priests to His God and Father" (Rev. 1:6), "bond-servants [who] shall serve Him" and "shall see His face" (Rev. 22:3–4).

14. At the end, the Lord Jesus will "[deliver] up the kingdom to the God and Father" after "He has put all His enemies under His feet" so that the Father "may be all in all" (1 Cor. 15:24–25, 28). The Son will have raised up to eternal life all that the Father had given to Him, all those who have believed in Christ (John 6:39–40).

15. The tears of godly sorrow that lead to repentance in those who are in sin and the tears of those who intercede for them are very precious to God. They are preserved in His bottle and recorded in His book of remembrance (2 Cor. 7:9–10; Phil. 3:18; Ps. 56:8; Mal. 3:16).

The tears of God, like those of a woman in the labor of childbirth (Gal. 4:19; Rev. 12:2), are shed as He births His children (Isa. 42:14). He also moans and weeps about the extermination He must carry out upon a nation like Moab because of its sins (Jer. 48:31–32). Jesus was a man of sorrows with regret in His heart over the loss those would suffer who reject Him (Luke 23:28–30).

16. In Scripture one's name may signify one's character, position, function, or destiny before God, the name being practically equivalent to the person. Jesus, along with every Jewish baby boy, was named at His circumcision to signify His entrance into the covenant (Gen. 17:10–12; Luke 2:21). To each believer who overcomes with Christ, a new and everlasting name will be given by the Lord. The saint will be called by this new name in heaven, and he will be forever in covenant with Him, the new name being permanently inscribed on a white stone (Rev. 2:17). The stone

His words struck me to the heart. “My Lord and my God,” I said quietly, “no one has ever loved me as You have…” I was choked with emotion. Slowly I continued, “Nor has anyone ever desired my company as…,” but I could not finish.

“None of flesh and blood can, Anna, for you belong to Me.” He looked me in the eye, and His eyes pierced through me. “I created you for Myself, and only I can satisfy you truly and fully.”

A Gift to God

I did not know what to say. I searched, trying to think of some reply. Finally I asked, “If I am created for You, Lord, what can I do for You? How…,” I groped for the words to convey that I wanted to give a gift to Him. “How do I give something to You?”

He searched my face for a moment and then smiled. “Sing for Me, Anna; that would comfort Me.” He leaned back against the large, apricot tree and closed His eyes.

I did not know what to sing. I swallowed hard. Then I looked out over the garden and prayed within myself. Soon, without knowing what I would say, I began to sing:

Where golden light becomes the red,
And red becomes the white,
Burning with the zeal of love,
A land devoid of night,
Powering the universe
From star to distant star;
Consume the dross, O Ancient One,
Let no aberrance mar
All that belongs to You alone,
Created by Your word;
All that is seen and understood,
All hidden and unheard.
Consume the sin, O Ancient One,
Consign it to the night;
For us there's oneness with our God,
The Everlasting Light.
No shadow dare exalt itself,
No darkness dare display,
Where God Eternal rules and reigns
The land of endless day.
Praise Him, all you heavenly host,
Praise Him, sons of men.

Turn your faces toward the Son,
God's "Yea" and His "Amen."

I had never heard that song before. At its completion I sat amazed. My right hand came up to cover my mouth.

That Which Is Coming

There was a long pause after the song ended. Finally He spoke, "Before the cock crows, Anna, three stages of betrayal will have been accomplished against Me in the world. Betrayal is multiplying, and many will be seduced by their own fear and need for survival.[18] They will betray to save themselves."

Three stages of betrayal of the Lord, as portrayed by Judas, are: (1) those who pretend to be His disciples but secretly love the things of the world (John 12:6); (2) those who secretly consort with His enemies (Matt. 26:14–16); and (3) those who openly side with His enemies (Matt. 26:47–49).

"Lord, unless You give us the grace, we will all betray You. Who is strong enough to think he can stand? You must strengthen us. Unless You rise up to pass these tests...," I was momentarily speechless at the thought, "...who would not, for the slightest reason, betray You? Help us! Rise up within us, Lord. Do not let us sin against You."

He opened His eyes and turned His head to look at me. "I have heard this, Anna." He continued to look at me silently, as if meditating upon my features. Then He sat up straight and said, "Walk with Me to the gate." He rose from the bench and helped me to stand also. We walked

is a witness to the sealing in covenant, as the stone was when Joshua made a covenant with the Israelites at Shechem (Josh. 24:25–27).

The Lord builds His church with living stones (1 Pet. 2:5), those who receive the revelation of Him as the Christ. Simon did, and his name was changed to Peter, meaning "a stone" (Matt. 16:16–18).

17. The Lord must call each person to Himself before the new birth can occur (Acts 2:39; 2 Thess. 2:14). Jesus said that "the [spiritually] dead shall hear the voice of the Son of God; and those who hear shall live" (John 5:25; Rom. 8:30). The words of Christ summoning a person to Himself "are spirit and are life," imparting the Holy Spirit to those who will receive them (John 6:63). He may begin calling a person while he or she is still in the womb (Isa. 49:1). The Lord Jesus experiences the pain of deep longing as He waits for those whom He created for Himself to stop trifling with the gods of this world (Isa. 65:1–2; Phil. 1:8).

18. As we enter the end times, many in the church "will fall away and will [betray] one another and hate one another" to save themselves from suffering (Matt. 24:10). "You will be [betrayed] even by parents and brothers and relatives and friends, and they will put some of you to death, and you will be hated by all on account of My name" (Luke 21:16–17).

silently to the golden filigree gate. The two doors of the gate opened as we approached. We walked out, and He closed the gates, looking into the quiet garden within the wall.

"It is very beautiful here," I said, also looking back at the garden.

The Golden Key

Jesus turned and handed me a golden key to the gate's lock. "Here is the key," He said. "Go in whenever you like." The key was large and antique in design. It hung on a red cord. "Here," He continued, and He dropped the cord with the key on it over my head.

"Will You meet me here?" I asked.

"Unlock the gate, and I will meet you here," He smiled.

I looked again at the garden.

"Whenever you wish," He repeated, "meet Me here." And then He disappeared.

I looked down at the white stone in my hand and the golden key resting on the area of my heart.

It was then that I heard the sound of singing, faintly at first. It was the sort of singing you might hear if your mother was making bread in the kitchen on a cold winter's day. I turned toward the sound and saw a bright light. In the center of this light sat a group of spirits.

The path lay right near them. I stepped onto the path to approach them.

Chapter Six

The Eagle's Nest

The light was as white and intense as the "incubating" light in the parts department. Within the light, four spirits sat together working. Intermittently each would reach up and take a blue ribbon from the air as it floated into the light. The ribbons also seemed charged with light as the spirits began to roll them onto large, silver spools. Then, with the ribbons wrapped, they would place the spools onto equally large, silver spindles that were suspended in midair.

Spirits of the Spools and Spindles

These spirits were not solid in appearance. They were closer to being transparent, but a bluish-silver light outlined their forms. Their shape was that of human beings. However, the light in which they worked made it difficult to see their facial features distinctly.

They did not seem to notice me as they sang together while they worked:

> Every little seam,
> Every little seam
> Sewn with the thread of life;
> Every little seam
> Joins the living stream
> Flowing to the river of life.

Then, without turning, they acknowledged me. "Hello, Anna," a spirit spoke from all that light. "Watching?"

"Yes," I said.

"We are getting the ribbons together for sewing. They represent the various streams that flow from the great river of life and back into it, even as the waters on Earth flow in and out but do not overwhelm the land."[1]

The "river of the water of life" in heaven is a visible representation of the Holy Spirit providing life to everything there (Rev. 22:1).

1. Even on Earth God grants to His faithful children "to drink of the river of Thy delights. For with Thou is the fountain of life" (Ps. 36:8–9). The Hebrew word for *river* means "a wadi or the channel of a watercourse that is dry except when it rains" (a symbol of the Spirit outpoured—Hos. 6:3), and then it becomes an overflowing river. This spiritual river is the powerful moving of the Holy Spirit supplying eternal life to and through those who obey Him (John 4:14; 7:38–39; Acts 5:32).

We are entering "the last days" (2 Tim. 3:1; 2 Pet. 3:3) when the Holy Spirit will be outpoured in a mightier way than ever

The streams that come out from the inspiration of the river of the Holy Spirit are the various movements (such as denominations) of the people of God in Christ who together form His living church on earth.

The sword of the Spirit is the living Word of God concerning Christ Jesus as applied by the Holy Spirit (Eph. 6:17; Heb. 4:12; Rev. 19:13–15).

"These streams are God's people," another spirit said.[2] "They come from Him and flow back to Him, the great Source."

"But they need to be sewn together," another said, looking toward me as if suggesting my participation.

"I'm not a very good seamstress," I laughed lightly.

"The needle here is the sword not of man.[3] The streams are being sewn together by the Spirit of God Himself so that the Father might rejoice to see His city filled with those who love His Son and one another. Even the city itself is made glad."[4]

"You are called to sew with such a needle, Anna," the first spirit said. "That we do know."

"We are placing the spools of ribbon on spindles so that they will unravel easily when ready to be brought together," the fourth spirit added.

"Is there some significance to placing them on spindles?" I asked.

Oil From Heaven

The spirits smiled at one another and sang:

There is oil in the spindles,
Oil right from God.
There is oil from the Spirit of God.
There is oil like a gusher,
Oil from the sky,
Oil that's been hidden until now.[5]
Hum-hum, oil from on high,
Oil that's been hidden until now.
Hum-hum, oil of the Spirit,
Oil that's been hidden until now.

Oil is a type of the anointing with power that the Holy Spirit bestows upon believers so that Christ Jesus from heaven will be able to minister through them for the bringing in of His kingdom here on Earth (Exod. 30:25, 30; Acts 1:8; 2:33; 1 Cor. 4:20).

One of the spirits turned to me and said, "These ribbons are being placed on spindles for you and others who will use the sword as a needle to prepare for the gusher."

Then they sang:

Sew the streams together
And catch the sacred oil;
And, oh, let it not be
Used for the profane.

"Your Father has the answers to the questions in your heart," the third spirit smiled. "We are those who wrap the spools and put them onto the spindles."

Ribbons of Blue

"They are all blue ribbons," I said.

"Yes, each became a stream when revelation came concerning a great truth about our God. But a truth *about* Him is not Him," the first spirit added. "Although the ribbons are being wrapped on individual spools, they are about to be sewn together into a river like the river of life from which they came."

"As we see the Lord bringing into completion all things relating to these times and seasons, we rejoice to be a part of His great roundup," the second spirit smiled.

The White Eagle

Suddenly the wings of a large bird passed over me.

The spirits to whom I was speaking looked up and rose to their feet immediately. I too looked up and saw a large, totally white Eagle. He was powerful, fierce, and majestic in flight. I had never heard of a completely white eagle.

before (Joel 2:28–29) as the promised "latter rain" that will bring in a worldwide harvest (Joel 2:23–24). The Spirit will then move through the earth—as the river described in Ezekiel 47:1, 5, and 9—to bring life wherever He flows.

2. These streams are not independent, for they not only drink from the one Spirit (1 Cor. 12:13–14), but they also add their particular contribution back into the flow of the Spirit in the one church (1 Cor. 12:7; Eph. 4:4, 16).

The coming descent of the Holy Spirit will be in such fullness of power that it will be necessary for these streams of God's people to be bound together in "one heart and soul" (Acts 4:32). This unity in the Holy Spirit (Eph. 4:3; 1 Cor. 12:25–26) will be needed to utilize in purity all the gifts and graces from the Spirit so as to preserve His work from corruption or waste.

3. In the coming days we pray that the Lord Jesus will send forth His Word to the various churches as He did in the second and third chapters of Revelation. He depends upon those who overcome by walking above their flesh, the world, and the devil: saints who no longer live for anything but for Him (2 Cor. 5:14–15; Phil. 1:20–21; 2:21).

The ribbons in the vision represent those streams or bodies of believers who are pliable and willing to be rolled up by the Spirit to wait for His use (Hab. 2:3; Mic. 7:7). The spindles are long rods on which the spools may easily rotate as the ribbons are unwound and sewn together.

4. The heavenly city of God is "the Jerusalem above [which] is free; she is our mother" (Gal. 4:26; Heb. 11:16; 12:22). The earthly copy of that city is the church of the living God described in Psalm 46:4–5: "There is a river [the Spirit flowing freely] whose streams make glad the city of God, the holy dwelling places of the Most High. God is in the midst of her, she will not be moved."

5. There is a vast supply of this oil that God has reserved for a fuller "salvation ready to be revealed in the last time" (1 Pet. 1:5; Rom. 8:18–19). It will come as a gusher, which is an oil well that spouts forth of itself without being pumped by man. The members of that unified, true church will dwell together as brethren, all of them having a share in the anointing oil that comes down from Jesus, who is their head (Ps. 133; 1 John 3:14). "Spindle Top" was one of the greatest oil gushers in recorded history.

"Stretch out your hands," He said as He began His descent.

The spirits bowed toward the Eagle. I did not know what to do but to stretch out my hands. The Eagle, as large as I, backed into me so that His eyes and beak were where my face was. Then just as quickly He was before me again, with His eyes piercing into mine.

I gasped.

The white Eagle is the risen Lord Jesus in His pure and righteous ministry as the prophet of God, for everything about Him is white (Matt. 17:2; Rev. 1:14; 3:4).

Just as quickly, the Eagle changed into the Lord. He said, "This is so you may know that 'the testimony of Jesus is the spirit of prophecy.'" Then He became the white Eagle again.[6] "Come," He said.

I put my arms around His neck, and we flew upward. I did not even think to say good-bye to the spirits who were wrapping the spools. As I lay down with my arms around His neck and my head near the back of His head, I could feel the motion of flying beneath me. His feathers were snowy, and His scent made me want to bury my face deep within His feathers. Beneath the white feathers the great Eagle's skin looked like pure gold.

His Nest

We came quickly to an outcropping of rock near the top of a mountain. An eagle's nest was positioned on this rocky thrust.[7] The nest was large, perhaps five feet across, and made of strong tree branches. I climbed from His back and stepped down onto small, downy feathers within the nest. The white Eagle perched on the nest's rim.

We were on Earth.

The view of the circling mountain range and valley below was breathtaking, but I did not know where we were. The air was clean there, and the view from such a high ledge was sweeping in its expanse. The mountains and the valleys were lush and green. There were passing clouds and shadows from the slant of the sun. Beautiful—but it was not Paradise.

As I viewed the surrounding mountain range, a string of very large paper dolls floated by.

The great Eagle spoke, "So much of what is happening now in the body of Christ is like paper dolls—one copying the other."[8]

The paper dolls disappeared, and an eagle of pure gold flew by. "I am looking for an eagle of gold, Anna—rare beyond measure." As He spoke, power like a surge of electricity ran all over the eagle of gold. It became pure white, like the great white Eagle. "The golden eagle becomes like Me," He said.[9]

Then a line of large, paper, cut-out eagles floated across the mountain range. They were hooked together as the floating paper dolls had been.

The White Eagle's Invitation

He continued, "There are many eagles, for I am generous with the gift of the Holy Spirit.[10] But, Anna, I am giving you an invitation to become an eagle of gold."

Suddenly I saw a rocket blast off from the earth and shoot into heaven. The great Eagle continued, "The golden eagle's nest is in heaven. The golden eagle does not even eat earthly food. It feeds above. The paper doll eagles catch fish, kill snakes, chase rabbits; but the eagle of gold breathes the ether above. It does not seek after or eat carrion. The golden eagle eats from the hand of God until it looks and smells and is like Me—pure white. There are many that *look* like Me, but you must eat from the hand of God to *be* like Me."

His eyes were aflame now. "Will you fly with Me, Anna, over streets of gold? Will you fly with Me over lakes so clear that the bottom is as the top? Leave the snakes, the bugs, the rabbits running rabbit trails. Come with Me and feed from the hand of God."

I paused to consider my answer—and He was gone.[11]

Hesitation or delay in following the Lord indicates that the allotted measure of the Lord's faith is not being exercised in the spiritual heart of the believer (Rom. 12:3).

6. The Lord quotes Revelation 19:10. A prophet, like the eagle, discerns clearly the things on Earth from the height of God's viewpoint; he speaks words from God (Deut. 18:18; John 7:16–18; 12:49–50). The Lord carried the children of Israel safely through their wilderness wanderings as "on eagles' wings" (Exod. 19:4), a figure of speech signifying His supernatural deliverance that, like the eagle's flight, the world cannot provide (Deut. 8:15–16).

7. An eagle's nest is used for many years; through the years the eagle may enlarge the nest up to six feet high and five feet wide. The white Eagle, the Lord Jesus, shares His nest, which is on a rocky ledge on a mountain height, with those who are learning to fly with Him in spirit. Spiritually, His nest represents a place of rest, quietness, and intimacy with Him (Ps. 31:20; 63:7; 91:1–2, 4, 9, 14). This is a place where one learns to trust Him as God's everything, and so as one's everything (Col. 3:11; John 3:35).

8. The paper doll Christians copy one another by using standardized methods of ministry employed in the church, or they attempt to reproduce the kind of ministry that was effective in the life of a famous minister of the past. They may try to duplicate the conditions that brought revival at another location. This use of patterns and formulas is actually a form of divination (a method of obtaining results in the spiritual realm without God's help), which He will not tolerate. Satan will often supply some of his limited power to this occult practice to advance his evil purposes. The false prophets in the Old Testament would repeat each other's words or pronounce prophecies that God had not given them (Jer. 14:14; 23:30; Ezek. 22:28).

The Pharisees obeyed complicated rules and rituals of behavior, but their reverence for God consisted of tradition learned by rote (Isa. 29:13). The Lord refused to copy both the customs of the Pharisees and the God-inspired fasting of John the Baptist (Luke 5:33). He listened and watched for His Father's instructions moment by moment (John 5:19–20, 30).

9. This kind of Christian is rare. This disciple "hates his [soul] life [mind, emotions, and will] in this world" so that he may have the soul life of Christ forever (John 12:25). He is not at home on Earth (2 Cor. 5:8; Phil. 1:23), for he cannot be satisfied by anything in this present world system (1 John 2:15, 17; 5:19). He desires only to feed upon the Lord Jesus as the hand of the Father shares His Son with him by the Spirit (Hos. 11:4; Ps. 78:23–25; John 6:32–35, 57).

Jesus's food is to please and honor His Father in everything (John 4:32, 34; 8:29). Jesus alone nourishes the Father (Lev. 21:6; Num. 28:2; Ezek. 44:7). As His Son is the true bread and drink (John 6:51, 55), Jesus alone sustains such a Christian. In time, this kind of believer will be perfected into oneness with the Son and the Father so that he is, acts, and looks like Jesus who is formed within him (John 17:21, 23; Gal. 4:19; 2 Cor. 4:10–12).

Back in Paradise

I found myself back in Paradise, seated alone on a high hill.

Did I pause too long to contemplate, weighing His passion against my inertia? Was I fearful? Of what? What kept me from leaping up in my spirit and shouting, "Yes! I accept the invitation! Take me to Your resting place above and make of me an eagle of gold. I want to eat from the hand of God. I yearn for the intimacy You are offering." Why did I hesitate?

Now from that place of solitude on the hill in Paradise, my heart cried out, "O God, I long for You alone. Do what You will with me, for I am Yours. Yours alone! Yours alone!" There was such longing in my heart's cry that I expected to see Him charging over the hilltop on a white horse in response, but He did not.

Instead, silence.

Passing Praise

Then, almost imperceptibly at first, I heard voices in the distance singing praises to God. The music came closer, but I could see no one. Instruments joined the song that now sounded as if it were being sung by a multitude of voices. The praise was rolling along like a flash flood in a wadi. Although I could see no one, the praise seemed to be passing before me on this hill and moving in the direction of the path below. My ears caught the words of the singing:

> Let my life extol the living God,
> The Father of all light.
> From the ends of the earth through the universe,
> Extol His mercy and might.
> Forever is not long enough
> To praise His glorious name,
> The forever of forever
> To shout His glory and fame.
> O celestial court, throw down your crowns
> 'Neath the ruler of the earth.
> Living creatures, sing your songs
> To the King of the universe.
> O joy unspeakable, joy foretold,
> Ever new and ever old,
> Before the Father's throne be bold
> To lift your songs of praise.

Then I saw one angel after another join themselves to this praise, seemingly riding along on it. They would rise when the music would rise, and sank down when the music lowered, like the tail of a kite. Evidently they could see the praise, although I could not, because they looked as though they were touching it and being carried along.

Then, from near me on the hill, came the clear, pure sound of a flute. I turned to see an exquisite angel dressed in green playing the instrument. Her eyes were closed in worship, and I knew that the music she was playing was joining the praise passing before my eyes.

10. The lofty eagle flies alone or with his mate, soaring effortlessly on the thermal currents; he builds his nest as high as possible. He has binocular vision, a symbol of the believer whose spiritual eyes Christ, the great Eagle, has opened (Matt. 13:16–17; Eph. 1:18–19). This Christian is at home in the godly spiritual world (1 Cor. 2:9–10; Phil. 3:20). He "[seeks] the things above, where Christ is," setting his mind upon the things of God (Col. 3:1–2).

The gift of the Holy Spirit enables the Spirit to bear witness of Christ in the saint (John 15:26), first to God the Father (Acts 2:3–4; 1 Cor. 14:2) and then to others (Acts 2:5, 9–11; 1:8).

11. Christ's love within that one has not become full (Eph. 3:19; Gal. 5:6). We see an example of this hesitation in the maiden whom Jesus is inviting to share more of His life (Song of Sol. 5:2–5). He asks her to open her heart to bear some of His sufferings. She delays by resorting to reasoning. She then agrees to His request, but He has gone away. She must now endure pain of another kind: the loss of consciousness of God's presence, as Jesus experienced on the cross (Song of Sol. 5:6; Matt. 27:46).

Chapter Seven

Obedience

The angel sat cross-legged on the ground playing a golden flute. Her hair was a rich auburn and plaited into seven large loops that were interlaced with gold. She wore a gossamer, green undertunic bound with a golden girdle, and a cloak with long sleeves, which was also green.

Within the sleeves of the outer garment were oversized pockets containing all manner of instruments used in the arts—all of gold.[1] There were various musical instruments, paint brushes, musical scores, ballet shoes, a quill pen—all within the sleeves. Her neck and hands had a slight tint of gold and so did the small portion of her bare feet that I could see.[2]

Gold is a symbol of Christ Jesus or the manifestation of the glory of that which honors God (Song of Sol. 5:11; Job 23:10). It is the one metallic element described in the Garden of Eden, indicating the value and beauty of the earth He had brought into being (Gen. 2:11–12).

Secured around her head was a golden cord; in the center of the cord was a small golden box. The box was in the middle of her forehead and similar to a frontlet for the housing of Scripture.[3]

Eventually she lowered the flute and opened her eyes peacefully, as one might who is still rapt in contemplation. Then turning her face toward me, she smiled. "Praise Him," she said. Her voice was gentle and melodious, and her eyes a limpid green.

I was too disquieted in spirit to share her peace, for thoughts were racing through my mind—with no resolution.

The Angel Judy

She smiled again, knowingly this time, but did not address my private conflict. "I am Judy," she said, "one who praises."

1. Ezekiel 28:13 describes Lucifer in heaven before he betrayed God. The end of the verse may be translated "and the gold, the workmanship of your tambourines and flutes, was prepared in you on the day you were created." Apparently he was connected in some way with worship in heaven. These musical instruments were "in" him, no doubt as part of his attire.

2. All the sacred objects in the tent of the tabernacle were of pure gold, for only the most precious metal was to be used to represent God in His dwelling place among the Israelites (Exod. 25:17–18, 24, 31; 37:25–26). This is true on Earth because it is true of the original tabernacle in heaven (Rev. 8:3).

3. Bound to the foreheads of the Israelites were little boxes, known as phylacteries, that contained verses of Scripture (Deut. 11:18). God instituted this custom in order to remind them that the truth of His words were to be impressed upon their minds and their hearts, so that they were on their lips wherever they were and whatever they were doing (Deut. 11:19). His Word says that all creation is to praise Him continually (Ps. 148:2; 34:1).

"Hello, Judy," I said without much enthusiasm, "I am Anna."

God assigns angels and other heavenly beings to serve on Earth "those who will inherit salvation" (Heb. 1:14; Gen. 48:16; Exod. 23:23).

"I know who you are," she smiled, "for I am assigned to you to assist you in praise of our God."[4]

"Assigned to me for praise?" I asked. Then excitedly I gestured toward the space in midair, "I saw..."

"Yes," she said, "angels traveling on praise."[5]

"Traveling on praise?"

"Yes," she reiterated, placing the flute into one of her oversized pockets.

"I do not understand."

"Praise has in it part of the heart and part of the spirit sent forth, and so it is tangible to us in this world of true light, life, and spirit. To us here, praise is as substantive as a trolley on Earth, you might say. You join yourself to it, and it will carry you along. It can take you for a ride," she laughed liltingly, "and the one joined to it adds to it."

I turned my eyes to look out over the valley. "How could this be?" I questioned within myself. Then I began to think, "Yes, yes, I can understand that. I know that if someone leads worship with an anointing on Earth, it can lift you in spirit to that person's level of praise. The other's anointing carries you with it, and you add your voice to the worship being raised to God. Yes, I can see that."

"Since all such praise travels to the Father," she continued, "it is like catching a ride on a passing trolley and enjoying the ride to the throne room. If the angels do not ride all the way there, still they have added an imprint to the praise. Therefore, they too have participated, if ever so briefly."

The sound of a single violin began to pass by. The violin was playing a tender, unaccompanied melody. A single angel was traveling with the adoration being expressed through this instrument and was adding to it.[6]

"Some praise on Earth is like a quiet stream, as is this," she smiled.

From a distance I could hear the sound of many voices singing. The sound was moving swiftly in our direction.

The living church of Christ Jesus is being watched with great anticipation by the host of heaven, both the redeemed there and the angels (Heb. 12:1).

"Some worship is like a tidal wave," she said. "All of it gives to the angels a joy they would not have if mankind did not lift up praises to God."[7]

The sound was coming more quickly now, rolling toward us. As it drew nearer, I could sense my spirit rising to join such exalted worship. It lifted us spontaneously to our feet. Judy raised her hands, tilted her head back, and joined the song:

Angels in their glory
Can never touch the flame,
The fire, pure incandescence,
That burns within Your name.
Let them gaze in wonder,
In awe, as they proclaim:
"Holy God, though ever new,
Eternally the same."

Frightened, frozen, fettered,
Those who seek to fight,
Numbed and gnawed and naked,
Those who choose the night.
But we are covered by His love,
Beneath His banner stand,
Hidden in the Rock above,
Sheltered by His hand.

Angels in their glory
Can never touch the flame,
The fire, pure incandescence,
That burns within Your name.
Let them gaze in wonder,
In awe, as they proclaim:
"Holy God, though ever new,
Eternally the same."

4. Angels may be assigned to a human being for life (Matt. 18:10), or for a certain period of time (Acts 7:38), or for one visit (Luke 1:26). The service rendered by angels includes assistance to believers in developing spiritual gifts and callings (Judg. 6:12–16). Judy is a feminine form of the biblical name *Judah,* which means "praise." A life of praise is so important for those who follow the Lord that God assigns angels to help believers express it in blessing God and in binding His enemies (Ps. 34:1; 149:6–9).

5. Praise is to be offered to the Father through the Son by the Holy Spirit in believers. The Son's words of praise to His Father contain something of the divine nature, heart, and life (John 6:63; Heb. 2:11–12). Therefore this true praise is substantial, active, alive, and visible in the spiritual realm (Heb. 4:12). Worship in the Spirit of God by the believers on Earth is joined to the praise in heaven because their resurrected, human spirits here are one with the spirit of the Lord Jesus there (Phil. 3:3; 1 Cor. 6:17; Eph. 2:6).

6. Praise to God may come from the playing of a musical instrument (Ps. 150:3–5). It is possible "to prophesy with lyres, harps, and cymbals," that is, to speak messages from God with their sounds (1 Chron. 25:1).

7. Paul says that "the anxious longing of the creation [including angels] waits eagerly for the revealing of the sons of God" in the last times (Rom. 8:19; 1 Pet. 1:5–6). Jesus said that "there is joy in the presence of the angels of God over one sinner who repents" (Luke 15:10). How much more do they exult when the church worships (Rev. 7:9–11).

In an ecstasy of devotion, Judy rose into the air from her place on the hill and began to move toward the passing praise.

"Take the path to find the Lord," she called, and she was swept along in the tidal wave of worship surging toward the throne.

The disappearing praise continued to engage my spirit. Finally I opened my eyes and realized that she had given me the answer I needed. I hurried down the hill to the path and began running in the direction of the vanishing praise.

Obedience

As I hastened, I heard the voice of Jesus say very clearly, "Obedience, Anna."

I stopped in my tracks.

The natural or earthly self is the greatest hindrance to following the Lord; therefore, it must be set aside (Matt. 16:24).

He continued, "I delight to show you your heavenly home, but for your safety, you must be trained in obedience.[8] There are grave dangers.[9] All doors to the enemy must be shut."

As I stood in wonder at the gravity of what He had said, an angel appeared on the path beside me.

The angel began talking to me as though he were continuing some conversation we had already begun, gesturing with his hand toward God's park. "All of this is for the children of God, but you, Anna, have chosen to eat from the hand of God. You must love your Father enough to choose obedience rather than gratifications on Earth.[10] Choose Him minute by minute. You are careless with His gifts, and you are careless with His love for you."

His overfamiliarity stunned me, as well as his knowledge of a decision I had only recently made, but yes, I was careless. As the Lord had drawn me into a deeper walk with Him, those things permissible a year or even a month ago were now no longer allowable. Somehow I could no longer get by with them, but I still lapsed into many of these faults.

The Thought Life

Elusive sins caused me to pay a high price in my relationship with the Lord. I thought to myself, "Let the wicked forsake his way and the unrighteous man his thoughts."[11] I had moved from the "way" category to the "thoughts." My mind did not focus on unforgiveness or covetousness or such obvious sins. My sins now were in engaging my mind in some area where I was not called, or in letting my mind dwell on the past, or in making a judgment that was out of my boundary of responsibility.

My life had become very constrained indeed.[12] If I walked without turning to the right or the left, I remained in the flow of God's grace. Any thoughts that were "vain in their imaginations" caused my mind to run in grooves around a track.[13] Such thoughts were driven by tormentors, it seemed.[14] But I found that I could stop them by repeatedly catching myself and halting the train of thought as I began to think on such vain thoughts.

The enemy has erected his fortresses in our natural minds in the form of man-centered attitudes, speculations, and beliefs (2 Cor. 10:4–5). From these citadels his demons can deceive and torment the believer, as happened to the slave with the unforgiving attitude in Jesus' parable (Matt. 18:33–35).

Of course, these thoughts would tiptoe back in, needing to be run out time and time again. Therefore I was halting them and throwing them out, standing against them with my will, as if my shoulder were against the door of access.

Still I was careless, as he had said, and was mentally running around many tracks in torment and weariness until each thought was taken captive to Christ.[15] Earlier in my life with Christ, my mind could usually do as it pleased, but not now.[16] Narrow and narrower was the way, but in this obedience to His Word was life.

8. All God's children must learn to obey Him, even as Jesus on Earth had to learn in His human nature to obey His Father in all things (Heb. 5:8; John 8:29). The natural person of believers is incapable of obeying God, for their "flesh" (the earthly body and soul acting on its own) desires only to do what it pleases (Rom. 8:7; 7:18; Eph. 2:3). Therefore our obedience must be learned by repeated acts of the will in freely choosing moment by moment the obedience of Jesus's perfect human nature in us (Eph. 4:24; Col. 3:10). The Holy Spirit can then reinforce the flow of the Lord's obedient life in us (Heb. 5:9; Phil. 2:13). Christ has been made unto us all things, including the obedience that the Father desires (1 Cor. 1:30; Col. 3:11). Believers need to let Christ manifest the life of obedience in them, for He is the only life in them (Isa. 26:12; 2 Cor. 4:10–11; John 14:13–14, 19; Col. 3:4).

9. The earthly soul life must be replaced by the soul life of Jesus's perfect human nature in us (Matt. 16:25). This exchange is called the salvation of the soul (Luke 21:19; Heb. 10:39; James 1:21; 1 Pet. 1:9). The Holy Spirit cannot protect us when we allow the devil and his demons to work through our old self (Gen. 4:7; Eph. 4:27; 1 Pet. 5:8–9). We give legal permission to them to inhabit the darkness in us because of sin (Eph. 5:11).

10. The glory of Christ's love meets all of the believer's true needs (John 17:24; Phil. 4:19). The enemy is capable of stimulating our natural desires so that we feel we must have certain earthly gratifications and have them now (1 Pet. 1:14). We can come to rely upon these substitutes and to love them instead of loving the Lord (1 John 2:15–16). We can discover that "the love of Christ [for us] controls us" (2 Cor. 5:14); that His love is better than wine (Earth's best stimulants) (Song of Sol. 1:2); and that His "love never fails" us (1 Cor. 13:8). It is no sacrifice to choose that which is of God in Christ—eternal, divine, truly pleasurable, and satisfying—instead of that which is temporary, created, a counterfeit pleasure, and a false satisfaction (James 4:3–4; 1 John 2:17).

11. Every believer must "forsake . . . his thoughts" because "every intent of the thoughts of his heart [is] only evil continually . . . from his youth" (Isa. 55:7; Gen. 6:5; 8:21). The Holy Spirit transforms us by helping us set our renewed minds (no longer conformed to this world) on God's interests (Matt. 16:23; Eph. 4:23; Rom. 12:2).

12. The Lord Jesus said that the path that leads to true life is narrow and restricted to walking step by step in Him who is the way (Matt. 7:14; 1 John 1:7).

13. Paul tells us that the imaginations and speculations of the mind of the natural person are vain and futile because they focus upon "the creature rather than the Creator" (Rom. 1:21, 25).

14. God said that the root of sin in mankind is in the thoughts of our hearts (Gen. 6:5). Jesus reiterated that truth (Matt. 15:18–19).

15. Paul says that the unruly mind can be reclaimed for Christ by casting down speculations and every proud argument that is contrary to the true knowledge of God in Scripture. The believer then takes control of every thought to make it obedient to Christ (2 Cor. 10:5).

The Angel Shama

The name *Shama* is a Hebrew word meaning "to hear with the intent to be obedient."

Without missing a beat, the angel on the path beside me said, "I am Shama."[17]

I saw no reason to give my name, for he seemed to know almost as much about me as I did myself.

"Shall we walk?" he continued.

Almost stumbling, I moved forward.

He had long, straight, silver hair that was caught at the base of his head and hung down his back. He was very muscular, and although his hair was silver, he looked perhaps forty. He wore a full-length white robe, which looked as though it had been stained with blood or the juice of red grapes. This stain was on the hem of the robe and on the cuffs of the long sleeves, discoloring the garment to the knees and elbows.

"You delight in God," he continued. "I have watched you and have seen that you desire nearness to Him. However, do you not know that disobedience creates a wall between you and Him?[18] It is a wall of your own making because you cannot curb your natural desires. He will replace with Himself every delight you push away, Anna."[19] In looking at me, his eyes caught sight of a hill slightly beyond us. "Come with me," he said.

Jesus in His human nature "learned obedience from the things which He suffered" (Heb. 5:8). Faith was perfected in Him as He endured the rejection and betrayal of those He came to save.

As we walked up the hill, he continued, "There is a type of suffering in obedience, but the rewards far, far outweigh the pain."[20]

The Prototypes Above

From the top of the hill, we could see a broad plain below. Herds of various kinds of creatures were grazing; among them were prehistoric animals.[21]

My hands went to my face in amazement.

"Heaven itself is like an ark, Anna," he said. "These animals do not have resurrected bodies but were part of the heavenly kingdom before the earth was created."

"Magnificent," I whispered.

"Aren't they?" he said, observing the scene. Then, almost with a sigh, he continued, "Let's return to the path." He was slightly ahead of me going down the hill, and he assisted me with the incline.

"Do you have hair?" I asked him.

"It looks like hair," he said. "We are creatures of light. We are spirit, Anna. We are not flesh and blood as humans are. Some of us in service to the King look like humans, but some do not."[22]

Celestial beings have bodies of spirit instead of physical matter; therefore they are able to appear or disappear (Judg. 6:12, 21) or to change their outward appearance (Exod. 3:2) as needed.

We returned to the path and continued to walk. "We can change our appearance," the angel said, "whereas you cannot. We are known by the essence of what we are, not by our outward appearance. On Earth this is often reversed, is it not? Humans often dwell upon appearances."

"You seem to know me," I queried.

"I know you better than you know me," the angel laughed.

The Stained Robe

"Why is your robe stained at the bottom and on the sleeves?"

"I am called to assist in child training—the kind that squeezes the child—like being in a winepress.[23] These," he looked down at the stains, "are visible signs of the child's development. The more stains, the greater the work has progressed within the child. Obedience is not learned easily, Anna. Some on Earth never learn it."

"Are you an angel assigned to help train me?" I asked.

16. The young apostle Peter was headstrong, bent on going wherever he wished (John 21:3). Jesus told him that when he grew old, he would have to follow his Master in the way of the cross where he did not wish to go (John 21:18–19).

17. An example of this word is spoken by Moses to the children of Israel to "listen obediently to the voice of the Lord your God." (Deut. 15:5).

18. God's "eyes are too pure to approve evil, and [He] canst not look on wickedness with favor" (Hab. 1:13). "Your iniquities have made a separation between you and your God, and your sins have hidden His face [intimacy] from you" (Isa. 59:2). The light of God cannot fellowship with darkness (1 John 1:6).

19. "Delight yourself in the Lord; and He will give you the desires of your heart" (Ps. 37:4). "In Thy presence is fulness of joy; in Thy right hand there are pleasures forever" (Ps. 16:11). "Thou dost give them to drink of the river of Thy delights" (Ps. 36:8). "God has prepared for those who love Him" things never seen or heard before, things beyond imagination (1 Cor. 2:9).

20. Having "emptied Himself, taking the form of a bond-servant," He became "obedient to the point of death, even death on a cross" (Phil. 2:7–8; Heb. 2:10; 12:2–3). Perhaps the worst suffering was the shame He endured from people believing He had been rejected by the Father (Matt. 27:42–44). He kept choosing at each trial to entrust "Himself to Him who judges righteously" instead of justifying Himself (1 Pet. 2:23). Jesus's perfected human nature, fully joined to His divine nature, is within the believer as his new nature: complete in Christ and becoming complete in its expression through His disciple (Col. 2:10; 3:10).

21. God created first in heaven the prototype of every animal that ever lived on Earth, and it still exists there in a perfect state (James 1:17; Heb. 8:5; 9:23). In the case of dinosaurs and other animals that ate meat on Earth instead of the grass and plants that God provided for them (Gen. 1:30), they remain in heaven as the gentle, herbivorous creatures that He made them. He will restore the carnivorous animals now on Earth to this condition during the Millennium (Isa. 11:6–9; Rom. 8:19–21).

22. Many have spiritual bodies that look like the physical form of human beings (Dan. 10:16, 18), but others are unique creations of God, as are the four living creatures around the throne in heaven (Rev. 4:6–8) or the wheels (Ezek. 1:15–20).

23. The Holy Spirit opposes the flesh in believers; He presses the power out of it in order that He may bring forth the obedience of Christ (Gal. 5:17; Rom. 8:12–13; Col. 3:5). The outward discipline that the Spirit custom designs for each of us is meant to bring us to accept God's "sentence of death within ourselves in order that we should not trust in ourselves, but in God who raises the dead" (2 Cor. 1:9; 4:10–11). This process is like pressing out the juice of grapes, leaving the "flesh" or pulp lifeless. Some Christians refuse

"I am assigned to you."

"Helping to train people in obedience cannot be a pleasant job."

The angel replied, "It is of great significance to the Father and absolutely necessary. By this time in your life, my robe should be entirely stained and my face and hands dripping, but there are only stains on the hem and sleeves. So may I suggest that you are hindering your growth through known disobedience. Immediate gratification can never replace serving the Lord with a whole heart. Such obedience releases joys untold."

Repentance

I looked out over the landscape, letting the truths he was sharing work within me. "I have sinned," I said quietly.[24] I did not wish to seem glib, but I did wish to show a willingness to repent promptly. "I ask the Lord to forgive me."

He put his arm around my shoulder and jostled me, as a coach might a football player. "And you know He does. This is a good day for new beginnings," he smiled. Then he removed his arm and looked ahead solemnly.

"I thank you for your patience and for helping me. I can see you are a powerful angel. If you were a human, I would say you 'worked out.'"

"We do 'work out,'" he laughed heartily, "but our workout comes from wrestling with humans.[25] I look as I do because you have given me so much resistance through your flesh. So," he laughed, "you might say I do 'work out.' I would suggest that you turn this very day so that my workout is less strenuous. Delight yourself in God, Anna, and reduce my exercise program," he smiled.

The heavenly host is watching how we believers on Earth run the course of obedience in Christ Jesus (Heb. 12:1).

Then he sobered rapidly. "Nothing, no one can compare to Him," he said. "Speaking for those of us who are assigned to you," he continued haltingly, almost as if he was going to reveal something deeply personal, "we would like to get a little closer to God." He almost stammered, "If it were only us, we would; but much depends upon you concerning that."[26] He seemed so embarrassed by what he had said that he vanished.

The Eagle Returns

Before I could puzzle over what he meant, I saw the white Eagle fly across the path. My heart leaped when I saw Him. I began to run after Him, calling, "Lord! Lord, please come back, please."

He must have heard me, for He made a wide bank in flight and landed before me. I was so overjoyed to see Him whom my heart adores that I hugged Him around the neck, clinging to Him. "I want to fly with You. I want to eat from the hand of God."

He became the Lord. I buried my face in His shoulder. He held me, returning my embrace, more like a lover than a friend.[27] This amazed me. Did He long for me as I longed for Him?

"Forgive me, Lord," I said. "I want to be with You. I long for You. I want to be and do whatever You want, as long as we are together."

"Anna," He said, pulling me away from Him so that He could look into my eyes, "do you trust Me?"

"Why, yes, Lord," I answered, surprised.

"Then come."

He became the white Eagle. I quickly climbed onto His back, and He began to fly. I put my arms around His neck and buried my face in the fragrant feathers of His head.

He flew...and flew...and flew...until He flew into deep darkness.

to accept and carry this individual cross as Jesus continually bears His private cross (Matt. 16:24). Therefore they have to continue in chastisements from God for years (Heb. 12:5–6).

24. Children in human families learn to obey by being disciplined or trained by their parents, and so do the children of God. Divine discipline also is meant to bring us to receive the gift of repentance, so that we change our attitude and direction and return to peace and right relationship with our heavenly Father by sharing in His holiness (Heb. 12:10–11).

25. Sometimes angels must strongly oppose us, as the angel with the drawn sword blocked Balaam's path (Num. 22:22–35). An angel also wrestled with Jacob at the ford of the Jabbok (Gen. 32:24–31).

26. When the sons of God are revealed in the last days as those who "will shine forth as the sun in the kingdom" (Matt. 13:43), "the whole creation," including the angels and the redeemed in heaven, will share in "the freedom of the glory of the children of God" (Rom. 8:18–19, 21–22; Col. 3:4). Christians have received "the promise" of the Spirit (Acts 2:39), who brings forth Christ as that "something better for us, so that apart from us they [the redeemed in heaven and the angels] should not be made perfect" (Heb. 11:39–40; 1 Pet. 1:10–11). All heaven also awaits the victory Jesus won over Satan and his host at Calvary to be enforced by the overcoming church, so that all of God's enemies will be cast out of that part of heaven that they occupy (Eph. 3:10; Rev. 12:10–12).

27. The Bible portrays the living church as the bride of Christ in graphically romantic terms in the Song of Solomon. An example is the Lord speaking to her, "Arise, my darling, my beautiful one, and come along!...For your voice is sweet, and your form is lovely" (Song of Sol. 2:13–14). The prophets speak of God's affectionate love for His people (Jer. 2:2; Ezek. 16:8). Human marriage is a type and foreshadowing of Christ's love for His bride, the overcoming church (Eph. 5:25, 29–30), to whom He will be joined before He returns to earth with her to reign (Rev. 2:11, 26–27; 3:21; 19:7–9; 20:6).

Chapter Eight

The Corrupted Strata

I could not discern if it was densely dark or if it only seemed that dark because we had come from a place so permeated with light.

The Sheepfold

The white Eagle flew down into a walled-in area that had a shelter within it. The wall was of uncut stones and fairly high. On top of the wall were branches brandishing large, painful-looking thorns.

God's people are called sheep throughout the Bible, for they are utterly dependent upon the Lord, their Shepherd, for nourishment, discipline, and protection (John 10:9, 29).

It was a sheepfold.[1] It was Christ's outpost in that corrupted strata occupied by Satan.[2] The enclosed area had but one gate. It appeared that the thorns were not so much to make entry by the demons impossible, but to serve as a warning. NO TRESPASSING—a visible command from Christ Himself. The sheepfold was His territory.

It occurred to me that perhaps one of the reasons the crown of thorns was crammed into Jesus's skull before His crucifixion was as a private slap in the face from Satan, for the sheepfold was crowned with thorns. Christ had dared to establish a place of safety within the enemy's hostile kingdom. That crown of thorns was an affront before His crucifixion; now, after His resurrection, it was an ever-present reminder of Christ's victory and His eternal lordship.

The white Eagle changed into the Lord.

1. Jesus Christ is "Lord of all" (Acts 10:36) "by the exertion of the [resurrection] power that He has even to subject all things to Himself" (Phil. 3:21; Eph. 1:22). He proclaims His lordship right in the midst of Satan's headquarters by the sheepfold where "no one [can] snatch… out of [His] hand" any believer whom Christ brings there (John 10:28). The Lord leads them in and out of this place of safety in the presence of their worst enemies (Ps. 23:5; John 10:3–4). He is the one and only door that leads to life (John 10:9), "who opens and no one will shut, and who shuts and no one opens" (Rev. 3:7).

2. The command post for the devil's worldwide organization of demons and fallen angels is in a lower sphere (Eph. 6:12; 3:10; Col. 2:15; 1 Cor. 15:24). God's throne is in the third or highest heaven (2 Cor. 12:2; Eph. 4:10). From his headquarters, Satan governs a wicked empire on Earth through lust, deception, and pride. The Bible calls this evil realm "the world" whenever it refers to the system of commerce, industry, finance, education, science, medicine, and law that makes man the measure of all things and omits God (1 John 2:15–16; James 4:4).

The shepherd's staff represents the Lord's authority and power (Exod. 14:16; 17:9, 11; Ps. 23:4).

There was scant light except for that which came from Him. "Stay with Me," He said. He had a tall staff in His hand.

By the gate were two pairs of porpoise shoes that were dyed red.[3] He put on a pair, and so did I.

"Touch nothing here, Anna; all is defiled."[4] We walked out the gate into the darkness. Jesus Himself was the light on our way.

Satan's kingdom aboveground includes the earth's surface (1 John 5:19), the atmosphere above the earth (Eph. 2:2; 6:12), and his headquarters in a lower part of the heavenly realm or midheaven (Luke 10:18). All three of these areas are interconnected; whatever he controls in one area of his kingdom, he also controls in all the other areas.

Weeping and sardonic laughter came from the darkness. They were human voices, but they sounded as if they were coming from animals.[5] Alarm gripped me. I stayed close to the Lord, walking in His footsteps. Although it was dark, I began to see dimly.

The Outskirts of the Strata

The surface on which we were walking was dank and sticky. There was a slight suction created on the bottoms of my shoes as we walked, as though I might become glued to the spot if I did not keep moving. Huge, slimy creatures would half roar, then lift themselves up and move threateningly toward us. They looked like giant slugs, but acted more like bull seals protecting their territory.[6] They tried to frighten us, but they ended up bowing before Jesus, a begrudging acknowledgment of His lordship.[7]

The River of Filth

The filthy, stagnant water is a pitiful imitation of the crystal clear river of life in God's heaven (Rev. 22:1).

We came to a levee that sloped down to a black lagoon. The water was filthy, sluggish, and stagnant. The smell was putrid.

Jesus helped me into a long pirogue. I sat down, but He stood and poled us across this narrow waterway with His staff. The water boiled and emitted steam every time His staff plunged into it.

Jesus said, "This is a river of filth. As the river of life is clear, so this one is putrid and defiling. It issues from the mouths of sinful man. As rivers of living water come from the belly of My righteous ones, so out of the blackened heart, through the mouth, comes this watery filth."

I could see creatures lying on the banks and hear them breathing. They appeared to be crocodiles, but they made blowing sounds through their nostrils like hippos.[8] Their eyes shone in the dark.

The Chained Ones

Caves lined the levees, and an occasional cry or moan came from them. I felt that the sounds I had heard when we walked through the gate came from these caves. They looked like dungeons with demons guarding the entrances. But who or what was imprisoned there?

The demons uttered low, guttural chuckles at the obvious pain of those imprisoned. They enjoyed someone else's pain.[9]

"Observe the misery," the Lord said. "My people participate in this, enjoying the downfall of another, laughing at the mistakes of others, and holding them in their chains instead of setting the captives free."[10]

The fleshly use of a Christian's tongue is demonic, whether he is cursing others or attempting to speak wisdom (James 3:6, 9, 15). When he speaks out of his earthly self, he seeks his own glory and so gives Satan the right to use him (John 7:18).

I looked toward the dark entrances of the caves. Within these dungeons the enemy held captive certain areas in the lives of humans on Earth. Christians, instead of helping to set the captive free, were tightening the chains of condemnation that held them in bondage. Christians were siding with the jailers against the Lord by nullifying the provision of forgiveness and reconciliation that He had made for them through His shed blood.

3. Porpoise skin is water repellent and so served as the outer covering on the tent or tabernacle (Exod. 26:14). Nothing of the sin and death in Satan's domain is to touch the feet of the believer! The shoes are red, a witness to the victory over the devil and his host won through the blood sacrifice of Christ on Calvary (Col. 2:15). The shed blood of the Lamb not only overcomes any accusations of the enemy, but it also cleanses from any possible defilement through being in his loathsome territory (Rev. 12:17; 1 John 1:9; 2 Cor. 7:1).

4. Sin and death have brought physical darkness to Satan's territory in the midheaven (Col. 1:13). Because of the vicious hatred there, the inhabitants also walk in spiritual darkness (1 John 2:11), the opposite of the love that enables one to abide in the Light of God (1 John 1:5; 2:10).

5. The sources of this torment are the areas of human soul life (mind, emotions, and will) on Earth that Satan and his demons control. Everyone is born with his soul faculties subject to the law of sin and death in his bodily members (Rom. 7:23), and hence he is dominated by "the [evil] spirit that is now working in the sons of disobedience" (Eph. 2:1–3). Satan therefore has a legal right to bring distress and suffering in every person's soul until that person believes in Christ Jesus. He is then joined to Him, submitting his soul faculties to the Lord as he begins to think, desire, and choose as He does. This is "the salvation of your souls" (Matt. 16:24–25; Luke 21:19; Heb. 10:39; James 1:21; 1 Pet. 1:9).

6. In Leviticus 11 and Deuteronomy 14, God separates the animal kingdom into two categories: the clean and the unclean. The clean animals were offered in sacrifice on the altar and used as food for His people. The unclean ones were not so acceptable. It would seem that Satan and his demons select many of these unclean animals to inhabit, as the legion of evil spirits asked Jesus to send them into the pigs (Mark 5:12–13). The hideous bodies of some demons are the result of living in an atmosphere of utter corruption apart from the light, life, and love of God. There is a hierarchy of rank among demons. A sluglike animal represents the lowest order—those that crawl on their bellies (Gen. 3:14; Lev. 11:42).

7. The Father has so highly exalted the risen Christ "that at the name of Jesus every knee should bow, of those who are in heaven, and on earth, and under the earth" (Phil. 2:10). "Every knee" includes every creature in Satan's domain, too.

8. The crocodile is an example of a reptile that the ancient Egyptians worshiped as a god. This culture often made idols of animals they feared, like serpents and lions. They considered the crocodile to have godlike qualities. It is also the only animal without a tongue, which the ancients considered godlike. Furthermore, it is almost impenetrable and seemingly afraid of nothing.

9. God has compassion on the suffering of His children (Exod. 3:7; Deut. 30:3) and is hurt by their unfaithfulness (Hos. 11:8; Mic. 6:3). In direct contrast, Satan and his demons find pleasure in defiling the children of God (Rom. 1:32) and rejoice in their sins, which is the opposite of love (1 Cor. 13:6). The enemy host compounds hatred in their kingdom by taking delight in refusing to give any relief to those who are in pain (2 Tim. 3:3).

10. When we enjoy hearing of the fall of another into sin or slander each other or presume to pass judgment on the guilt of another, we are usurping God's place and are participating in Satan's sins (Rom. 14:10; James 4:11–12; Rev. 12:10). We are thereby withholding the blessing of God that we "were called" to give others (1 Pet. 3:9). We are even to "bless those who persecute [us]; bless and curse not" (Rom. 12:14). Christians have the great privilege of asking God for life for any brother or sister whom they see committing a sin (except sins for which the sinner deserves to die) (1 John 5:16).

The Levee

WE stepped onto the opposite bank and began to walk up a wide path to the crest of that levee. Moans came from every demon we passed. Christ's appearance among the demons tormented them, and they ran away from Him.[11]

"Light is very painful to them," Jesus said, indicating the fleeing demons. "They suck up darkness and breathe out venom—lost, corrupted forever, darkness inside and out. These who once ate the food of angels, these who stood in My Father's light, these who knew the companionship of the trustworthy—now they slither and cringe from the light, cursing the darkness and cursing the light—they are doubly damned. They eat vomit—three or four times over." (I felt that He was equating vomit with slander.) "In community with those of their kind, they laugh at each other's misery and deny each other relief—turning, forever turning upon one another, therefore always alone."

"Leave us," a voice said, and a hyena giggled.

All is damp or watery because satanic creatures fear the coming flames of hell (Matt. 8:29; Luke 8:31). Jesus said that they are even tormented by dry places on earth (Matt. 12:43).

As we topped the levee, the land as far as I could see was slimy mud, a murky wasteland.[12]

"Wet," Jesus said, "for they fear the fire. They are tormented even by dry places."

Numerous dead trees stood within the mud.

"The trees are a memorial to the vile groves of false gods. Here these trees are seen for what they actually are: broken, bare, without life—the home of snakes and birds of prey."

Counterfeit Unity

Indeed, black snakes were in these dead trees, as well as covering the brackish mire. They were hissing and writhing, constantly moving over one another as if mating.[13] "A false unity, a joining in the black mind," I thought. It occurred to me that as the Lord is bringing together a oneness in Himself, so the devil is birthing a counterfeit unity.

We are to walk before the Lord with nothing in our lives concealed from Him (Eph. 5:11–12). Everything is continually exposed to let His presence cleanse and transform all into His light (Eph. 5:13–14; 1 John 1:7).

Jesus spoke, "The spawn of demons. How Satan promotes his imitation fruit. These goad tormented souls to vomit forth slanders, lies, and cursing—rivers of putrid water in which the demons swim."

His ear caught the sound of a cry from a cave by the lagoon. He turned His head to hear, saying, "There are labyrinths also within some believers: dark corridors where the light has not shown, hutches that have not been delivered from darkness.[14] But the true light is ready to travel every corridor and touch every dark corner so that all within each believer may be of the light. Darkness is heavy with sin; it is dense and murky. My freedom is light. For the redeemed, all within them must be delivered over to light. Light must flood every corridor, and every lurking malady must be healed."

Jesus then took my hand, saying, "Come."

The Demonic Temple

Suddenly we were within some sort of huge temple.[15] Large, gray concrete pillars supported this main area. The room was hazy with incense, and the cloying odor of blood was mixed with that smell.

Around the perimeter were several stories of rooms, some closed and some open. They looked like caves of horn.[16] It was possible to reach only the lower rooms by foot; all the others required flight, like bats.

A horn symbolizes the power of a king or kingdom for good or evil (Rev. 5:6; 12:3).

11. The demons in Scripture found the presence of Jesus tormenting to them (Mark 5:7). "For everyone who does evil hates the light, and does not come to the light, lest his deeds should be exposed" (John 3:20). The true nature of "all things become[s] visible when they are exposed by the light" of God (Eph. 5:13). Since "God is light, and in Him there is no darkness at all," there can be no fellowship (but rather enmity) with Him for those who walk in darkness (1 John 1:5–6; Rom. 8:7).

12. On one occasion thousands of demons who were in a person asked the Lord to send them into a herd of pigs so that they could go with the animals into the lake (Mark 5:12–13). The devil has long secured worship of himself on Earth with sacred trees and tree trunks or pillars called Asherim that represent female deities of fertility (Deut. 16:21–22). These tree trunks are dead, as are all idols (Hab. 2:18–19).

13. Snakes or serpents are a major symbol for Satan and his demons in Scripture (Rev. 12:9; Luke 10:19). One reason is that God cursed the serpent in the Garden of Eden because it was used by the devil to deceive Eve (Gen. 3:1, 14). Jesus said that Satan must maintain unity among those in his evil kingdom (Mark 3:24–26), a oneness built upon hatred of God and His creatures (John 15:25; Ps. 69:4).

14. All believers "were formerly darkness" before receiving the light of the nature of Christ Jesus within them (Eph. 5:8; 2 Cor. 4:6). Their old nature was darkness because they had grown into the image of their father, the devil (Matt. 13:38; John 8:41, 44; 1 John 3:8, 10). Remnants of their old, dark ways of thinking, desiring, choosing, and acting may remain unnoticed if Christians continue to rely only upon their natural observation and perception. To perceive only the things of this world admits the old darkness again (Matt. 6:22–23; 2 Cor. 4:4). Their spiritual eyes need to be enlightened to the reality of Christ and be focused on Him (Eph. 1:18–19; Heb. 12:2). Of course, anything the believer does secretly with a guilty or doubtful conscience is hidden away from the light of fellowship with Jesus (1 John 1:6).

15. Satan has counterfeited all the things in heaven that are possible to him, an example being his guise as an angel of light (2 Cor. 11:14). Above all else, he craves to be worshiped (Matt. 4:8–9). Praise and homage come to Satan's temple from the great multitude of idolatrous places of worship throughout the world by means of the demons who inspire this worship (1 Cor. 10:20; Rev. 9:20). The worship of false gods even infiltrated the first temple in Jerusalem during the reign of many kings of Judah (2 Kings 23:4; Ezek. 8:9–16). The first recorded instance of satanic worship occurred in Babylon around 2150 B.C. A rebellious host of people erected a tower whose "top reach[ed] into heaven," meaning that the devilish signs of the false zodiac were used for divination there (Gen. 11:4). The antediluvian patriarchs knew the true meaning of these constellations of stars, for God tells the story in the night sky of salvation in Jesus Christ (Gen. 1:14 ["signs"]; Ps. 19:1–2).

16. Satan undergirds heathen kings on Earth to increase their treasuries of silver and gold, which the Bible calls "treasures of darkness, and hidden wealth of secret places" (Isa. 45:3). He increases their earthly wealth in exchange for their homage and praise through false gods (Isa. 65:11). In the first temple in Jerusalem, there were "upper rooms" called "treasuries" (2 Chron. 3:9; 2 Kings 12:18). Gold and silver that had been dedicated to the Lord for His purposes were stored in these rooms. These treasures came as gifts from the king or wealthy people and from the spoils of war (1 Kings 7:51; 1 Chron. 29:6–7; Num. 31:48–54; 2 Sam. 8:9–12). At times the kings of Judah gave these treasures away to try to gain military protection from enemies instead of relying upon God (1 Kings 15:18–19).

There were six staggered levels of rooms on the left side: six at the back and six on the right side. But how many cave rooms were there in all, I could not tell.

I could see black creatures covering the walls of the hollow rooms that were open. They looked like dark, unhealthy jellyfish, each with only one eye. These were like a fungus on the walls. Their eyes were constantly looking to and fro. Nothing escaped their notice.

Stolen Treasure

The Lord spoke, "The enemy has hidden stolen treasure within the darkness of these rooms. Prying eyes guard this treasure. These spies are rewarded for their vigilance. The infested caves are a vortex, throbbing with suspicion. Here there is fear of exposure—the opposite of covering—because of love. The time has not yet come, Anna, to release these captives from the caves [meaning the stolen treasure], but all that is of Me and is Mine will be cleansed and come to Me."

A time is coming when everything belonging to God that Satan has stolen will be released from his headquarters, then cleansed and restored to the highest heaven (Heb. 9:23; 2 Pet. 3:12–13; Rev. 21:1, 5).

I did not understand what He meant. He continued, "Just as tears and prayers can be stored above, so can praise be taken captive by the evil one and stored in caves of horn. The enemy bathes in stolen worship—renewing himself in that which belongs to God, putting his hands all over that which is sacred and secret. Since Satan cannot create but only imitate and defile that which belongs to God, his greatest joy is to desecrate that which is of the Light. My Father will one day have all that belongs to Him. The temple vessels were captured and hidden away in Babylon, desecrated by being mocked and used to toast false gods. Just as these were returned and reconsecrated to God, so all that belongs to My Father will be cleansed and consecrated to Him alone.[17] The enemy is in dense darkness, doing that which is foul in order to relieve his pain, but instead only multiplies his pain. But My Father will set free all that belongs to Him. He will cleanse it from the filth of deception and idolatry corrupting it so that it might rise to Him."

I saw demons flying into these caves of horn to defile the hidden things of God there, like spiders sucking the life out of their captured prey.

Promised Day of Deliverance

The Father will signal the beginning of His judgment on all of Satan's host by raising His sword and by severing all that is His from the enemy (Deut. 32:41; Ps. 7:12; Heb. 12:26–27; Hag. 2:21–22; Zeph. 3:8).

Jesus continued, "There is coming a time when God Himself will raise His sword in the midheaven.[18] He will come forth in His own behalf; the fat from false sacrifices and from offerings to other gods, who are not gods, will be His.[19] The fat is His, and they have robbed Him. The praise is His, and they have stolen it from Him. They have stored it for themselves. But He will raise His sword to sever the fat

17. The valuables taken as spoil from enemies of the Israelites in war had to be purified either by fire or by water (Num. 31:21–23).

18. Not only will the stolen treasures be cleansed and returned to God, but the very terrain will be completely purified from the effects of darkness, sin, and death (as in the natural, see Ezekiel 36:6, 8–9, 13–15).

19. "All fat is the LORD's" (along with the blood) of the animal sacrifices on the brazen altar, "an offering by fire for a soothing aroma" (Lev. 3:16–17). God commanded this from the beginning with Adam, Eve, and their sons (Gen. 4:4). Animal fat burned on the altar symbolizes nourishment and fragrance to the Father (Ezek. 44:7; Lev. 4:31). It represents the "sacrifice of praise" that is "continually offer[ed] up" (Heb. 13:15) through the Son (Acts 2:33) by the fire of the Holy Spirit (Lev. 3:3–5) from the people of God (Acts 2:3–4, 11). The Father seeks such worshipers (John 4:23). The main purpose of fat is to be "burned" (oxidized) to produce energy. The physical fat of the animal sacrifices was removed from organs in the abdominal cavity, which is the location in Christians of the human spirit from which praise and worship proceed (John 7:38).

The fat (and the blood), God's portion of the sacrifices, was offered first on the altar—before the rest of the animal—in order to rise in smoke toward heaven (1 Sam. 2:15–16; Lev. 4:34–35). Likewise, the first order in approaching the throne of God in spirit is to "enter... His courts with praise" (Ps. 100:4; 96:8). As fat is that which abounds, believers are to abound in praise to our God. The word *fat* is an expression used to designate the best part, for example, "living on the fat of the land." Praise to God is surely the best part for human beings (Ps. 147:1). When we worship anything of the earthly realm, we violate the first two commandments and allow demons to capture this spiritual fat.

20. Israel is often compared to a female (Isa. 54:5–6; Hos. 2:14, 16, 19–20). So is the church as the bride of Christ (Song of Sol. 4:8–10; Rev. 19:7). God designed human marriage on Earth to prepare the two mates for eternal marriage to Jesus Christ (Eph. 5:25–27, 31–32; Rev. 21:9). The church is the spiritual womb in which the children of God are conceived, born, and reared (Song of Sol. 8:5; Rev. 12:1–2, 5). From the earliest days Satan has perverted this sacred imagery into licentious worship of female deities of fertility. In all the nature religions of history, there have been "mother goddesses" (Acts 19:27; 1 Kings 11:5). The Bible often calls this idol "the queen of heaven" (Jer. 7:18; 44:17–19). During many periods Israel worshiped "the Baals and the Ashtaroth" (Judg. 10:6; 1 Sam. 12:10). The idolatrous church in these last days is pictured as a harlot queen called "Babylon the Great." She is ruled by demonic powers just as the first Babylon in Genesis 11:4, 9 was ruled by them (Rev. 17:1, 4–5). She is foretold in Isaiah 47:1, 7–9.

21. Israel has been a captive nation in political terms and in spiritual chains for most of her history (Ps. 106:41–42; Isa. 52:2). Many present Christians have been "conformed to this world" system (Rom. 12:2). They are caught in "the snare of the devil, having been held captive by him to do his will" (2 Tim. 2:26). The captive church ensnares her converts with an illusion of grandeur—prosperous, outward appearance—and activities that are actually "dead works" and "devoid of the Spirit" (Heb. 9:14; Jude 19). This worldly church chains her members by teaching them to idolize the religious organization and by binding them to perpetuate it through traditional and rote forms of worship (John 11:48; Isa. 29:13).

22. Honey at times represents the false comfort that Satan provides through the fleshly church: smooth, sweet words based on earthly wisdom that is soulish and demonic like the words of an adulteress (Prov. 5:3; James 3:15).

23. King Solomon built a magnificent throne of ivory and gold, like no other throne on earth (2 Chron. 9:17–19). Furthermore, "he went up to the house of the LORD" by a stairway of such grandeur that it took the visiting queen of Sheba's breath away (2 Chron. 9:3–4). His love of opulence was a root from which grew other idolatrous sins. Satan will give the coming Antichrist the power and authority of his throne to use on the earth (Rev. 13:2).

24. An evil "spirit of divination" spoke through a slave girl in Acts 16:16 to foretell the future. The Greek word for *divination* means "python." Python was the name of a mythical serpent that guarded the Delphic oracle where secret knowledge was thought to be revealed. God forbids the evil art of people who seek to discover knowledge about the future that He Himself has not revealed to them (Deut. 18:10–11). The devil cooperates with this ungodly practice and supplies some of his limited knowledge if it will suit his purposes. Psychics, astrologists, fortunetellers, and adherents of the so-called New Age religion use modern divination.

25. God on His throne in heaven is attended by the redeemed "from every tribe and tongue and people and nation" (Rev. 5:9–10). In evil imitation, Satan's court is composed of ruling, fallen angels known as "princes" (Dan. 10:12–13, 20). These angels control the heathen rulers, nations, and areas throughout the earth for the devil's purposes and bring their homage to Satan's throne (Rev. 17:1–2, 15).

26. Through consorting with Satan's evil, spiritual empire on Earth, which the Bible calls "the world" (Matt. 4:8; John 14:30), the false church receives the "bodies and souls of men" (Rev. 18:13, NIV) whom she holds on to for display. God calls her the Esau church because she cares more for her comfort, gratification, and convenience than for her spiritual birthright (Gen. 25:29–34).

27. All along God has sent true prophets to speak for Him to His people, but time and time again they have been rejected in favor of false prophets who prophesy by means of an evil spirit what the people want to hear (Jer. 2:8; 23:13–17, 25–32). Jesus said that false prophets would arise in the last days "to mislead, if possible, even the elect" (Matt. 24:24).

28. In the last days, Jesus said that people in whom Satan is working will show "great signs and wonders" (Matt. 24:24; 2 Thess. 2:9–11; Rev. 13:13–15).

29. There were female and male cult prostitutes during periods of Israel's history (1 Kings 14:24). Along the outer walls of Solomon's temple in the three stories of side rooms that were built for the priests on duty, there was cult prostitution at times (2 Kings 23:7;

Nothing that is not of God will be able to stand before His divine light, for "the powers of the heavens will be shaken" (Matt. 24:29; Isa. 34:4; Mark 4:22; Eph. 5:13).

from them and to release the praise stored for generations. A great holocaust will occur when the fat of many generations finally rises to Him. When He unsheathes His sword and rises up in His own behalf, none can say to Him, 'Nay!' None can call to Him, 'Hold!' None can turn Him back at the gate. He will cleanse the midheaven and set it free. Then His light will touch every corner and purge the malignant growth from generations of corruption, thievery, and lies. When He lifts His sword and releases His light, surrogates will flee like roaches; mighty ones in the strength of wickedness will shrivel and slither away."

He spoke to the midheaven, "O promised day of deliverance, a time has been appointed, and you will be free." He turned back to me and said, "When He raises His sword in heaven, praise will be released like a bird from a cage, never to be imprisoned again."

The Demonic Masquerade

A drone or monotonous tone in ritual incantation is used in some heathen worship to contact the power of the spirit world. The Lord expressly rejected the use of such mantras (Matt. 6:7).

We began to hear a drone, like that of bees swarming or flies gathering on a dead carcass, coming from a distant area of the temple. As those creating the monotonous sound drew nearer, I could hear the hypnotic rhythm more clearly. They were chanting a mantra.

Suddenly they burst into view. It was a large and lavish procession accompanied by loud, discordant music.

The massive concrete columns within the temple obscured our presence from those entering, so we stepped out of view.

Dancers and musicians came before a woman splendidly dressed.[20] Jewels adorned her long robe and crown. She held innumerable chains in her hands just as a person would hold dog leashes. Shackles were around the necks of demonic beings she held captive, who bowed continually, kissing the ground where she walked.[21] They looked like naked humans.

Everything about the evil one and his kingdom is false and an imitation of the true (John 8:44). The true fire of God "burns up the chaff" in believers and ignites the new heart to become a living flame of love for God (Matt. 3:12; Song of Sol. 8:6). The false fire of the enemy merely torments and destroys (John 15:6; Rev. 9:17–18).

Her retinue was very large and seemed to comprise those from various nations—perhaps every nation. She turned in our direction. Her eyes were red with false fire; when she opened her mouth, fire came from it.[22] We were too far away for the fire to touch us, however. When the fire ceased, honey dripped from her mouth; those in chains licked up the drops that fell to the ground.

She went up by stairs to a high throne in this incense-filled hall.[23] When she sat, her attendants wrapped the long train of her robe around her feet. The train looked like a python.[24] Those in chains groveled on either side of her throne.

False Homage

The kings of the earth came with presents for this woman.[25] They also brought jugglers, prophets, and magicians to entertain her and her court.

The team of jugglers juggled all manner of objects of unequal weight, including gold bars and apes. But the object that fascinated me the most was a cage on which was written THE SOULS OF MEN.[26]

The prophets were almost as showy, jumping around and speaking great boasts concerning her and others present.[27] Those gathered would laugh and throw money to these false prophets.

The showiest of all, however, were the magicians, who looked extremely grave, wise, and dignified; they performed mighty signs and wonders.[28] Everyone clapped and bowed before them in awe.

The devil is able to perform signs (miracles) and wonders (marvels) through his human servants on Earth. He did this, up to a certain point, through Jannes and Jambres, the magicians of Pharaoh's court (Exod. 7:11–12, 20–22; 8:5–7, 18; 2 Tim. 3:8). Simon the magician astonished the people of Samaria with his diabolical arts (Acts 8:9–11).

Each king would take a golden coin from this woman's tongue like tokens taken while standing in line at a store counter. A number was on each coin. They would return them to her later as she went from side room to side room, servicing these kings like a prostitute with many clients.[29]

The woman's face was old and caked with makeup, but from a distance she looked beautiful and splendid. She was drinking from a jewel encrusted cup, and her eyes looked glazed.[30]

"Who is this?" I asked the Lord.

Hos. 4:14). The fallen church has committed adultery through her friendship with the world system masterminded by the devil, adopting many of its values and methods, thereby making herself "an enemy of God" (James 4:4; Rev. 17:1–2; 18:3, 9).

30. In the last years before Christ returns, the corrupt church will be in league with Satan's Antichrist (Rev. 12:3; 13:1; 17:3, 7). This human beast and his armies will turn and destroy her with fire in one day (Rev. 17:16). God executes this judgment against her for "corrupting the earth with her immorality, and He has avenged the blood of His bond-servants on her" (Rev. 19:2). The "cup of demons" is that which sustains them (1 Cor. 10:21). With Christians it is the cup of Christ's blood (1 Cor. 11:25). With Satan's host it is the "cup full of abominations and of the unclean things of her immorality" (Rev. 17:4).

31. God will separate out the true and living church of His Son (Rev. 18:4; Isa. 52:11; Jer. 51:6). This emerging church has only one standard by which she measures everything: Christ Jesus. The true Christians will allow the fire of God's Spirit to burn up everything that is not of Christ in them and in their lives. The members of the false church will not allow the fire to deal with the ungodly use of their bodies and their natural self life (the flesh) or their love for the things of Satan's evil system (the world). The enemy will still have access to them. The Lord says in this vision, "Many will go with her [the false church]." Many of those who call themselves Christians will remain with the spiritually dead church. As in all past generations, only a remnant will be saved (Isa. 10:20–22; Zech. 8:12; Matt. 7:13–14).

The fleshly church will "become a dwelling place of demons and a prison of every unclean spirit" (Rev. 18:2) when God completely withdraws the light of the Spirit from her (2 Thess. 2:7, 11).

"The false church," He replied.[31] "She makes herself a queen, and those enslaved eat of the honey from her mouth. She has given herself to every demon. She services them. Many will go with her."

I looked at her, horrified.

"I have brought you to see the false masquerading as the true," He said. "Mark well the content. Mark well the consequences and outworking of the decision to embrace the darkness instead of the light. All manner of corruption breeds in darkness. Come," He said, and once again He became the white Eagle. "We go now to the bowels of the dragon."

Chapter Nine

Bowels of the Dragon

The white Eagle flew into a darkened tunnel that seemed to be a passageway through a mountain, but the walls were like part of a living organism, resembling an intestine. The sides of the walls seemed packed with fecal matter, and the stench was nauseating and overpowering.[1]

An Attack: The Flesh

Although I was with the white Eagle, the filth and blackness shocked me. I was afraid. I tried to maintain some sort of spiritual equilibrium, but fear began to paralyze my faith.

Hopelessness, oppression, and despair were within the very walls of this tunnel. I knew that Jesus was protecting me, but the presence of evil was suffocating.

Then, like a trapped animal, my mind began to search for an escape: "Where am I going? Why am I here? What if I fall off in this place? How can I get out of here?"

Once doubt had gained an entrance, panic soon followed, bypassing all assurance of the Lord's protection. Now, thoughts like wild dogs began to lunge at me. Did they come from within or from the tunnel? I did not know, but I was frantic with fear: "I won't make it; I can't hold on. They'll hurt me. They'll kill me!"[2]

At times the Lord allows the thick darkness from the enemy to come upon the believer, together with a limited assault by demons. This is not an unloving thing for Him to do; it is necessary for us to experience the hideous depth of corruption in the flesh (Gal. 5:19–21; 2 Tim. 3:2–5).

1. Among the laws given by God to the Israelites was one that required them to have bowel movements outside the camp, digging a hole and covering up the excrement. They were to keep the camp clean and sanitary, for the holy God walked in the midst of His people (Deut. 23:12–14). In his headquarters, Satan deliberately defies the laws of God, particularly the laws concerning His purity and holiness. Within the tunnel there were foul odors of feces; the evil host enjoys being indecent and defiling the lower part of the heavens to which God has assigned them for a time. This is one of the reasons why Scripture calls demons "unclean spirits" (Mark 5:13).

2. This pollution is ever present, together with Christ's victory in us over the power of the flesh (Gal. 5:24). The Spirit tests everyone (as Jesus was tried in the wilderness) before they are given added responsibilities. The flesh, our worst enemy, is the earthly expression of the old, outer person who was born captive to the law of sin and death within (Rom. 7:23; Eph. 2:3). Evil spirits have helped fashion this natural person into the image and likeness of Satan during the years before we came to Christ (Eph. 2:1–2; John 8:44).

The flesh is a storehouse of memories, attitudes, and emotions stemming from the resentments, injustices, and pain we have experienced in the past. The reason these are still with us is because the flesh cannot forgive or love, anymore than the devil can forgive or love. Demons can tap this reservoir of hatred within us at a moment's notice if God or the believer allows it. The flesh cannot love anyone but itself, for it hates God, the source of love (Rom. 8:6–7; 1 John 4:7–8). It will always be in bondage to the law of sin and death (Rom. 7:18, 23–24). The flesh cannot be redeemed. It will remain bound by sin for the duration of one's earthly life, as it cannot repent (Heb. 12:17).

If the Lord had not shielded me, I believe these thoughts would have torn me to shreds. I clung to the white Eagle. "Jesus, Son of David," I cried, "have mercy upon me."[3]

I could not tell what happened, but slowly the sense of almost being eaten alive lessened. Jesus, my Savior, had come forth in me. He had shown mercy.

I was in shock, though, and dazed, rather like a person who has been attacked by a pack of ravenous wolves and escaped only with her life. I was left weakened and trembling, badly shaken.

No human being can possibly survive the full assault of the enemy, but the Lord sets limits to the severity of a trial (Job 1:12; 2:6).

The Lord strengthened me, and I sighed, relaxing my grip somewhat.[4] He would protect me. He would not let me fall.

"I am all right," I sighed. "I am all right." My trust in God had returned.

Then silently, more like vapors than thoughts, insinuations reached for me like tendrils of smoke.

An Attack: The World

It has always seemed strange to me that after a severe attack by the enemy, the most dangerous period of time appears to be after the battle is over and the victory secured. Perhaps one is vulnerable because of weariness, allowing vigilance against attack to be relaxed. But stranger than this is the fact that after the heat of battle, I always forget this truth.

I forgot again.

The insinuations reaching for me were disarmingly subtle; they made the world, which is Satan's heaven, seem to be all that I could ever desire or should ever desire.[5] Promises sweeter than honey enveloped me, promises of having Satan's heaven now and God's heaven later.

Suddenly the tunnel lost its stench; instead, it emitted a tantalizing fragrance. I thought to myself, "Why am I doing this? I can have anything I want simply by applying myself. I don't need to live like this. In fact, I'm tired of living like this."

I began to think of ways to make money—and not just to make money, but to make a fortune. "Only a fortune can lift me above this sort of trial," I thought. "Only a fortune can give me luxuries commensurate with my taste, which deserves to be expressed and enjoyed. There is so much beauty in the world, and I want to surround myself with this loveliness. There's nothing wrong in that. I can do it with hard work. All I need to do is to center myself upon this goal and head for it, give myself to it...head for it and give myself to it...head for it and give myself to it..."

"Wait, wait," I said to myself. "This isn't right. Giving myself to a life of accumulation, just satisfying my senses, can't be right." Such an idea was a siren song whose allure, if it did not bring shipwreck, certainly would have seduced me into a spiritual limp. Deadly.

"No!" I said silently. "Choose you this day whom you will serve, and I choose Christ. I choose Christ," I cried aloud.[6]

The vaporous fingers ceased reaching for me and silently slid away. Again, the Lord strengthened me. I sighed deeply as before, relieved.

An Attack: The Devil

By this time I thought I saw some light at the end of the tunnel. I started to become anxious for relief. I wanted out. Out.

Then, as if in my own voice, I heard, "Jesus may love you, but it's a strange sort of love that would bring you into a place of such great danger. And I can't see that He's protecting you as He should. Of course, if He'd told you beforehand what you would be facing... but He didn't. If you could acquire more knowledge yourself, you

Victory over the power of the flesh was won by Christ on the cross when the old, corporate heart (the power source of the flesh) of the human race died with Him there (Ezek. 36:26; Rom. 6:6; 2 Cor. 5:21; Col. 3:3). When He rose from death and ascended to the Father, a new inner person of heart and spirit in the likeness of Jesus's resurrected heart and spirit became available to set every believer free from the dominion of the flesh (Eph. 4:24; Col. 3:10; 1 Pet. 3:4; Ezek. 36:26–27; Rom. 8:2; 1 Cor. 6:17). The love of Christ now has the power to control us rather than the flesh (2 Cor. 5:14; Phil. 3:21).

We must be brought to hate our flesh and every expression of it (Jude 23; Luke 14:26; John 12:25). We are to put no confidence in ourselves but in Him who raises the dead (2 Cor. 1:9). God gradually reveals to us the depth of the hideousness of our flesh (Gal. 5:19–21; Col. 3:5, 8). He reveals it so that we may vehemently oppose it in the power of the Holy Spirit (Rom. 8:13; 13:14; Gal. 5:17, 24). We also may remain hidden within Christ, trusting His presence to be all that every situation requires in the Father's eyes (Col. 3:3; Phil. 4:6–7).

As we live on Christ's level and share all things with Him in loving submission to His needs, His presence in us will meet our needs and the needs of others (Ps. 16:11; Phil. 4:19).

3. This was the same cry of another person who was in darkness: the blind beggar Bartimaeus (Mark 10:46–47). The Spirit helps us to counterattack the enemy with the spoken word of Scripture, as He helped Jesus on earth (Matt. 4:4; Eph. 6:17; Rev. 12:11).

4. Angels strengthened Jesus in His trials (Matt. 4:11; Luke 22:43). Second Thessalonians 3:3 says, "The Lord is faithful, and He will strengthen and protect you from the evil one." (See also John 17:15; Ephesians 3:16; Philippians 4:13; Hebrews 2:18; 1 Peter 5:10).

5. This world system based upon earthly pleasure, gain, and glory was offered by its ruler, Satan, to Jesus in His temptations in the wilderness (Matt. 4:8–9). To love the world system is to love its prince and to be without the love of God in oneself (James 4:4; 1 John 2:15–16; Luke 16:13). Jesus gained the victory over Satan's kingdom on this earth on the cross. The world system was crucified (separated by death) to us and we to the world (Gal. 6:14; John 12:31; 15:19). When resurrected in spirit with Christ Jesus (Eph. 2:5–6; Col. 3:1), the life of the redeemed is "far above all rule and authority and power and dominion" of the enemy (Eph. 1:21). Jesus will manifest in us His overcoming of the world (John 16:33; Rev. 3:21).

6. Joshua admonished the children of Israel to choose between serving the false gods of this world or serving the living God (Josh. 24:14–15). The greater Joshua, Jesus Christ, said that a person cannot live for God and also live for the world: "No one can serve two masters" (Matt. 6:24).

wouldn't need to rely upon Him for protection. You could protect yourself. You deserve better than this."

Pride in its most heinous form is the effrontery of overstepping the bounds of the dependent creature so as to presume to judge God and others (Gen. 3:5; Num. 11:1, 5–6; 21:4–6; Matt. 7:1–2; James 4:11–12; 5:9).

There it was: pride, presumption, unbelief, accusations against the Lord's loving-kindness, and an invitation to be independent of Him, better than Him—in other words, rebellion. All of these were the deep things of Satan.[7]

"Oh, God," I said within myself, "forgive me. That I would think I could do anything by myself, when I know that apart from You there is no life. I love You, and I know that You love me. You alone are the victor, You alone. You alone will do all and be all and are all; I trust You, my Savior and my Lord, my God in whom I trust."[8]

When believers are tested by trials or temptations, it is for the purpose of having Christ's own faith within them tested in order to demonstrate to them its genuineness (James 1:2–4; 1 Pet. 1:7).

With great passion I cried out within the tunnel: "I have been crucified with Christ, and it is no longer I who live, but Christ lives in me!"[9]

The Gigantic Cavern

Joyously the white Eagle burst through the far mouth of the tunnel. Now we seemed to be flying inside a gigantic cavern within that mountain, but I could not be sure, for I was unable to see the top. Within this cavern, if it was a cavern, the atmosphere was gray and deathly still, but electric, as it might be in the eye of a hurricane.

Tunnels honeycombed the encircling mountain, both up high, as was the one we had traveled, and at the base.

Satan's Palace

Just ahead of us was another mountain rising from within the center of this cavern. It looked as though it was made of shiny, jagged coal. On its top was an exquisite palace, as perfect and lustrous as a jet gemstone. A thick, yellow liquid oozed from beneath the structure and slid down the mountain. The air reeked of sulfur.[10]

Dragons in Satan's kingdom are not imaginary or mythical creatures. They are demons with serpentine bodies (serpents being venomous reptiles) that have grown to be monsters.

At the base of this mountain, large red dragons luxuriated in a cesspool moat, as wild beasts might cool themselves in muddy water on the Serengeti.[11] Their heads rested against the base of the mountain. Slight fire would come from their nostrils; when this fire touched the yellow liquid sliding down the mountain, a flame would ignite but quickly go out. They rolled their eyes up at us, but we must have been outside of their designated patrol area, for we did not raise their ire enough to protect the castle.

The palace itself was ingenious in design—imaginative and tasteful, but dark, cold, uninviting, and foreboding.

"Satan's mountain and his palace," the white Eagle said.[12–13] He continued to fly toward it.

7. The basic sin of Lucifer in heaven was arrogant presumption in claiming God's giftings and grace to him as his own to be used to make himself like God (Isa. 14:14; Ezek. 28:17; 1 Tim. 3:6). The presumptuous sin of the Israelites in the desert was passing judgment on God for not being faithful in providing for them (Exod. 17:7). In the wilderness Satan brought a temptation against Jesus to be presumptuous and put God the Father to the test by requiring Him to prove His faithfulness (Luke 4:9–12).

Satan could find no pride in Jesus (John 14:30). When He suffered unjustly, He did not retaliate but "kept entrusting Himself to [His Father] who judges righteously" (1 Pet. 2:23).

Believers hold their position in Christ, clothed in His victory over the enemy, to resist being moved from that place of His triumph (Heb. 2:14–15; Col. 2:15; 2 Cor. 2:14). Unmoved by the schemes of the enemy, we stand firm and proclaim the Word of Scripture as supplied by the Spirit (Eph. 6:11, 13, 17).

It was necessary for Jesus to have complete victory over the enemy during His forty days of fasting in the desert in order that He might then return to Galilee "in the power of the Spirit" (Luke 4:14). All believers need to experience the power of Christ's triumph within them so that they might become steadfast during any proving of Christ's faith in them that God allows the devil to bring (James 1:2–4). In this way they can begin to reign with the Lord even in this present life (James 1:12; Rom. 5:17; Rev. 2:10; 3:10–11).

8. We have nothing of our own with which to pass these tests. Jesus's faith was perfected through His suffering every trial we may face and His remaining obedient to His Father (Heb. 2:18; 4:15; 5:8–9).

Our part is to obey Him by trusting Him as our victory; His part is to be that obedience in us that is necessary to demonstrate His victory in our present testing. We must not rely upon anything of ourselves to obey God. To clearly teach us this truth, Jesus gave one commandment that He called "My commandment": to love others just as He loved us (John 13:34). It is, of course, humanly impossible for us to love as He loves. To establish this truth even more firmly, Paul added two more humanly unattainable commands: to forgive one another just as the Lord forgave you (Eph. 4:32; Col. 3:13), and to accept one another just as Christ accepted us (Rom. 15:7). Jesus must be that love, forgiveness, and acceptance of others; He must be all things unto us (1 Cor. 1:30; Col. 3:11). He said, "As the Father has sent Me, I also send you [into the world]" (John 17:18; 20:21).

9. In times of temptation, we are to proclaim to the devil and his demons that Jesus Christ is our victory over them, for we died with Him on Calvary and now share His risen life (Gal. 2:20; Col. 3:3).

10. The word *brimstone* in Scripture means "sulphur." Sulphur is a yellow solid that becomes a liquid when its temperature rises, and it burns with a suffocating odor. It is part of the molten rock called magma that is in the mantle or layer that extends some eighteen hundred miles beneath the earth's crust. Hence sulphur is found plentifully in volcanic regions. Burning sulphur is poured out from heaven by God in judgment upon the sins of mankind (Gen. 19:24; Ezek. 38:22). The abyss or "bottomless pit" deep within the earth is a prison for the most evil spirits, who will be loosed in the last days to spew burning sulphur from their mouths against unrepentant humanity (Rev. 9:18). Sulphur oozes from beneath Satan's palace as a constant reminder from God that his house is built upon that which cannot stand (Luke 6:49). It is also a reminder that his final place of abode will be the lake of burning sulphur in hell (Rev. 19:20).

11. The principal Hebrew word meaning "dragon" is *tannin,* which is also translated "serpent" and "sea monster" (Ps. 74:13; Isa. 27:1; 34:14). The root of the Hebrew *tannin* is the word *tan,* which means "jackal," a wild dog that often subsists on the remains of animals slaughtered by other carnivores. Another Hebrew word used to describe dragons is *saraph,* translated as "fiery serpent" (Deut. 8:15). It is the same Hebrew word that is also translated "seraphim," the plural of seraph, who are an order of fiery, heavenly beings stationed above God's throne (Isa. 6:2). As the blessed seraphim burn with the holiness of God, so the fiery, serpentine dragons are diabolical fiends that have grown to resemble the character of the evil one whom they guard. In the Bible the words *dragon, serpent,* or *sea monster* are also used as figures of speech to describe the literal, bloodthirsty ferocity of Satan or the heathen kings and nations that he controls (Rev. 12:4; 13; Ezek. 32:2).

12. Mountains in Scripture are often symbolic of kingdoms. Again in imitation of heaven, the devil has erected his dwelling place on a mountain, for God dwells on Mount Zion (Ps. 2:6; 9:11; Heb. 12:22; Rev. 14:1). "Out of Zion, the perfection of beauty, God has shown forth" in radiant splendor (Ps. 50:2). The plan of the evil one was to set up his throne in heaven above all the other angels and to reign there like God (Isa. 14:13–14). Such was the utter folly of his deluded mind, corrupted by arrogance and ambition (Ezek. 28:17; James 3:14).

13. Satan's palace is more like a castle, which means a large and stately residence that is fortified against an enemy. It is also a palace in the sense that such mansions are usually where kings live. We see the devil's dwelling reflected in the palace of the king of Babylon, whereby they both claimed the power and the glory for themselves (Dan. 4:28–30). There are no palaces or castles in heaven, for God does not seclude Himself in a castle—He has nothing to fear from His enemies (2 Chron. 6:18; Ps. 2:1–5). The devil, on the other hand, rules by fear, lies, and torture; he must isolate himself in his headquarters and surround himself with guards.

Attack of the Harpies

These harpy angels that protect Satan are a supreme example of once beautiful creatures who dwelt in the light of God's presence in heaven but chose to follow the evil one into utter degradation.

Suddenly, dark angels by the thousands poured out from the tunnels and began encircling us, like bats leaving caves at sunset. They had the heads and torsos of women and the wings, tails, legs, and clawed feet of rapacious vultures.[14]

"They cannot touch us," the white Eagle said. "Remain calm."

These harpies would pass by us closely, crying and taunting, but they never obstructed our view of the palace nor hindered the white Eagle's relentless flight toward it.

The Prince of Darkness

High in the black palace at a lightless window, a solitary figure appeared, looking at us.[15] From a distance, one could sense his power, authority, and extreme loneliness. Yes—loneliness—separation, isolation, and a cold, cold heart.

He looked like a Spanish prince. He wore an elegant black velvet robe encrusted with jewels; he was tastefully and perfectly groomed. He was handsome, almost perfectly handsome, with shiny black hair and dark intelligent eyes.

He waved his hand, and the harpies flew away as quickly as they had come, retreating into the honeycomb of tunnels. The sound of thousands of leathery wings dwindled away, leaving the cavern quiet in comparison.

After that he continued to stand unmoving at the window, his eyes fixed upon us: lonely, like a king who is also a rejected lover.

I thought to myself, "There he is: he who was so full of light that he was named 'the shining one'—now 'the prince of darkness,' he whose executive ability still is such that he manages a vast, global empire of deceit, seducing the whole world."

Ezekiel 28:12–19 tells us more about Lucifer than any other Scripture (the name given him in Isaiah 14:12, KJV). In Ezekiel 28:14, the Holy Spirit reveals that he was "the anointed cherub who covers [or guards]." He was the highest of several cherubim who surrounded the Father continually as a kind of honor guard to His radiant glory (Ezek. 9:3; 10:18).

Seeing his impeccable, ageless beauty, I could not help wondering what he must have been like before his fall, for he was created sublime in order to hold the most exalted position in the heavenly court. He was "the anointed cherub who covers." I wondered if once there were three cherubs guarding the throne of God, one on either side and one above? Was that why he was created so beautiful, wise, and powerful? To guard the throne from that elevated position?

He walked amid the coals of fire, sharing the very heart of God, intimate with the Godhead. Did he betray the One who loved him by striking at Him from above? Is that the reason he boasted that he would exalt his throne above the stars of God?[16]

"There he is," I thought to myself, "still superior, but superior now only in evil, and because of his vaulting pride, isolated—beyond mercy's reach and beyond asking for it."

The white Eagle turned from the palace and began to fly back toward the tunnel.

Taunts of the Black Raven

A huge black raven suddenly appeared beside us.[17] Its feathers were a brilliant ebony, and its eyes flashed a fiery red. "Why have You come?" hissed Satan. "Does it please You to shame me before my subjects? Does it please You to bring love and warmth here to torment us? You are cruel!"

The Lord said nothing.

"Don't You miss me?" Satan continued. "Did You come here because of Your loneliness for me? Would You like to come here more often to be with me, just to see me?" The raven cracked a hard, cruel laugh. "You miss me and love me still," he exulted. Then in tones venomous with

14. In classical mythology, a harpy was a winged monster with the head and upper torso of a woman and the lower body and claws of a vulture. This predatory creature was very fierce, starved-looking, and loathsome. It lived in an atmosphere of filth and stench, contaminating everything it came near. A dreadful example of this type of demonic creature is described in Revelation 9:7–10.

15. Satan is consumed with hate for God and therefore with hate for His children. Since the day the evil one deceived Eve, his strategy has been to corrupt the church in order to make void the working out of the cross of Christ (Gen. 3:15). His bitter enmity is focused upon the Son of God who humbled Himself to be born as a human being, to die as a common criminal, and to carry His perfected human nature into heaven. The Lord's goal is to grant to anyone who receives Him the right to share both His human and divine natures forever. It must have been very difficult for this supremely beautiful, wise, and blameless cherub, who was one of the guardians surrounding the Father (Ezek. 28:13–14), to accept His plan: to make mere earthly people a part of Himself and fellow heirs of all that He had given to His Son (John 17: 21–23; 3:35; Rom. 8:17). To have mortal human beings advance to intimate union with God beyond what he could ever know (1 Pet. 1:12) and to have these adopted children share in Christ's reign over him and the other angels (Rev. 20:4; 22:5) must have been a humbling he could not accept (Ezek. 28:17; 1 Tim. 3:6).

16. The other main Scripture that describes Lucifer's fall is Isaiah 14:12–15. In verse 13, he aspired to sit upon a throne that would be elevated above all the other angels, who are called "the stars of God." Other examples of the Scriptures describing angels as stars are in Revelation 8:10 and 9:1–2. In truth, Lucifer was the most gifted and glorious of the heavenly host, but God so endowed him in order that he might better honor God and serve others rather than exalt himself.

17. God declared the raven to be an unclean bird (Lev. 11:15). Noah sent it from the ark to determine the extent to which the water had subsided (Gen. 8:6–7). Being a carrion eater, the bird may have subsisted on dead carcasses and did not return to Noah. The bird's name has become the source of words such as *ravenous,* a word meaning "rapacious" (seizing by violence) and "voracious" (devouring). No wonder the evil one chose to take the form of this darksome bird. Good angels can change their appearance (Gen. 18:1–2; 19:1) and so can Satan, since after his defection he retained his former rank and giftings in corrupted forms (2 Cor. 11:14; Rom. 11:29).

bitter scorn, he mocked: "You are a fool to love me even now, Jesus of Nazareth."[18]

The Lord's silence infuriated the raven.

Lucifer once walked in closest fellowship "in the midst of the stones of fire," which means intimacy within the very heart of the Father (Ezek. 28:14). The Bible speaks of the fire of God (Ezek. 1:4, 27). At that time Lucifer loved the Son of God very deeply, but now as Satan, he has only absolute hatred for the Lamb of God who denied Himself in being born as a human being and in submitting in love to the Father unto death on a cross: the complete opposite of the arrogant presumption of Satan.

"Don't come back to shame me before my subjects! I am king here. Stay away! I don't love You, and I wish all manner of exquisite torments upon You to express my contempt. Stay away!" Satan spewed vehemently.

Having said that, the raven made a sharp turn and flew back to the palace.

The white Eagle continued through the tunnel from which we had come. A void, deathly silence was in that darkness now.

Return to the Sheepfold

He flew to the sheepfold and stopped before the gate. I climbed down from His back. He became the Lord again with His shepherd's staff in His hand. He opened the gate and led me inside.

We both removed our shoes and stood barefoot within the sheepfold. I was shivering, and He put His arm around me.

"It is all right, Anna," He said. "You needed to see that Satan is cruel. Rest now."

Warmth began to flow into me, and I tried to breathe deeply, settling myself.

"Why did You show me these things?" I asked.

"To you it has been granted to know," He said. "Mark well what you have seen and heard."

The Vision of Judgment

"Look," He continued, gesturing toward the ground in front of us within the sheepfold. The area opened to reveal the world spinning some distance beneath us.

As I looked at the globe, I heard huge footsteps, as if giants were walking, shaking the earth.[19] The ground of earth trembled, and mountains began to break apart.

"Look again," He said, gesturing above Him.

Heaven opened, and I saw something dropping from the center of the bright angels.

"What is it?" I asked.

"A plumb line," He answered.[20] The weighted plumb line dropped from heaven through the sheepfold to the earth.

"Our great God has relented twice before, but now He has dropped the plumb line."

Twice in the history of the Israelites, God determined to destroy them completely and to begin again to build a new nation with Moses as its leader (Exod. 32:10, 14; Num. 14:11–12, 20). At Moses's intercession, the Lord relented by granting mercy instead of strict justice.

As the plumb line reached Earth, great rejoicing began in heaven. It was as though every created being there was singing, and the sound began to shake the celestial realms:

> His righteousness is from everlasting to everlasting.
> His judgments are sure and will be withheld no longer.

As the thunderous rejoicing increased, fire came out of heaven and traveled the plumb line, passing before us and sweeping down the line to the earth. Suddenly the whole world was aflame.[21]

18. Satan here mocks the Lord by simply calling Him "Jesus of Nazareth." The unclean spirit in the synagogue used these words to Him (Mark 1:24). The words "Jesus the Nazarene" were part of the inscription that the devil moved Pilate to write in derision and have placed on the cross (John 19:19). In those days to say that a person was a Nazarene was a term of reproach (John 1:46).

19. The human offspring of fallen angels who mated with earthly women are called Nephilim, which means "fallen ones." (In Genesis 6:2–4; Job 1:6; 2:1, "sons of God" are angels, creatures brought into being directly by God and not born.) They were later known by the names of Rephaim, Zuzim, Zamzummin, Emim, and Anakim. These were people of monstrous size and wickedness as they were truly children of Satan (Gen. 6:11–13). The flood became necessary to preserve the human race from being completely corrupted by these abnormal human beings (Gen. 6:5, 7; 2 Pet. 2:4–5; Jude 6).

The "giants" here represent modern people of renown and great gifting, especially those in the fields of science and technology, who are able to cause the earth to tremble in awe at their natural knowledge and power to accomplish wonders. "Mountains" in Scripture are sometimes symbols of monumental obstacles or problems (Zech. 4:7; Matt. 17:20). Modern science seems capable of overcoming any earthly obstacle. When Christ returns to rule the earth, His almighty power will cause "mountains" to melt away (Mic. 1:3–4; Ps. 97:5). Nothing can stand before His presence, but all must bow to His authority as Lord of all (Mal. 3:2; Acts 10:36; Phil. 2:10).

Giants also represent powerful fallen angels who will be loosed by Satan as we move toward the end (Rev. 9:1–11). Even the most powerful of the enemy's forces cannot stand before the power of our God.

20. A plumb line is a cord with a weight on one end; it is used in building construction to test whether something is perfectly vertical. It is used figuratively in Scripture of God's action in measuring the uprightness or vertical dimension of His people (His "building," 1 Cor. 3:9). The major scripture for God's dropping the plumb line to earth is Amos 7:7–8, where the apostate northern kingdom of Israel does not measure up to God's standard; the Lord "will spare them no longer." He destined this northern kingdom for destruction, with the people carried away into exile and scattered into oblivion (Amos 9:10; 2 Kings 17:5–6, 20, 23).

21. Consuming fire is a part of God's being (Heb. 12:29). It is one expression of His holy love for His Son (John 3:35). His fiery love is both zealous and jealous (Exod. 20:5; Deut. 4:24; Ezek. 36:5; Zeph. 3:8). There is a good and godly jealousy (2 Cor. 11:2). Both words convey the passionate ardor of the Father's heart to see His Son reproduced in His adopted children and manifested in all creation (2 Cor. 4:10–12; Num. 14:21). The fire of God's love is part of His glory (Exod. 24:17; 33:18–19; 34:6–7). The fire of His glory purifies and transforms His repentant and obedient children (Matt. 3:11–12; Mal. 3:2–3; 2 Cor. 3:18). It sets their hearts aflame as a living sacrifice (2 Chron. 7:1; Song of Sol. 8:6), "an offering by fire as a soothing aroma" (Num. 29:13). But for the unrepentant and rebellious, the fire of His unrequited love brings judgment (Isa. 66:15–17; Ps. 97:3; 1 Thess. 1:7–9; Heb. 10:26–27).

The False Church Judged

As God stretched over Edom "the plumb line of emptiness" and "desolation" (Isa. 34:11), so it will be with the church of Edom in this closing period. God will withdraw all light from her; she will be in total spiritual darkness and be destroyed by fire (Isa. 60:2; Jer. 13:16; Joel 2:1–2; Rev. 17:16).

As the chant in heaven continued, Jesus spoke, "Edom will be judged.[22] To the world she looked pure, but she will be stubble before the wrath of God. The children of the living God will see Him on His holy mount. But to the church of Edom, He will hide Himself in darkness, never to reveal Himself again.

"The mountain of Edom will melt like wax before the flame of the Lord, but the righteous will thrive amid the flames. Indeed, the righteous will be a flame before the Lord.

"The righteous will be counted as nothing by the enemies of our God. They will be mocked, a crown of thorns pressed into their brows, but God, our God, will consume the thorns with His fire and heal their wounds with His balm.

"The plumb line has dropped. The earth shakes as giants walk the land. God's power will be seen. No giant can stand before His power. No giant can walk into His flame. The righteous will look up and rejoice with the whole assembly of heaven. In one mighty chorus they will proclaim His righteousness and His power. His justice will prevail, for the plumb line has dropped and will not be removed.

"Fear, O you who lie with the adder, you who drink the venom of vipers. The day is coming and now is when the Word of the Lord will cut you in two, and you will writhe in the agony consigned to those who embrace idols.

"The heavens proclaim His righteousness and His throne; like a great rock, He will fall upon the wicked. The righteous will look upon His face, but deep darkness will shroud Him from the eyes of Esau.[23]

"Woe to those who embrace idols. They couple themselves with demons. Fire has traveled the plumb line. Lightning has flashed from His hand. Indeed, the world will see it but will remain deceived. When giants walk the land, the mountains tremble; but when God walks the land, the mountains melt.

"As the chant of God's righteousness goes forth in heaven, there is a splitting, a separation, a falling away, and a letting go: ruin follows the reverberation of that refrain. Division that could not be measured until the plumb line dropped from heaven to Earth.[24] All of heaven has joined in the song, and all of Earth will hear and not hear. Judgments are in the land. The righteous will grow in righteousness, and the wicked will gnash their teeth and curse God.

Unless the church is manifesting the life of God and proclaiming His Word, there is no hope for those who do not obey the gospel of God (Eph. 2:12).

"Hold fast to God, Anna. Hold fast to God. Once He relented, even twice, but now judgments have begun with the household of God.[25] The righteous will shine like the sun, and the corrupt church, rich though she be, bedecked in beautiful gifts from God, will be stubble before Him.[26] For He will relent no longer, and the mountain of Esau will be leveled. A man will kick at the dust of that mountain and say 'Where is she? Not even a mound as high as an ant hill remains. Where is she?' Her rocks and earth will have been ground to powder and blown away. In her place there will be a desert wasteland that none will turn aside to see because nothing will remain.

22. Edom is the nation that descended from Esau, Jacob's older brother (Gen. 25:24–26). Esau founded Edom, a word derived from a root meaning "red," which represents the color of the earth from which the human body was formed (Gen. 25:30; 36:1, 8–9). It also spiritually denotes a fleshly person rather than a spiritual one (1 Cor. 3:1, 3). The Edomites showed no mercy to the people of Judah when the latter were defeated and led into exile (Ps. 137:7; Obad. 10). Therefore they are the only neighboring country to God's people that was not given any promise of mercy from the Lord. They disappeared from history in A.D. 70 (Isa. 34:5, 10).

23. The church of Esau (or Edom) lives by natural wisdom and energy instead of taking one step at a time by the leading of the Holy Spirit (Gal. 5:16, 25). As Esau sold his birthright as the first-born son to his brother, Jacob, for a bowl of lentil stew and bread, so the Esau church of today is controlled by the worldly spirit of immediate gratification and glory. She has no heart for the things of the Spirit (Rom. 8:7–8). The idolatries of the outward appearance of success and of recognition by man have replaced the desire for the hidden life in Christ (Matt. 6:1; Col. 3:3; Rev. 17:4; 18:7).

24. Already the separation of the servants of Christ from the idolatrous, unbelieving church has begun. The holy people of God are commanded: "Come out of her, my people, that you may not participate in her sins and that you may not receive of her plagues;...for...in one day...she will be burned up with fire" (Rev. 18:4, 8). At the instigation of Satan, Nimrod originally instituted this false religion at Babylon (Gen. 10:9–10; 11:4, 9). It substitutes a god made in the image of man for the God of the Bible. This substitution is done together with the practice of good works that gain merit for the worshipers (known in Scripture as "the works of their own hands," Jer. 1:16).

25. "For it is time for judgment to begin with the household of God" (1 Pet. 4:17; Heb. 10:30–31). God does not hold the pagan world primarily responsible for the deception that abounds; He holds the church accountable, for salvation in Christ is through His body, the church (Mark 16:15–16; Eph. 1:22; 3:10).

26. The righteous church will suffer great persecution in the last days by the corrupt church being in league with the world system of Satan (Rev. 17:3, 6). The redeemed and the angelic host will declare with one mighty voice in heaven: "Hallelujah!...He has judged the great harlot who was corrupting the earth with her immorality, and He has avenged the blood of His bondservants on her" (Rev. 19:1–2). "All the arrogant and every evildoer will be chaff; and the day that is coming will set them ablaze;...But for you who fear My name, the sun of righteousness will rise with healing in its wings" (Mal. 4:1–3; Isa. 60:1–3, 19).

27. These saints will join with the "loud voices in heaven, saying, 'The kingdom of the world has become the kingdom of our Lord, and of His Christ; and He will reign forever and ever...Thou hast taken Thy great power and hast begun to reign'" (Rev. 11:15, 17).

28. God's children who overcome His enemies and learn to live above in Christ are promised "hidden manna" that will nourish them, food from heaven about which the world does not know (John 4:32; Rev. 2:17). They will "walk the streets of gold" in the celestial Jerusalem while still alive on Earth, meaning that their inner person will live in Christ's realm (John 14:3; 17:24; 1 John 1:3; Heb. 12:22–24).

29. Satan inserted the thought in Eve's mind that she was more righteous than God, who was not respecting her rights (Gen. 3:4–5). Job "justified himself before [more than] God" (Job 32:2; 35:2), saying, "I am righteous, but God has taken away my right" (Job 34:5). God reproved him with the words: "Will you condemn Me that you may be justified?" (Job 40:8). God is the only one who has rights.

30. "Flesh and blood [that which is of the earth] cannot inherit the kingdom of God; nor does the perishable inherit the imperishable" (1 Cor. 15:50). That which stems from the natural person is cursed (Gen. 4:11; Jer. 17:5; Gal. 3:10). "Christ is all in all" in His kingdom (Col. 3:11), and only that which is of Him passes through God's flame (Rom. 15:18; 1 Cor. 3:11–15; 2 Cor. 3:5).

31. The Holy Spirit must bring all those in the kingdom of Christ to the full measure of development found in Jesus by their "grow[ing] up in all aspects into Him, who is the head" (Eph. 4:13, 15). He is the "precious corner stone" of God's house, the stone to which the Spirit aligns everything else (1 Pet. 2:5–6).

The righteous church will see "the mountain [kingdom] of the Lord" established on Earth after Christ returns.

"The mountain of the Lord: the righteous will see it and be glad.[27] They will join in the mighty chorus of heaven. They will walk the streets of gold and feed upon the manna.[28] They will stand beside the plumb line and not be ashamed. Righteousness and justice are the foundation of Your throne, O righteous God.

"O Just and True, mankind has thought itself more just than You; but to the righteous You will reveal Your righteousness, and to the just, You will reveal how just You have always been."[29]

Join the Chorus

Christ Jesus has been made the throne of God, that is, the authority and power for the universe in His person (Isa. 22:23; Heb. 1:3; Col. 1:17). He is coming to "sit on His glorious throne [to exercise that dominion]" (Matt. 25:31; 28:18; Eph. 1:20–22; Rev. 3:21).

The Lord continued, "Join the chorus of the sons of God. Proclaim His righteousness forevermore. Let the sound of our cry fill the sky. Let the sound of our cry fill the earth. Join the rejoicing as the chant goes forth, falling with a weight mightier than giant's steps, falling with the weight of the throne of God Himself.

"Rejoice, O heavens; weep, O world. Rejoice, O righteous, and tremble, O flesh. For fire has come from heaven, traveling the plumb line, and only the Son of God will pass through this flame.[30] Rejoice, O heavens, and be glad, for judgments have begun; the final redemption is near. Our God will settle all accounts. The plumb line will not be removed until all lines up with the Son of God.[31] Rejoice!"

The Lord turned to me and said, "Mark well what you have seen and heard, for these things are and will be; no hand will stop them. Come."

He took my hand, and together we followed the flaming plumb line into heaven.

Chapter Ten The Throne of God

As we rose, the light became multicolored, vibrant, alive almost. The sound of the chant intensified a hundredfold as we followed the flaming plumb line into the third heaven:

> His righteousness is from everlasting to everlasting.
> His judgments are sure and will be withheld no longer.

Paul speaks of "the third heaven," which Nehemiah calls "the heaven of heavens," which is the place of God's throne, His dwelling place (2 Cor. 12:2; Neh. 9:6; Ps. 11:4; 2 Chron. 6:33).

Jubilant Celebration

When Jesus appeared on the "sea of glass," a great shout went up; those singing burst into spontaneous rejoicing at the sight of Him.[1] We had entered the third heaven at what seemed to be the back of the throne room.

The redeemed began to dance as one—sidestepping in a swift, gliding movement, as dancers on Earth might in an old-fashioned courante.[2] The movements were vigorous and joyful. Those passing near us would reach out a hand to touch Jesus; He reached out to touch hand after hand of those passing by in the dance. All were laughing. I was certain the dance was spontaneous. The redeemed were dancing by the power of the Holy Spirit, thousands upon thousands led by the Spirit Himself.[3]

Jesus glanced over at me. "I am needed, Anna," He said. He motioned for someone to draw nearer to us. It was the large formal angel whom I had met on the moving path. As the Lord spoke to me, He was still

1. The floor of the throne room looks like "a sea of glass," clear as crystal (Rev. 4:6; 1:22, 26; Exod. 24:10). The angels and the redeemed there may stand or move about on this great expanse created of light from the Father (Rev. 15:2).

2. The Bible enjoins the redeemed on Earth and in heaven, as well as the angels, to praise God with dancing (Ps. 149:3; 150:4). King David certainly obeyed the injunction (2 Sam. 6:14). Devotional group dancing in an orderly manner was part of the worship of God in ancient Israel (Exod. 15:20–21) and in the earliest centuries of the Christian church. In the fourth century, the bishop of Caesarea wrote: "Could there be anything more blessed than to imitate on earth the ring dance of the angels?" The courante originated in the sixteenth century as a lively, folk dance with quick, running steps. Singing to the Lord has always been a major part of praise on earth and in heaven (Ps. 47:6; Rev. 14:3). The biblical psalms were written to be sung (Ps. 47:7; Eph. 5:19).

3. Paul says that his spirit is able to pray or to sing by the working of the Holy Spirit within him (1 Cor. 14:14–15). The same Holy Spirit who is able to speak through believers on Earth (1 Cor. 12:3, 7, 11) is also able to give the same song and the same dance movements to the multitude of the redeemed in heaven at the same time (Rev. 14:1, 3). This is possible because the unity of the Holy Spirit (1 Cor. 12:13; Rom. 8:14) with their spirits (1 Cor. 6:17) is pure and unobstructed, so that the Spirit flows freely to all. An example of this is in Revelation 5:13, when "every created thing which is in heaven" was saying the same words of praise to God.

Epaggelias is the Greek word that means "promises."

smiling and touching the hands extended to Him. "Epaggelias will be with you."

The Angel Epaggelias

"So that is his name," I thought to myself, smiling inwardly.

The angel bowed from the waist to Jesus. The Lord smiled at me, reached over and squeezed my hand, and was gone.

Epaggelias and I continued to watch the exuberant dancing.

"You have come at a joyous time," Epaggelias said.

"Why?" I asked.

The hosts in heaven are able to see us on Earth and rejoice over every sinner whom God saves (Luke 15:7; Heb. 12:1; Rev. 18:20; 19:1–2).

He answered, "We rejoice daily for those who have recently come into the kingdom, but this celebration is in response to your Father's proclamation that a great ingathering is about to commence.[4] His children are filled with thanksgiving to Him for His faithfulness, for He is about to do a quick work and redeem many of their brothers and sisters through Christ Jesus our Lord."

"That is exciting," I smiled. "Thank you for telling me, Epaggelias."

He bowed in acknowledgment and smiled in spite of himself, for it was a private joke between the two of us that Jesus had just given me his name.

The thousands of dancers gathered into circles, each circle containing about twenty-four dancers. They began circling and weaving in and out within the rings. Some were laughing, but everywhere there was rejoicing. They began to sing as they danced:

> Again and again we sing of His glory,
> Again and again rejoice in our God.

All were executing the same movements, twirling and whirling within the circles, and singing the same song everywhere on the sea of glass.

Silent Worship

Then, as by the Spirit's leading, the music slowed to a sigh, a pause, a selah.[5] The redeemed paused also, silently with arms raised, abandoned to God. I remembered Psalm 65 where it states, "There will be silence before You…praise in Zion, O God." Silent worship.

After a long pause, a slow, stately melody began. Besides the tone of the instruments I recognized, some of the music was being played on instruments I had never heard.[6] Perhaps they were from other cultures or of ancient design. In harmony with the instrumental music was another lovely sound. It was not singing, nor was it being played by musicians. What was it?

Dance of Worship

The redeemed responded to the music by beginning a majestic dance of worship. The movements were regal and noble, and they executed them with great care and intensity. Perhaps a pavane is the dance on Earth most closely resembling this worship of the redeemed. I felt they were dancing to express their respect. Their dancing was homage. The change of pace allowed me to get my bearings.

The pavane was a majestic, processional, court dance in the sixteenth century, characterized by slow, formal movements. In southern Spain, it was performed in Christian churches on solemn occasions.

The Throne of God

The throne room was as brilliant with light as Satan's kingdom had been dark.

The surface on which the redeemed were dancing was a pavement of light that looked like a translucent blue. The area was as immense as a huge plaza. At the far end of this expansive "sea" was a dazzling white light, in the center of which was the throne of God.[7]

A great yearning welled up within me, and a whisper involuntarily escaped: "Daddy." His presence drew me with the cords of love. Epaggelias looked down at me and smiled.

4. Of the three annual feasts appointed by God for all males in Israel—the Feast of Unleavened Bread, the Feast of the Harvest (first fruits), and the Feast of the Ingathering (Exod. 23:14–17)—only the last one is yet to be fulfilled in Christ. Known also as the Feast of Booths, as in Leviticus 23:34, the Feast of the Ingathering occurred each year at the close of the growing season when the final harvest of produce was made before winter (Lev. 23:39). It became the most important and joyous of the three feasts in the presence of the Lord (Exod. 34:23; Deut. 16:13–15). This last ingathering with respect to the celebration will begin to take place with the fullest outpouring of the Holy Spirit ever to occur, known as the "latter rain" (Joel 2:23, 28–29). There will be a great harvest, for "whoever calls on the name of the Lord will be delivered" (Joel 2:32).

5. *Selah* is the transliteration of this Hebrew word that is inserted repeatedly in the Psalms, mainly for the purpose of having the worshiper pause and consider the connection between the verse before and the verse after (Ps. 3:2).

6. Mankind began to make musical instruments on Earth in the seventh generation (Gen. 4:21). King David made the musical instruments that were used in giving praise to God in the first temple (2 Chron. 7:6). Many of these no longer exist on Earth, but those made by God in heaven exist forever (Rev. 8:13; 15:2).

7. The throne of God in heaven is a literal and magnificent seat upon which the Father sits (Rev. 4:2–3; 5:7). The Bible records the testimony of six different people who saw Him sitting on His throne: five of them in visions (1 Kings 22:19; Isa. 6:1; Ezek. 1:26; Dan. 7:9; Rev. 21:5) and the sixth, Jesus Christ, who has lived there (Matt. 23:22).

The Father's being is manifested by light of an indescribable whiteness. His uncreated glory radiates outward in all directions to form a great sphere of awesome colors.[8] From a considerable distance this radiance looks like an eye with a dazzling white pupil. Perhaps the sphere is due to the reflection upon the sea of glass. I could not tell. But I remembered that often the early church had mosaics or frescoes of the "eye of God" in its buildings.[9] Standing on the sea of glass, I wondered if they were seeking to depict the glory of the Father as well as His omniscience.

The *Shekinah* is a Hebrew word meaning "resting" or "dwelling," and it refers to that manifestation of the reddish-gold radiance of God's presence when it rests or dwells among His people on earth. The root of *Shekinah* is the Hebrew word *shokhen*, meaning "neighbor" or "intimacy." God's glory appeared first to the Israelites in the midst of the cloud that went before them when they left Egypt (Exod. 13:21–22; 16:10).

The splendor of His person radiates out into bands of color, like a bow whose hues blend from white to yellow, to gold, to the Shekinah reddish-gold, and on through the color spectrum of reds, purples, blues, and ending with green. The rainbow on Earth is a type of "My [God's] bow."[10]

Moving Closer to the Throne

Transfixed, I was lost in the wonder of Him. Epaggelias touched my shoulder to draw my attention to that which he was about to say. "Come with me," he said, and with that he began to move toward the throne area. We began to pass through those worshiping, sometimes ducking beneath a dancer's arm as we made our way forward.

The light into which we were entering began to intensify, as well as the sense of power. As we moved nearer to the throne, the radiance looked more like the waves of light in the aurora borealis when it forms an arc of lights across the sky.[11]

The light of God is part of His nature (1 John 1:5). Therefore it is alive, active, and powerful like His Word (Heb. 4:12). It will transform the darkness of sin, sickness, and death in the natural person into the light that is Christ (John 12:46; Eph. 5:8).

The blazing light was not blinding as would be the earth's sun if you gazed at it. One could experience, feel, and even look at this light.

Angelic Praise

Thousands of angels were circling above the throne area, and thousands more seemed to be arriving to join them.

Countless numbers of angels were already within the bow of the corona around the throne. Each group wore the color of that particular hue. They were making musical sounds by flying at different levels and speeds and patterns.[12] Just as a whirling stick might make a different sound—increasingly higher or louder by the speed with which it is whirled—so these angels in their flying brought forth various sounds of praise. The tones that their flight made were different from singing or the playing of instruments. This must have been the musical sound whose origin I could not detect earlier, rare in its beauty.

They seemed to be unbelievably happy, swimming, as it were, in the glory of God. I too felt this joy; forever would not be long enough to praise Him and to receive His joy back from Him.[13]

At times some angels would fly together, producing a tone different from the sound of those in flight in a single color.

One With Praise

The melodies, like the light in the throne room, went right through me. The music of praise entered me and passed through me, and I became one with the sound. It was as though I became praise. I remembered that in the Book of Psalms David said, "But, I prayer"[14]—meaning that he was prayer. So it is with praise in the throne room.

Epaggelias paused amid the dancers and spoke, "The harmony, the unity, and the desire of these here to give to the Father His due—constantly giving of themselves and receiving more of Him when they praise and adore—bring forth a sweet music."

"Yes," I agreed.

We watched and listened a moment before moving forward again.

8. There is "one God, the Father, from whom are all things" (1 Cor. 8:6). His nature is the source of true light (1 John 1:5; John 1:9; James 1:17). The form of the Father is light of incomparable whiteness similar to the glory manifested in Jesus on the Mount of Transfiguration (Mark 9:3; John 5:37). His light illumines all of heaven (Rev. 21:23).

9. God "looks to the ends of the earth and sees everything under the heavens" (Job 28:24). His eyes see every step taken by every person, and He understands all their works (Job 34:21; Ps. 33:13, 15). He knows every person's attitude toward Him, for God "looks at the heart" (1 Sam. 16:7; Jer. 12:3).

10. Ezekiel and John compared the upper half of the radiant sphere of colors surrounding the Father on His throne to a glorious bow (Ezek. 1:28; Rev. 4:3). This aspect of the light of His glory God calls "My bow," and the rainbow represents it on earth (Gen. 9:13, 16).

11. "The heavens are telling of the glory of God; and their expanse is declaring the work of His hands" (Ps. 19:1). God created and arranged the stars and constellations to picture the gospel of salvation in Christ. Another luminous phenomenon seen in the night sky, particularly in the northern arctic region, is called the aurora borealis. It appears in streamers of light ascending in the shape of a fan or as an arc of light across the sky from east to west.

12. Ezekiel heard the flight of heavenly beings whose wings emitted sounds on certain occasions. Some of these sounds were like the voice of God Almighty, like many waters, like the tumult in an army camp, and like a great rumbling (Ezek. 1:24; 3:12–13; 10:5). We see by this that their flying can produce many kinds of sounds.

13. When one is in the presence of the Lord, there is fullness of joy (Ps. 16:11). We come into His courts (His nearer presence) with the offering of sacrifices of praise, the psalmist says (Ps. 27:6; 96:8; 100:4). God creates the praise within us, and we give it to Him (Isa; 57:19; 2 Chron. 7:6). In return, He imparts His joy to us (Neh. 12:27, 43; Ps. 71:23).

14. The Bible describes the sound of the wings of heavenly beings in flight as "like the voice of God Almighty when He speaks" (Ezek. 10:5). The speaking of God penetrates and becomes a part of believers (Ezek. 3:10; Job 22:22). In the original text of Psalm 109:4, David said of himself, "But I am prayer," in the same way that he described himself as "I am peace" (Ps. 120:7). Christ can impart both His prayer and peace to us by the Holy Spirit (Rom. 8:6, 26–27, 34; Eph. 2:14; 6:18; Col. 3:15; John 15:16).

The nearer we come into the presence of the person of the Father in heaven, the clearer our spiritual sight and our perception of spiritual realities become.

As we drew nearer to the throne, it was as though I began to see praise.[15] It was translucent, almost invisible, but I could see it. It seemed to have different properties. Some kinds of praise were like fabric, some like particles. Thanksgivings looked similar to bird flights of light.

Praise Purified

The angels in flight gathered some of the praise from the sea of glass and wove it into their praise within each color of the bow (that is, the radiance around the Father) before it went to Him. Some worship went to a small altar on which there appeared to be smoldering coals.[16] I wondered why some went one way and some another.

Epaggelias addressed this unspoken question. "Some praise is already in harmony with heavenly praise, but some must pass through the fire," he said.[17]

Angels of His Presence

The angels at the altar of incense are among those who attend upon the Father in close proximity. Their pale purple robes with deep purple and gold embroidery indicate that they are in the retinue of the divine king.

Angelic beings in pale lavender were at this small altar. Their robes were embroidered with deep purple and gold on the sleeves and hem, and they were bound with golden girdles. The palms of their hands were also tinted with the purple color. I felt that they must be angels of His presence.[18] They took great care with all that was going to the Father. There was a delicacy in handling that which belongs to Him, like a shepherd encouraging and assisting a newborn lamb. Whether being woven into the angelic harmony within each color of the radiance, or like a homing pigeon, drawn into the coals on the small altar—all, all goes to Him.[19] Nothing is carried away or stolen.

There is a oneness to everything created in heaven because everything originates from the Father through the Son by the Holy Spirit. Therefore, the nature of everything living in the kingdom of heaven is spirit (1 Cor. 15:50). That which is produced by the Spirit is spirit (John 3:6; 1 Pet. 2:5; Eph. 1:3). As a result, there is a oneness to the sight, sound, and odor there.

Interwovenness

I became more aware of the pleasant fragrance around the throne area and of the interwovenness of sound and color and smell.[20] These cannot be woven together on Earth the way they are blended here in heaven. We below can experience them simultaneously, but above they seem to have the same properties. It is more like water being poured into water. Water, having the same properties, can be mixed. So it is here with sound, light, and fragrance. It seems strange to see sound, hear color, and for smell to have a tangible quality to it; yet in heaven it all seems natural and right and even obvious.

Seven Great Flames

There were seven great flames of fire, seven torches, before the throne.[21]

Epaggelias spoke, "These are manifestations of the Holy Spirit. They burn before the throne continually. He reveals Himself here [above] and on Earth. The Lamb embodies these, and the Spirit takes of Him. Of the created, heavenly hosts, the seraphim, burning in holiness, most closely resemble these lamps of the Spirit.[22] They burn above, and the lamps burn before [the throne]."

Seraphim

I looked up to see heavenly beings burning right above the most intense light of the throne. Each had six wings. Now and then I could see their faces or the movement of their wings. They burned like blow torches. From them came the sweetest and purest music I had ever heard.

15. Moses was able to see the glory of the goodness of His character (Exod. 33:18–19; 34:5–6). Isaiah saw the depth of his and others' sin (Isa. 6:5). Ezekiel knew the living beings to be cherubim (Ezek. 10:20). John heard all creation praising God (Rev. 5:13).

16. In the wilderness tabernacle, the golden altar of incense stood in front of the veil separating the holy of holies from the holy place (Exod. 40:26–27). Here was burned the holy incense that represents the prayers of the saints (Rev. 5:8). The true altar of incense is before the throne of God in heaven (Rev. 8:3).

17. Some of the earthly praises of the saints have to pass through the fire on the altar of incense that is before the throne to be purified before going to the Father (Rev. 8:4).

18. There are certain angels who stand in the immediate presence of God (Luke 1:19). John saw "the seven angels who stand before God" (Rev. 8:2). Paul indicates that there are certain angels who are chosen to stand in His presence (1 Tim. 5:21). Jesus spoke of these angels when He said, "I will confess [the believer's] name before My Father and His angels" (Rev. 3:5).

19. All things are from the Father, and all things are to Him (Rom. 11:36). Sin had separated all things from being able to return to the Father, but through Christ He reconciled all things to Himself, "having made peace through the blood of His cross" (Col. 1:20).

20. The sweet aroma around the throne area is due to several aspects of Christ Jesus, who is the fragrance to God (2 Cor. 2:15): His prayers, His praises, the sacrificial offering of Himself to the Father (Num. 28:2; Eph. 5:2), the odor from the mountains of spices of His perfections (Song of Sol. 8:14), and the manifestation of Christ's triumph in the redeemed (2 Cor. 2:14).

21. These flames of fire are manifestations of the Holy Spirit (Acts 2:3; Matt. 3:11–12) before the Father's throne (Rev. 4:5; 1:4). The fullness of the Holy Spirit in His sevenfold perfection is in Jesus Christ (Isa. 11:2; Rev. 3:1; 5:6) and Christ in Him (John 16:14).

22. Fire is a part of the holy being of God the Father and represents the absolute purity of the righteous perfection that is His alone (Isa. 5:16). Of all creatures, the fiery beings called seraphim most closely witness to the holiness of God. This order of heavenly beings, the plural of *saraph,* is a Hebrew word derived from a root meaning "to burn." They are described in the Scriptures only in the vision to Isaiah where they testify to the purity of His righteousness by their words extolling His holy name (Isa. 6:3) and by the fire of God purifying the lips of the prophet so that he might speak His holy words (Isa. 6:5–7). It therefore follows that the singing of the seraphim should be the sweetest and purest known to mankind.

The Twenty-four Elders

The twenty-four beings around the throne of the Father are called "elders," a term signifying the governmental authority of those of faithful seniority. Their delegated rulership is seen in their wearing golden crowns, which at times they cast before the throne and prostrate themselves in worship (Rev. 4:4, 10).

In the midst of the intensely white light of the throne area, there stood twenty-four very tall beings with crowns on their heads.[23] Each wore a chain with a single gold medallion hanging from it. The hair on their heads was white, and they were full of light. I could sense that they were ancient, wise, and bore much authority.

Epaggelias led me into a clear area nearer the throne.

Four Living Creatures

Within the greater light, I could see four living creatures.[24] Each was whiter than white, so full of light were they. Each had six wings. One looked like a calf, one like a lion, one like an eagle, and one like a man. Their heads and their feet, paws, hoofs, or claws were golden. They were full of eyes, awesome and very beautiful.

The living creature of light that looked something like a man wore a transparent garment with a collar that came up high from the neck to the ears. This collar looked like an open fan of white lace interwoven with golden thread. A golden yoke and front panel completed the center of the robe. Through the gossamer fabric of his clothing, I could see that his body was covered with eyes. Beneath the wings of each of these living creatures were hands.

When the redeemed dropped to their knees during the dance, these four bowed before the King.[25] Within their hands they held golden bowls that they presented before the throne.[26]

They represent four great divisions of animate creation: the wild beasts, the lion; the domesticated beasts, the calf; humanity, the man; and the birds, the eagle. God includes these four categories of creatures with breath in the covenant He made with Noah and his sons after the flood (Gen. 9:8–10).

Epaggelias spoke to me: "These represent four great divisions of animate creation. The Word says that all things are to praise Him.[27] These are the remnant of creation that fulfill that Word. That which they do is attributed to all that God has made."

"Why do they have golden heads?" I whispered.

"Gold shows their place among those representing creation before the throne," he answered. "It is a precious metal on Earth and representative of Christ here, so their color reflects that which is precious: worshiping God. God deals with the remnant. These four are a certain remnant. Before the throne, God the Almighty, the glorious One, is being praised and worshiped by His creation. The white represents the innocence of all He brought forth originally. It reminds Him that what He created was created pure and uncorrupted in the beginning."

Concluding the Offering of Praise

The offering of worship and thanksgiving by the redeemed was drawing to a close. As one, the redeemed saints stepped forward, their arms around each others' waists. They knelt on their right knees before the throne, bowing their heads in reverence. The twenty-four ancient ones and the four living creatures knelt, saying *amen* at the conclusion of the dance.[28]

The myriads of angels praising Him aloft within the radiance stood still. They looked like thousands upon thousands and tier upon tier of organ pipes as far as I could see.

In the silence that followed, God spoke.

23. They praise God in song and speech, play instruments, and present the prayers of the saints before God (Rev. 5:8–9). An element of their authority, the one that is mainly portrayed in the Book of Revelation, is to humbly lead in worship (Rev. 5:8, 11). Many scholars believe that these elders are the eldest angels who assist in the administration of the other angels and in some way the administration of the universe for God.

24. Closer to the throne than the elders are the four living creatures described in Revelation 4:6–8. These four "give glory and honor and thanks" in praise to the Father on behalf of all of His created beings (Rev. 4:9, 11). They are covered with eyes, indicating a completeness of discernment through spiritual perception with understanding (2 Kings 6:17; Acts 26:18; 1 Cor. 2:9–10, 12, 14). They are one form of several kinds of cherubim, an order of heavenly beings who are mainly assigned to honor and guard the radiant glory of God wherever it is (Ezek. 9:3; 10:18–20). The cherubim in one vision to Ezekiel said, "Blessed be the glory of the Lord in His place" (Ezek. 3:12–13).

25. There are times when the redeemed take the initiative by the Spirit and begin to worship before the throne, and the angelic host joins in (Rev. 7:9–12).

26. The four living creatures and the twenty-four elders hold before God "golden bowls full of incense, which are the prayers of the saints" (Rev. 5:8). These prayers are first placed on the golden altar of incense before the throne, and they are also offered to God in incense burned by angels in a golden censer (Rev. 8:3–4).

27. All things were created to praise the living God, as Psalm 148 enunciates. (See also Psalm 48:10; 69:34; 100:1.)

28. The heavenly beings declare their agreement with the praise of the redeemed in heaven (Rev. 7:9–12).

Chapter Eleven The Father's Lap

"Beautiful, children," God the Father said. "Now rest."

Those who had been dancing broke formation and began talking among themselves in small groups. The warmth of their fellowship was as children around an open fire in the presence of a loving father.

Epaggelias leaned over and spoke to me. "Now watch," he said.

The Children's Offering

An angel began to play a simple melody on a recorder as hundreds of children came before the throne.[1] Angels and the redeemed carried the very young in their arms. They led other children by their hands.

The children took small bouquets of flowers to Jesus and to the Father.[2] Jesus kissed each child, and both He and the Father talked with them. Huge hands of light came out from the throne area as the Father received the flowers. He touched every child and blessed each one. "Thank you," the Father said to each child, calling each one of them by name.[3]

The Bible repeatedly shows us that God the Father has hands of light in the form of human hands with fingers. Examples of the use of His hands are writing with His finger (Exod. 31:18), covering someone with His hand (Exod. 33:22–23), touching someone's lips (Jer. 1:9), handing someone a cup of wine (Jer. 25:15), putting a scroll into someone's mouth (Ezek. 3:2), and picking up someone by his hair (Ezek. 8:3).

Epaggelias continued to me privately, "These are ones who died young."

Instantly I knew that some of the children had died through miscarriage, and some had been aborted; how I knew this, I do not know.

Epaggelias continued, "They are raised to maturity here. Both angels and their own brethren—the redeemed—are their tutors."

1. The modern recorder is a type of flute with eight finger holes. The Bible says that the sound of the flute brings rejoicing and gladness of heart (Job 21:12; Isa. 30:29; 1 Kings 1:40).

2. The Father designed flowers to show forth the glorious aspects of the beauty of His Son. The flowers and all living things in heaven do not wither or die, for "everything that God does will remain forever" (Eccles. 3:14).

3. If God counts the number of the millions upon millions of stars and calls them all by their names (Ps. 147:4; Isa. 40:26), then surely He knows the name of every human being. He has recorded the names of His redeemed children in the "book of life of the Lamb" (Rev. 13:8).

I looked from the children to search Epaggelias's face. He saw my perplexity.

The Holy Spirit must breathe upon the speck of an embryo in the womb for it to have a human spirit and begin to live (Gen. 7:22; Zech. 12:1; John 6:63). From its beginning, a human spirit has all of its faculties for hearing and deciding about God (Ps. 22:10; 58:3; Isa. 49:1, 5; Jer. 1:5).

"Anna, many of the mysteries of our God are unfolding now.[4] For some, the book of understanding is open." He looked back at the children. "Our God can speak to the spirit of a child from conception. Its spirit can respond from the beginning of life in the womb."

I too looked back at the children. I suddenly realized that John the Baptist had responded to the Spirit of the Lord from the womb.[5] If the Holy Spirit can search the mind of God Himself, as the Word says, of course the Spirit can communicate with a child's spirit even before birth.[6]

The children who had been aborted presented small branches of henna as a way of showing the Father that they had forgiven those responsible for their deaths and also asking Him to forgive them as well.[7]

As I watched, the magnitude of the fairness of our God overwhelmed me. He had given each child the opportunity to come to Christ, and all who had chosen Him were here.[8]

Epaggelias spoke, "None are lost from the hand of Jesus, Anna. None."

Song of the Seraphim

As the children began to leave, the seraphim sang:

> O Jewel beyond every jewel, our God,
> Prize beyond every prize.
> God eternal, God sublime,
> God before our eyes.

While looking at the intense light of the Father, my eyes had become more accustomed to the brilliance, I suppose, for as the children began to clear the throne area, I could see more of the throne itself.

The Throne

Beneath the armrest of the throne on either side were two very large cherubim.[9] They were looking out at me through the blazing light. Each cherub seemed to be a composite of the four creatures represented in the living creatures. Each had the face of a man, the wings of an eagle, and one portion of each body was that of a lion and the other part that of an ox. They guarded either side of the throne of God.

They were exquisite and so impregnated with light that they were like lightning with a pale lavender light defining their shape.

The throne on which the Father was sitting was bejeweled with intangibles: righteousness, justice, holiness, mercy, and other virtues.

The throne of God is resplendent with the most valuable of all: the divine character and virtues of the Father. These comprise His authority and that by which He rules. Righteousness and justice are the foundation of His throne (Ps. 97:2). He is righteous and just (Ps. 11:7; Zech. 9:9). He loves righteousness and justice (Ps. 33:5). He works righteousness and justice (Ps. 99:4).

The Priceless Above

Epaggelias spoke as he saw me gazing more intently into the light surrounding the throne, "It is the things that are not that are in heaven, Anna."

I felt that he meant the things that are not tangible.

Epaggelias continued, "The priceless is uncreated. These the enemy wants, for their value is beyond gold. He will give mere gold and silver for them, but it is not a fair exchange. Wisdom, prudence, joy, peace, truthfulness, faithfulness—these adorn the throne of the almighty One. Mere jewels cannot compare. The streets here are gold, but faith is a jewel beyond compare, mercy a commodity more precious than diamonds."[10]

I looked into the awesome light of our God. "Daddy," I whispered again.

4. The English word *mystery* is from the Greek word *musterion,* which means "a sacred secret that only God can reveal." He has been unveiling His mysteries in Scripture beginning in Genesis. In Christ Jesus "are hidden all the treasures of wisdom and knowledge," for He is the full understanding of all the mysteries of God (Col. 2:2–3). The Lord revealed many of these secrets of God to His disciples (Matt. 13:11) and to Paul (Eph. 3:2–5). He promised that He would make more known about the Father's name—His character and work (John 16:25; 17:26).

5. While in his mother's womb, John the Baptist was filled with the Holy Spirit, and he leaped for joy when the Spirit spoke through the virgin Mary to his mother (Luke 1:15, 44).

6. "The Spirit searches all things, even the depths of God... the thoughts of God no one knows except the Spirit of God" (1 Cor. 2:10–11).

7. As Jesus and Stephen were dying, they asked the Father to forgive their murderers (Luke 23:34; Acts 7:60). The Word says, "Love your enemies, do good to those who hate you... pray for those who mistreat you" (Luke 6:27–28). We are also told to "overcome evil with good" (Rom. 12:21).

The leaves of the henna tree yield a red dye; the Hebrew word for this tree means "a redemption price," deriving from a root word meaning "to forgive."

8. God knows the children who will be aborted, miscarried, or die too young to be able to choose the Lord Jesus, so the Holy Spirit presents that choice to these in the womb. All those who believe in Him will go to heaven when they die (John 6:39–40).

9. The letters of the Hebrew root word for *cherub* mean "holding something in safe keeping." The two cherubim on either side of God's throne serve as an honor guard or "chariot" to uphold the glory of the Creator of all (1 Chron. 28:18; 2 Sam. 22:1). The Bible refers to cherubim as those above whom the Father "sits" or "is enthroned" (Ps. 99:1, literal Hebrew; 80:1). They are a composite of the four categories of living creatures because God created them to live in harmony together (Gen. 2:19) before sin shattered their unity (Gen. 9:2; Hos. 4:2–3). The man is the head of these composite cherubim because he was ordained to rule for God over the other animate creation (Gen. 1:28). These two "cherubim of glory" (Heb. 9:5) were represented on Earth by the golden figures on either end of the mercy seat in the tabernacle where God met and spoke with Moses (Exod. 25:18, 21–22).

10. True gold, like every created thing in heaven, is transparent because it exists to be illumined by God's glory (Rev. 21:18, 21, 23).

The Father

No human being can see the brightness of the glory of God's face and live through the experience (Exod. 33:20; 1 Tim. 6:16). Angels are able to behold His countenance (Matt. 18:10), and believers in their resurrected bodies will see His face (Rev. 22:4).

Within the resplendent light, part of my Father's form could be seen.[11] I could see what appeared to be His feet and that which looked like a garment falling in drapes to the sea of glass. Flashes of lightning were in this garment.[12] Within the searing light, I could see something of His hands and the loose sleeves covering His arms. Above His waist, the light emanating from Him was so blinding in its intensity, purity, and holiness that I could see no further.

As Jesus was handing the last baby back to an angel who would carry it from the throne room, my Father spoke to me.

"Anna, My child," He said.

Jesus turned to smile at me. Epaggelias gestured for me to move forward, closer to the throne.

Standing Before the Father

I did so, rubber-legged, moving nearer to that all-consuming light. After I got to the area where the children had been, I dropped to my knees and bowed my face to the sea of glass.[13]

Jesus stepped over to me and helped me to rise, strengthening me as He did so. "My sister is here to see You, Father."

As I rose to my feet, the Father's arms of light came out from all that splendor and picked me up, lifting me high into the air. The action seemed as natural as a father picking up his child.

Our Father's Lap

He set me on His lap.[14]

I was so overwhelmed with love and gratitude and relief, that without thinking, I held up my arms and buried my face into the light. The response was like that of a child who would bury its face in the parent's clothing.

"Daddy," I said, sensing peace, unbelievable peace.

"You are precious to Me, Anna."

"I love You, Daddy."

"And I love you, Anna," He said, drawing me closer.

As we sat there enjoying one another, He began to address my innermost thoughts.

Hope

He said, "Those who are called to draw near to Me will share in My peace.[15] But only those who have hope have peace, continual peace.[16] If hope is gone, the soul is tossed to and fro seeking safe harbor, Anna. I want My children's eyes set on Me, hoping in Me, not looking at the passing panorama of earthly events being played out before them. I want them to look beyond, to look up, to see at last the distant shore toward which they are sailing, filling their hearts and minds, their eyes and ears with Me. This will bring the hope that gives peace."

Christ Jesus is our hope of drawing near to God the Father and to dwell in Him with His Son even while we still walk the earth (1 Tim. 1:1; Heb. 7:19; John 17:21; Col. 3:3; Rev. 3:12).

I sat up and looked into the greater light of the area that would be His face if I could have seen it.

Deeper Into God

My Father continued, "If they delight in Me, Anna, their desires will carry them deeper into Me. Then, as they are drawn into Me, so will they leave the earth's orbit in greater and greater degrees. Soon, like gravity, the pull from My realm, the desire for Me—to know Me and to experience the eternal while in the temporal—will become so strong that they will be set free from Earth's orbit and will be drawn more and more swiftly into Mine.[17] I do not wish to dwell in a dark cloud

11. Jesus said that His Father has a "form," a figure or shape that can be seen (John 5:37). Many people saw His bodily form: Moses alone (Num. 12:8) and again with all the leaders of Israel (Exod. 24:9–11). The body of the Son of God is like His Father's appearance, for the Son is in His image (2 Cor. 4:4; Phil. 2:6; Col. 2:9). Jesus said, "He who has seen Me has seen the Father" (John 14:9).

12. The divine light that is of God flashes through His garment in heaven like lightning as an indication of His awesome power (Rev. 4:5; 16:18). The power of the Lord Jesus on Earth also permeated His garment (Luke 8:43–46; 6:19).

13. The primary Hebrew word translated "to worship" literally means "to bow down," not a matter of words or feelings but an act of humbling oneself. An example is Moses in the presence of the glory of God's grace (Exod. 34:8). When the glory cloud of God filled the temple, none of the ministering priests were able to stand (1 Kings 8:10–11).

14. The same words translated "lap" in both Testaments are also translated "bosom." When one sits, the lap is almost the equivalent of the bosom. This represents the intimacy that the Son has "in the bosom of the Father" (John 1:18).

15. The Lord has made His disciples to be "a kingdom, priests to His God and Father" (Rev. 1:6). Priests are chosen and brought near to God to dwell in His courts (Ps. 65:4). God gave His covenant of peace to the Aaronic priesthood through Phinehas (Num. 25:11–13). The Melchizedek priesthood of those who have believed into Jesus includes a greater covenant of peace (Heb. 7:17, 24). Christ is their peace (Eph. 2:14).

16. He is "a hope both sure and steadfast and one which enters within the veil, where [He] has entered as a forerunner for us" (Heb. 6:19–20). Having entered within the veil in spirit, "we look not at the things which are seen, but at the things which are not seen" (2 Cor. 4:18). Our desires and minds are set on "things above, not on the things that are on earth" (Col. 3:2).

any longer.[18] I want My children to know their Father. I want them to see Me and hear Me, for I am a loving Father to them, Anna, and I care for every breath they take. Truth, who is My Son, came into the world. Many have 'seen' and walked out of the prison doors. But My Son came to reveal Me.[19] Now that revelation will become present reality. The unfolding, the accomplishment of that earthly mission, which began with the unveiling of My Son, will reach a present clarity unaccomplished before."

Vision of Troubled Waters

One meaning of "waters" in Scripture is "peoples and multitudes and nations and tongues" (Rev. 17:15). Troubled waters symbolize heathen peoples in an uproar (2 Chron. 15:6).

I saw a hand moving back and forth in a pool of water, disturbing any clear reflection from being seen.

"As the waters of mankind become more and more troubled," my Father said, "the spiritual pool will become clearer."[20–21] (Then I saw a hand held over a clear pool and reflected perfectly within the water.) "My children will know Me. Will you help Me, Anna?"

Offered a Responsibility

God has ordained that the salvation of the Lord Jesus be carried out on Earth with the free consent and cooperation of those in the one body of His Son, those who have been made a part of the risen Christ (Eph. 1:22–23; 2:16; 3:10; 5:23, 25–27, 30).

"If you need me, Daddy," I said.

"I have raised you up in this hour to see into the heavenly realm, to fly in the rarified air with the white Eagle, to rest in the Eagle's nest, and to taste of the delights that are to come by eating from My hand so that you may eat and others digest what you have eaten."[22]

"How, Daddy?"

"By giving them hope by allowing them to see and experience through your eyes and experiences. I will say through you, 'Hope,' for I am doing a new thing in these days; all who hunger and thirst for Me will eat and drink. You will be My chancellor."[23]

"Like of the exchequer?" I blurted out before I knew it (for I had only heard the term mentioned in these days on the British Broadcasting Corporation).

"No," my Father laughed, "My secretary."

"Oh," I said relieved, for I thought I might be able to handle a secretarial assignment—*with the Lord's help,* I quickly added to myself.

Letters From Home

My Father continued, "You will tell of what you have seen and heard. You will reveal My heart and give hope by revealing 'home' to others. Your words will be like letters from home to those in the field. When a soldier is on the battlefield, a letter from home telling of the people and places of home gives the soldier great hope. He keeps going because he longs for home and realizes that he is greatly loved. Hope, Anna, is a gift to mankind. Without hope, they languish."

The hope of returning to heaven, our true home, to know our true Father, our true Brother, and our true Friend, the Holy Spirit, lies deep within the new, human, spiritual heart (Ezek. 36:26; John 17:3; 2 Cor. 5:8; Phil. 1:23). The resurrected spirit of each believer is already there in Christ (1 Cor. 6:17; Eph. 2:5–6; John 12:26; 17:24).

"Why have You chosen me, Daddy?"

"Because you are simple, Anna, and know little. Before the foundations of the world, I called you, not because you are wise or intelligent, but because I delight in you.[24–26] My Son delights in you. The Holy Spirit delights in you. And I have brought you to Myself this day to ask for your help."

17. "Delight yourself in the Lord, and He will give you the desires of your heart" (Ps. 37:4). If we "[desist] from [our] own ways, from seeking our [own] pleasure, and speaking [our] own word, then [we] will take delight in the Lord" (Isa. 58:13–14). He will move us beyond the heights of the earth by drawing us after Him (Song of Sol. 1:4; John 6:44).

18. The Lord God dwelt within a dark cloud when He visited the Israelites at Mount Sinai (Exod. 19:9; Deut. 4:11; Ps. 18:9).

19. "[No one knows] who the Father is except the Son, and anyone to whom the Son wills to reveal Him" (Luke 10:22). "He who has seen Me has seen the Father," Jesus said (John 14:9).

20. Jesus said that there would be "dismay among nations, in perplexity at the roaring of the sea and the waves, men fainting from fear and the expectation of the things which are coming upon the world" (Luke 21:25–26).

21. The more the judgments of God come upon the earth at the end of the age, the more clearly His glory will appear upon His children. They will begin to "shine forth as the sun in the kingdom of their Father" (Matt. 13:43; Isa. 60:1–2).

22. "Open your mouth and eat what I am giving you" (Ezek. 2:8). "Thy words were found and I ate them; and Thy words became for me a joy and the delight of my heart" (Jer. 15:16). "Write in a book what you see...and the things which are, and the things which will take place after these things" (Rev. 1:11, 19). "Blessed is he who reads and those who hear the words [with understanding]...and heed the things which are written in it; for the time is near" (Rev. 1:3).

23. The word *chancellor* is from the Late Latin *cancellarius,* meaning a doorkeeper or a secretary to a king. God's chancellor is one who opens the door for others to come to know Him through a written record of proceedings in heaven and their substantiation by the Scriptures. As the risen Lord opened the minds of the eleven apostles and those who were with them to understand the things concerning Himself in all the Bible, now He is opening the mind of His church to deeper revelation of the Father's heart (Luke 24:27, 33, 45; John 16:12–13, 25).

24. God knew each of us in Christ before we were born into the world (Jer. 1:5; Ps. 139:16). "He chose us in Him before the foundation of the world" and called us according to His purpose (Eph. 1:4; Rom. 8:29–30; Gal. 1:15).

25. Human wisdom and the reasonings of worldly thinkers are useless nonsense to God (1 Cor. 1:20; 3:20). "God has mainly chosen the foolish people...the weak...the lowly and despised, even those considered nonentities, in order to nullify those who think themselves to be somebodies—so that no one may boast before Him" (1 Cor. 1:27–29, paraphrased).

26. The Father delights in one He has called to fulfill His purposes because of the apportionment of the grace of His Son's character, life, and ministry that He chooses to allot to that person (Gal. 5:22–23; Rom. 12:3, 6; 1 Cor. 12:7, 11; Eph. 4:7, 15–16).

"Yes"

"Of course I will help You," I said, "but Daddy, please help me to refrain from sinning against You. I want to represent You truly. Please keep me pure so that I might not defile this gift or the trust that You have placed in me."

Only in Him

There is nothing good and trustworthy dwelling in the natural state in which we were born, that is, in our "flesh," which hates God and refuses to obey Him (Rom. 1:30; 8:7). Christ Jesus is the only good and trustworthy thing in us, for He has been made all things for us from God (1 Cor. 1:30; Col. 3:11).

In the end times, God's family will be restored to Him (Mal. 4:5–6; Eph. 3:14–15; Mark 9:12) from the captivity of a double heart (Ps. 12:2), so that they no longer go limping between two opinions (1 Kings 18:21, KJV).

I continued listening to my Father speak to me. "In Him, Anna, in My Son. I trust only in Him.[27] It is His life, His ministry, and the work of the Holy Spirit through you. My dear child, you are completely untrustworthy. As the life of My Son increases within you, it appears that you are more trustworthy, but actually, it is only Him; it always will remain only Him."[28]

He paused briefly before continuing. "Now, Anna, you must give yourself time to be with Me. Chancellors must grow into their duties and anointing and authority.[29] My child, My heart is turned toward the children. Show them My heart that they may turn toward Me."[30]

He picked me up from His lap and placed me before Him on the sea of glass as He said, "Now, stand before Me."

The Awesome Convocation

Within the throne room something tremendous seemed to be happening. From all directions there was a great gathering of angels converging upon the throne area. Some that were flying had wings; some did not. There seemed to be myriads and myriads of angels aloft within the throne room, and those within the radiance joined them.

A ripple of sound began near the throne and moved out through the angelic ranks. As the tone increased, singing began until it reached a crescendo at the outer edges of the heavenly host who was in flight. It was as though whatever originated near the throne passed through the others, allowing the singing to swell and then be released outward. The sound was exhilarating:

> Praise You beyond the highest heaven.
> Praise You beyond the lowest depth.
> Praise You for Your loving presence.
> Praise You for Your judgments blest.
> Praise You, sun and moon together.
> Praise You, whirling wheels and stars.[31]

Praise You, angel chorus sounding.
Praise You near and praise afar.

Children sing Your praises, Father.
Maidens praise You, holy Son.
Holy Spirit, we adore You.
Finish now what You have begun.
Started long ago, hallelujah,
When together we did sing,[32]
Blessed Father, Son, and Spirit,
To You, O God, our praise we bring.

(The redeemed joined in the chorus.)

Praise Your holy name, hallelujah,
Praise Your holy name, hallelujah,
Praise Your holy name, hallelujah,
Praise Your holy name.

Suddenly, angels without number began blowing trumpets. The sound was awesome, electrifying, glorious. As the trumpets sounded, everyone present began to proclaim fervently:

Glory to God.
Glory to God.
Glory to God.
Glory to God.

The trumpets were blown in heaven on this occasion for one of the same reasons that the two silver trumpets in Israel were sounded to gather everyone together: to rejoice in worshiping God in His immediate presence (Num. 10:2–3, 10).

27. The Father has placed His entire trust in His Son, giving Him all authority to bring all creation to completion (John 3:35; Matt. 28:18; Eph. 1:22). The Son warrants this trust because He laid Himself aside from eternity out of love for His Father in order to fully obey and manifest His Father rather than Himself (Phil. 2:6–8; John 5:19, 30).

28. The natural expression of the earthly person in soul and body, called in Scripture "the old self" (Eph. 4:22; Col. 3:9) or "himself" (Matt. 16:24), must be denied and laid aside as worthless to God. The Holy Spirit will enable us to keep it incapacitated on the individual cross that He provides each of us, as Jesus bears His personal one (Matt. 16:24). The life of God in Christ alone is to be manifested in us (Eph. 4:24; 2 Cor. 4:10–11). The natural or old person cannot be changed, for it is hopelessly centered on itself rather than God. Christians change only by having more of Christ Jesus, the one new man, formed in them (Gal. 4:19; Eph. 2:15; 4:13).

29. God the Spirit causes believers to grow up together in all aspects into Christ (Col. 2:19; Eph. 4:15): in His salvation by the Scriptures (1 Pet. 2:2), in the grace of faith and love and of the knowledge of Him (2 Thess. 1:3; 2 Pet. 3:18), and in being fitted together into a holy temple in the Lord (Eph. 2:21).

30. The Father is unveiling more of His heart so His people may know that He has turned their heart back again (1 Kings 18:37) and that He has given them a heart to know and understand Him (Deut. 29:4; Matt. 13:15) and that they may love Him with all their heart (Deut. 4:29).

31. Whirling wheels accompany certain cherubim (Ezek. 1:15–20; 10:13).

32. When God created the earth, the host of heaven "sang together and . . . shouted for joy" (Job 38:7; Rev. 12:4, "stars of heaven"; Job 1:6, "sons of God").

33. The Israelites usually used a trumpet made of a ram's horn called a *shofar,* the transliteration of the Hebrew *shophar.* One of the purposes of their blowing the shofar is the same as that for which it was blown now in heaven: to solemnly prepare everyone for a new revelation or act by God (Exod. 19:13; Josh. 6:5; Joel 2:15).

I had never been a part of anything so powerful. It took my breath away. At the end of the proclamation, the elders threw down their crowns and fell on their faces before the throne, and so did the four living creatures and all the redeemed and angels who were on the sea of glass within the throne room. I too fell on my face before God, for who could stand? The angels aloft held their places at attention.

Then one lone shofar blew.[33] It seemed that the sound echoed throughout heaven. As the sound died away, fire and peels of thunder and lightning began to belch from the throne.

God Almighty spoke, "Stand to your feet, Anna."

I stood, but I was trembling. Everyone else stood also.

Chapter Twelve

The Installation

The thunder and lightning increased within the throne, and fire streaked upward at times.[1]

The Witness of Two

Jesus spoke: "Father, she is Mine and belongs to My kingdom.[2] She is ready to fulfill the commission You have given to her." He stepped toward me. "I verify this commissioning, for this is the witness of two. Both My Father and I witness to this."[3]

The Golden Chain

My Father's huge hands of light came from the throne area and placed upon me a large golden chain made of twenty-four linked medallions. An even larger center medallion hung over my heart.[4] As I looked down at the chain, I realized that beneath the chain I was wearing the multicolored robe given to me by Jesus earlier.[5]

The number twelve signifies the perfection of government: the twelve patriarchs and the twelve apostles. Twice twelve, or twenty-four, expresses heavenly government or leadership. Twenty-four insignias on one chain represent the heavenly authority delegated to one in an office of responsibility.

My Father's Name

Then my Father touched my forehead with His hand.[6] It burned like a brand. "My name is on her forehead," He said in a voice that sounded

1. Thunder, lightning, and fire coming from the Father are part of the manifestations of His presence. Often in Scripture they indicate that He is going to speak or act. This was true before He spoke the Ten Commandments to the children of Israel on Mount Sinai (Exod. 19:16–18; Job 36:33).

2. All belongs to the Father (Job 41:11). When the Father draws a person to His Son (John 6:44) and that one is born again of the Spirit, he is given to the Son to be brought to resurrection (John 6:39) and finally to be returned to the Father (1 Cor. 15:24; Eph. 1:4). The Lord Jesus confesses the name of His own before the Father and His angels (Rev. 3:5).

3. The Lord Jesus quoted His Father's words spoken to Moses: "By the mouth of two or three witnesses every fact may be confirmed" (Matt. 18:16; Deut. 19:15).

4. The new, spiritual heart is the vital life link between the hidden, inner person and the outer person (Prov. 4:23; 1 Pet. 3:4; 2 Cor. 4:16).

5. The wearing of the cloak or mantle (chapter 5, note 1) signifies spiritual anointing for a ministry of the Lord Jesus to be exercised through a believer. Such was the passing of Elijah's mantle to Elisha (1 Kings 19:19; 2 Kings 2:9, 13–15).

6. From the Gospel account of what Jesus did on Earth, we learn what His Father does in heaven (John 5:19–20). We therefore know that one reason God the Father lays His hand upon someone is to initiate a supernatural work in them as Christ did: healing (Luke 22:51), strengthening (Rev. 1:17), or blessing (Mark 10:16).

God's name placed on one's forehead indicates His ownership and the impartation of the spiritual capacity to know Him (Rev. 14:1; 22:4).

like mighty, rushing waters. He reached out again with a scepter and touched my shoulders.[7] "She is My chancellor."

Jesus acknowledged, "I bear witness to this."

The Spirit, who is invisible, spoke from the left side of my Father, "I bear witness to this."[8]

Impartation by the Ancient Ones

Then another voice spoke. "Do you trust God?"

"I do," I answered, turning to look at one of the twenty-four ancient ones around the throne.

In the same way that human elders represent the church when they lay their hands upon a believer to impart graces and giftings (1 Cor. 1:3; Acts 8:14–17), so the angelic elders represent the heavenly host as they bestow such blessings.

"Come here," he said. He put his hand upon one of the golden medallions on the chain and spoke with great authority and solemnity: "All the gifts and graces given to me, I now impart to you." Then he motioned for me to pass to the next ancient one, and I did.

Each one of the ancients asked me the same question as the first. Each placed his hand on a different medallion of the chain with the same impartation.

"Your Heart Belongs to Me"

Then my heavenly Father spoke again. "Come here," He said. "Look at the insignias." The gold of the twenty-four medallions was shining like diamonds under an intense light. "The gifts and graces that are Christ are yours," He said.[9] Then He put His hand upon the center medallion and said with great tenderness, "Your heart belongs to Me. Your heart belongs to Me. Your heart belongs to Me."[10]

The Finger of God

Shoulders symbolize strength to carry responsibility (Isa. 9:6). God's right hand touching both shoulders of a person confers power and blessing (Gen. 48:17–18; Mark 14:62). We carry the shield of faith with one hand and the sword of God's Word with the other (Eph. 6:16–17).

After this He touched my eyes with His forefingers. It was like lightning shooting through me. "The finger of God has touched your eyes, Anna."[11] Then He put the lower part of the palms of His hands upon my eyes, and the power almost bent me over backward.[12] He moved His hands and placed His fingers into my ears; another bolt struck me, then one on my nose. "Open your mouth," He said, and He touched my tongue, searing as a coal from the altar.[13] "Lift your hands," He continued. Lightning shot into my fingers and palms. He placed His hands on my shoulders, and then He crossed His hands and laid them on my shoulders again. He moved to my heart and diaphragm, my thighs and knees; then God stooped over and placed His hands on my feet.[14] Power shot into them like nails.

The Sword Not of Man

"I am giving into your hand this day the sword not of man. This sword is two-edged. It can bar or open the way to the tree of life." He spoke to someone near. "Bring the sheath to her."

The sword is the living, moving, powerful, Spirit-energized Word of God concerning Christ Jesus that reveals the true condition of our spiritual hearts (Heb. 4:12–13). It is truth as it is in Jesus, and it overcomes the lies of the enemy (Eph. 4:21; 6:17; Rev. 12:11).

A large, powerful angel knelt and gave the sheath into the light surrounding the throne. Two cherubs were on either side of the angel. These cherubs must have been over eight feet tall. Each had two faces. One cherub had the face of a man in front and a lion in back. The other had the face of an eagle in front and of an ox in back.[15] Each had two wings with hands under their wings. Their legs were straight like a man's but ended in hooves. Taupe-colored feathers covered their bodies like fish-scale mail. They were full of eyes around their bodies and within their wings. I had seen no celestial beings that held such terror as well as majesty.

"Step forward," my Father said. "Let Me buckle this on you." The scabbard was very fine, pure gold and hung on the left side. "Now, the sword," He said.

From the Light that is my Father came the most beautiful sword. It appeared to have a blade of white gold or diamond with a golden handle that was jeweled. I could see through it. It was all light and fire, and it hovered in the air. Jesus stepped forward, and He and my

7. A scepter is a short staff borne by a king as an emblem of authority. The strong scepter of the Lord Jesus was stretched forth from Zion (Ps. 110:2), a scepter of uprightness (Ps. 45:6).

8. The Holy Spirit, proceeding from the Father through the Son, bears witness of the Son's witness (John 15:26; 16:13).

9. All things that the Father has belong to His Son (John 16:15). The children of God are also fellow heirs of the Father with Christ (Rom. 8:16–17).

10. Another reason God lays His hand upon someone is to designate that person as belonging to Him (Ezek. 3:14; Phil. 3:12). He alone gives the measure of the faith, hope, and love of His Son by the Holy Spirit to the spiritual heart of His children (Eph. 3:17–19; 1 Tim. 1:1). The three persons of the Trinity are meant to dwell there, for the new heart belongs to them (John 14:23; Gal. 4:6).

11. The fire of the Spirit of God tests the quality of the way we use our eyes, and it burns up the chaff (Matt. 3:12; 1 Cor. 3:13). The fire of the finger of God, the Holy Spirit, also casts out any darkness from the work of the enemy that may be present in us (Luke 11:20; Matt. 6:23).

12. Great power issued forth through the hands of Jesus Christ when He laid them upon the eyes of the blind (Mark 8:25). God "covers His hands with the lightning [His power], and commands it to strike the mark" (Job 36:32).

13. One of the seraphim touched the lips of the prophet Isaiah with a burning coal from the altar in heaven, declaring his iniquity removed and his sin forgiven (Isa. 6:6–7).

14. These words speak of the humility of God: "I bent down and fed them [His people]" (Hos. 11:4). We see the Son's humble heart in His kneeling to wash the disciples' feet (John 13:4–5).

15. Scripture describes cherubim with one, two, or four faces (Ezek. 1:10; 41:18; Rev. 4:7). In the vision of a new temple, there were cherubim with the faces of a man and of a lion carved on the walls (Ezek. 41:19). The Lord Jesus is "the Lion that is from the tribe of Judah" (Rev. 5:5).

Father put their hands on it. It glowed even brighter. It was as though lightning and thunder or an explosion went off within it. They then removed their hands, and a beautiful sound of music or singing came from it.

"Grasp it," my Father said.

The sword of God's Word in our hearts can be wielded by the Spirit through our actions (hands) or spoken by the Spirit through our mouths (Matt. 10:19–20; Col. 3:17). That Word wars against the enemy and strengthens the brethren (Rom. 12:21; Eph. 6:17–19; Col. 3:16; Rev. 2:16).

"Anna," Jesus said, "let Me help you." He came to my right side and put His hand on mine; together we reached for the sword. It leaped into my hand. Jesus smiled at me. "You may wield this sword because we are one.[16] This sword is sheathed on the outside, but it is also hidden within for the hand and the mouth."

Suddenly, the sword became a red quill pen and an inkwell full of golden ink.[17] Jesus continued, "The Holy Spirit writes for the Father. The Holy Spirit is ever proceeding, never initiating, Anna."[18] Pure, pure water with flicks of fire in it began to flow from the pen. "He writes for Me and for the sake of the kingdom." The pen and inkwell changed back into the sword. Jesus continued, "With the sword not of man, chains will be cut asunder and yokes of iron severed."[19]

Jachin and Boaz

My Father spoke. "Jachin and Boaz will go with you now," He said, referring to the two cherubs.[20] "They guard the sword.[21] They are very powerful and most loving; they will be your friends." He addressed the cherubim, "Guard well." They bowed and then turned around and bowed again. Their bodies had two fronts and no backs. Then my Father spoke again, "Now, Anna, the mantle."

The Mantle

From the left side of the Father, where the Holy Spirit had spoken, came forth a shimmering mantle that hovered in midair. Jachin and Boaz moved over to stand on either side of it. The mantle was both visible and invisible, like a gossamer, with thousands of lights within it. The material was like breath, but breath that was full of living light.

The whirlwind is a visible representation of the powerful moving of the Holy Spirit as on the Day of Pentecost "like a violent, rushing wind" (Acts 2:2). The Greek word for *wind* in John 3:8 is the same word that is translated "Spirit" in the New Testament.

"The mantle that you are to wear," my Father said, indicating the cloak.

The Whirlwind

I slid the sword into its sheath in order to put on the cloak. I expected Jachin and Boaz to help me, but instead, a huge whirlwind stirred before the throne. The garment swirled up into the whirlwind. The angels aloft joined with it by flying within the whirlwind, around and around.

"The Holy Spirit bestows His own mantle," my Father said.

As the cloak began to come down, there was lightning within it. Light changed and pulsated around it, and the Holy Spirit began to proclaim through the singing of the angels:

The Holy Spirit's Song

Let the brush of angels' wings
Never blind the eyes
Of those who see beyond the veil
To gaze at Paradise.
Gaze on, gaze on past the golden rim,
Gaze on past streets of gold,
Gaze on past all created things
To the new One, ever old.

Ever old and ever new,
Ancient of Days is He.
Infinity within His hands,
Light eternally.
Compassionate God, He who is good,
Compassionate God of might,
Life as a river flows from Your throne
To those who turn from night.

16. The sword of God's Word is empowered by the Holy Spirit who takes that which is of Christ Jesus and discloses it to those who are one with Him (John 16:14; 1 Cor. 6:17).

17. There are many books that God the Holy Spirit has written personally (Exod. 32:32; Dan. 7:10) with His fiery-red pen and golden ink. Examples are the Book of Life (Rev. 20:12), the book of the days ordained for each person (Ps. 139:16), the book of our tears (Ps. 56:8), the book of those recorded for life in Jerusalem (Isa. 4:3), and a book of remembrance of those who fear God and esteem His name (Mal. 3:16).

18. "The Spirit of truth . . . proceeds from the Father" through the Son (John 15:26). "The Spirit of truth . . . will not speak on His own initiative, but whatever He hears, He will speak" (John 16:13).

19. The Spirit of truth as it is in Jesus sets us free (John 8:31–32): from bondage to sin (Rom. 6:12–14), self (Rom. 6:6), and the world (Gal. 6:14); from oppression (Isa. 10:27); from the prison of darkness (Ps. 107:10–14); from sickness (Luke 13:16); from the Law (Gal. 5:1–4); and from death (John 11:25–26).

20. The two large pillars supporting the roof over the porch of the temple that Solomon built were named Jachin, "He establishes," and Boaz, "In Him is strength" (1 Kings 7:15, 21). In the spiritual sense, the pillars stood guard at the entrance to the holy place, as cherubim also guarded the entrance to the Garden of Eden (Gen. 3:24).

21. David, Solomon's father, said that God made him understand all the plan for the temple to be built, including the porch, "in writing by His [the Holy Spirit's] hand upon me" (1 Chron. 28:11, 19). The two cherubim named Jachin and Boaz are assigned to stand guard over the revelation of the words of God in writing by the inspiration of the Holy Spirit.

Let the cherubim in awe,
The seraphim in praise,
As those who see beyond the veil,
Upon Him ever gaze.
Gaze on, gaze on past the golden rim,
Gaze on past streets of gold,
Gaze on past all created things
To the new One, ever old.

As the mantle neared the sea of glass, what seemed to be electricity was popping and arcing within the cloak; colors were rippling within it like the changing colors of a certain type of jellyfish in the ocean. The two cherubs stepped to the side to make room for the mantle. It was suspended in midair in front of me.

"What do I do?" I asked.

"Wait, Anna," my Father said.

There was silence in heaven.[22] It was as though everything held its breath. Everyone in the throne room was silent. Gradually, with a gentle, pleasant breeze, the garment moved toward me. I held out my arms as if someone were going to help me put on a coat. The mantle was shimmering. It was like breath. As I slipped into it, however, I realized that I became transparent, invisible in certain areas. The only parts of me that could be seen were my hands, my feet, and my head.[23]

Before I could think about this further, Jesus said to me, "Anna, take these."

"What are they?" I asked.

The Shoes

"Shoes of porpoise," He said.[24] I felt this was a play on the word "purpose," but I did not know why.[25]

A strong ankle is needed to walk well. A spiritual walk is behavior that rests upon supernatural faith in and manifestation of the Lord Jesus in love (John 6:29; 15:5; Eph. 5:2). Only the Holy Spirit can bring this forth (Gal. 5:16). He strengthens us to be able to allow Christ to be and do this in His strength (Phil. 4:13).

I looked at them. They too were gossamer. They laced up the front like high-top work shoes that covered the ankle, but there were no soles in the shoes. "They have no soles," I said.

Jesus smiled, "No, the Godhead is to be the expression of the soul."[26] (He seemed to enjoy His pun.) "These shoes keep your feet naked, touching the holy ground above, but leave you unjustified before mankind.[27–28] You will be invisible to man but intimate with God. These cover the ankle and the heel also. Invisibility will work the cross in your life to the point that there will be no exposed heel or any strength in the natural man displayed."[29–30]

I sat on the sea of glass to put them on. "These are the strangest shoes I have ever seen," I said.

"Yes," Jesus answered. "Few want to wear them. They are out of style."

"Will they stay on?" I laughed.

"Yes, unless you yourself take them off. You can expose your walk before mankind, but there will be no life in it.[31] The worm of death will crawl in and out of that exposure, Anna."[32] Then He asked, "Can you walk in the fire of invisibility that mankind will not give you glory? Few alive today will wear these shoes, for they want their glory from mankind instead of God."[33]

I finished lacing the shoes and stood. The tops of my feet were invisible. "Lord," I asked seriously, "am I going to be able to do this?"

"No," He smiled, "but I will, if you will let Me."[34]

I searched His face. "I believe," I said softly. "Help my unbelief."[35]

22. At times there is silence in heaven, as when the seventh seal is broken, with the host there waiting to behold what God would do (Rev. 8:1). "It is good that [one] waits silently for the salvation of the LORD" (Lam. 3:26).

23. The hands of a believer represent the visible work (Matt. 5:16). The feet stand for the walk or conduct that is seen (2 Cor. 4:2). The head is the place of spoken thoughts (1 Cor. 2:11–13). The Holy Spirit reveals only Christ, not Himself, and He does the same thing in the believer.

24. A porpoise skin covering over the tabernacle in the wilderness hid its true purpose from the eyes of the world (Exod. 26:14).

25. Jesus as the Christ was hidden from recognition except by divine revelation (Luke 10:21). The believer's life is hidden in God (Col. 3:3), so that only Christ Jesus in him may be manifested (2 Cor. 4:10–11).

26. Jesus said that "whoever wishes to save his life [Greek *psuche*, the expression of his own soul] shall lose it [when he dies], and whoever loses his life [soul] for My sake [so as to express My soul], he is the one who will save it [for eternity]" (Luke 9:24).

27. Everyone in heaven is without shoes, for all the ground there is holy (Acts 7:33).

28. Jesus rebuked those who justified themselves, seeking to be considered righteous in the sight of people (Luke 16:15) rather than before God, who alone is the One who declares us righteous in His Son (Rom. 8:33).

29. Part of the individual cross, which is continually offered to each believer, works the invisibility to others of one's self (Luke 14:27; Eph. 4:22).

30. An exposed heel means anything in one's walk (behavior) that makes one vulnerable to being wounded or tripped up by the enemy (Gen. 3:15; Matt. 18:7; 1 Cor. 3:3; 1 Pet. 5:8–10).

31. Nothing good dwells in or originates from our "flesh," the earthly person (Rom. 7:18). On the cross God removed all spiritual life support to this old self (Rom. 6:6).

32. The functioning of the natural person can only produce spiritual death (Rom. 8:6, 13).

33. Jesus said, "I do not receive glory [honor or fame] from men. . . . How can you believe [trust in God] when you receive [and trust in] glory from one another, and you do not seek the glory that is from the one and only God?" (John 5:41, 44). The rulers of His day "loved the approval of men rather than the approval of God" (John 12:43).

34. God maintains a sufficient degree of freedom in our will to enable us to choose for or against Him in every matter. He respects that freedom and waits for us to be willing. "Whosoever will, let him take the water of life freely" (Rev. 22:17, KJV).

35. "I do believe; help my unbelief," the father of the epileptic boy cried out to Jesus (Mark 9:24).

A Burning Flame of Love

Suddenly, the throne became a towering column of fire, roaring louder than any forge on earth.[36] I involuntarily stepped backward, for the fire seemed hotter than the furnaces that melt iron ore into molten magma.

"Anna," my Father said with a voice of thunder, "can you live within the fire?"[37–38]

"Father," I said hesitantly, "I cannot wish for painful experiences, but I can wish for You. Give me the grace to desire You more than life itself."

Huge hands of fire reached out to me. "Come," He said.

With a big gulp, I began to move forward slowly.

Jesus took my hand. "I will go with you," He said gravely.

The conditions for a saint to abide within God the Father and His Son (and They in him) are to abide in His love and in His Word (John 14:23; 1 John 2:24).

Suddenly, when Jesus took my hand, my yearning for my Father grew more intense. I began crying out in my desire for more of Him: "Daddy, Daddy, Daddy, Daddy!" As I began to call to Him, it was as though God opened Himself with a great, silent cry of hunger on His part to have me closer also. It was as though we were instantly sucked into Him.[39]

We were standing amid coals that were white from the intense heat.[40] I too began to heat up. The light was so bright that I could barely see Jesus for the glory within the blazing, white haze.

Fiery Comets

Then fire resembling great, flaming comets began to hit me from all sides. Two hit my eyes, and my eyes burst into flame.[41] As these fiery missiles assailed me, my Father began to speak, "The fire of My holiness, the fire of My love, the fire of My compassion, the fire of My wisdom, the fire of My understanding, the fire of My knowledge, the fire of My zeal, the fire of My purity, the fire of My mercy…"[42]

The fire of God must burn within the inner person (spiritual heart and human spirit—1 Pet. 3:4) as well as the outer person (2 Cor. 4:16) of the soul expressed through the body.

My fingers went to my burning lips. "Prudence," He said. "Breathe in." I sucked in fire. Fire now was outside and inside of me.

The Beautiful and Terrible Eyes

In the midst of the coals of fire, I saw two huge eyes aflame: beautiful, terrible beyond description. The eyes looked at me. I could not turn my own eyes away; they were so awesome in both beauty and dreadful wonder.[43]

"Your eyes are beautiful," I said. "I wish to see as You see."

"Fix your gaze upon Me," He said, and His eyes came into mine and then back again. I continued to look and burn until I felt as though my eyes were burned out of their sockets.

He spoke, "Let Me look through your eyes.[44] Let My heart look with mercy upon My children and upon the lost.[45] Let My lips speak."[46]

Passionate, all-consuming love welled up within me. "Make me a burning flame of love for You," I cried from the depths of my being.

The Lord in His Glory

Suddenly Jesus was standing directly in front of me within the coals of fire. Brilliant, white light was coming from Him; tongues of fire radiated out from Him at intervals. His eyes were aflame also. He spoke, "As My heart is represented by the garden in Paradise, each believer's heart is likewise represented as a locked garden wherein we meet. The

36. The "great fire" of the jealous, holy love of the Father infuses and envelops Him (Deut. 4:24, 36), as it does His throne (Dan. 7:9). The whole top of Mount Sinai was enveloped by His fire (Exod. 24:17).

37. "God thunders with His voice wondrously" (Job 37:5).

38. "Who among us can live with the consuming fire?" (Isa. 33:14).

39. The Scriptures speak plainly of a place within God the Father (the Greek *en,* translated "in," means "into or within") where the believer may live in spirit and may fellowship with Him and His Son. An example is: "God [the Father] is light.... If we walk in [within] the light... we have fellowship with one another [the Father and the believer]" (1 John 1:5–7). As the Son abides in the Father, so we are to be perfected into the oneness that They have (John 15:10; 17:21–23), for the Son has prepared this place for us (John 14:3; 17:24).

40. Ezekiel saw visions of "burning coals of fire" (Ezek. 1:13; 10:2) and of something like fire near the form of God (Ezek. 1:27).

41. These projectiles of God's fire were to purify and to intensify the spiritual perception.

42. God is a consuming fire (Deut. 4:24). By His Word He burns up the refuse in us and infuses the remainder with the burning purity of His love (Jer. 23:29; Matt. 3:11–12; Heb. 12:27–29).

43. The Lord Jesus's eyes are "a flame of fire" (Rev. 1:14; 2:18–19). These eyes indicate His intuitive knowledge through the "eyes of [His] heart" (Eph. 1:18), the same way that the Father knows all things by "the eyes of [His] heart."

44. Paul prays that the Father would give the saints to know intuitively with the eyes (perception with understanding) of their hearts as God knows (Eph. 1:17–18).

45. The Father looks with compassion and mercy upon His people and the lost, as Jesus did on earth (Mark 5:19; 6:34).

46. "Whoever speaks, let him speak, as it were, the utterances of God" (1 Pet. 4:11).

47. Divine love is "the very flame of the Lord [God]," the burning, all-consuming, everlasting passion of His heart (Song of Sol. 8:6; Jer. 31:3).

48. Many are invited to walk with God as Enoch did, in oneness here on Earth, but few are chosen because the path of living by His life is a narrow one (Gen. 5:24; Matt. 7:14; 22:2–5, 14; John 6:57; 17:21; Col. 3:3). Few will enter it (Matt. 7:14). Fewer yet will go all the way (Phil. 2:20–21; 3:12–14). The Father zealously yearns for His children to put His Son both as a seal over their hearts so that they will be completely His (2 Chron. 16:9) and as a seal on their arm (He is their strength—Ps. 18:1): that they may become an unquenchable flame of His love on Earth (Song of Sol. 8:7) and within Him in heaven (Rev. 3:12).

49. Scripture describes Christ's love for His Father as four dimensional, the fourth being expansion or growth (Eph. 3:18). Divine love is ever abounding (Exod. 34:6) in the Lord Jesus (Eph. 3:19) and in those joined to Him (Phil. 1:9; 1 Thess. 3:12).

At every stage of sanctification, God must call each of us, saying, "Seek My face" (Ps. 27:8). If we freely respond, He will choose us to receive the grace for His Son to be and do that in us (2 Tim. 1:9).

Father's heart is represented by these coals of fire, aflame with love.[47] The heart of our Father is pure, aflame, and holy. You must be invited to walk amid the coals of fire, for although our Father loves all, not all are invited within.[48] For those whom He invites, complete oneness is the only thing that will satisfy: consuming and being consumed, where all sin is unthinkable and painful in the extreme. Like a moth to a flame, one is drawn closer and closer into holiness. Any thought of darkness that hinders perfect union with Light—any wavering in obedience, any thought that is not love—becomes painful; for to that degree, the perfect oneness with the Father is disturbed. Love desires more and more of the Beloved. There is pain in separation. Darkness causes blockages, but love seeks more and more of the Light—more, ever more, until the child also is a walking flame of love in constant communion with Love Himself.

"My heart yearns in ever increasing multiplications for My Father. His love consumes Me, and I hunger and thirst for more.[49]

"Let this desire so be in you—that His goodness draws forth thankfulness and praise, that His mercy draws forth adoration, that His holiness draws forth worship, that like a true child of the Father, Love begets love and trust."

With that, He took my hand and led me out of the coals of fire.

Conclusion

The Return

Jesus led me back to the great assembly. As we emerged, my Father stood and proclaimed, "Let it be recorded. She has passed through the coals of fire; My name is on her forehead. She is My chancellor." He placed His hands on my shoulders and turned me around to face those on the sea of glass.

"I accept this responsibility," I said.

"So be it," He said.

Then all of heaven broke into high praises of God for His faithfulness—music and choirs, fragrances and colors, with angels beyond number bowing before Him who sits on the throne. Joy abounded.

Quietly I told Jesus that I was not sure of all that my new duties entailed.

He leaned over and whispered, "Write what you have seen and heard."

"Oh," I nodded.

A lively circle dance began, and the angels came down from their stations above and joined in the circles with the redeemed: *mahanaim.*[1]

As I stood there, two angels brushed me off with their wings, for I was covered with ashes. I felt a bit fuzzy also, as though I had gone through something and had not recovered or stabilized. My eyes felt stretched.

To enter the fire of God involves a burning to ashes of that which is not of Him, in the way that silver or gold is refined (Zech. 13:9; Mal. 3:3; Ezek. 22:18; 1 Cor. 3:11–15; 1 Pet. 1:7).

The Gift of a Venerable Angel

While the celebration continued, my Father spoke to me privately. "Anna," He said. Jesus and I turned to face Him. "I have a gift for you."

1. The Hebrew word translated *Mahanaim* means "two camps." This is the name Jacob gave the place where he and his household camped and where the angels also camped (Gen. 32:1–2). In another context it is the name of a dance of two companies (Song of Sol. 6:13).

A large, old-looking angel came to stand beside me. He seemed slightly blue because of the blue light emanating from him. He had a partially bald head and a very long white beard. He wore a full-length, sleeveless mantle woven with various shades of blue. Underneath was an even deeper blue robe. Light flashed within the cloak.

The Father shared His heart with His friends like Abraham and Moses (Gen. 18:17; Exod. 33:11; Isa. 41:8). Jesus shared all that He heard from the Father with His friends (John 15:15).

"This is a friend of Mine, Anna," Jesus said to me. "He has come to train you."

My Father said, "Elijah is a gift from My hand. He is beloved of Me and revered among the angels. He will be with you now during your journey on Earth." He said to the angel, "Elijah."

Elijah knelt before the Father.

"Will you help to train My daughter?" my Father asked.

"I will," Elijah replied.

"My friend," Jesus said. Jesus took Elijah by the hand, raised him to his feet, and kissed both of the angel's cheeks. "This is My Anna, Elijah," Jesus said. "She is beloved of Me."

"Hello, Anna," the angel said and took my right hand into his hands. "I am honored to be of assistance," he said. "It is my desire to serve the great and living God."

"Thank you," I said. "I hope to be a good student."

The Father's Exhortation

"Anna," my Father continued, "My people wait for the hope that will seal My covenant of peace. Are you ready?"

"Yes, Daddy."

"Well then, My Anna," He said, "let us bring them into the throne room and into My heart."

His glory came from Him and kissed my forehead.[2]

Jesus leaned over and kissed my hand. "I am with you," He said, looking deeply into my eyes.

"Thank you," I smiled, continuing to gaze at Him whom my heart adores.

He squeezed my hand.

Departure

Then Elijah and I bowed and turned to leave. Before we reached the area where the dancing was taking place, I turned again to look at my Father. The mercy, splendor, and faithfulness of our God overwhelmed me. I choked a little as I said, "I love You, Daddy."

"I love you, Anna," my Father replied.

I smiled again and began to walk from the throne room with Elijah. Epaggelias followed right behind us, and Jachin and Boaz dropped in behind him and slightly to either side.

As we walked through the dancers, the redeemed acknowledged our passing. Their looks were warm. I was as comfortable as being among loved ones on Earth, and more so. "What a family," I thought to myself. "What friends."

Clara waved to me from among those dancing. I looked for other angels that I knew now, but there were so many of them circling around that it was difficult to distinguish quickly one face from another.

On the Path

Almost immediately we were walking on the path in Paradise.

"Another promise kept," Epaggelias said, speaking aloud to himself.

The promise made by the Lord many years ago concerned seeing into heaven (chapter 2, note 3). He also promised the disciples around Him on Earth that they would "see the heavens opened" (John 1:51).

I turned my head to look at him.

He chuckled to himself, "My, He is faithful."

Jachin and Boaz showed respect for the depth of Epaggelias's gratitude. They nodded solemnly.

Questioning Elijah

"Elijah," I said.

He looked at me.

2. The Father is able to act and speak through the radiant glory that surrounds His Person and is a visible form of His infinite goodness (Exod. 33:19). He causes this glory to appear or disappear (Exod. 16:10; Matt. 17:5), to move from one place to another (Ezek. 10:4; 11:23), to be reflected upon the face of a person (Exod. 34:29; 2 Cor. 3:7), and to transform His children from within (2 Cor. 3:18) as Jesus was changed on the mountain (Matt. 17:2). Believers bless in God's name by laying their hands in prayer upon the head of another (Gen. 48:14). God the Father may bless a believer by touching his forehead with His glory (Prov. 10:6).

"Why did the Lord give me a new name?"

Elijah answered, "Because you are new. Your mission, your call, your direction on Earth have changed. You are called now to reveal the Father's heart, and I am to be of assistance to you in doing this. So few understand, Anna, but they long to understand.

"The world is too much with the children of God. It is as though the earth, from which their frames are made, has too much of a hold upon them. Truly their vessels of clay should not dictate the course of the lives of the redeemed, but they seem to have difficulty separating the vessel from that which the vessel contains—seepage. It is as though their clay is still wet and has seeped into their souls.

At the new birth, God gives us a new spiritual heart that is clean (Ps. 51:10; Ezek. 36:26). But it must be kept clean in the conscience part of it by confession of sins and by faith in the cleansing power of His blood (Heb. 9:14; 10:22; 1 John 1:7, 9; Acts 15:9).

"However, this manner of life will no longer suffice. The times are coming and now are already here when the separation between soul and spirit, between body and soul, together with cleanness of heart, must take place for survival.[3–4]

"Anna, there is a spirit in the land that distracts continually from the true.[5] Because of this, our God is sending again the spirit of Elijah.

"The greatest need is still to know the Father. He must reveal Himself in greater measure before the end of these times. I have come to help reveal the heart of the Father to the children, for His heart is for them, and to prick their hearts to seek Him in order that they might know Him. The Father has brought you forth at this time to be one" (I felt that "among many" was implied) "to reveal His heart.

"When the spirit of Elijah is in the land, there are judgments, droughts, and visible confrontations with the enemies of God. As it was with those who worshiped Baal, always there will be violent confrontations and great exhibitions of God's power; but first, Anna, the Father's children must have a greater certainty of His love.[6] They must be rooted and grounded in Christ, empowered by the Holy Spirit, and their eyes looking above and fixed on Him.

"You will enjoy revealing the Father's heart, and I will enjoy assisting you."

The Dark Cloud

I asked, "What is the dark cloud about which my Father spoke, Elijah?"

He replied, "The dark cloud that surrounds God is actually the dense oil of the Spirit, a great good, a visible sign of the magnitude of the anointing, incomprehensible to mankind and therefore seemingly dark.[7] To the majority of mankind, He is hidden in darkness. Light that they cannot see emanates from Him. To many of His children He seems hidden, but the fire of His love is burning through the density of that oil now and will allow His children to see His love, His mercy, and His fatherly compassion, as well as the startling reality of His holiness.

"This fire will burn all that is wood, hay, and stubble in the lives of His children. They must desire the fire and long for His holiness. His heart is turned toward them, and the fire of His love will reveal this. The hearts of the children will long to turn toward Him, to walk through the fire of purification, and to rest in His arms. As the enemy hates the fire, so must God's children love it, for in and through the fire, they will see God."

At the Stairport

We had arrived at the stairport. Elijah smiled at me, "Are you ready to go to work?"

"Yes," I smiled in return. I took his hand in mine. "Thank you, Elijah, and all of you," I said, turning to Epaggelias, Jachin, and Boaz. "Thank you. I bless you in the name of the Lord Jesus."

"Thank you, Anna," they replied together. "We receive that."

We stood there awkwardly.

"Now what do I do?" I asked.

3. Those portions of the Scripture that are made powerfully alive by the Holy Spirit to a believer pierce the depths of the individual's spiritual heart. There the Word divides or discerns between that which comes from his natural soul (mind, emotions, and will) and that which issues from his spirit (Heb. 4:12).

4. The earthly capacities of the soul (mind, emotions, and will) must be governed (2 Cor. 10:5), renewed (Eph. 4:23), and supplied by the Holy Spirit with Christ's soul life (Mark 8:35) through the new inner person (spiritual heart and spirit, 1 Pet. 3:4). The transformed soul must govern the body, never the body controlling the soul. God's dealing with the body is a work of disciplining its members (such as the mouth, eyes, and ears) so that the saint presents them continually to be used to glorify God (Rom. 6:13; 12:1; 1 Cor. 6:20). There is a permanent law of sin in the body that prevents the independent use of its members from ever being redeemed (Rom. 7:23).

5. Jesus said that "the worries of the world, and the deceitfulness of riches, and the desires for other things enter in [a person] and choke the word" from growing up in his heart and producing the fruit of Christ's character (Mark 4:18–19). The spirit in the prophet Elijah was undistracted by these idolatries.

6. The Holy Spirit in Elijah confronted the four hundred fifty false, idolatrous prophets in Israel and overcame them when the fire of God fell and consumed his offering. He had prayed "that this people may know that Thou, O LORD, art God, and Thou hast turned their heart back again" (1 Kings 18:18–40).

7. Within earthly oil is latent power to move the machinery of the world. There is literal oil (as there is literal water) that comes directly from the Holy Spirit, by whose power the Father accomplishes all His working (Gen. 1:2; 1 Cor. 2:4; 12:11). The anointing oil applied to the priests and to the articles of the tabernacle (Exod. 30:22–33) and the oil used in the golden lampstand (Exod. 27:20) were symbols of the true oil of the Holy Spirt (Song of Sol. 1:3; Ps. 45:7; 89:20).

"You return," Elijah chuckled.

"And what about you?" I asked.

All four faces of Jachin and Boaz said, "We go with you, Anna. Remember?"

"Oh," I said perplexed, "right."

I turned to walk toward the docking station, and they disappeared, though I knew they were with me.

Azar Reappears

Azar appeared, leaning on the docking post. "Ah, here you are—well, parts of you anyway," he smiled, referring to my visible head and hands.

I looked down at my cloak and shoes. I could see right through them to the path.

He began to remove the red cord from the post. "And your Father has revealed to you the reason you came?" he grinned broadly.

"Yes," I smiled, and then the wonder and mystery of it all swept over me. "Yes," I repeated with a greater sense of awe.

"Are you ready to return then?" he continued, trying to help me gather my scattered focus.

"Oh, yes," I said, suddenly realizing that I needed to concentrate on the task before me. I moved toward the stairs.

"Remember not to look down over the sides of the stairs when going back. It takes a little getting used to, but we need to learn sometime, don't we?" He sounded ever so like a nanny.

He began to let down the stairs.

"Thank you for your help, Azar."

"That's my name," he chirped. "Still I hope we don't see each other too often. Naw, just kidding," he said. "If you slip on the steps, I'll steady you."

I laughed at him, shaking my head.

"Give me your hand," he said, leading me to the top of the stairs. "Now be careful with the first step. Light isn't slippery, but it does have a different feel from materials on Earth, you know."

He held my hand until I had taken the first step and then the next.

"All right!" he cheered, and began whistling through his teeth and clapping loudly as one would at a sport's event. "Take care, luv."

The Descent

I could not help but smile, even while steadying myself on the stairs. As I began to descend, he called after me, "Remember the stairports are all over the world and ready for your use."

"Thank you," I called back to him loudly; I lifted my hand without looking back. I could sense that he was watching me the full length of the stairs. He continued to hold the end of the cord.

When I reached the bottom, I turned and waved, although he was only a speck. The cord tightened; the stairs in its first stage retracted, then the second, then the third, and disappeared.

On Earth Again

I was back at the location from which I had escaped. Far away in the distance, I could hear the sound of a fierce battle in progress. Quickly I clawed my way to the top of the sandy hill again. I wanted to see if any of the city remained after the battering ram's attack.

Where the walled city had stood, now there was only debris, scattered stones, and pockets of burning. Still I knew that the stones, the living stones of Christ's true church, were safe. They may have climbed some stairway, or hidden in caves, or floated on the water; but the living stones had survived.

I stood there a moment looking at the devastation before me. Then I looked up, cocked my head to one side, and smiled. "Reporting for work, Daddy."

Afterword

How It Happened

You will receive a visitation." With these simple words our lives were blasted from one realm into another, although we did not realize it at the time.

My husband and I received this promise at a dinner party a few days before we left the city. Four years before, the Lord had brought us to that large metropolitan area after my husband's retirement from the pastoral ministry. We brought together pastors and intercessors—crossing denominational lines—in a citywide prayer movement.

After the Lord raised up leadership from among the pastors, we turned the prayer ministry of the city over to them. At our last citywide gathering with the ministers, they laid hands on us, blessed us, and sent us out to serve the larger body of Christ.

"You will be in a cabin at the season of Hanukkah when you receive this visitation," the dinner guest had continued. He was a friend of ours who had an internationally recognized prophetic ministry. Although we had known him for several years, he had never spoken words from the Lord to us personally.

I had seen angels intermittently while we were in the city and had even seen the Lord several times from a distance, but a visitation was far beyond anything my husband or I had ever experienced. To say the least, we were skeptical.

However, our God is merciful as well as full of surprises.

On the eve of Hanukkah, 1994, in a cabin on a lake in Texas, suddenly, the heavens opened as the Spirit ushered me into the very throne room of God. I saw with such startling clarity that I could not deny what I was seeing. Everything I saw and heard was different from what I had thought: more extraordinary, yet comfortable. It seemed as though I were at home.

I began to visit heaven on a daily basis. Although at first the visits were tiring, I was careful to journal them. I do not think of these visits as visions, for I believe that what I saw is actually there. John told of such an experience in Revelation 4:1. John reported what he saw and heard when he was summoned to heaven in the Spirit.

There were visions also. This book begins with a vision. Visions seem to be a pictorial language—visual aids representing truth from God in which one may or may not participate. One example of the visions given to John while he was in heaven is Revelation 9:17.

When I shared these revelations with my husband, the Lord allowed my husband to experience what I was experiencing by being there.

Then on January 1, 1997, the Lord asked us to compile a book from some of the early revelations and to include an addendum containing scriptural verification and illumination concerning all that was seen and heard. He asked us to complete the entire manuscript in one year.

This book is in response to the Lord's request. My husband and I can truly say that we do not believe this book is our own. We have never served the Lord in any way that has been so completely Him. Everything in this book is true. If there are errors in the way things are described, the errors are entirely our doing.

All those who are born again in Christ Jesus sit with Him, in spirit, in heavenly places. However, He has been gracious to allow some of us to see into that realm, according to His Word in John 1:51.

Moreover, we found that these revelations were not for the two of us alone, as we had first thought, but for the body of Christ, of which we are members.

We, who are bondservants of Christ, bless you in His name.

—Anna Rountree

PART II

Revealing the Mystery of Our Betrothal to God

The Lord's incredible love for His bride shows through the Rountrees' writings, revealing the intimacy that is available to those who choose to walk a life of obedience and holiness, dying to the things of the flesh. The bride of Christ needs to live the crucified life in order to experience His resurrection power daily.

—Suzanne Hinn

This section by Anna Rountree is an invitation for believers to participate in the bridal process of preparation to walk in an exalted privilege of intimacy as the bride of Christ. As you read this revelation of Jesus's love for His bride, you will be overwhelmed with the incredible marvel of your destiny as the object of the Bridegroom's infinite love.

—Mike Bickle
Director, International House of Prayer

This section is a glimpse into eternity, a preview of the consummation of the ages. It is right that God should give the bride of Christ this final "love letter." It will help her to prepare her soul for the day of her betrothal to her Beloved.

I love the way the angels join with all of heaven in sending us the message, "He comes!" even as they did to the shepherds of Bethlehem long ago. And the Holy Spirit echoes back, "The bride hath made herself ready!"

Thank you, Anna, for giving us a glimpse into the eternal chambers of love! We know that the words of love your Beloved spoke to you are for each one of us, and we are comforted as we wait.

—Gwen R. Shaw
President, End-Time Handmaidens

Part II

Contents

Revealing the Mystery of Our Betrothal to God

. . . for I betrothed you to one husband,
that to Christ I might present you as a pure virgin.
—2 Corinthians 11:2

Preface

Often men identify with the priesthood of Christ and women with the bride of Christ. But in reality, neither the priest nor the bride has anything to do with our own gender. Our heavenly Father is looking only for His Son in us.

He is looking to see if we exhibit the holiness and righteousness that was to be displayed in the lives of His biblical priests. He is looking to see if we exhibit that single-eyed devotion so apparent in a loving bride—the one who wishes nothing more than to live in perfect union with her husband—even as Christ lives in perfect union with His Father.

Since only perfect union will satisfy our Father, He created us so that only perfect union will satisfy His children. The ancient betrothal process in the Bible is a spiritual road map for the believers' "rite of passage" into this consuming intimacy with God in Christ.[1]

All of the Father's adopted children will know full union within the family of God in the New Jerusalem on the new earth (Rev. 21:3). Gathered closely around the Father, we shall behold His face in joy unspeakable (Rev. 22:3–4).

When we are born again, we are joined to Christ in spirit, translated out of the kingdom of darkness into the kingdom of the Son of His love, seated with Him in heavenly places and made coheirs with Christ Jesus of God the Father.[2] We begin as high as we can get, but not as deep. Depth is a journey.

If in this journey we seek the Lord for His sake alone, if we long to know Him as He knows us, then He will draw near to us in startling reality. He will ratify the betrothal covenant into which we entered (arranged by our heavenly Father) at the time of our new birth.[3]

The betrothal occurs at the new birth, but one is a spiritual baby when this happens (1 Cor. 3:1).

1. God desires "to bring you near to Himself" (Num. 16:9). The Father's heart longs for intimacy with many children like His divine Son (1 John 3:2). "He [the Father] chose us in Him [Christ] before the foundation of the world, that we should be holy and blameless before Him [the Father], in love" (Eph. 1:4, MARGIN).

2. "For by grace you have been saved through faith; and that not of yourselves, it is the gift of God" (Eph. 2:8). Each person must choose to receive the gifts of repentance, forgiveness, and saving faith through hearing the Word concerning Christ (Rom. 10:17). Each must believe in and confess Him as Lord (Rom. 10:8–10). That is our part. Everything else connected with our spiritual birth is entirely God's doing (Ezek. 36:26–27; Rom. 8:16–17; Eph. 2:5–6; Col. 1:13–14).

3. Many remain unaware that they have entered into covenant to share one life with the Lord Jesus forever (Hos. 2:19). However, every Christian will eventually have to complete the training by the Holy Spirit before that one can be presented as part of the sanctified bride (Eph. 5:26–27). The Spirit will bring each one to be holy and blameless, sharing Christ's heart, soul, and spirit (Col. 1:22–23).

4. God declares, "I also swore to you and entered into a covenant with you so that you became Mine" (Ezek. 16:8). If we respond with heart longings like "Draw me after you, and let us run together," He begins the courtship. Later He will say "Arise... and come along... [to] the secret place of the steep pathway" (Song of Sol. 2:13–14). He is asking the betrothed one

There comes a time when each Christian is to embrace this eternal covenant. Christ will then take the initiative by giving us the ardent desire to be His.

Passionately He will draw us after Him and usher us into that stage of our Christian growth that the Bible describes as "the time of love" (Ezek. 16:8, KJV). The New International Version says this: "I looked at you and saw that you were old enough for love" (Ezek. 16:8), describing this stage as *courtship*.[4]

For the betrothed, this is a time of intense joy and severe testing. An acute longing begins to grow within such believers.[5] They realize that nothing will satisfy this hunger except a deeper union with Christ Himself.

One of the meanings for the Hebrew word *yada* is to know another person through conjugal relations (Gen. 4:1).

If we will persevere, seeking consolation for our hearts in Christ alone, the Lord will draw us into a spiritual oneness.[6] Once we have been brought into a more complete melding, we "know" Him—oh, not as we will know Him later, nor as we will know Him when we have full salvation by receiving our resurrected bodies. But we know Him as the One who will say to us, as He said to Abraham, "I *know* him" (Gen. 18:19, KJV, emphasis added). The Hebrew meaning of the word can be translated: "I am *intimate* with him" (emphasis added).[7]

There are three distinct stages within the bridal process. The individual experiences two of these, and one is corporate.

This book is an actual account of such a journey—a journey (open to all believers) into a consuming intimacy with Christ. I am sharing my love letters with you because the One who gave them asked me to share them.

His visitation to me on Earth, as well as these particular visions and revelations experienced in heaven, occurred between July 5, 1995, and July 5, 1996 (with two related visions given later). They were recorded word for word in journals. They chronicle a relentless, passionate drawing by the Lord unto Himself, culminating in a glorious, spiritual union.

It is my great hope that these will be an encouragement to all who wish to live in God as deeply as possible while on Earth—and to know Him above all others and above all else both on Earth and in heaven.

For you, Christ has love letters of your own awaiting.

The chart on the next page shows each stage, the work accomplished and what is received in each stage.

Many of us have some grasp of the first and third stages of this process. But some of us have not comprehended the depth of the impassioned commitment on the part of Christ toward His chosen ones, nor the poignant intimacy with Him that is possible during this lifetime within the second stage.

Who experiences this stage of salvation	Work accomplished	Received in this stage of salvation
1. Individual	a. New birth/betrothal[8] b. Bridal price[9] c. Dowry[10] d. Clothed with Christ[11] e. Spiritual gifts to the bride[12] f. Marriage contract[13] g. Formal acceptance[14] h. The covenant cup/first cup of wine[15]	• Repentance and forgiveness of sins (Acts 11:18;10:43) • Declared righteous in Christ (Rom. 10:4) • The Holy Spirit (John 7:39) • New spiritual heart and new human spirit (Ezek. 36:26) • Adoption as heirs (Rom. 8:17) • Eternal life (Rom. 6:23)
2. Individual	a. Ongoing sanctification[16] b. Ratification of betrothal with accompanying gifts[17] c. Esther's preparation/testings[18] d. Deeper union with Christ[19] e. Formal betrothal (with the status of being married; the bride is a married woman, the groom a married man, but they are not yet a married couple)[20]	• Transformation of the soul life (Matt. 16:24–25) • Consecration of the body (Rom. 12:1)
3. Corporate (realized after passing from this life)	a. Resurrected body[21] b. Linen garments of righteous deeds[22] c. The corporate bride of Christ[23] d. The Father's blessing[24] e. The cup of new wine/second cup of wine[25] f. Married/the bridal week[26] (full marital status) g. Marriage supper of the Lamb[27] h. Reigning with Christ on earth[28]	• Salvation of the body (Phil. 3:21) • Full salvation • Married

to rise above self, the world, and sin—and come away with Him. If this one clings to the Lord, He begins a hidden time of leading that person apart. There He will "speak tenderly to [that one's] heart" as never before (Hos. 2:14, AMP).

5. David cries, "My soul longed and even yearned for the courts [the heavenly presence] of the LORD" (Ps. 84:2). "My soul pants for Thee, O God. My soul thirsts . . . for the living God" (Ps. 42:1–2). Jesus said that those with this kind of hunger and thirst "shall be completely satisfied" (Matt. 5:6, AMP).

6. The Lord Jesus interceded with His Father for all those who would believe in Him to "be perfected in unity" with the Father and the Son. He asked that they "be one [with Us] just as We [the Father and the Son] are one" (John 17:23, 22).

The Father has one great purpose in creating the human race. It is to have each child of His grow up to share in the complete union that He and His Son experience, so that the revelation of the Father in the Son will be seen in all.

7. God knows us (as He did Abraham) in the most private way possible. He knows "the hidden person of the heart" (1 Pet. 3:4; 2 Chron. 6:30; 1 Cor. 8:3).

8. Jesus said, "One is born [again] of water [of the Word] and the Spirit" (1 Pet. 1:23; John 3:5). Believing "the word [gospel] concerning Christ" brings saving faith to those who are thirsty (Rom. 10:17, MARGIN; John 7:37).

Paul said of those who received the gospel he preached, "I betrothed you to one husband, so that to Christ I might present you as a pure virgin" (2 Cor. 11:2).

9. In ancient Israel the groom, or his father, paid a price to the father of the bride for the right to marry her. The clearest example in Scripture concerns Dinah, Jacob's daughter (Gen. 34:11–12). Other examples are Rebekah in Genesis 24:51–53 and Leah and Rachel in Genesis 29:18, 26–27. This bridal price paid to the bride's father is different from the gifts given later to the bride.

Our heavenly Father gave His only divine Son as the bridal price (John 3:16). The Son shared in that payment by the sacrifice of His life on the cross (Acts 20:28; 1 Cor. 7:23).

10. The dowry is the sum of the items of value that the bride brings to the marriage. Pharaoh, king of Egypt, gave a captured city as a dowry to his daughter who became the wife of Solomon (1 Kings 9:16).

What riches can anyone bring to his or her union with Christ Jesus? The Father owns everything on Earth and has made His Son the heir of it all (Ps. 24:1; Heb. 1:2). Therefore, Christians bring nothing of their own to the marriage.

11. "For all of you who were baptized into Christ have clothed yourselves with Christ" (Gal. 3:27; cf. Rom. 13:14). This means that He alone is to be seen in His disciples.

12. The individual bride of Christ receives a multitude of spiritual gifts at that person's new birth (2 Pet. 1:3–4). The greatest gift from God is His own divine life by the Holy Spirit who comes to dwell within (John 10:28; 2 Cor. 1:21–22). Other major presents of grace given are repentance, forgiveness, righteousness in Christ, a new spiritual heart, a new spirit and adoption as heirs. Please see the Scripture references in the chart on the previous page.

13. In the Jerusalem Bible, Raguel gave his daughter, Sarah, as wife to Tobias. "He drew up the marriage contract . . . according to the ordinance in the law of Moses" (Tobit 7:14, the Apocrypha).

The Jewish nuptial contract, called in Hebrew a *ketubah*, spells out the mutual obligations of the partners in marriage. The groom promises to love and to provide for his bride her food, clothing and conjugal rights, except in the case of her possible adultery (Exod. 21:10). She obligates herself to be lovingly faithful in her responsibilities in the home.

The new covenant sealed by Christ's blood on the cross is the marriage contract for His disciples (1 Cor. 11:25). Our Bridegroom promises betrothed Christians that eventually each one will know Him intimately, with their sins forgiven and no longer remembered (Jer. 31:31–34; Heb. 8:8–12).

14. Among Israelites there can be no valid betrothal unless the bride freely consents. Rebekah's family asked her, "Will you go with this man [Abraham's servant]?" And she said, "I will go" (to become Isaac's wife) (Gen. 24:57–59).

Jesus offers the water of eternal life through union with Him to any who are thirsty—"a free gift to all who desire it" (Rev. 22:17, NEB). But we must come willingly to Him and drink (John 7:37).

15. At the traditional Jewish betrothal ceremony, the bride and groom drink from the same cup of wine. The wine has been blessed by giving joyful thanks and praise to God for the holiness of human marriage.

The Lord Jesus spoke His betrothal to His disciples at the Last Supper before He died. They shared a common cup of wine that He had blessed (Mark 14:23). He was instituting the new betrothal covenant to be sealed by His blood on the cross (Luke 22:20).

16. "Aaron was set apart to sanctify him as most holy" unto God (1 Chron. 23:13). The Christian's "sanctification [is] by the Spirit and faith in the truth" as it is in Christ Jesus (2 Thess. 2:13; see also Ephesians 4:21). It begins with the gift of repentance and includes a new spiritual heart and a new spirit (Acts 11:18; Ezek. 36:26).

The Holy Spirit also yearns to present our bodies as a holy sacrifice and to save our fleshly souls in Christ (Rom. 12:1; Luke 9:24). This means that we are called to be sanctified entirely—heart, soul, spirit, and body (1 Pet. 3:15; 1 Thess. 5:23).

17. One listing of betrothal gifts that God gave to His people Israel is found in Ezekiel 16:8–14.

The Lord Jesus ratifies or confirms His betrothal to a Christian when the person has matured sufficiently to embrace the commitment to deeper union with Him. Christ grants gifts to the disciple at this time to equip that one for a share in His ministry to the Father and to others. The anointing of the Holy Spirit and fire is a foundational gift that Jesus desires to come upon all of His betrothed ones who obey (Matt. 3:11–12; Acts 2:3–4; 5:32).

18. Esther was prepared by first being beautified with oil of myrrh (Esther 2:12). This signifies for Christians the incapacitating of the flesh by the Spirit with the sentence of death applied to its operation (2 Cor. 1:9; 4:10–11). After six months Esther was then given spices and cosmetics to make her desirable for the king. These represent the virtues and perfections of Jesus's resurrected life to be manifested in His betrothed ones (Rom. 6:5, 13).

Her tests came when she had to face the possibility of death in approaching King Ahasuerus uninvited (Esther 4:11–16). Later an edict of the irrevocable law of the Medes and Persians condemned the Jews to death. Esther again risked death by disclosing that she was a Jewess (Dan. 6:8; Esther 7:3–6).

Each disciple of the Lord Jesus must deny (or die to) one's self (that is, the fleshly expression of the soul through the body) in order to manifest only Him (Matt. 16:24–25).

19. Deeper union with Christ means sharing one life with Him in God the Father (Col. 3:3). That life begins to flow through the new heart capacity given to every person who receives the risen Lord Jesus (Ezek. 36:26; Rom. 10:9–10). As this new spiritual heart becomes filled with Jesus, the Christian's own soul life (mind, emotions, and will) is to be gradually replaced by the soul life of the Lord (Eph. 3:17–19; Matt. 16:24–25). The culmination of union with Christ on Earth is the sanctified human spirit being made one with His human spirit. "The one who joins himself to the Lord is one spirit with Him" (1 Cor. 6:17).

20. Mary and Joseph were officially betrothed. This meant that the people of Nazareth considered each of them to be married though not yet living together (Matt. 1:18). Therefore, when he considered putting her away, he would have to get a divorce. The ceremony in the spiritual realm of a Christian's official betrothal to Jesus means that before witnesses in heaven they are now considered to be married to one another in heart, soul, and spirit (Ezek. 11:19; Phil. 1:27).

Complete union with the Lord will occur at the wedding of His corporate bride in resurrected bodies (Rev. 19:7). "Thus we shall always be with the Lord" (1 Thess. 4:17).

21. Jesus said, "All who are in the tombs will hear His [the Son's] voice, and will come forth: those who did the good deeds to a resurrection of life, those who committed the evil deeds to a resurrection of judgment" (John 5:28–29). Every human being will eventually receive a resurrected body. The children of God will receive a body like Christ's glorified body (1 Cor. 15:42–44; 1 John 3:2).

22. At "the marriage of the Lamb," His corporate, priestly bride is provided with "fine linen [robes] bright and clean; for the fine linen is the righteous acts of the saints" (Rev. 19:7–8). Each bride also comes as a priest in clothing like the Old Testament priests who wore white, finely woven linen robes (Exod. 39:27). The grace of the righteous Christ in each one will make it possible for them to accomplish these righteous acts. They do the acts because they *have been* joined to Him, not in order to *be* joined to Him (Eph. 2:10; 1 Cor. 15:10).

23. "Let us rejoice and be glad and give glory to Him [God, the Almighty], for the marriage of the Lamb has come and His [corporate] bride has made herself ready" (Rev. 19:7).

24. In Scripture, Rebekah's family at home blessed her as she was leaving to marry Isaac, Abraham's son (Gen. 24:60). Every Jewish bride thereafter is blessed at her wedding. It is fitting for Christians that God, the Father of the Bridegroom, should bless the members of the corporate bride at their marriage in heaven, His home (Eph. 1:3). The Father's first blessing over a husband and wife was also to "be fruitful and multiply" (Gen. 1:28).

25. At Jewish weddings the bride and groom sip from a cup of consecrated wine after the traditional matrimonial blessings are spoken over them. Jesus said, "I will not drink of the fruit of this vine from now on until the day when I drink it new with you in My Father's kingdom" (Matt. 26:29). He was referring to the corporate wedding ceremony that will take place in heaven. There He and the members of the resurrected bride will share a cup of new wine (Rev. 19:7; John 2:10–11). This cup represents a life of new joy with Him never before realized by human beings.

26. In ancient Israel the bride and the groom would be alone in the bridal chamber for seven days (Gen. 29:27–28). There they would consummate the marriage and come forth later for the marriage supper with their friends. After the corporate wedding ceremony for the resurrected, priestly bride of Christ, there also will be a bridal week (possibly the seven-year period of the tribulation on Earth). They will be alone with the Lord Jesus during this time. Then they all will gather to celebrate the marriage supper before returning with Christ to Earth to share in His reign (Rev. 20:6).

27. At the celebration of a Jewish wedding on earth, there is a time of feasting and dancing with much joy (Matt. 22:2).

The Lord's disciples renew their betrothal covenant to Him at every celebration of His communion supper on Earth (1 Cor. 11:20, 25). At the completion of the corporate marriage to Christ in heaven, there will be a glorious celebration that includes "the marriage supper of the Lamb" (Rev. 19:7, 9).

28. Christ will establish His kingdom on this planet (Rev. 11:15; 19:15–21). The corporate wife will serve also as "priests of God and of Christ and will reign with Him for a thousand years" (Rev. 20:6).

Chapter One The Visitation

The edges of the air were on fire.

I raised my hand to shield my eyes from the searing light. The very molecules of the air within our apartment were burning white-hot from a central point.

Swiftly the Holy Spirit spoke: "Rise, Anna." At the time I was down on my knees in prayer asking for more of God. Now, however, I had stopped praying, for I was struck by the wonder materializing before my eyes. The air sizzled and curled.

From the center of this phenomenon, the fiery glory of the Lord began to burn through the wall of our apartment. The Holy Spirit had to set me on my feet, for I could not stand. Seeing the Lord's glory while on Earth and in one's body is very different from seeing Him above while in spirit. His glory is almost more than the physical body can bear.[1]

Angels of His Presence

As I rose to my feet, stately angels of His presence stepped through the center of the blazing light to enter the room.[2] They came in pairs but separated as they touched the room's atmosphere. Four angels stood before me in a semicircle to my left, four angels in a semicircle to my right. They wore pale lavender robes embroidered with deep purple and gold on the sleeves and hem. Golden girdles bound these garments across their chests.[3] Each angel carried something in his hands in the manner of an emissary.

Christ Jesus wears a golden girdle as the great High Priest to the Father (Rev. 1:13).

1. The Lord Jesus visited the apostle John in a vision while he remained on the earth at the island of Patmos (Rev. 1:9). He was so overcome that he "fell at His [Christ's] feet as a dead man" (v. 17; cf. Acts 9:3–5). But later John was taken up into heaven in spirit where he was able to look upon the Lord Jesus as well as the Father on His throne without being physically overcome (Rev. 4–5).

2. The apostle John saw "seven [of the] angels who stand before God" to do His bidding (Rev. 8:2). We know that among the angels of His presence is Gabriel, who told Zacharias that he "stands in the presence of God" (Luke 1:19). These angels are chosen for this special responsibility (1 Tim. 5:21).

3. The colors of their robes signify that these angels stand in the presence of Christ the King (John 19:2–3). The golden girdles across their chests indicate their priestly service to God (Rev. 15:6).

4. "All that the Father gives Me will come to Me," Jesus said (John 6:37). The Father "gives" or betroths His children to His Son here on Earth at the time when each one is born again of the Spirit and enters the kingdom (John 3:3, 5–6).

For the Christian the *chuppah* is "in the bosom of the Father" Himself. The Lord calls this "My Father's house" where His own on Earth are to abide in spirit even now (John 1:18; 14:2–3; 17:24; Col. 3:3).

The presence of the canopy symbolizes the fact that Jesus is coming from His Father's house in this instance. The *chuppah* itself represents the Father as signified by the word *love*.

The canopy is called the *chuppah* in Hebrew and means "a chamber." It represents the place in his father's house that the bridegroom in ancient Jewish ceremonies had prepared for the couple to begin life together.

Then four additional angels, similarly dressed, entered the room through the burning air. Each of these held one pole of a canopy, the sort one might see in a Jewish wedding. As they moved forward, the word *LOVE* could be seen at times in the canopy's fabric.[4]

King Jesus

The Holy Spirit stirred and swelled into a whirlwind in response to the One who now stepped beneath the canopy. King Jesus, brighter than the sun, entered the room.

The Lord Jesus comes not only as King but also as Priest according to the order of Melchizedek (Heb. 5:6).

Through the shock of unbelievable light, I could see faintly that He was wearing a rich purple cloak that opened in the front and hung in folds to the ground. It had long sleeves and was edged with a wide, gold brocaded border. Beneath this garment was a white robe that also reached to His feet. The robe was grappled across His chest with a golden girdle. On His head was a golden crown that was similar in some respects to the crowns used to cap Torah scrolls.[5] He was terrible in majesty, awesome in holiness, splendid in beauty.

The Holy Spirit swirled around me to strengthen me, for the intense light and power emanating from the Lord made it difficult for me to stand.

Gifts

Spiritual wisdom is primary among the Holy Spirit's giftings, for "all desirable things cannot compare with her" (Prov. 8:11; cf. Isa. 11:2). Therefore she is represented by a crown of gold (Prov. 4:8–9; Ezek. 16:12).

Then, as if by some silent command from Jesus, the nearest angel in the semicircle stepped toward me. In his hands he held a golden crown, which he carefully placed upon my head. "Wisdom," he said, smiling slightly.[6] Then crossing his arms over his chest, he nodded respectfully and stepped back into the semicircle.

The angel opposite him in the semicircle stepped forward with the gift he was carrying. He placed golden earrings on my ears. "Knowledge," he said.[7] Then he too folded his arms over his chest and moved back to join the other angels.

Rings on every finger can mean that the sword of the Spirit (the living word from God) is to be fully grasped and communicated in writing to others (Eph. 6:17; Rev. 1:11, 19).

One by one each of the remaining angels of His presence brought the gift that he held in his hands. After the physical gift was placed upon me, the angel named the spiritual gift it symbolized. The gifts these angels presented included a golden heart that hung on a chain over my own heart—*understanding*;[8] golden bracelets on each wrist—*discretion*;[9] a golden nose ornament—*discernment*;[10] golden rings on each finger—*the ability to communicate*;[11] and a golden necklace—*the fear of the Lord*.[12] The eighth angel stepped forward and blew a mist of gold over me. It covered me like a veil from my head to my feet.

"Favor," he said as he smiled.[13] He too nodded and stepped back into the semicircle.

All of the eight gifts given here are manifested in some form of a circle, symbolizing that they are of the Father Himself and eternal, without end. God empowers these endowments to operate as the Christian follows the leading of the Holy Spirit (Heb. 2:4; Rom. 11:29).

The Response

I was stunned. I had never received such an immediate and extravagant answer to prayer. I looked down at the gifts that I was able to see. They were princely—gifts of my Father from my Father.[14] But why the canopy?

"Lord," I said, "let all of these gifts be within for Your pleasure."[15]

5. Melchizedek was king of Salem and priest of God Most High eternally (Gen. 14:18; Heb. 7:1–3).

The purple robe attests to Christ's royalty (John 19:2–3). The white robe with the golden girdle across His chest signifies His priesthood. Jesus appeared to the apostle John in the same white robe with the golden girdle (Rev. 1:13).

The crown He wears covers the top of His head in filigree work of gold. It is similar to the ornamental crowns placed on top of the Torah scrolls, the written Word of God in synagogues. The Lord Jesus is the Word of God (John 1:1).

6. The dictionary gives the meaning of human *wisdom* as knowledge of what is true or right, coupled with just judgment in applying it to obtain the desired results. But "the wisdom of this world is foolishness before God," for natural wisdom is hopelessly flawed by sin (1 Cor. 3:19; 1:20).

The wisdom of God the Father from the beginning has been encapsulated in the person of His Son (1 Cor. 1:24; John 1:2). Those who receive Christ Jesus are put into Him by God, so that the Son becomes for them all things including divine wisdom (John 1:12; 1 Cor. 1:30; Rom. 8:32).

7. The dictionary defines human *knowledge* as acquaintance with information learned from study or from experience. Golden earrings signify the divine knowledge from the Father that Jesus receives for the Christian. Christ said that "He [God] awakens My ear to listen as a disciple... and I was not disobedient" (Isa. 50:4–5).

The Holy Spirit reveals to the disciple the knowledge the Lord Jesus has received for that person (1 Cor. 2:10–11). One category of such knowledge is the spiritual gift called *the word of knowledge* (1 Cor. 12:8). It is a direct disclosure of knowledge that was not seen, heard, or thought by the Christian (1 Cor. 2:9).

Another area of supernatural knowledge is in the disciple's conscience where the Spirit reveals what is in accord or not in accord with the life of Christ in that person (Rom. 9:1).

8. The human definition of *understanding* is insight or comprehension with the mind of the meaning or the significance of something. The golden heart hung on a chain over a disciple's heart represents the spiritual heart of Christ being reproduced in that person (Song of Sol. 8:6). King Solomon asked God for an understanding heart to administer justice in the natural realm (1 Kings 3:9, 11). The Christian is given a spiritually minded heart to understand things of God in the supernatural sphere (Ezek. 11:19; 1 Cor. 2:14; Isa. 6:10).

The renewed human spirit is to know intuitively in the conscience when some thought, word, or act is from God or not, but the heart is to understand its meaning. What the mind or the spirit cannot understand, the heart does because it is the seat of faith by which we understand spiritual things not seen (Heb. 11:1, 3; Rom. 10:9–10).

9. One of the meanings of human *discretion* is the capacity to act judiciously, being circumspect in exercising sensitivity regarding the effect of one's conduct.

The main Hebrew word for *bracelets* is derived from a root word meaning "to bind or join." Bracelets on the wrists of the Christian signify being bound or attached to the Lord Jesus (1 Cor. 6:15, 17).

In New Testament times, prisoners were bound to their guard by a chain around their wrists (Acts 12:6–7). Paul considered consecrated disciples to be willing prisoners of Christ Jesus (Rom. 16:7). As such we are to be restrained by the Spirit in not being able to do or say what we please, but are to act as the Spirit leads (Gal. 5:17–18).

10. The dictionary defines *discernment* as the faculty to make distinctions accurately between things.

The nose ornament is a symbol of spiritual discernment because the nose instantly recognizes the presence of an odor. It distinguishes between pleasant and offensive smells without reference to the mind or to sight (Ezek. 16:12; 1 Sam. 3:8). Discernment is meant by the common expression, "sniffing out a matter."

The first thing to determine in spiritual discernment is whether the matter at hand is of God or not. If it is not of God, the next distinction is whether it is of the flesh (coming from the natural person) or of Satan (demonic). This spiritual gift can be a manifestation of the Holy Spirit called *the distinguishing of spirits.* It enables believers to identify the kind of spirit that is operating in a particular situation, group or person (1 Cor. 12:7, 10).

11. In ancient Jewish betrothals, for the right to marry the girl, the groom's family gave gifts—called *the bridal price* (Gen. 24:53; 29:18, 26–27; 34:11–12). The giving of money or some other gift of value constituted the engagement to be married. In more recent Jewish betrothal ceremonies, the groom gives the bride a ring and says "Behold! You are consecrated to me with this ring according to the Law of Moses and Israel."

The mysteries of God are those truths concerning Him that cannot be known except that He reveals them.

He smiled at me. "Because you have asked that these be for My pleasure, they will be [for My pleasure] and will also be experienced by others.[16] These gifts will unlock My heart to you and to My body. All mysteries are bound up, locked away in Me, Anna. But the mystery of My love is the greatest revelation of all."[17] Moving toward me, He said, "My chosen one, My love, a fruitful bough, an orchard of fruitfulness."

"Lord," I replied, "I am barren." (I had never borne physical children.)

He smiled again as He answered, "You will bear and be more fruitful than if you had borne physical children. I have withheld your bearing. But now I place My hands upon you that you might bring forth good fruit—many children, all heirs, kings and priests to their Father."[18]

Women in Scripture who were childless felt great disgrace (1 Sam. 1:5–7, 10–11).

He placed His hands upon me. Fire and power surged through me. He continued to speak, "No longer will you bear shame because of unfruitfulness."

Ratification of Betrothal

The Bible speaks of the Lord as the husband of His people (Isa. 54:5; Rev. 21:2). The Father instituted human marriage on earth in order to prepare His children for eternal union with His Son.

"Cleave to Me," He said. "I am your Husband.[19] Let My covering be on your head."[20] His eyes burned into me as He continued, "I am the Lord your God, and none is like Me. I am the beginning and the end. I am your health, your protection, and your fruitfulness. Thousands upon thousands of heirs will you bear, those who will walk right into My kingdom, those who will be at home in My chambers.

"Anna," He said in a more intimate tone, "you are more beautiful now than earlier. My heart is turned toward you. My desire is for you. You have captured My heart. Lock this away in your heart, for My promises are true and sure."[21]

I could hardly breathe. "Lord," I whispered, "let it be soon."

All judgment has been committed to Christ Jesus, who alone has the authority to render righteous verdicts with divine mercy (John 5:22; James 2:13).

"It is already accomplished," He said. "Bear fruit for the kingdom. Shun pride.[22] Point not the finger."[23]

The Departure

He bowed at the waist as a sign of His departure and stepped back under the canopy. Once under the canopy, He turned and walked through the burning opening in the wall of the apartment. The four angels holding the poles of the canopy also bowed and walked out with Him, holding the canopy over His head as He disappeared. The angels of His presence also signified their departure, and two by two they followed the Lord.

When one is betrothed to the Lord Jesus, a spiritual ring on the finger is a constant reminder that one is consecrated (set apart) unto Him. It also represents His pledge of faithfulness to endow the person with spiritual gifts and grace needful to carry out the Father's calling upon that person.

12. In the Bible a golden necklace is an emblem of authority for a person who is under greater authority (Gen. 41:42; Ezek. 16:11). An example is King "Belshazzar [who] gave orders and they… put a necklace of gold around his [Daniel's] neck" giving him "authority as the third ruler in the kingdom" (Dan. 5:29). The neck represents the human will, either in yieldedness to authority or in being obstinate and stiff-necked (Prov. 1:8–9; Matt. 8:8–9; Acts 7:51). The Father gave His Son authority over all things (Matt. 28:18; John 3:35). However, the Lord Jesus humbled Himself always to the authority of the Father's will (John 5:30).

Because of His love and respect for the Father, Jesus feared to ever act independently of Him, but found delight in obeying Him (Ps. 40:8; Isa. 11:3; John 5:19–20). Christians will find rest only in having the same yoke about their necks (Matt. 11:28–30).

13. The betrothed, Rebekah, asked the servant, "Who is that man walking in the field to meet us?" The servant said, "He [Isaac] is my master. Then she took her veil and covered herself" (Gen. 24:65). It was a custom in early times in the East for a future bride to be veiled, set apart until she was married. A disciple of Christ accepts the spiritual veiling of one's whole being in consecration to Him (1 Cor. 6:19–20).

The word for *favor* is usually translated as "grace" in the Bible. The veil of divine favor (grace) surrounds those who embrace their consecration to Jesus. Each can say (with David) "You surround [me] with favor as with a shield" (Ps. 5:12).

14. Through his servant, Abraham gave gifts to Rebekah, the betrothed of his son Isaac (Gen. 24:53). Our Father God gives gifts of His splendor through His Son to those who welcome their betrothal to Christ Jesus (James 1:17). These presents cause the bride to be "exceedingly beautiful" in God's eyes. He said that the "beauty [is] perfect because of My splendor which I bestowed on you" (Ezek. 16:13–14).

15. The author of the Book of Hebrews says that Psalm 45 is about God's Son (Heb. 1:8–9). It is a wedding song of the marriage of Christ the King and His bride. In Psalm 45:13 the bride is described as "all glorious within." This refers to the "hidden person of the heart, with the imperishable quality of a gentle and quiet spirit, which is precious in the sight of God" (1 Pet. 3:4).

16. King Solomon asked God to "give Thy servant an understanding heart to judge Thy people to discern between good and evil." God said to him, "Because you have asked this thing and have not asked [things] for yourself… I have done according to your words… [and] I have also given you what you have not asked" (1 Kings 3:9, 11–13).

17. The supreme mystery of God is Christ Jesus who incorporates all other divine mysteries within Him (Col. 2:2–3). The mystery of the ever-expanding love that is manifested in Christ is the greatest mystery of God. It can never be fully known (Eph. 3:17–19; Luke 10:22).

18. "Rejoice, barren woman who does not bear; Break forth and shout, you who are not in labor; For more numerous are the children of the desolate, than of the one who has a husband" (Gal. 4:27; cf. Isa. 54:1).

19. Adam was "a type of Him [Christ] who was to come" (Rom. 5:14; cf. Gen. 2:24). Husbands and wives on earth are to become "one flesh," meaning that the two think and act as one. In full union with Christ, the betrothed one becomes one heart, one soul and one spirit with Him (Ezek. 11:19; Acts 4:32; 1 Cor. 6:17).

The Bible calls Joseph the "husband" of Mary. After their betrothal they were considered married but without the physical consummation (Matt. 1:19). This is also true with betrothal to the Lord Jesus (2 Cor. 11:2).

20. In two instances of betrothal in Scripture, the groom places his garment over the intended bride.

(1) God spread His skirt over His people of Jerusalem that His love might cover their nakedness (the exposure of their sinful nature) (Ezek. 16:8; 1 Pet. 4:8).

(2) The widow Ruth asked her relative Boaz to spread his covering over her as a sign of his willingness to be her protector as redeemer (Ruth 3:9, 12–13; Deut. 25:5–7).

Jesus as our head covering in betrothal means that we walk under His favor, protection and authority. This is so that our "minds should [not] be led astray from the simplicity and purity of devotion to Christ" (2 Cor. 11:3).

21. The passionate heart of Christ for His betrothed ones is represented by the ardor of the shepherd for the maiden in Song of Solomon 4:9: "You have made my heart beat faster, my sister, my bride. You have made my heart beat faster with a single glance of your eyes."

22. "… the boastful pride of life, is not from the Father but is from the world [system ruled by Satan]" (1 John 2:16). *Pride* is claiming for oneself glory that belongs to God (John 5:44). All glory belongs to God. He has said, "I will not give My glory to another" (Isa. 42:8).

The Son of God "is the radiance of His [Father's] glory," but He did not claim that glory as His own (Heb. 1:3). It remains the Father's alone.

The light of God's glory shines within the hearts of disciples, but it is not their possession (2 Cor. 4:6). They are "reflecting" it, as in 2 Corinthians 3:18, where "reflecting" is the better meaning of the Greek word usually translated "beholding."

23. Isaiah spoke of abstaining from "the pointing of the finger," which means passing judgment on other people (Isa. 58:9).

24. David said the same thing to Saul when the king offered his daughter to him in marriage: "Who am I… that I should be the king's son-in-law?" (1 Sam. 18:18)

25. "What do you have that you did not receive?" (1 Cor. 4:7). "Every good thing bestowed and every perfect gift is from above, coming down from the Father of lights" (James 1:17; John 3:27). Even our own beings now are a gift from God because His Son purchased us on the cross of Calvary from our former master (1 Cor. 6:19–20; Rev. 5:9).

Then the Holy Spirit swirled before me again, this time gathering up all of the remaining fire and light. He too passed through the apartment wall. Instantly, the gifts became internal and no longer adorned me externally. The wall closed.

God says that when we are betrothed to His Son, we are "advanced to royalty" (Ezek. 16:13).

Silence.

"Father," I whispered, "who am I to marry a King?[24] I come with nothing.[25] I have no dowry.[26] I do not even have a hope chest with linens and..."

Before I could continue, my Father thundered audibly in the room: "Can I not provide linens for My children?"[27]

Immediately, I heard a knock at the front door of the apartment. Although engrossed in all that was occurring, I managed to cross to the door and open it.

The Caravan

A Bedouin is a wanderer with no permanent abode on Earth. "Let the nomads of the desert bow before him [the King of kings]" (Ps. 72:9).

"Hello, Anna," blurted a tall angel. I say that he was an angel because he called me by the name that at the time was known only in heaven.[28] Also, he was dressed in Bedouin attire (uncommon apparel for this continent). Beyond him in the parking lot I saw a caravan of twenty-four camels with Bedouin attendants.[29]

I shot a quick glance around the apartment complex. My husband and I were living in a low-rent housing facility in Florida. We had adjusted fairly well to these living conditions since we had learned to duck when the neighbors were shooting at each other. However, I was not sure how they might react to a camel caravan. Although usually the complex was alive with adults and children, no one was in sight.

Hope Chests

The hope chest was a sturdy trunk or a box with a lid in which a young, unmarried woman collected clothing and linens for a future home in the hope of using them in married life. Twenty-four chests certify that heavenly authority sends them.

The angel continued. "We have brought your hope chests," he said effusively. "Twenty-four chests. Where would you like them?"

My hands went to my face in amazement. I was flooded with so many mixed emotions that I began to laugh and cry at the same time.

"It is all right, Anna," the large angel said comfortingly. "Do not be troubled. Your Father loves you."

In the parking lot the Bedouin attendants signaled the camels to kneel down. These angels began unloading the chests.

Between the laughing and crying I said, "Can you stack the chests in here [meaning in the living room]?"

"We certainly can," he brightened. He whistled to the other angels and indicated with his head to bring the chests. Then he turned his attention to me again. "Hope is of God, Anna.[30] Each chest your Father gives to you is hope that you can share. This is a greater gift to your Husband than laces and embroidered towels," the angel smiled.

The dictionary defines human *hope* as the feeling that what one desires will be obtained.

The attendants began carrying the chests into the living room with two angels holding each chest. All of these angels wore camel-colored, desert clothing.[31] After delivering a chest, each pair of angels smiled broadly like those wishing to show themselves extremely agreeable. Then they returned to the caravan.

The chests seemed to be covered in camel skin. They were large and looked something like treasure chests. The five straps encircling each chest were gold, and the two handles for carrying were an intense blue.[32] The opening for a key on each chest was encased in gold, with the shape of the keyhole itself being a cross.[33] No one ever gave me a physical key, however.[34]

Almost every chapter of the Bible that is numbered five or contains a number 5 describes human weakness and inability and therefore our absolute need for the grace of God. An example is John 5:2–3.

The Receipt

Because of their size, the chests stacked up to, and then through, the apartment ceiling.

The large angel rocked back and forth on his heels enjoying the sight. "Yes," he smiled, "there is great hope here." Then he took a pencil from behind his ear and pulled out a clipboard that held a receipt. "Sign here, please," he said, extending the clipboard to me.

"What name should I use?" I asked.

"Anna would be fine."

I wrote "Anna" on the white receipt and then handed the clipboard back to him.

"All right," he said with a sigh that denoted closure of a mission. He pulled out the under copy of the receipt and handed it to me. "Here is your receipt. Twenty-four chests full of hope."

Rebekah

Suddenly, I remembered Rebekah and how she had watered the camels as well as drawn water for Abraham's servant.[35] "Would you like some water or something?" I asked haltingly, not sure of what to say.

"Oh, no," he laughed. "We have better water than your city's water system can supply. We will be going now before we draw a crowd."

Jesus said that He would give the "living water" of the Holy Spirit who would become in a Christian "a well of water springing up to eternal life" (John 4:10, 14; 7:37–39).

"Thank you for bringing the chests," I said.

"Our pleasure," he smiled. "*Shalom.*"

The attendants whistled and clicked their tongues for the camels to rise. The large angel grasped the reins attached to the headgear of the lead camel and guided him around so that the caravan could reverse its direction in the parking lot. Then he and the camels with their attendants began to leave. Suddenly, they disappeared.

Just as suddenly, life in the apartment complex returned to normal.

I closed the door and leaned against it looking at the chests piled through the ceiling. "Thank You, Daddy," I whispered.

It is by God's choice that one is taken in spirit to heaven from Earth. The person experiences whatever is granted one to see and hear there.

My Father spoke audibly again. "You have a bigger and better hope than any princess brought to her wedding day.[36] Now," He continued, "come up here."[37]

Amazingly, in my spirit, I began to rise.

26. "Pharaoh king of Egypt had...captured Gezer...and had given it as a dowry to his daughter, Solomon's wife" (1 Kings 9:16). A bride's *dowry* is the material wealth that she brings to the marriage.

There are no riches that anyone can give to God's Son whom the Father "appointed heir of all things" (Heb. 1:2). His Father owns "the earth and all it contains" (Ps. 24:1).

27. The linens to which God refers are the white, finely woven linen robes such as those worn by the Aaronic priests (Lev. 6:10; Exod. 39:27). These garments represent the righteousness of Christ with which "it was given to her [Christ's bride] to clothe herself in fine linen" (Rev. 19:8; cf. Isa. 61:10; Rom. 3:22). *Fine linen* symbolizes righteous acts that the Holy Spirit accomplishes through the saints to glorify the Lord Jesus (John 16:14; Rom. 15:18–19).

28. One of the promises Jesus makes to each Christian "who overcomes" (who shares in Christ's overcoming of all the enemies of God) is a new name. "I will give him a white stone, and a new name written on the stone which no one knows but he who receives it" (Rev. 2:17). The name is engraved on a stone to indicate that the believer will be called permanently by this name in heaven. Only the person receiving the name knows the basis upon which God gives the new name.

29. The root of the Hebrew word for *camel* is a verb meaning "to deal fully with." Psalm 116:7 translates this verb as "the Lord has dealt bountifully with you."

Camels transport goods of some kind. God has been bountiful in sending this many animals. Twenty-four camels imply that this caravan is under the authority of heaven. An example of the number twenty-four signifying heavenly authority is the group of twenty-four elders who rule from thrones surrounding God's throne (Rev. 4:4).

30. "Christ in you [is] the hope of glory" (Col. 1:27; 1 Tim. 1:1). Everything good that we could desire is found in Him. "For no matter how many promises God has made, they are 'Yes' in Christ" (2 Cor. 1:20, NIV; Col. 2:9–10; 3:11).

31. The camel-colored desert clothing of the attendants shows that they are not of this evil world system but are sent from God. The prophets like Elijah and John the Baptist wore hairy robes of camel skin (2 Kings 1:8; Matt. 3:4; Zech. 13:4).

32. The five golden straps encircling each chest denote the grace of God that keeps the hope of Christ secure in the believer (Heb. 6:19–20).

The two handles of blue indicate that this hope was brought from heaven. Sapphire, a gem of blue color, describes the color of God's throne, as well as the pavement under His feet (Ezek. 10:1; Exod. 24:9–10).

33. The shed blood of Jesus on the cross paid the price to unlock for us all that is His from the Father (Heb. 10:19–22). "Behold, I [the Lord Jesus] have put before you an open door which no one can shut"—the way to the Father in heaven (Rev. 3:8; John 14:6). It remains unlocked through Christ (Eph. 2:18).

34. The blood of Jesus on Calvary paid the price for our access to "the unfathomable riches of Christ" (Eph. 3:8). "He who did not spare His own Son, but delivered Him up [to the cross] for us all, how will He not also with Him freely give us all things?" (Rom. 8:32).

35. Rebekah "gave him [Abraham's servant] a drink...[and] she said, 'I will draw also for your camels until they have finished drinking'" (Gen. 24:18–19).

36. A Christian becomes a family member of the reigning Monarch of the universe (Rev. 22:5; Eph. 2:19). As His children by adoption and grace, we are "heirs of God and fellow-heirs with Christ" (Rom. 8:17). And by betrothal and then oneness with Jesus our Bridegroom, we become heirs of all that He is and inherits (1 Cor. 1:30; Gal. 2:20; Eph. 1:22; Phil. 3:21).

37. In Revelation 4:1, God commanded John the Apostle to "come up here" into heaven. He spoke the same words to the two witnesses on Earth (Rev. 11:12).

Chapter Two

The Ascent

As I rose, I realized that a protective shield surrounded me. It was clear and round. I wondered if this shield was present at all times, even though I did not see it.[1] I sat down, drawing my knees up to my chest with my arms hugging my legs.

The Deeper Life

I began to reflect during this ascent.[2] "How did all of this begin? Certainly when I was born again," I thought to myself. But I wanted to think beyond Christian infancy and adolescence. "No," I thought, "it began when I decided that I wanted to live as deeply as possible—to touch the essence of life itself. The only way to do that was to know truly Life Himself."[3]

God "Himself gives to all life and breath and all things" (Acts 17:25).

I had come to a place in my life where I did not want to live like a pebble skipped across the water. I wanted to experience deeply. I wanted to know Him.

As I reflected, I realized that it had taken me twenty years as a Christian to come to this conclusion. Twenty years to be persuaded that to know and to fellowship with God is the noblest pursuit of mankind.[4] "Why," I wondered, "had it taken me so long?"

The foremost commandment is to "love the Lord your God with all your heart . . . with all your soul . . . with all your mind . . . and with all your strength" (Mark 12:30). This means with all your being.

The Ambush

As I neared the second heaven, I had a sense of foreboding.[5]

1. In Job 1:10, Satan says that God has "made a hedge about him [Job] and his house and all that he has, on every side." David sang that God "is a shield to all who take refuge in Him" (2 Sam. 22:31).

2. While the body of John the Apostle remained on the earth, he was taken "in the Spirit" to heaven. There he appeared and walked about in a spiritual body (Rev. 4:1–2; 10:8–10).

3. In addition, "God has given to us [who believe] eternal life, and this life is in His Son" (1 John 5:11). Eternal life is God's own life that He gives to His children because they are "heirs of God [Himself]" (Rom. 8:17). For Christians to live by God's life is to be able to know the Father and the Son in loving companionship as members of the heavenly family (John 17:3; 1 John 1:2–3; Eph. 2:19).

4. The Father has always considered loving Him by being with Him to be greater than doing works for Him (Gen. 3:8; Lev. 26:11–12; Mark 3:13–15).

A primary thing Jesus desired from His Father was that Christians "be with Me where I am" in heaven even while they are still on Earth (John 17:24; Phil. 3:20).

5. Paul says that he "was caught up to the third heaven . . . into Paradise" on one occasion (2 Cor. 12:2, 4). "The Lord's throne is in [this highest] heaven," together with the holy angels and the redeemed who are there (Ps. 11:4).

Suddenly, in the distance the atmosphere ripped, and a black swarm poured through the opening. From my perspective, the swarm looked like locusts or bees. Whatever it was, it was rapidly heading in my direction.

Demons—black, red-eyed, putrid smelling—surrounded the shield. They looked like winged gargoyles. They began screaming curses at me. I felt trapped, cornered.

In Job 20:12–15, wicked persons are described as those who feed upon evil and then "vomit . . . up . . . the bile of cobras within" (vv. 14–15, literal Hebrew).

These spirits began to vomit a sickly green bile onto the shield.[6] The bile must have had the properties of acid, for it began to burn into the surface, causing it to warp and thin like heated plastic. Then with sharp claws, the demons began to dig through these weakened areas.

"Lord, help me," I cried.[7]

Angelic Help

Immediately, shrieks came from several of these demons on the outer edge of the pack. Quickly they turned their attention from me to two warrior angels clothed in bright armor and to the angel Azar.

I was very glad to see Azar. When I had seen him before, he had told me that he was an angel of "helps" assigned to protect me.[8] Well, I certainly needed help now.

He was dressed in work overalls over which he wore a thin, brown robe. A white tool pouch hung from his belt. Two suction cups that had a handle between them also hung from this belt. (These cups were the kind used to move large sheets of glass.) In addition, he had a tank harnessed to his back. I cheered when I saw him.

The weapon that the Holy Spirit uses against the enemy is "the word of God" (Eph. 6:17).

The warriors were dressed in armor similar to that worn by centurion guards—except that the armor was shot through with light. Instead of swords, they carried long rods that displayed the Word of God.[9] The demons recoiled at the touch of these rods as if receiving a violent shock. Like wild animals with a fresh kill, however, they fought viciously to retain their prey.

While the warriors were fighting the enemy, Azar pulled out a hose that was attached to the tank harnessed to his back. Quickly he hosed down the bubble to stop the bile from eating through the surface. Just as rapidly, he attached the two suction cups to the bubble. Then he grabbed the handle that was between them. With a great heave, he started to pull the shield upward, away from the battle. The demons began to scream when they realized we were getting away.

The warrior angels held the demons at bay while we made our escape. As we climbed higher, I saw that the warriors were routing the enemy, driving them back toward the rip in the atmosphere. I sighed in relief.

The Corridor

As we arose, the sound of demonic clamor faded. A great sense of peace came over me.

Azar had pulled the shield into an invisible passageway. On either side of the bubble, thousands of angels were flying in a slow, upward spiral. They formed a magnificent, shimmering corridor to Paradise. They smiled at us as we passed.

Laserlike streaks of light flashed by us going up and down. These were angels who were traveling the passageway.[10]

Paradise

Before we entered a greater light at the end of this corridor, Azar veered off to carry me into Paradise a different way. Suddenly, the bubble surfaced through an opening in the turf of God's perfectly groomed park.

As soon as the shield touched the grass, it went "pink," bursting as easily as a fragile soap bubble. "Sorry to burst your bubble," Azar joked.

"Thank you for helping me, Azar," I said with great relief.

In Jacob's dream he saw that "a ladder was set on the earth with its top reaching to heaven; and behold, the angels of God were ascending and descending on it" (Gen. 28:12). The root of the Hebrew word for *ladder* denotes "a highway." Christ Jesus is the highway that connects heaven and earth (Heb. 10:20; John 14:6).

This phrase, *burst your bubble*, is a play on words that means to shatter another person's impression that something is permanent.

The first or lowest heaven is the visible, celestial atmosphere above the earth. The Bible calls this "the expanse" or "firmament" (Gen. 1:8).

Because there is a third and a first (lowest) heaven, there is a second heaven in between. This is the area allowed by God to Satan and his host. There they organize and direct their evil strategies (Eph. 6:12; 3:10). The devil and all those with him there will be "thrown down to the earth" in the last days before Christ returns (Rev. 12:7–9).

6. Eternally sick (damned) creatures vomit that which they have fed upon. Demons subsist entirely on evil (as does Satan), and so they vomit it up.

7. God hears the cries of His children for help. He answered the pleas of "many [Christians who] were gathered and were praying" for Peter's release from prison (Acts 12:6–8, 11–12).

God sent a great earthquake to open all the doors of the prison where "about midnight Paul and Silas were praying and singing hymns of praise to God" (Acts 16:25–26).

8. "For you have made . . . the Most High, your dwelling place . . . He will give His angels charge concerning you, to guard you in all your ways" (Ps. 91:9–13). This is said about the angels of helps who respond to the cry of disciples. These angels are instantly available, as was Azar, whose name is a Hebrew word meaning "to help or relieve."

9. The rods or staffs wielded by the two warrior angels carried the same kind of authority from God's written Word that Moses exercised with his staff when it was empowered by spoken words from God. For Moses it thereby became "the staff of God" to defeat the enemy in Egypt and to release God's people (Exod. 4:20; 8:16–19).

"We aim to please," he drawled in a cowhand accent. He pulled out a clothes whisk and began dusting me off. I suppose I had bubble flakes on me.

I looked around. How at home I felt here now. Even though I had visited Paradise many times, the beauty and grandeur of God's park always overwhelmed me.

Azar continued concerning the demons, "They're just a nuisance. Those have no real power. That's the reason they travel in packs. They're a bother, though. They can slow you down."[11]

"And the warriors?" I asked.

The evil angels are required to "keep their own domain" and not abandon "their proper abode" (Jude 6). Angelic watchers are warriors on the borders of heaven to insure that Satan and his host stay within their boundaries assigned by God.

"Well," he smiled, "sometimes I need help myself. Those were Watchers, part of the border patrol.[12] They refuse to take any nonsense from those wishing to interfere." He stepped back, looking at me, "So, how do you feel?"

"I feel fine," I said. "Will you thank the Watchers who helped me?"

"I will," he smiled. He began taking his arms out of the straps that held the tank to his back. "Are you going to see your Daddy?" he asked.

"Yes," I smiled, handing him the suction cups that had fallen to the ground when the bubble burst.

Angelic Escorts

Two angels who looked like lovely young women came flying by.[13] They wore pale blue robes and had no wings. "Come fly with us, Anna," they called.

Azar smiled, "They will escort you to the throne room."

"Will you come with us?" I asked Azar.

"I need to test this equipment before I store it," he said. "Go on," he continued. "You'll enjoy the flight."

I lifted my arms toward the angels, indicating that I wanted to join them. Laughing, they swooped down and picked me up, one on either side. Immediately they executed two loop-the-loops that took my breath away.

Azar laughed and called after me, "Have a good time with your Daddy."

Off they flew with me between them. They were like precision stunt flyers executing perilous aerobatics over the terrain of Paradise. They banked, rolled, dove, and looped-the-loop. I knew they were trying to share an experience with me that I could not have on Earth. However, I was beginning to be grateful for that fact. They were as exuberant as children.

The Throne Room

We arrived very high in the throne room and rather far away from the throne. However, from this vantage point I had a panoramic view of the glorious bow of colors emanating from my Father, the thousands of redeemed on the sea of glass, the angels coming and going, the elders, the four living creatures, and the activity around the throne (which I supposed to be official business of the kingdom).[14]

"I wonder if I should disturb my Father?" I asked myself.

I did not wonder long. "Come here, Anna." My Father spoke in that loud but soft voice that penetrates to the core of your being.

The angels who were carrying me responded instantly to His request. They made a steep turn and flew toward the throne area—too rapidly for comfort, I might say. Right before we arrived at the throne, the angels dipped down and made an abrupt landing at a respectful distance from the activity. Unfortunately they released me too quickly, and the momentum caused me to slide on. Those conducting official business

10. While on Earth, Jesus was seen by His disciples to be the living way into heaven, for "the angels of God [were] ascending and descending on the Son of Man" (John 1:51).

11. It is possible for demons occasionally to hinder those passing through the devil's assigned territory in the middle heaven. The evil angelic princes stationed by Satan to control the Persian Empire withstood for twenty-one days the passage of God's angel who was sent from heaven to Daniel in Persia. "Then behold, Michael, one of the chief [angelic] princes [of God] came to help" him. In the skirmish other demonic rulers over Persia joined the fight (Dan. 10:12–13).

On the way back to heaven, God's angel who had come to Daniel was going to have to battle through the evil angels over Persia and over Greece. He would again have the help of Michael, God's chief angel assigned to the Jewish nation (Dan. 10:20–22; 12:1).

12. These watchers also keep track of the enemy to be certain that he does not exceed the limits he is allowed to go with people on Earth. "An angelic watcher, a holy one, descended from heaven" and announced the decree of God to permit the devil to afflict King Nebuchadnezzar in a certain way and for a set time (Dan. 4:13–17).

13. Some angels look, talk, and dress like men; other angels appear like women. At least three Scriptures support this differentiation:

(1) In Matthew 22:30, Jesus said, "For in the resurrection they [the saints] neither marry, nor are given in marriage, but are like angels in heaven." If the angels were not representative of both male and female, the Lord's analogy would make no sense.

(2) In Acts 12:12–15, Peter is miraculously released from prison and goes to a house where believers are in prayer for him. A servant girl did not open the door at Peter's knock and call but recognized his voice. When she told those in the house that Peter was outside, they said, "It is his angel." They knew that the voice of an angel sounds like the Christian to whom that angel is assigned. Peter's angel sounded masculine.

(3) Zechariah 5:9 says that "two women were coming out with the wind in their wings" to lift up an evil person from the earth to deposit her in a foreign land. The two winged women seem to be evil angels. It is, however, true that at times the spirits in the highest heaven appear to have distasteful assignments (1 Kings 22:21–23). However, Satan cannot create. Whether good or now evil, these winged women originated with God.

moved out of the way, being unsure of how far I might travel. I was incredibly embarrassed, and the angels who brought me were abashed.

But like a powerful head of government whose two-year-old stumbles into his office, my heavenly Father was more concerned about my feelings than His own.

"Not bad," He chuckled, commenting on my landing.

"Just out of the nest, Daddy," I sputtered, trying to help the situation.

He spoke graciously to the escort angels, seeking to relieve their distress. "Thank you for bringing My child," He said. They bowed deeply, shaking their heads and biting their lips as they excused themselves.

I turned in an apologetic way to those who had been in conference. "I did not realize so much was going on up here." I looked back at my Father, "Are You busy?"

There was a pause—then God laughed.[15] The elders laughed. The redeemed and the angels laughed. I laughed. It was a laugh that rolled and continued to roll throughout heaven.

My Father

The Father's figure is composed of divine light (1 John 1:5). Jesus spoke to others about His Father's form (John 5:37). It is only the brightness of the Father's face that people still living in their earthly bodies are not able to look upon (Exod. 33:20).

After the sound subsided, my Father said, "Come here, My child." He picked me up and set me on the armrest of the throne.[16] Those who had been meeting with Him bowed and withdrew.

I looked up toward the area of His face. Our Father is light—dazzling light.[17] He has a form and even looks clothed in a garment of light.

From His chest upward it is impossible to see His face because of the brilliance. The white light of His presence radiates outward to create an aurora of jewel-like colors. Resplendent.

God sees every human being (Ps. 33:13–14). He knows each heart (Ps. 33:15). He is aware of what each one thinks, does, and says (Ps. 139: 2–4). He is everywhere, knows all, and has all power (Ps. 62:11; 139:7; Heb. 4:13).

Even though He embodies holiness and majesty, to be near Him is to have the deepest sense of coming home. I felt completely safe and utterly loved.

"There must be millions of people speaking to You right now," I said to my Father.

"Millions," He affirmed, "but each of My children has a personal relationship with Me. Each feels like an only child, receiving all of My attention."[18]

14. The apostle John gives the best description of the grandeur of the scene in the throne room of God, with the unfolding of glorious events there, in chapters 4 and 5 of the Book of Revelation.

15. God the Father laughs. "God in heaven merely laughs! He is amused by all [the] puny plans" of the heathen nations that think they are able to establish their own kingdoms in opposition to "the Lord and His Messiah, Christ the King" (Ps. 2:4, 2, TLB). Our God even shouts for joy over His people (Zeph 3:17).

16. God the Father stretched out His hand and picked up the prophet Ezekiel (Ezek. 8:2–3). Another time He fed Ezekiel with His hand (Ezek. 2:3, 9). Sitting on His throne, the Father held a book in His right hand (Rev. 5:1).

17. Human beings have an outer form that is in the same shape as the Father and as the Son, being made in the image of both of Them (Gen. 1:26; Ezek. 1:26–27).

18. How our Father God is able to hear and respond to millions of people at the same time is beyond our comprehension. David said, "Such knowledge is too wonderful for me. It is too high, I cannot attain to it" (Ps. 139:6; cf. Job 9:10).

19. The golden eagle Christian is in the juvenile stage of learning to share in Christ's ministry as the great white Eagle (see note 25).

One of the offices of Christ Jesus is that of the Prophet long foretold (Deut. 18:18–19; John 6:14). The "flying eagle" symbolizes His prophetic ministry from heaven, one of the four living creatures who surround the throne of God (Rev. 4:6–8). Flying eagles are equipped to see objects on earth from a great height—their "eyes see it from afar" (Job 39:29). The Lord Jesus as the Prophet discerns clearly from God's perspective what the Father is speaking to those on Earth. Christ then reveals the Father's acts and words to certain eagle Christians on Earth who will speak or write "for edification and exhortation and consolation" of others (John 12:49–50; 2 Pet. 1:20–21; 1 Cor. 14:3).

20. The Lord Jesus calls golden eagles to live in spirit and heart with Him in heaven. They are "hidden with Christ in God," though they walk on the earth (Col. 3:3). The revelations given to them mainly concern the life in heaven where our eternal family and home are. The Father feeds them with the true manna that is Christ (Hos. 11:4; Rev. 2:17; John 6:32–35). They are to become white like Jesus as the great white Eagle (Ps. 51:7; Lam. 4:7; Matt. 28:3).

21. Here the greatest number of eagle Christians are called and gifted to serve. The altar of burnt offering there represents the blood of Christ's sacrifice on the cross of Calvary to release people from the guilt and power of sin. This is to bring them to consecration and to peace with God in His Son (Lev. 1–5).

The Lord may minister through an eagle Christian in the outer court all the days of that one's adult life. However, He may move that eagle into another area of the tabernacle. Wherever one serves, the ministry is always first to God and then to people in His name.

22. The revelations from the Father through the Lord Jesus are given for different purposes in the front area of the tent of the tabernacle known as the holy place (Exod. 29:30). At the golden lamp God gives divine light to eagle Christians from His written Word (Exod. 25:31; 27:20; Ps. 119:105). At the table of "the bread of the Presence," disclosures are granted concerning life in close fellowship with Christ Jesus (Exod. 25:30). The supernatural illumination from the lampstand and the heavenly life from companionship with the Lord are both supplied to help those Christians who are called to a ministry of prayer. Prayer is represented by the altar of incense situated before the veil in the holy place (Exod. 30:1, 7; Rev. 5:8; 8:3–4).

23. He is also the great high Priest before the Father according to the order of Melchizedek (Heb. 4:14). As High Priest he offers food to His father in the form of "the fat and the blood," both of which were reserved for God in the Old Testament sacrifices (Lev. 3:16–17; Ezek. 44:7, 15). In deepest, loving fellowship with the Father, He offers the fat of thanksgiving, praise, and worship as a soothing aroma (Heb. 2:11–12; cf. Lev. 1–3). He also presents the blood of Calvary in intercession (Heb. 7:25; 9:11–12). The altar sacrifices of the Old Testament priesthood represented Christ Jesus, who alone nourishes the Father (Lev. 21:6; Num. 28:2).

24. Those who would draw near to God in Christ in the holy of holies must die to their sinful nature.

God's Word concerning our human nature

God declared that the human nature we have at birth "is flesh" (Gen. 6:3). The Bible uses the word *flesh* in several ways. It may mean the soft covering of the bones, all mankind, or corrupt human nature. Paul said, "I am of flesh, sold into bondage to sin" (Rom. 7:14). "Nothing good dwells in me, that is, in my flesh" (Rom. 7:18). There is an irreversible "law of sin which is in my [bodily] members" (Rom. 7:23). This law always leads me to sin whenever I use my body or soul (mind, emotions, and will) independently of the leading of the Holy Spirit (Eph. 4:22).

The salvation of the soul

The saving of the soul and the control of the body for Christ does not mean the annihilation of their God-given faculties. It is only their fleshly, self-centered use that must be kept inactive. As we continually choose Christ Jesus instead of ourselves, the Spirit will keep the flesh confined as a prisoner is kept on death row. Without freedom to do as the flesh pleases and without the possibility of any change in our flesh, all hope in our natural selves will wither away. The "flesh is hostile toward God" and cannot obey Him (Rom. 8:7). It is under the curse of God (Jer. 17:5). We will come to hate the flesh operating in us as the Holy Spirit reveals the hideousness of its corruption (John 12:25; Col. 2:18).

The impartation of Christ's soul life

Allowing the Lord's soul life to be manifested in us is the salvation of our souls (Heb. 10:39; 1 Thess. 5:23; James 1:21; 1 Pet. 1:9). It is an ongoing process (Luke 21:19). We accept the individualized cross that the Spirit arranges day by day for each of us "so that you may not do the things that you please [wish]" (Gal. 5:17). As we bear about this spiritual cross to our flesh life, the Spirit gradually bestows the soul life of Christ—His mind, emotions, and will (2 Cor. 4:10–12).

This process is what Jesus meant when He said, "Let him [the disciple] disregard his own interests, and let him at once and once for all pick up and carry his cross day after day, and let him take the same road with Me that I take as a habit of life. For whoever desires to save his soul life shall ruin it [for heaven]. But whoever will declare a sentence of death upon his soul life for My sake [to have Mine], this one shall save it" (Luke 9:23–24, WUEST).

The Golden Eagle

"So," my Father continued, "how is My golden eagle today?"[19]

I supposed that He referred to me as a juvenile eagle because of my inglorious landing near the throne. "I am fine, Daddy," I said. "How long does it take a golden eagle to mature?"

The Father likens the outer court of the desert tabernacle to Christ's prophetic ministry concerning the needs and problems in people's lives on Earth (1 Cor. 14:24–25).

"When your feathers become pure white, you are ready to nest above. You must fly the mountains and valleys of heaven, though, and you must eat from My hand.[20] Do not seek that which the eagles below seek. They seek fresh meat [fresh revelation], but their game is earthbound, and so is their revelation—times, seasons, natural signs, and consequences of sin. I have given them to see into human souls, but all of it concerns the needed revelation for the outer court. Most eagles labor there for the need is great."[21]

He continued, "There are those eagles who fly in the holy place. They minister to Me more intimately. They fly among the branches of the golden lampstand. They, like David, are in communion with My Son, eating the shewbread. Their revelation is used to assist those who minister at the golden altar of incense. Fewer minister in the holy place.[22] But who ministers to Me before the ark?"

The ascended Lord Jesus is the great white Eagle in the utter purity of His ministry as the Prophet foretold (Deut. 18:18–19; John 7:40).

The Great High Priest

"The High Priest, Daddy," I said.

"Yes, My Son. He is the great white Eagle as well as the great High Priest.[23] He is the sacrifice, and His is the blood sprinkled. How many enter into that place [meaning the holy of holies]?"

The more believers die to their own self-expression, the more they live by Christ, the true manna (Mark 8:34–35; John 6:32–33). As He fills their emptied souls with His mind, desires, and will, more of Him will be formed in them (Matt. 16:24–25).

"One," I answered.

"One," He reiterated. "He is the Door, the Way, the Truth, and the Life. He draws near to minister to Me. And when you, joined to Him, eat from My hand, when you eat from the hand of the One who sits upon the throne, you too become white. Narrower and narrower is the way, Anna. Fewer and fewer are those who will continue. But for those who will be drawn near to Me—for those who will lay their hands upon the ark and die to the fleshly use of their own souls—they will live between the cherubim and will bear much fruit for the kingdom."[24–25]

Natural eagles have a type of dance when courting whereby they lock talons at a great height above the earth. Then they start turning over and over like a Ferris wheel as they plunge downward.

Suddenly, He opened my eyes in vision to see two white eagles cartwheeling. He continued, "I have chosen you, and you have chosen Me, and I have chosen you..."[26] It was as though the cartwheeling could go on and on, like an eternal wheel. The vision ended.

My Father continued, "Let nothing turn you to coarser food, helpful though you think that would be to mankind. Eat from My hand and sleep between the cherubim."

Golden Manna

When the vision ended, I realized that a golden rain of light was falling on me. It piled up on my head, my shoulders, and then my upturned hands. It was soft like snow but not cold.

"Golden manna, My child. Food for the golden eagle."[27] He scraped the manna from my head, shoulders, and hands and held out His hand of light from which He wanted me to eat. "Food from the hand of God, Anna."

I ate from His hand. He continued, "That which goes in your mouth will issue forth through your hand so that you may write what you see and hear."

The golden rain ceased.

Betrothal

"Now for the reason I summoned you, Anna," my Father continued. "You must make yourself ready. Since your betrothal to My Son, you are no longer your own. You belong to Him. Prepare yourself as Esther did.[28] We love you, and you are called and chosen. Therefore, the need

Christ's personal cross from eternity

In bearing our personal cross, we follow the Lord who from eternity denied Himself in His own soul expression so that the heart and soul of His Father could be revealed through Him (Phil. 2:5–7; John 5:30; 12:44–45). His ongoing cross is different from the cross of Calvary. There He died once to redeem us from sin unto fellowship with the Father (Rom. 6:11). The cross to His soul life, however, still continues.

25. The area in the tabernacle tent called the *holy of holies* represents the prophetic, priestly ministry of Christ Jesus to His Father (Exod. 26:33–34). In that room the divine presence rested above the ark of the testimony "where I meet with you," God told Moses (Num. 17:4).

In heaven the Lord Jesus as High Priest serves in the holy of holies of His Father's heart. Together with Him are those who have answered the call to abide there in spirit (John 1:18; 14:2–3; 15:4). The night before He died, Jesus asked the Father that "they also, whom You have given Me, be with Me where I am" (John 17:24). The revelations given there to "white eagle" Christians primarily concern the heart of the Father and heavenly life with His Son (John 17:26).

The great fruitfulness for the Son comes from believers abiding hidden in Him in heaven through their spiritual person (1 Pet. 3:4). As a consequence of these disciples yielding the entire course of their earthly existence into the hands of God, the persons of the Trinity will make their home in them on Earth and bring forth much fruit (John 14:16–17, 23; 15:5).

26. The Father explains that this cartwheeling is symbolic of Him choosing a believer to receive certain grace. If that person responds to that grace, the Father will then choose that one for more grace, and on and on (Matt. 22:14).

27. "To him who overcomes, to him I [Christ] will give some of the hidden [spiritual] manna" (Rev. 2:17). The Lord Jesus is the golden manna in heaven that juvenile golden eagles are fed by the Father in order to mature.

28. The beginning of the preparation of betrothed ones to abide continually in the Lord Jesus is for them to ask Him for the baptism of the Holy Spirit (Acts 1:4–5; 2:33; 19:2–6). The Spirit, like the king's eunuch Hegai in the Book of Esther, knows how to prepare each one the Father has chosen for union with King Jesus (Esther 2:2–4; Rev. 19:7). Esther found favor with Hegai, who

The little foxes represent habits and patterns of thought, desire, choice, and conduct from our old self-centered life. "The Spirit constantly has a strong desire to suppress the [old] evil nature . . . so that [the old] you may not do the things that [the old] you desire[s] to do" (Gal. 5:17, WUEST).

is not eliminated for the all-important training that lies in obedience. Your obedience must arise out of a perfect love for Me—not under constraint, but for love's sake.[29] Catch the little foxes, Anna, that My harvest may be full."[30]

He continued, "This time will pass swiftly. We want you to treasure all of it. Courtship is a memorable time, a suspended time. It is a time when lovers walk hand in hand, a time of growing in knowledge and understanding concerning the other. The time of courtship on Earth is sweet. But you, Anna, are in a courtship with My Son, the Prince, none more perfect and beautiful, none more powerful and glorious—My Son. Abandon yourself to the experience of the time."

The Flesh vs. the Spirit

The word *perfected* means "reaching one's full and intended end, lacking in nothing" (Matt. 5:48; James 1:4).

"I do not want you to live by what your eyes see or your ears hear or by what you reason," He said. "I want you to live by every word that proceeds from My mouth to you.[31] The arm of the flesh can never do My will. Try My way, Anna. You have given your own way a princely chance. Now take the way of the Prince Himself—the mind of Christ, the emotions of Christ, the will of Christ. All of Him. None of your flesh.[32] Complete and total union.[33] He deserves nothing less, does He not?"

"Yes, Daddy," I said quietly.

"That is My girl," He said, picking me up and placing me onto the sea of glass before Him.

The Emerald

My Father held out a large emerald to me. "For your crown, Anna," He said.

I took it. "Oh, Daddy, it is beautiful!" I replied (although I did not know to what crown He was referring). "Thank You."

There was a pause. Then He asked, "Would you like to see your Beloved?"

I felt embarrassed, for He had read my innermost desire. I ducked my head and pulled out the golden key that hangs from a scarlet cord around my neck. Jesus had given the key to me. It unlocks the golden filigree gate to the enclosed garden of my heart in Paradise.[34] The Lord had told me that if I wanted to see Him that He would meet me there. I held up the golden key and smiled at my Father.

"Go to Him," my Father said tenderly. His glory came from Him and kissed my forehead.[35]

Instantly, I was before the walled garden.

The glory of God is the awesome brilliance of the goodness of His love (Exod. 33:18–19; 16:7, 10). It is therefore not surprising to witness God's glory move outward from the throne to express the Father's tender affection.

provided her with the best help possible to be beautified before being brought to King Ahasuerus (Esther 2:8–9).

In the way Esther was prepared, the Spirit provides betrothed Christians the oil of myrrh. This represents "the fellowship of His [Christ's] sufferings, being conformed to His death" (Phil. 3:10). It is sharing His victory over sin, the world, the flesh, the devil, and death (Rom. 6:6; 1 John 5:5; Gal. 5:16–17; Rev. 12:10–11; John 5:24).

Afterward the Spirit applies heavenly spices of the heart virtues of the Lord Jesus, as Esther was beautified (Esther 2:12; Exod. 30:23–24, 34–35; Song of Sol. 4:13–14). Because of the divine splendor bestowed upon each one, the loveliness of a priestly bride will be perfected by the time each one is presented individually to Christ (2 Cor. 11:2–3; Ps. 45:11, 13–15; Ezek. 16:14; Song of Sol. 4:10).

29. The Father who loves perfectly will only be satisfied with the perfect love of His divine Son (John 17:1; Luke 10:22). We see this love of the Son in the perfect obedience that Jesus learned "from the things which He suffered" on Earth (Heb. 5:8). Jesus is the loving obedience that His Father desires in His children. The Lord did "nothing of [out from] Himself," for He said, "The Father in Me does His works" (John 5:19; 14:10). He does not ask His disciples to be what He has not always been.

Consequently, Jesus's love for His Father (the same as His Father's love for Him) is poured into our new hearts by the Holy Spirit (Rom. 5:5; John 17:26). The Spirit then wills and works the Son's obedience within us to be expressed in our souls and bodies (Phil. 2:13).

30. The Father is quoting Song of Solomon 2:15. The Beloved asks His bride to "catch the foxes for us, the little foxes that are ruining the vineyards, while our vineyards are in blossom." The young foxes gnaw on the tender shoots that are in bloom and prevent them from bearing fruit.

31. In Matthew 4:4, Jesus quoted the Father's words to Moses about the Israelites wandering forty years in the wilderness: "Man shall not live on bread alone, but on every word that proceeds out of the mouth of God" (Deut. 8:2–3; Rom. 10:17; 1:17). Jesus did not make decisions by His bodily senses and reason but by faith in the Father communicating His will to Him at that moment (Isa. 11:3; John 5:30; 12:49–50). The Lord wants to continue to communicate His way of life by the Spirit in every disciple (Rom. 8:2; 2 Cor. 5:14–16; Phil. 3:9).

32. Jesus said, "The flesh profits nothing" (John 6:63). Paul said, "Nothing good dwells in me, that is, in my flesh" (Rom. 7:18). There is no hope for that fleshly self, for there is a law of sin and death in our bodies that always demands to keep this old self active (Rom. 7:20; Gal. 5:17). The soul life can be renewed with the gradual impartation of the soul life of Christ, but the law of sin in the body remains until we die (Matt. 16:24–25; Rom. 7:22–24).

33. The union between the Father and the Son is complete and total (John 10:30). They will be satisfied with nothing less than that for those who are "heirs of God and fellow-heirs with Christ" (Rom. 8:17). Jesus prayed, "As Thou, Father, art in Me and I in Thee, that they also may be in Us... that they also may be perfected in unity [with Us]" (John 17:21, 23).

34. The "hidden person of the heart, with the imperishable quality of a gentle and quiet [human] spirit... is precious in the sight of God" (1 Pet. 3:4). The Christian's new person of heart and spirit is both within the disciple on earth and is also within Christ in heaven. This makes it possible for one to fellowship with Christ in one's heart on Earth and also in heaven. (See Ephesians 3:17; Colossians 3:1–3.)

In the vast park of Paradise in heaven, each betrothed one's new heart is represented by a private, enclosed garden (Song of Sol. 4:12). No one else has a key to the lock on the gate. The more we abide in love with the Lord in our heart garden in heaven, the more He abides to fill the garden in our heart on Earth (John 15:4; Eph. 3:16–19).

35. The splendor of this supreme grace continually surrounds Him upon the throne in heaven (Ezek. 1:26–28; Eph. 1:5–6). That magnificent brightness is also able to move about and appear at other places by the manifestation of the Holy Spirit (Ezek. 10:4, 18–19; 11:23; 43:2, 4).

Chapter Three

The Beloved

Quickly I placed the key into the lock and opened the gate to the enclosed garden. I dropped the scarlet cord back around my neck, quietly stepping inside the gate. As it closed behind me, it clicked shut.

Within the Garden

What stillness and peace were there.

I stood facing the three-tiered fountain in the center of the garden.[1] Cool, clear water flowed from its top and gently pooled in its widely rimmed basin. The large, flowering apricot tree arched over the fountain, with the bench for two at its base.[2]

In the garden of the Christian's true heart in heaven, the three-tiered fountain represents the persons of the Trinity of God who are also to occupy that one's heart on Earth (John 14:23; 2 Cor. 1:22).

I let my eyes rest upon the colors and varieties of the plantings within the walled area. All sorts of scented herbs grew among the jonquils, tulips and daffodils. The fruit-bearing trees and vines were heavy with flowers, but they also had leaves and the rudiments of both summer and fall fruit.[3] As with the trees and vines, the flowers of spring, summer, and fall were blooming at the same time within the beds.

The bench represents the quiet rest of Christ's own faith that He gives to the betrothed one. "In His shade I took great delight and sat down" (Song of Sol. 2:3; Heb. 4:1–3).

1. All that is good and true is from God, originates in heaven, and comes down to Earth (James 1:17).

In Scripture, flowing water symbolizes the divine life that comes from the Father, the Son (the Word), and by the outflowing river of the Spirit (Father—Rev. 21:5–6; Son—Eph. 5:26; Spirit—John 7:38–39). "And he showed me a river of the water of life, clear as crystal, coming from the throne of God and of the Lamb" (Rev. 22:1).

2. The apricot tree is not mentioned in most editions of the Bible by this name. The Hebrew word *tappuach* is usually translated "apple" but probably refers to the apricot. Apples at that time in history were of very poor quality. Luscious, fragrant apricots were in cultivation in Israel early in its history.

The apricot tree is a reminder of heavenly grace (which Paul calls "the Jerusalem above... our mother") that brought the person to new birth in Christ (Gal. 4:26–29; Eph. 2:4–5). "Beneath the apricot tree, I [Jesus] awakened you; there your mother ['the Jerusalem above'] was in labor and gave you birth" (Song of Sol. 8:5, MARGIN).

3. Plants on Earth produce leaves, blossoms, and fruit only at certain seasons of the year. In the eternity of heaven, there are no atmospheric seasons. In the garden of the Christian's heart in Paradise, there is growth. God designs that garden continually to bear herbs, flowers, and fruit according to the spiritual maturity in the heart of that Christian. These three signify the fragrance, beauty, and nourishment of the character of Christ (John 15:5; Gal. 5:22–23).

The spiritual heart in the disciple on Earth is to "bear fruit [that is Jesus], and [which]... should remain" in all seasons as one's heart in heaven matures (John 15:16).

4. "Awake, O north wind, and come, wind of the south; make my garden breathe out fragrance, let its spices be wafted abroad. May my beloved come into his garden and eat its choice fruits!" (Song of Sol. 4:16). Whether the circumstances arranged by the Holy Spirit on Earth are harsh ("north wind") or pleasant ("the south"), the disciple's heart on Earth is to sustain the growth of Christ's fragrance there (2 Cor. 2:14–15). This private garden belongs to the betrothed one and to Christ. It is only for the pleasure of the Lord Jesus and His "friends," the Father, and the Holy Spirit (Song of Sol. 5:1).

In the garden of the disciple's heart, the growth shown by bearing fruit indicates Christ being formed to the point where He becomes fruitful through that person (John 15:4–5).

A slight breeze blew across the garden stirring the aromas.[4] The fragrance was unique. On Earth we do not experience the three growing seasons together. I was reminded of Aaron's staff that sprouted, blossomed, and bore fruit at the same time.[5] I wondered if the three seasons being represented within the garden had something to do with the priesthood of believers.[6] But I did not know.

I breathed in deeply and exhaled slowly. Peace.

Not Alone

Suddenly I heard someone clearing His throat in order to call attention to His presence. I looked up. Jesus was sitting in the large apricot tree. "My Lord," I said in amazement, "what are You doing up there?"

To be "up a tree" means to be in a difficult situation.

"I am up a tree, Anna," He said.

I laughed. "What are You doing up a tree?"

"You want Me up here," He replied.

"I want You up a tree?" I laughed, for I thought He was joking.

"Yes," He answered. "I am localized, and you know where I am. You can come to the base of the tree and ask Me questions, and then go about your life. I am in a portion of your heart, but I do not have free access to the whole garden."

I was cut to the quick. I swallowed hard. "Come down, my Lord," I said. "Forgive me. These mysteries are so exciting…well, forgive me that…"

"…that you have begun to use Me?" He asked, jumping down from the tree.

"The very thing I have hated, I am doing," I said.

He walked toward me. "What do you want of Me, Anna? Information? There is a vast supply. Is that what you want?"

"No, of course not," I replied. "These mysteries are so…"

"…titillating?" He asked.

"Well, they are…"

"…seductive?" He added.

"Yes," I affirmed.

"But they are part of Me—and you have been given all of Me. It seems a poor exchange."

"Oh, my Friend," I continued, "forgive me. I love You and want to be with You. I want You to have access to the entire garden."

"You are called to know mysteries, Anna, but not to use Me," He said.

To Still the Soul

I was speechless. When years before I had decided to pursue the Lord earnestly, I withdrew my senses from the overstimulation of worldly input. I felt that I needed to still my soul if I wanted Him to come knocking at my heart.

The withdrawal from keeping myself entertained with the world was exceedingly painful. But now the Lord was saying that I had replaced the worldly with spiritual entertainment—desiring more and more spiritual knowledge—a subtler and less objectionable substitute, but still a substitute for Him. I did not know what to say. I was stunned.

He took me by the arm and guided me gently to the rim of the fountain. "Sit down," He said quietly. He sat beside me. I looked into His face. The beauty and clearness of those eyes were beyond compare. He took my hand and held it.

5. Moses settled the question of God's authority being vested in Aaron (and Moses) of the tribe of Levi. He placed the rods or staffs of Aaron and the leaders of the other eleven tribes before the ark of the covenant overnight. The next day Aaron's rod "had sprouted and put forth buds and produced blossoms, and it bore ripe almonds" (Num. 17:6–8).

6. The priests under the old covenant were limited to the family of Aaron of the tribe of Levi. Under the order of Melchizedek, all Christians are included in the priesthood of the new covenant (Rev. 1:6). One is spiritually born into this priesthood, but each must mature in sharing the priestly duties under the High Priest, the Lord Jesus (1 Pet. 2:5).

The overcoming Christians represent a remnant of the kingdom of priests according to the order of Melchizedek in the church in Philadelphia (Rev. 3:12). They are called *pillars* because they serve in spirit within the temple of the heart of God the Father, in strength and steadfastness of the Spirit though their bodies are on the earth (John 14:2–3; 12:26). With Christ the High Priest, they live to bless the Father in prayer and praise (Heb. 2:11–12). They do not live by the system of this world, for God brings them near to Himself (Num. 16:9; John 17:16, 24).

7. The Lord Jesus calls disciples to be with Him and to share His life (Mark 3:14). They are to be wholly given to Christ as He is to the Father (1 Cor. 3:23). Claiming nothing as their own, they are to receive all from Him (Luke 14:33; Rom. 8:17, 32). They know the unearthly joy of blessing God and others in His name (1 Pet. 3:9).

8. The passions of Christ are the pure spiritual fires of His love that have burned from eternity for the Father and for those whom the Father has given Him in betrothal (Luke 10:22; John 6:39). "I have loved you [My people] with an everlasting love" (Jer. 31:3).

9. Christ has shed tears from eternity. He has known heartache because of the rebellion of the angels. From the beginning "the Lord was sorry that He had made man on the earth, and He was grieved in His heart" (Gen. 6:6). There is sorrow for those whom He knows will not receive the gift of salvation (Matt. 7:13–14). He has continuing sadness because He knows that many of those who will be joined to Him will be lukewarm in their response (Rev. 3:16). His regret for their loss does not diminish the ardor of His heart that yearns for all of these (Jer. 31:20).

10. It is the wisdom of the Father that the full stature of His Son will be shown forth by His body, the church (Eph. 4:13). Each member of the bride has been chosen and called to manifest that portion of God's Son that the Father in His inscrutable wisdom designs. Hence the full stature of the Lord Jesus will one day be reflected corporately in the Father's children (Eph. 4:4, 7, 10; Gal. 4:19).

11. The root of the Hebrew word for *myrrh* means "bitter."

A True Friend

"My Anna," He said, "be a true friend to Me, as I am to you. I want you to desire My company. I am a King, but I desire to be with you, as any lover would long to be with the one he loves. I do not command your love; I humbly ask for it. I do not dictate that you be with Me. I long for you to seek Me. Therefore I wait for you, Anna."

I dropped my head. "Lord," I said, "I am selfish. I am using You for my own pleasure."

Even a King

He lifted my chin. "Anna, look at Me," He said. "Even a King wishes to be loved for Himself, not for the gifts He bestows." He smiled at me. "If you do not enjoy being with Me now, why do you believe you will enjoy My company for eternity?" He looked down at my hand. "The pursuer wants to be pursued also," He said gently.

He looked up and then over to the gate. "Have you ever thought of standing at the entrance to the garden with the gate opened, waiting for Me?"

"No," I replied.

"You have expected Me to travel the entire distance to you. Do you not think I would be pleased to have you waiting, with part of the distance covered so that we might see each other sooner?"

"Yes," I said quietly.

He smiled at me. "Come, My love, let us walk." He helped me to rise and put His arm around my waist. We began to walk the path that circles the garden. "I have called you to Myself," He said looking down at me. "Few understand what this means.[7] Would you like to know, Anna?"

The Levites, including the priests, were called by God and set apart to stand before Him as a holy remnant. They were to belong to Him in order that He might bless the rest of the Israelites (Deut. 10:8; Num. 1:53). God took them for Himself to be wholly given to Him (Num. 8:15–16).

"Yes," I said tentatively. "I say this in fear and trembling because I fear not getting something I want."

He laughed. "I know this. What does that say about our relationship?"

"It sounds like I do not trust You," I said.

"That is what it sounds like," He agreed.

"Is it true?"

"Yes," He replied.

"Well, Lord, help me!" I pleaded. "I want to trust You."

"My wonderful girl," He said, "My love. Do you not understand? My desire is for you. My passions burn with eternal fires.[8] No mere tear could quench them. It would take the tears from eternity, and still the fire of My passion for you would not be quenched.[9] Why would you not trust the One who loves you as I love?"

There is a Hebrew word used only three times in Scripture that means "intense longing" such as the longing of the Son for each betrothed one who was created for Him. When the bride realizes this, she uses that word when she says, "I am my beloved's, and his desire [longing] is for me" (Song of Sol. 7:10).

I could not answer. I did not know why I did not abandon myself to God. I shook my head. "Who am I to deserve such love?"

"You are chosen for Me by My Father," He said earnestly. "With wisdom that is beyond wisdom, He has chosen you."[10]

"Then increase my desire to be with You," I said, "to desire You more than an anointing or spiritual knowledge or..." I could not think fast enough to enumerate. I shook my head in frustration and then blurted out: "I love You." I clung to Him, burying my face in His chest. "You are the dearest Friend I have...I love You!"

He placed His arms around me lovingly. "My own," He said. He dropped His head back and laughed as in pain mixed with joy. Then, bringing His head to mine, He spoke softly, "Anna, Anna." There was great pain in His voice. "Please do not do this again." He held me trembling. "Anna, do not do this again."

I had hurt Him deeply by treating Him presumptuously, casually—like someone with whom I had to deal in order to receive that which was my primary interest. But He loved me. He wanted my company and wanted me to desire His. That which is the deepest desire of every human heart was mine, and I was seeking secondary rewards.

The bark of the myrrh tree is pierced so that the gum from the heartwood oozes out and hardens in red drops called "tears." These are crushed to make the spice myrrh.

My heart began to break. The pain was excruciating. The garden responded also. The smell of myrrh flooded the area. I glanced at the myrrh tree. Red tears of the aromatic gum were slipping from the heart of the wood.[11]

Myrrh signifies the bitter sufferings of Jesus at Calvary. "He was pierced through for our transgressions, He was crushed for our iniquities" (Isa. 53:5).

It also represents His present tribulations (Phil. 3:10; 2 Cor. 1:5). Christ Jesus is still bearing shame and sorrow because Christians deny Him by cooperating with His enemies (Heb. 6:4–6; 10:26–29).

It is necessary for the church to bear its portion of His afflictions as His body, as part of Him. "Now I rejoice in my sufferings for your sake, and in my flesh I do my share on behalf of His body [which is the church] in filling up [completing] that which is lacking in Christ's afflictions" (Col. 1:24).

12. The other Hebrew word for husband, *Baali*, is translated "my master." It is the same word used for the god Baal. Hosea says that this word will not be used again for Israel's husband (Hos. 2:16–17).

13. The human race was created to reflect the life, character, and glory of God's own Son who is the image of the Father (Rom. 8:29; Col. 1:15). Christians cannot themselves in any way bring forth this divine fruit. It can only be the Lord Jesus formed in them by the Spirit (John 15:5; Gal. 4:19).

14. The three persons of God share one divine life (called in Scripture simply "life" or "the life") (John 5:26). They are the source of all lesser forms of existence (John 6:63). When Jesus says, "I and the Father are one," He means that They have one eternal life together (John 10:30).

15. Please see notes 18, 19, and 22 of chapter 2.

I pulled back, holding Him at arm's length, looking into His eyes. "My God, my God," I said. "I am not worthy of You. I cannot even respond correctly to the depth of Your love. *Ishi*, if You do not give to me a love that matches Yours in intensity..." The pain in my heart was so severe that I could not finish the sentence.[12] With all that was in me I pushed past the extreme pain to cry out, "Oh, please help me to love You as You love me. I am willing, Lord, but I cannot do this myself.[13] You must do this through me! Please!"

Ishi is a Hebrew word meaning "my husband."

The Impartation

He looked at me intently. Then He took my right hand into His, turned it over, and tenderly kissed the center of it. "Receive," He said. Immediately I could feel the Spirit surging through me. "There is no greater closeness than to share one life," He said.[14]

In the blur of light and power that followed, I saw worlds collide and millions of people being born. I saw death and life. Wave upon wave of ecstasy rolled over me. I thought I would burst into a million pieces, being unable to contain such heights of love. I lost track of where I was or even who I was. I lost track of everything but Love Himself. How long this impartation lasted I do not know, but when the power began to subside, the garden slowly came back into focus for me. I was fuzzy, though, blurry and unstable. I had to be steadied.

He spoke reassuringly, "This quiet place [meaning the garden] is within you, Anna, where you may meet with Me at all times."

My vision cleared finally. I looked into His face. He smiled at me. "My Anna," He said, "I will show you another garden."

Instantly, He became the white Eagle.[15] "Come, Anna," He urged. I climbed onto His back and lay down with my arms around His neck, as I had done in the past. Then with one mighty movement of His wings, He flew over the garden wall. Immediately, we were on Earth.

Vision of the Bride

We flew over a vast desert.[16] In vision we were approaching what seemed to be a garden in the center of this wilderness.[17] The white Eagle spoke, "I will show you the bride, Anna."

Spiritually the vast desert represents the earth-wide expansion of the lifeless, evil order that Satan masterminds (Ps. 107:4–5, 10; 1 John 5:19).

At the center of this garden in the wilderness I saw a lovely young woman (the corporate bride of Christ).[18] She was clothed in the glory of God.[19]

The white Eagle continued, "The Holy Spirit is training the bride.[20] I have taken her into the wilderness to teach her to sing.[21] She is a virgin, undefiled by idols.[22] She will not name them or consider their beds.[23] Her eye is single, and I fill all her sight.[24] She will not lust for idols or cut her eyes to entice them. My beloved will desire Me alone."

Spiritual virginity from idols means not giving honor in one's heart to that which is of human or satanic origin.

The young woman began to sing:

> Daystar of the morning,
> Dawn before our eyes,
> Rise that we might see Your face,
> Prince of Paradise.
> Clothe Yourself in splendor.
> Clothe Yourself in might.
> Trail supernal righteousness,
> Quintessence of all Light.[25]

Jesus Christ is that quintessence for He is the light that is God made visible in the world (John 3:19).

The Lord continued, "The Holy Spirit will be a pillar of fire and a pillar of the cloud of God's glory.[26] As with the children of Israel, He will lead her in the wilderness, and He will protect her. The glory of God will rest upon her."[27]

A *pillar* signifies what is established and strong from God (1 Kings 7:21; Rev. 3:12).

God's glory is the splendor of the goodness of His unfathomable love (Exod. 33:18–19; Eph. 1:6).

16. Satan's purpose is to exalt himself through the human self and nullify love for God (Matt. 4:8–10; 1 John 2:15–16).

17. The coming physical and spiritual wilderness will be caused by love for God and people growing cold in the face of worldwide catastrophes (Matt. 24:7–12).

Like the first Garden of Eden on Earth, this garden represents the spiritual heart of God's Son. His true heart is manifested by the garden of God in heaven where the tree of life still grows (Ezek. 28:13; Rev. 2:7).

18. The bride is pictured as a woman to represent the church for whom Jesus provides and that He holds dear as human husbands are to provide for and hold dear their wives (Eph. 5:28–32). The bride is seen standing in the center of the garden of Christ's heart. This means that she seeks to be one heart with Him, to know Him as intimately as possible (Jer. 24:7; Hos. 2:19–20).

19. The corporate bride of Christ is to be clothed with the brightness of the glory of God as Adam and Eve were when they walked with Him in the Garden of Eden (Gen. 3:8).

20. When we are God's children, we are disciplined because He loves us and desires our eternal good, "that we may share His holiness" (Heb. 12:5–6, 10). To be disciplined by the Holy Spirit in the area of our flesh "seems not to be joyful, but sorrowful; yet to those who have been trained by it, afterwards it yields the peaceful fruit of righteousness" (Heb. 12:11).

21. "Therefore, behold, I will allure her [the betrothed ones], bring her into the wilderness, and speak upon her heart... And she will sing there as in the days of her youth... And it will come about in that day," declares the Lord, "That you will call Me Ishi [my husband]" (Hos. 2:14–16, MARGIN).

22. *Idolatry* is putting anything before God:

(1) in spiritual matters where one uses God for selfish reasons (1 Tim. 6:5–6), or

(2) in the exaltation of anything of earthly origin. This includes one's natural self, other people, fleshly morality, wealth, position, financial enterprise, pleasure and such like (Luke 8:14; John 12:25).

23. God said to the Israelites in the desert, "Do not mention the name of other gods, nor let them be heard from your mouth" (Exod. 23:13). Not to "consider their beds" means that Christians will not allow idols to bed down in their hearts.

Intimacy of the Garden

"Our Father is restoring the intimacy of the garden, Anna. He is giving Me a bride who will walk with Me hand in hand."[28]

He continued, "The pillar of fire will consume all that is not of Me.[29] The pillar of cloud will cover her. The Holy Spirit passionately desires that I have a pure bride. He will teach her and lead her. He will give her the oils and the perfumed spices.[30] He will feed her manna from above—as He fed the children of Israel in the desert—so that within and without she might be prepared.[31] Nurtured and warm, she will grow and bloom for Me alone. The fragrance of her perfumes will be for Me alone, and she will sing—sing for Me alone. The glory will be a shield for her, blinding the eyes of the wicked. The cloud will cause them to stumble and fall. They will grope as in the darkest night, but they will not find her."[32]

Come to the Garden

To be "in Us" means living with Christ in the Father, even as They desire to abide in our hearts on Earth (Col. 3:3; 1 John 2:24; John 14:23).

"The call has gone out from the very halls of heaven to come to the garden. But most will remain outside. I, Myself, call, 'Come to the garden!' But many who do enter are content to eat the fruit nearest the gate. Few seek Me in the center of the garden. However, for the few who do make the journey, searching for Me, they find an open door to the Father's heart.[33] For in the center of the garden is the entrance to My Father's heart, and within His heart, I live and move.[34]

"As for you, Anna," He said, "leave behind all that has been an anchor to your soul. Loose the rope, trim the sails, and let Me set the course. Come into the wilderness. For in the wilderness there is a secret garden, and in the center of that garden, the doorway to God."

We began to fly away from the garden in the wilderness.

The Mountains

Suddenly, the vision ended. I found that we were actually flying up to a mountain range on Earth. Beneath us the valley lay lush and green. On several of the encircling mountains there were apple orchards. These were laid out in neat rows and were carefully tended. The sun shone on what seemed to be a river winding through the valley far below. However, as we drew nearer, I realized that it was a road.

Before us near the top of the highest mountain was a large, protruding rock. It formed a ledge. The white Eagle had taken me to this rock before.

I buried my face in His scented feathers as I clung to His neck. He was taking me to His nest.[35]

24. "Your eye is the lamp of your body. When your eyes are good [sound, pure], your whole body also is full of light" (Luke 11:34, NIV). Disciples focus their eyes upon one thing: the Lord Jesus (Heb. 12:2). "He Himself might come to have first place in everything" (Col. 1:18).

25. God the Father in His nature is Light (1 John 1:5). The "quintessence of all Light" means the most pure and perfect embodiment of divine light.

26. "The Lord was going before them [the Israelites in the wilderness] in a pillar of cloud by day to lead them on the way, and in a pillar of fire by night to give them light, that they might travel by day and by night" (Exod. 13:21).

27. The glory of God when seen on Earth is a manifestation of the Holy Spirit (2 Cor. 3:18). He is called "the Spirit of glory and of God" who can rest upon disciples at times (1 Pet. 4:14). As the Spirit of glory, He moved about or remained stationary in the vision of the new temple (Ezek. 43:2, 4–5; 11:23).

28. Adam and Eve had close fellowship with Christ in His preincarnate form in the Garden of Eden, as did Moses in the wilderness (Gen. 3:8; Exod. 33:11).

29. The Holy Spirit "will burn up the chaff with unquenchable fire" in those whom Jesus has baptized with the Spirit and fire (Matt. 3:11–12).

30. Please see note 27 of chapter 2. For further reading, see Esther 2:8–13.

31. The spiritual manna imparted by the Holy Spirit is the soul, heart, and spirit of the resurrected Lord Jesus in His perfect human nature as joined fully to His divine nature (Heb. 5:8–9; Col. 2:9). Each bride will know that "it is no longer I who live, but Christ lives in me" (Gal. 2:20).

32. See also note 10 for this chapter.

33. The Lord Jesus prays "that they may all be one; even as Thou, Father, art in Me and I in Thee, that they also may be in Us" (John 17:21).

34. The Father's heart is "My Father's house... [where] I go to prepare a place for you... that where I am, there you may be also" (John 14:2–3). The resurrected Lord Jesus lives within His Father's heart but is also able to walk about in heaven and to appear on Earth at times (Rev. 1:12–17; Acts 26:16; 9:10).

35. To abide in the nest of the great white Eagle on Earth signifies living by means of the Holy Spirit. Living inwardly by the Spirit is the means of walking in outward conduct by the Spirit (Gal. 5:25). The nest represents a place or position in the realm of the Holy Spirit where the Christian's spirit is continually joined as one to the spirit of Jesus (1 Cor. 6:17). It is a state of rest from one's own works in full dependence upon Christ for everything (Heb. 4:10; Phil. 4:6). There is continual sharing of the person's heart with the Lord (Ps. 62:8). It is a condition of being alert in spirit to what the Holy Spirit may be speaking to magnify Jesus (John 16:14; Rev. 2:29). It is keeping one's spiritual eyes open to perceive the hand of God operating (Ezek. 3:14). It is learning to know the things of God by the Spirit (1 Cor. 2:12). It is abiding in Christ where one was placed by spiritual birth (John 15:4; 1 John 2:27). See also note 10 for this chapter.

Chapter Four

Lesson of the Birds

We continued to fly higher. Before we neared the tallest mountain, I saw vultures circling the valley below us. Their bald heads looked raw, unclean, repugnant.

The white Eagle spoke, "Pay no attention to them. They seek that which is dead, not the living."[1] I diverted my eyes.

Jesus is saying that Christians should not be distracted by demons or learn from them.

Chimney Swifts

Suddenly, thousands of small, dark birds began to pass us. The sky was filled with them. They chattered loudly among themselves. The sound of their wings added to the commotion of their flight. They were so noisy and gabby that they did not recognize the white Eagle flying among them. They called past us to confer and reconfer with one another.

"Chimney swifts," the white Eagle said. "They live in soot. They rise, but not from fire. Covered with charcoal, they rise from the darkness of hiding among that which is charred. Their tails are like snakes' tongues. Do not fly with them."

Chimney swifts are dark birds that love the blackness of old, dirty chimneys where they congregate in huge colonies. There they live so close together that they overlap each other. The width of their open beaks is huge, and they have distinctive forked tails.

Hearing their communal chatter, the word *gossip* came to mind—"for poison is in their tales," I thought.[2]

An updraft mercifully carried us higher than their piercing calls. I was troubled by the Lord's warning and began to ponder what He had said.

Often conversation among the brethren did seem to be more like a checkout counter tabloid than the admonition from Paul to "let no unwholesome word proceed from your mouth" (Eph. 4:29). "Indeed," I thought, "how can we fly higher if we are earthbound by our

1. The Lord Jesus said, "Wherever the corpse is, there the vultures will gather" (Matt. 24:28). These birds of prey feed upon carrion. The eyes of a carcass are the first things that they eat. Vultures here represent demons on Earth that prey upon people who are not saved by Christ. "The god of this world has blinded the minds of the unbelieving, that they might not see the light of the gospel of the glory of Christ" (2 Cor. 4:4). Paul warned the early church about "paying attention to deceitful spirits and doctrines of demons" (1 Tim. 4:1).

2. These loudly chattering birds with big mouths do not rise up on the warm air currents from the fire (of the Spirit). They come forth out of the cold, lifeless depths of an empty chimney. With forked tails, they exemplify those people with forked tongues who "spread tales" about the sins or faults of others. "He who goes about as a slanderer [defaming others with malicious or false reports] reveals secrets; therefore do not associate with a gossip" (Prov. 20:19; Lev. 19:16).

fascination with hearing of and talking about sin—not only the world's sins, but also sin among the brethren? Our earthbound focus has driven a stake into the ground to which our spirits are tethered."

Hawks

I blinked back into the present moment as a dark bird of prey passed beneath us.

To *hawk* something means to peddle it in crafty ways.

"Hawk's hawk," the Lord said.[3] "Do not fly with them."

"Hawking your wares," I murmured to myself.[4] I had not thought of that phrase in years—and certainly not in connection with the work of the kingdom. However, now that I thought about it, it seemed that in trying to reach the world for Christ, some of us had become remarkably like the world. We rivaled sideshow barkers in our flamboyant peddling. Could it be that we were cheapening the depth of commitment to which the Lord had called us? Was the salt losing its savor?

Bird-eating hawks know the flying patterns of other birds and quickly recognize the way the weak ones are flying so as to attack them.

Falcons

Before I could consider this further, a falcon swooped passed us.[5]

"Falcons will con you," the white Eagle said. "The lie will run your life afoul.[6] Do not fly with them."

"With whom may I fly, Lord?" I asked.

"Fly with Me, Anna. Fly with Me. Eagles nest high.[7] They do not travel in flocks like ducks [following one another instead of the Lord]. They do not roost together like chickens [seeking protection from others instead of Christ]. They do not hunt bugs together like geese [seeking provision from other than the Lord]. Eagles nest high. Do you wish to fly with Me, Anna?"

Eagles live in a realm high above all the confines of Earth. There is effortlessness in their awesome flight on thermal updrafts.

"Yes, Lord," I said.

"Stop trying to be a part of the flock [that does not follow the Lord]. Turn into the wind, and let the currents lift you higher."

The Rock

Immediately, the wind swelled beneath His wings.

"We will soar, Anna. We will soar," He exclaimed. We did soar, higher and higher. "Leave your father's and your mother's house.[8] The King desires your company." With a mighty upsurge of wind and power, we soared to the rock near the top of the mountain.

Disciples are not to be controlled by allegiance even to the closest family relationships, but to be governed by complete loyalty to Christ.

The great white Eagle gently descended. He settled upon the rim of His large nest. I climbed from His back and sat down near its center.

The nest was made of strong tree branches. When I was seated on its floor, the rim was about chest high.

Frankincense

Within its circumference, there was the pungent aroma of frankincense.[9]

Frankincense is a main ingredient of incense that is burned before the Lord to represent the godly prayers of His people rising to the throne (Exod. 30:1, 9, 34–35; Rev. 5:8).

"Purity," I thought to myself.[10] "That is what the Lord has been saying through the lesson of the birds. It is not enough to love Him and want to be with Him. He wants a bride who is pure—one who is free from the world, the flesh, and the devil. Also one who will not participate in the sins of immature Christians—one who is willing to be transformed into His likeness."

I folded my arms on top of the nest and rested my head on my hands, looking out. We were very high above the valley. You could see for miles. The land looked fertile.

I had noticed a few white feathers within the nest when I sat down. As I looked out over the valley now, I wondered how many of my own juvenile feathers had been replaced by the strong, mature, white ones.[11]

A Christian learning to fly as a juvenile eagle means maturing in moving by the wind of the Holy Spirit in hearing and obeying the Lord (Deut. 32:11; Isa. 40:31).

3. Some hawks feed upon other birds. Hawks try to give these birds the impression that they are harmless. But they are actually watching from a concealed perch to catch their unsuspecting prey.

4. There are some people that prey upon others by "proclaim[ing] Christ out of selfish ambition rather than from pure motives," "peddling the word of God" as a huckster would (Phil. 1:15–17; 2 Cor. 2:17).

5. Falcons are highly aerial, many of them catching and killing other birds in midair. Some people consider them the ultimate predatory bird.

6. Eve was "conned" into believing a lie. She acted upon this lie and became the first person to sin. There is one great lie by which Satan deceives human beings. It is the illusion that a person can be what one wants to be (Gen. 3:5). One can live to suit oneself. The enemy, like the falcon, cons many into thinking that they can fly their own way in safety. He then kills them in flight.

7. This typifies God's rest in disciples who trust the wind of the Spirit (a power that is not their own) to carry them higher in Christ (Prov. 30:18–19; Heb. 4:9–10; John 3:8). The majestic, soaring eagle is memorialized before the throne of God as one of the four living creatures (Rev. 4:6–7).

8. Speaking prophetically to one who is betrothed to Christ Jesus the King, the psalmist says, "Listen, O daughter...Forget your people and your father's house [household]" (Ps. 45:10; Matt. 19:29). Earthly human devotion is so far beneath eternal fidelity to the Lord that the difference is as hate is to love (Luke 14:26). Jesus left His earthly father's small household to be committed to the members of His divine Father's family (Matt. 12:49–50; 19:29).

9. A portion of this prescribed incense was not burned but simply placed before the ark in the holy of holies. God said that this is "where I shall meet with you; it [this incense] shall be most holy [the holiest] to you" (Exod. 30:36). It is most holy because it represents the prayers in heaven between the Son and His Father.

10. The word *frankincense* is from a Hebrew root meaning "pure" or "white." This is because of the milk-colored drops of aromatic resin that flow from the slashed inner wood of the tree.

"Pure and holy" biblical incense contains genuine frankincense, which burns with ascending, white smoke (Exod. 30:34–35; Rev. 8:3–4).

11. The natural eagle learns to control every aspect of its flight with fractional adjustments of the wings and feathers. It develops massive wing muscles to move the large, outermost flight feathers. There is continual renewal as the entire plumage is shed gradually over and over again.

"Am I growing up? Am I being transformed? Am I willing to pay the price?"

The Question

In Part I, the Father commissioned His chancellor. A chancellor is like a secretary to a king.

My heavenly Father had asked me this question when I became His chancellor (a secretary to a king). I answered that I was willing. Sometimes, however, I find that I answer before I know the cost—the real cost.

The Father can give the Lord Jesus and His adopted children no greater inheritance than Himself, which includes everything else that is good (1 Chron. 29:14; 1 Cor. 3:22–23).

Now I wanted to ask myself the same question: "Am I willing to pay the price?[12] Really willing? Do I want to give up habits that I consider minor infractions—the ones about which the devil whispers to me, 'It's all right this time'? Am I willing to let the Holy Spirit bring me into a disciplined life, the life of a disciple?" My thoughts continued. And my motives: "Do I want success, or am I willing to allow Him to work through me, freely embracing the visible outcome or lack of visible outcome—whichever He chooses? What reward do I seek—Him or my own glory, being the bride He desires or becoming a marketable commodity? What reward do I seek?"[13]

The Rose

I turned to look at the white Eagle. He had changed into Jesus. The Lord now was sitting on the rim of the nest with His feet on its floor. In His left hand He held a large, pink rose.

"The flesh may look good," He said, "but the thorns on this rose can cause many wounds." Suddenly in His right hand appeared a bouquet of (what looked like) red tulips. "This is the rose of Sharon," He continued. "It grows within My garden. I want you to be such a rose, Anna, a rose without thorns."[14]

The Holy Spirit tests us, whether we will walk by God's Word or by our flesh (Exod. 16:4).

The pink rose disappeared as He continued, "Testings crack the grip of the flesh. Let yourself be poured from vessel to vessel so that the cracked sediment can be left behind."[15] He handed to me the bouquet of the red rose of Sharon. "For you, Anna," He said.

"My Lord, they are beautiful," I responded. "But will they not die here on Earth?"

The Reward

"They will not die," He smiled. "When you are rewarded by the Reward, life, even life on Earth, becomes electric, mysterious, pulsating with true, eternal life.[16] You become a life-giving spirit, for My Spirit touches others through you."

He continued, "When I in greater measure flow through you, My reward is with Me.[17] Fortresses tumble, walls crack and fall—more life rushes through your spirit and overflows to others. But you too benefit. You too are invigorated by being a channel of My life."

The choice was clear—life or death. If I wanted more life—more of Him—it would cost me. "What will it cost me?" I quickly asked myself. "Everything," I quickly answered. "Everything else.[18] But what is that everything else?" I again asked myself. "Death. Everything outside of Him is death, death wearing a mask, mere delusion. No," I thought to myself, "let others have more of the world. I want more of God."

I got up from the floor of the nest and sat beside Him on its rim. I looked into those clear eyes. "I want You as my reward, Lord. Since You have promised to be my reward, the only reward I will accept is

12. From eternity the Son of God freely chose to reveal only the Father. To do that, He had to lay aside all expression of His own soul life (Phil. 2:5–7). We know this is true because as Jesus was in His earthly body, so He was forever in His divine form. "Jesus Christ is the same yesterday and today, yes and forever" (Heb. 13:8). Jesus on Earth revealed only the words and work of His Father (John 5:19–20, 30; 12:49–50).

To be a disciple of someone is to become like that person (Matt. 10:25). The Lord Jesus tells anyone who wishes to become His disciple that he must count the cost. It is to "forsake all that he has" of his own in order that all that he has may be of Christ (Luke 9:23–24; 14:28, 33, NKJV).

13. God "is a rewarder of those who seek Him" (Heb. 11:6). As children of our heavenly Father, we are "heirs of God" in the same way that His divine Son is (Rom. 8:17).

14. Thorny plants were apparently not a part of God's original creation because He gave "every green plant for food" (Gen. 1:30). It was only after God cursed the ground because of Adam's sin that thorns sprang up (Gen. 3:17–18).

Human nature with the law of sin inherent in it is what the Bible calls *the flesh* (Rom. 7:23). Most of the deeds of the flesh listed in Galatians 5:19–21 cause wounds to other people. Only the character of Christ in the hearts of those on Earth causes no injury to others (Eph. 3:17; Rom. 13:10).

15. In wine making, after the grapes are crushed, there are small particles in the juice that must be removed. This sediment is called the *lees*. The wine is poured off several times after the lees settle to the bottom. The wine is thereby clarified.

Spiritually speaking, this takes place when the Holy Spirit tests us to remove the dregs of our flesh. When we refuse to allow Him to dismantle some part of our flesh, we put God to the test (Exod. 17:7; Matt. 4:5–7). God describes a nation that refused to be tested: "Moab has been at ease since his youth; He has been undisturbed, like wine on its dregs, and he has not been emptied from vessel to vessel" (Jer. 48:11–12).

16. The only life that Christians have is Christ (Col. 3:4). We live by His resurrected, human life united with His divine life. The power of His life is to flow through and continually renew the mortal bodies and souls of God's children (Rom. 8:11; 12:2; 2 Cor. 4:10–11). One of the signs of being filled with the Holy Spirit is the distinct awareness that the life within you is not your own (Gal. 2:20). Christ's life in the disciple is charged with glory because the Spirit has the power to exalt the Lord in every circumstance where one chooses Jesus (Phil. 1:20).

17. Jesus said, "My reward is with Me, to give to every one according to his work" (Rev. 22:12, NKJV). The Lord Jesus Himself is the reward. "It is the Lord Christ whom you serve" (Col. 3:24).

18. Paul said, "I consider everything a loss compared to the surpassing greatness of knowing Christ Jesus my Lord, for whose sake I have lost all things. I consider them rubbish, that I may gain Christ" (Phil. 3:8, NIV). God created human beings to show forth only His Son, even as the Son only manifests the Father (2 Cor. 4:10–11; John 17:6). All that is not of Christ in a person is worse than worthless (Rom. 7:18; 2 Cor. 3:6).

19. "Friendship with the world is hostility toward God" (James 4:4). Jesus deliberately refused to accept any reward or honor that people could give Him (John 5:41). He refused any glory but the glory from His Father (John 5:44; Matt. 4:8–10).

20. Christ Jesus loves His betrothed ones with all His heart. We know this because He said, "Just as the Father has loved Me, I have also loved you" (John 15:9). We know that the Father loves the Son with all His heart because the Father has made Him heir of everything, which includes all of His love (John 3:35; Rom. 8:17).

Another way of understanding this is that God has commanded us to love Him with all our hearts (Matt. 22:37). There is no way

Once and for all, each Christian must settle this matter of love for the things of this world, or one's love for God will be compromised (1 John 2:15).

You."[19] Laying the bouquet in my lap, I put my arms around Him, resting my head on His chest. "You, Lord. I want my Lover, my Friend; I want my Husband and my strong tower. I love You and will be satisfied with nothing but You."

"My little princess," He said, kissing me softly on my forehead, "I love you."

I tilted my head to look up at Him. "Thank You for loving me," I said. Then I returned my head to His chest. How secure I felt with His arms around me, how happy, how complete and totally at peace. I asked quietly, "Did You watch me grow up?"

"Yes," He answered tenderly.

"I wish I could have watched You grow up," I said.

Alone Together

We sat together quietly, holding one another. "We do not need words, do we, Anna? Give Me your hand," He said.

He took my hand and placed it over His heart. I could feel and hear His heart beating. He looked down at His hand covering mine. "My heart beats for you, Anna."[20] When I looked up into His face, His eyes were full of tears. "I love you," He said.

Blue Spirits

Twenty-four is the number of heavenly authority, indicating that these spirits are acting under the jurisdiction of God (Rev. 4:4).

Suddenly, before us in the air were twenty-four spirits.[21] They were ice blue, like clear gemstones.[22] I could see right through them.

In a stately manner they began to dance to heavenly music that seemed to come from nowhere. They danced on the air as if it were a floor. However, when they made a circle, it was vertical, like a wheel.[23]

Their demeanor was reverential. They began to sing:

> Let the earth hear heav'n declare.
> Hear, O Earth, its voice.
> Paradise breathes out a prayer.
> Trees and rocks rejoice.
> Every minute, every hour
> Singing songs unsung,
> Praising mysteries of His power,
> Blades of grass a tongue.
> Endless wonder, endless awe,
> Endless pure delight,

Life and love the Spirit's law
In heaven, land of light.
Ever seeing, yet unseen
Spirits join as one,
Extolling God, our gracious King,
Extolling Christ, His Son.
Hear, O Earth, as heaven sings.
Echo back its praise,
Silent, joyful thunderings
To God, th' Ancient of Days.

After their song ended, the dance continued to heavenly music. I remained with my head resting on the Lord's shoulder as I watched the spirits complete their dance.

Most birds have one mate at a time, and some are joined for life. During the courtship period, the male is focused on attracting the female. After building the nest in the male's territory, they give their attention to hatching the eggs and then feeding the young.

I wondered if the Lord would be wooing me always as He was doing now. "Will it always be like this?" I asked.

He smiled, "No, Anna. As on Earth the preparation for marriage is not marriage, so with the birds—a couple in mating rituals is not the couple after consummation and nesting begins.[24] Yet each period of

for us to do this unless He and the Son love us first with all their hearts (1 John 4:10).

21. There are good spirits in heaven who have transparent, ethereal forms in the shape of human bodies. They differ in manifestation from angels who have more visible and touchable bodies, but they are all ministering spirits (Heb. 1:14). God at times may assign these spirits to perform some task for Him on Earth (1 Kings 22:19–23; 2 Kings 19:7).

22. The central place in heaven is the throne of God. Directly before it is the pavement that is called "a sea of glass like crystal" (Rev. 4:6). Two kinds of blue gems—sapphire and lapis lazuli—are used in Scripture to describe the marvelous color of these two areas (Exod. 24:10; Ezek. 1:26; 10:1). Hence, *blue* is the biblical color representing heaven.

23. The reason that these spirits made upright circles in their dancing was because they were celebrating a coming event between heaven and earth. They were acting out clues that could not be understood until later.

24. During the wooing period, the Lord and His bride attend to each other (Song of Sol. 6:3). After deeper union is reached, much of their concern is in ministering together to the Father and to others (Rev. 1:6; Song of Sol. 6:11–12).

25. Salt remains a stable substance for millions of years in salt mines. It is used in preserving food because it inhibits the growth of microorganisms. Therefore, salt is a biblical symbol of permanence in the enduring covenants between God and His people (Lev. 2:13; Num. 18:19).

The color blue signifies heaven (see note 22 of this chapter). *Blue salt* represents a covenant with the heavenly realm.

26. The third stone on the Aaronic high priest's breastpiece was an emerald. This is a green gem representing Jacob's third-born son, Levi (Exod. 28:15,17). Some kings of Israel appointed Levites to minister unto the Lord—"to celebrate and to thank and praise" Him with joy (1 Chron. 16:4; 2 Chron. 29:30). This was a prototype of the service of praise and prayer by which Jesus the great High Priest attends His Father (Heb. 2:12; Rom. 8:34). Praise and thanksgiving in Christ's name is a high form of sacrifice by which His children are able to bless their Father (Heb. 13:15; Ps. 50:23).

The rainbow around the throne of God in heaven appeared to be mainly emerald green to John (Rev. 4:3). The Father is enthroned upon the praises of His people (Ps. 22:3).

27. By His inconceivable power, the Father knows and can respond to all that every human being is thinking, saying, and doing (Ps. 33:13; 139:2–4). "Christ [is] the power of God" to act for His Father in this way also (1 Cor. 1:24; John 5:19–20).

28. The Bible speaks of an everlasting (eternal) gospel in only one place—Revelation 14:6–7: "And I saw another angel flying in midheaven, having an eternal gospel to preach to those who live [literally, "sit"] on the earth . . . and he said with a loud voice, 'Fear God, and give Him glory, because the hour of His judgment has come; and worship Him who made the heaven and the earth and sea and springs of waters.'"

The everlasting gospel is the good news from eternity that the Father bore as "witness concerning His Son" (1 John 5:9).

All things concerning the kingdom of God that are fulfilled on Earth were first proclaimed in heaven (John 16:13).

time is rich in itself. You do not like a static routine. Why should you mind change? Eat what is set before you. Enjoy the journey today."

The spirits completed their exquisite offering. The music ended. I sat up. *Ishi* and I both clapped in appreciation.

"Deeply meaningful, dear friends," He said to the spirits. He turned to me, "Hold out your right hand."

I did. Instantly the spirits flew to me.

Blue Salt

Each spirit poured into my hand a small deposit of blue salt. Then each spirit flew back to stand before us.

Salt is a chemical compound formed by the violent reaction between a gas (chlorine) and a soft metal (sodium). This makes a totally different substance called *sodium chloride,* or table salt.

"Eat, Anna," the Lord said. I ate the blue salt. It was good. He continued, "This covenant of salt is for the heavenly realm."[25]

The spirits seemed exceedingly pleased to have represented heaven in helping to make this covenant. "Thank you, My dear friends," Jesus said. They bowed deeply from the waist, then disappeared.

The Emerald

"Come, Anna," the Lord said, rising. He helped me to stand. I picked up the bouquet. Instantly it became a large emerald.[26] I blurted out a laugh, because it startled me.

"For your crown, Anna," He said.

"Thank You, Lord," I smiled in return (although, as with my Father, I did not know to what crown He was referring). "How do You spend so much time with me?" I asked.

The job description of a particular position of employment is an analysis that describes the responsibilities of the job.

"It is in My job description," He laughed.[27] He held out His hand to me saying, "Come." I gave Him my hand. We began to rise from the nest.

Wheel of the Everlasting Gospel

As we rose, I saw an unrolled scroll with writing on it. It extended from heaven to Earth and then back to heaven again. It formed a huge wheel touching Earth and heaven. We rose right beside it.

"I have never seen this, Lord," I said.

Christians proclaim the gospel of Jesus Christ here on Earth, and God fulfills it in heaven (Heb. 2:3–4).

"The everlasting gospel made visible, Anna," He said. "Proclaimed in heaven, fulfilled on Earth—proclaimed on Earth, fulfilled in heaven.[28] Come."

Chapter Five

The Pool of Reflection

After we arrived in Paradise, I found that I was sitting alone near a clear, round pool of water. On the opposite side of the pool, shrubbery was growing in geometric shapes—squares, rectangles, triangles, and circles. These shapes were reflected perfectly within the pool.

Stacte was blooming behind the geometric shrubs.[1] Each of these bushes was covered with waxy white blossoms that gave a mild, pleasant fragrance. I remembered that stacte was a spice used in the holy incense. But I could not remember the meaning inherent in its name.

The name of the spice *stacte* is from a word whose Hebrew root means "to fall in drops" or "to prophesy."

It was unusually still by the pool, like being in the eye of a hurricane. I swung my legs around, putting my feet into the water. They hardly made a ripple. Strange.

"Where am I?" I asked aloud.

"The pool of reflection," a child's voice answered from behind me.

Crystal Clear

"Uh oh," I said within myself because I recognized the voice. "Crystal Clear," I smiled faintly as I turned to face her.

There she stood, her hair still tousled as if from play. She was wearing the same pale shift and pinafore. She looked five or six years of age.

1. It is thought to be a liquid gum that flowed in drops from incisions in the bark of the storax bush. The hardened resin was combined with other sweet spices that God prescribed for making the sacred incense to be burned daily in the tabernacle (Exod. 30:34–35).

2. Crystal Clear is the name of a ministering spirit in heaven. God teaches truth through her in very pure, simple, unmistakable and unavoidable terms. Even her bodily form is clear or transparent. She taught a vital lesson in Part I, pages 12–14.

3. The fleshly body and soul are unalterably opposed to God (Rom. 8:7, 13). This outer person was born and reared in the image of Satan (John 8:41, 44). Human nature lives a lie, without any truth in it (John 8:44). It relies on its own rules and reason, hence is "sly, legalistic, and evasive," as Jacob was (Gen. 30:41–43; 31:36–41).

4. "If we judged ourselves rightly, we would not be judged" (1 Cor. 11:31). We oppose the Holy Spirit by being "stiff-necked [stubborn and contrary] and uncircumcised in heart and ears [a stony heart that does not want to hear and obey God]" (Acts 7:51; Zech. 7:12).

5. "The kindness of God leads you to repentance" (Rom. 2:4). He gives His repentant disciples:

(1) a change of attitude when we see our sin profaning the life of Christ within us (John 16:8–9);

(2) godly sorrow for the sin (2 Cor. 7:9–10);

(3) power to forsake the sin and to choose Christ in its place (Isa. 55:7).

6. Jesus roundly castigated those Jewish leaders as hypocrites who pretended to be righteous (Luke 20:20).

However, she had old eyes. At times I could see through her arm or leg. She was a spirit.

"You have come back to see us," she exclaimed cheerily. "We L-O-V-E, love you," she continued, spelling out the word *love* as if it were in a child's song.

I sighed painfully within myself as I remembered the last time I had seen her.[2] "But," I thought, "perhaps this time will be different." I decided to ask her about the pool. "What is the pool of reflection?"

"It is a place where you can see yourself very clearly," she said.

The *flesh* means the human nature with which we are born (Ps. 51:5; Eph. 2:3).

I was not sure that I liked that idea. "Does one wish to reflect upon oneself?" I asked coolly, my flesh suddenly rising up and being as sly, legalistic, and evasive as the flesh always is.[3]

She continued as though she did not notice. "You might want to take a look to see if you are cooperating with God or resisting Him.[4] Do you want to look into the pool?" she asked brightly.

The Decision

Of course I did not want to look into the pool. However, I was beginning to hear in my own voice, as well as in the hardness of my heart, my resistance to correction.

Shortly before arriving at the pool I was telling the Lord that I would give up anything and everything in order to gain more of Him. Now with my first opportunity to allow this declaration to become experiential in my life, I was balking. "Do you think I should look?" I asked limply.

"It might help," she replied.

With a sigh I took my feet out of the water and lay down on my stomach to look into the pool. I was amazed. I saw Jesus's face reflected in the water instead of my own. But there were geometric objects stuck onto His head and face. "What are these objects?" I asked.

"Blocks," she said. "You are blocking Him. They make the face of Jesus look really ugly."

"How do I get them off?" I asked with alarm.

She leaned over to look at my face in the pool. "*Hmmm,*" she said, as if making a diagnosis. "You need to unstick the glue."

"Unstick the glue?" I asked. "How do I do that?"

Repentance

"Repentance," she said matter-of-factly.[5] "Repentance unsticks the glue." She pulled back to look at me directly instead of at my reflection.

I sat up to look into her face. She shook her head from side to side as children do when correcting one another. Speaking in a slow, singsong manner, she said, "You're too old to play with blocks." Before I could answer her, she vanished.

One meaning of the Hebrew word for the spice *stacte* is "to fall in drops" gently. A similar meaning is "to speak forth words from God," that is to prophesy the "truth [as it] is in Jesus" (Eph. 4:21). Therefore, *stacte* symbolizes speaking the truth of Christ with mercy (Matt. 18:33).

Stacte

The strong smell of stacte flooded the area. I looked at the bushes. The fragrant gum was running down the branches.

"Truth with mercy," I said glumly, remembering now the inherent meaning within the name.

7. The flesh keeps telling us that we need many earthly things in order to be happy and secure (Mark 4:18–19; Luke 10:41–42). Believers trust Christ Jesus as their true treasure, in whom are included all the lesser treasures (Col. 2:2–3; 1 Cor. 3:21–23). Our deepest needs are for God in His glorious presence (Phil. 4:19).

We store up treasures in heaven each time we choose Christ Jesus instead of ourselves (Matt. 6:20). In time the main thing we will pray for is that which is needed to have Him exalted in each situation (Phil. 2:20–21; 1 Cor. 6:20).

8. If one seeks to be honored by people, he has no honor from God (Matt. 6:1; John 5:44). One cannot love the things of this world and love God, too (1 John 2:15).

While on Earth Jesus said that He did not receive glory from people (John 5:41).

9. "Therefore, just as through one man [Adam] sin entered into the world, and death through sin... so death spread to all [people], because all sinned" (Rom. 5:12).

"We know by experience that our old heart person was crucified once and for all with Jesus on the cross. Thereby the heart power to the sin nature in our body might be broken and that nature kept inoperative. Consequently, we should no longer be slaves to our sin nature, for the person who has died [with Christ in one's old heart] is freed from the power of sin [and death]" (Rom. 6:6–7, paraphrase).

10. The three main categories of moral wrong in Scripture are called sin, transgression, and iniquity (Exod. 34:7; Ps. 51:1–2). *Sin* is falling short of the glory of Christ that the Father has offered through the Scriptures (Rom. 3:23; 2 Cor. 4:4). *Transgression* is rebellion against God's authority. It is aligning oneself with Satan's primary sin (1 Sam. 15:23). *Iniquity* is deviating from what is inherently known to be right (Rom. 1:18–21).

11. "Let the Holy Spirit direct your lives, and you will not satisfy the desires of the human nature [the flesh]. For our human nature constantly has a strong desire to suppress the Spirit, and the Spirit constantly has a strong desire to suppress the human nature. These two are enemies, and this means that you cannot do what you want to do" (Gal. 5:16–17, WUEST). If the Christian is willing, the Spirit will apply one's individual cross daily to the fleshly deeds of the body and the self-centered use of the soul faculties (Rom. 8:12–13; Matt. 16:24–25; 2 Cor. 4:11).

12. "Therefore, since we are surrounded by such a great cloud of witnesses [the redeemed and the angels in heaven], let us throw off everything that hinders [and weighs down Christ's faith in us] and the sin that so easily entangles, and let us run with perseverance the [long-distance] race marked out for us" (Heb. 12:1, NIV; Luke 15:7).

13. This was like the cry of Aaron for his sister, Miriam. They had disputed Moses's authority alone to hear God. She was then struck with leprosy (Num. 12:1–2, 10). Aaron pleaded with Moses: "Oh, do not let her be like one dead, whose flesh is half eaten away when he comes from his mother's womb!" (Num. 12:12). He implored that she not be left with the living death that results from sin.

14. "He made Him [Christ Jesus] who knew no sin to be sin on our behalf, so that we might become the righteousness of God in Him [Christ Jesus]" (2 Cor. 5:21).

15. "Put my tears in Thy bottle. Are they not in Thy book?" (Ps. 56:8). The tears of those who cry out to God are preserved in heaven. The fact of their weeping also is recorded.

There are several books in heaven where matters concerning the lives of people on Earth are written (Rev. 20:12). An example of this kind of journal is the "book of remembrance [which] was written before Him for those who fear the Lord and esteem His name" (Mal. 3:16).

With a sigh I turned back to the pool. I looked into the water again. The face, and therefore the life of Jesus, was definitely blocked from flowing to others. I gathered the courage to look at the blocks more closely. Each had writing on it. I squinted to decipher the lettering.

The Blocks

The Greek word for *hypocrite* means "one who speaks behind a mask that one holds in front of one's face." They are like those on the stage who perform roles of people whom they are not.

"Hypocrite" was written on one block.[6] "Hypocrite," I said with self-righteous indignation. Although indignant, I dared not try to refute this because I knew it to be true. That which people on Earth might not see was plainly visible in heaven. Perhaps I might hide this from others, but I could not hide it from myself or from God. "I am a hypocrite," I said, "and You see it. I say that I am doing what I do out of obedience, not caring about the results, but I do care. I care greatly. I want success. I want to feel that I am accomplishing something." I could not look at that block any longer.

I decided to look at another block. "Money" was written on it.[7] "Oh, no," I moaned. "Well, it is true. I say that I do not mind being poor, but I mind a great deal. I do not like being poor. I know that to live by faith pleases You, and I want to please You. But truthfully, it is easier to talk about faith than to live by it. At times I think, 'If I just had enough money, I would never need to think about money again.'" My confession made me uneasy. I decided to look at another block.

By the word *glory*, the Bible usually means "honor and respect."

"Being a star" was written on this block.[8] My hands went to my face in embarrassment. "True again," I confessed. "It is difficult for me to live a hidden life. I want respect. I want honor. I want to be known. I want..." I almost said "glory." As I confessed this sin, I was struck by the seriousness of it. "God, help me," I said. "I want *Your* glory." I shook my head. "This is serious, very serious. How have You taken me as far as You have taken me? How can You love me? How can You want me to be Your Son's bride? In my spirit I know that I want to be on the inside that which I present on the outside. I know that I want to live by faith. I know that pride is a great sin. Satan wanted Your glory. How am I better?"

The Blood

Jesus Christ on the cross of Calvary paid the price for the forgiveness of every form of evil against God (Eph. 1:7; Heb. 8:12).

Saying that galvanized my thinking. "I am in a better place before You, Father, for my Lord and Savior died to release me from the penalty of death due to sin.[9] And I can plead the blood of Jesus before You and ask that You forgive me for every sin, as well as for every transgression.[10] I can proclaim to You that the Holy Spirit was sent to apply the cross to every act of the flesh within me.[11] I am in a better place.

"Then, Daddy," I cried, "I ask for correction by the Holy Spirit. I ask for the cross. I ask that I be clean inside and outside. I want the life of Jesus to flow through me unhindered. I mean, Daddy, that I do not want one hindrance.[12] I give You permission to bring me into a pure walk before You. I know it will hurt. I know it. But I give You permission to ignore my whining."

Tears

"O God, do not leave me as one dead."[13] I began to cry. "Forgive me. Wash me clean with the blood of Jesus—He who paid the ultimate price with His shed blood and death on the cross so that I might stand before You clean, in His righteousness."[14]

I continued, "Deal with my flesh. Override my protests. Discount my whimpering. Please, please do not let me go around this mountain one more time. I do not want to live a halfhearted life, compromising at every turn because I do not want the pain of the cross." I wept bitterly. "And I miss Jesus," I cried. "I am in pain when we are apart!"

I realized suddenly that a very bright angel was near me catching in an alabaster bottle every tear that I cried.[15] The tears would start down my cheeks and then automatically, obediently even, go into the vial. I was fascinated.

16. Of the angels assigned to the author, Judy is the one who assists her in living a life of praise to God (Ps. 34:1).

17. Some of the Levites were set apart on earth to minister to the Lord in giving Him thanks and praise (1 Chron. 16:4). Judy's green garment shows that she is set apart to that ministry in heaven.

Angels who minister in the temple in heaven wear golden girdles (Rev. 15:6).

18. God instructed the Israelites to bind small, black boxes on their foreheads and on the back of their hands. These little cubes contained parchment on which certain scriptures were written. This was to help impress God's words upon their hearts, souls, and strength in whatever they were doing (Deut. 6:5–8).

19. These words of Scripture, "the mantle of praise instead of a spirit of fainting," describe an aspect of the anointing of the Holy Spirit upon God's people (Isa. 61:3). The mantle of praise is intended for all Christians to set them apart as holy, so that they may bless God (Ps. 34:1).

20. Before the world was created, Christ was assigned to die for our sins. The people on Earth who believe in Him have their "names... written in the book of life belonging to the Lamb that was slain from the creation of the world" (Rev. 13:8, NIV).

It is possible for Christians to "again crucify [reject] to [within] themselves the Son of God, and put Him to open shame" before His enemies (Heb. 6:4–6; 10:26–29). But He died once, "never to die again" (Rom. 6:9).

21. *Galbanum* was one of the spices used to make the holy incense that was burned daily in the desert tabernacle (Exod. 30:34; 35:1, 6–8). The word comes from a Hebrew root meaning "fat" or "the best portion." Of the animal sacrifices in Scripture, the fat was reserved for God and burned as a soothing aroma to Him (Gen. 4:4; Lev. 3:14–16). Fat represented the sacrifice of joyful praise and thanksgiving to honor the Father by His Son and His disciples (Ps. 50:23; Heb. 2:12; 13:15).

22. The Hebrew word for the spice *cassia* is similar to the word meaning "to bow down," "to pay homage." *Homage* in Scripture means to honor another by bending low in deep respect (1 Chron. 29:20). Jesus said, "I honor My Father... I do not seek My glory" (John 8:49–50).

The name *Judy* comes from one of the tribes of Israel, *Judah*, a word that is derived from a Hebrew root meaning "praise" (Gen. 29:35).

The color *green* stands for the tribe of Levi, the third son of Jacob, represented by the third stone, a green emerald, on the high priest's breastpiece (Gen. 29:34; Exod. 28:15, 17).

A biblical mantle is a spiritual empowering and authority granted by the Father to His Son and exercised by the Holy Spirit in the disciple.

The Angel of Praise

I was so fixed upon this sight that I jumped a little when my name was called from behind me. It was Judy, the angel of praise.[16]

She was dressed in a gossamer green undertunic bound with a golden girdle.[17] Over this was a deeper green cloak that had long, oversized sleeves. These sleeves contained pockets that held all manner of golden musical instruments. Her neck, hands, and feet had a slight tint of gold. Her auburn hair was plaited into seven loops interlaced with gold. On her forehead was a small golden box, housing Scripture.[18] She began to speak. "Anna, rejoice that you are loved. I am sent to comfort you with the mantle of praise."[19]

"What is that?" I asked, wiping my eyes with my hand. The bright angel with the vial for tears disappeared.

Hymn of Praise

"*Shh*," she said, putting her finger to her lips. "Let me help to calm your soul. Rest." She became a small, green whirlwind. The wind and movement caused all the instruments within her robe to play together. The sound of praise was so pure that it seemed to draw angels from the air. They gathered in a large circle around her. She began to sing:

O great I AM, Eternal One,
Fountain of life within the Son,
Wellspring of blessing,
Wellspring of light,
Infinite mystery hid from our sight.

Searched by the Spirit,
Revealed through the Son,
Mystery unfolding, though ever begun.
Beginning and ending, great circle of light
That shatters the darkness, confounding the night.

All beauty, all joy, all splendor in One,
His grace freely shared through the life of His Son.
His life and His death and His life evermore,
Though crucified ever, to die nevermore.[20]

All hail, Great Redeemer,
All hail, Mighty King
Of Life and of Truth and of Light do we sing.

All praise, adoration, and thanksgiving,
Through time never ending, our homage we'll bring.

Galbanum and Cassia

As she sang, the aroma of galbanum and cassia filled the air. Galbanum bespeaks worship, adoration, thanksgiving, and praise.[21] Cassia urges homage to God alone.[22] I needed both. I needed the idols in my heart to be cast down. Also, I needed to be lifted up, out of myself, through turning my eyes toward Him in praise. Her song was like a mantle dropping upon me—lifting my spirit but settling my soul.

Christians are to be humble toward all people (1 Pet. 5:5). But they are to bow down in homage to God alone (Phil. 2:10).

At the end of the song, the many angels that had gathered withdrew discreetly. Judy spoke. "Worship God, Anna. He alone is worthy." Then she too disappeared.

God at Work

I was alone again. But the stillness near the pool was no longer a vacuum. It was closer to the stillness within my soul. The Lord had accomplished a work within me, although I did not know the nature of the work or how He had accomplished it. But I felt that I could see more clearly, that in some way I was different.

The answer seemed simple. Jesus overcame the flesh when He walked the earth. Now He could overcome the flesh in me.[23] He would work, and I would rest in Him. I felt cleansed, washed, with my soul as still as the round pool before me.

Jesus, as the "new man" on Earth, gained the utmost victory in learning to obey His Father always (Eph. 2:15; Heb. 5:8–9).

However, the stilling of my soul made room for a greater longing for Him.[24] The ache within my spirit had grown painfully acute. I missed Him. I wanted to be with Him. The pain was becoming a wracking hunger.

Cassia was considered inferior to other plants in the laurel family. God, however, honored it by designating it as one of the spices to be used in the holy anointing oil (Exod. 30:24). The leaders considered Jesus of little account because He came from Nazareth, but His Father glorified Him (John 8:54).

23. Jesus was "made perfect" in every way, including the denial of the flesh, the merely human use of His soul and body (Luke 9:23). "Hence, also, He is able to save completely those who draw near to God through Him" (Heb. 7:25, MARGIN).

24. Martha was a distracted and worried soul when Jesus came to dine in her home (Luke 10:38–42). She had such a great longing to be approved by others that she could not enjoy having Jesus there. Her sister, Mary, quieted herself at His feet and desired only Him.

25. "No eye has seen, no ear has heard, no mind has conceived what God has prepared for those who love Him—but God has revealed it to us by His Spirit. The Spirit searches all things, even the deep things of God... We have not received the spirit of the world but the Spirit who is from God, that we may understand what God has freely given us" (1 Cor. 2:9–10, 12, NIV).

26. The natural or earthly-minded person comprehends things of the world. "Whatever is true, whatever is noble, whatever is right, whatever is pure, whatever is lovely, whatever is admirable—if

Two Angels

Suddenly two angels came strolling down the path near the pool. They looked like young men of about twenty-five years of age. One had brown hair and wore a brown robe. The other had blond hair and wore a blond robe. There was something comical about them. But I did not know why I felt this way. Salt and pepper came to mind when I looked at them. They were laughing and talking.

"Hello," I said. "Who are you?"

"Sense," bowed the angel in the brown robe.

"Nonsense," bowed the angel in the blond.

"What?" I laughed. "God is not into nonsense."

"Oh, yes," said Nonsense. "There is more understood by the spirit than the mind."[25]

"And much that the mind is given to comprehend as true," Sense added.[26]

"That reminds me of a song," said Nonsense.

"Oh, dear," said Sense.

"We will sing it for you," added Nonsense.

"We will?" asked Sense.

"Why not?" replied Nonsense. "You always like my songs."

"I do?" Sense asked incredulously.

"They certainly are better than yours," Nonsense quipped. "Yours sound like math problems."

Sense roared with laughter. "All right, all right," he said. "You start it."

Nonsense sang:

> What is it like to live above?
> What is it like above?
> Walk blind you see, walk deaf you hear,
> That's what it's like above, above.
> That's what it's like above.[27]

There was a long pause. "Is that it?" Sense asked.

"Well, I'm not singing an aria here," Nonsense answered. "That is it."

There was another long pause. "I like it," Sense said wholeheartedly.

"Thank you," Nonsense said begrudgingly. "Shall we sing it together?"

"Very well," Sense nodded. "Would you like to join us, Anna?"

"If I can remember it," I said.

"Just jump in when you can," Nonsense added. Nonsense began to sing the song again. We joined in when we could.

When the song ended, Nonsense asked, "Shall we sing it again?"

Laughing, Sense and I said, "By all means." Sense continued, "Come, Anna, we will walk with you down the path."

We began to walk and sing the song again. We sang it again and again and again. The more we walked and sang, the funnier everything seemed. We all began to laugh uproariously. In fact, we laughed so much that we could hardly stand. At times we had to hang on to one another just to remain upright.

"Your songs are better than I remembered," roared Sense.

We almost fell down laughing because the song was true, but absolute nonsense. We walked and sang and laughed until we neared a large verdant garden, the entrance to which was guarded by two enormous cherubim.

"We leave you here," said Sense.

I wanted to ask, "Where?" But before I could ask, Nonsense said, "Whenever you need a little traveling music, just let us know." They bowed laughing and were gone.

I was left on the path leading to the garden. Just ahead of me was a sign in the shape of an arrow pointing to the entrance. The lettering on the sign read: THE GARDEN OF GOD.

anything is excellent or praiseworthy—think about such things" (Phil. 4:8, NIV).

27. Jesus of Nazareth walked and worked on Earth, but He lived above in His Spirit within the Father (John 1:18; 14:20). On Earth He did not judge by what His eyes saw or by what His ears heard (Isa. 11:3). He relied upon the Holy Spirit to teach Him all things (John 14:26).

Chapter Six The Garden of God

The brief reprieve of laughter had vanished with Sense and Nonsense. The dull ache of longing returned. It was becoming acute, alarmingly so. It was multiplying, galloping in intensity.

I had asked to desire the Lord more than life itself. I did not realize that receiving such love would be excruciatingly painful. It was as though a javelin had been driven through my stomach. I could not pull it out. I was skewered with longing.[1] But I pushed forward toward the garden. Perhaps I would see Jesus there. He and He alone was my cure. That I knew.

The Angel Elijah

Suddenly the venerable angel Elijah joined me on the path. He was large, old looking, and slightly blue because of a blue light emanating from him. He had a partially bald head and a very long white beard. He wore a full-length, sleeveless mantle woven with various shades of blue. Underneath this cloak was an even deeper blue robe. Light flashed within the mantle as if a distant thunderstorm was raging within the fabric. Earlier my heavenly Father had assigned this angel to travel with me for the remainder of my life on Earth. He had become a friend.

Thunder and lightning are symbols of God the Father speaking or acting with power beyond human control or comprehension in blessing or in judgment (Rev. 4:5; 8:5). The blue color of the angel signifies the heavenly revelation that is given to him.

"Elijah," I smiled, acknowledging him.

"May I walk with you?" he asked.

"Please do," I replied.

He did not address the pain I was experiencing, for which I was grateful. As we walked, he began to speak. "Life in the Spirit is being known intimately and knowing intimately—trusting the Beloved One, preferring the Beloved One, thinking of the Beloved One, honoring the Beloved One, holding the Beloved One to your heart."

1. David said that God's "lovingkindness is better [more to be desired] than [his earthly] life" (Ps. 63:3). His longing for God was so great that it was like thirsting where there is no water (v. 1). This longing can become so intense that the psalmists describe it as "panting for" or even being "crushed with longing" (Ps. 42:1; 119:20). So the maiden says that she is "lovesick [faint with love]" for her beloved in the Song of Solomon (2:5; 5:8).

He looked at me as he continued, "Your heavenly Father has provided marriage on Earth to demonstrate the bond of growing love between the loved ones, maturing in love, deepening in love, not seeking to expose but to nourish, being vulnerable to the beloved and tender toward others."[2]

He continued, "Because our great and mighty God has created all, all has dignity. The One you love is mercy poured like warm oil on the wounds of the world, the balm of Gilead. The anointed One gave Himself for all, for He has compassion on all, though few will cling to Him."[3]

We approached the entrance to the garden. It had no walls around it. However, it looked as though it grew up to an invisible wall and then stopped.

Cherubim

The first mention in the Bible of *cherubim* (plural) is Genesis 3:24. God stationed them at the entrance to the Garden of Eden "and the flaming sword which turned every direction to guard the way to the tree of life." The letters of the Hebrew root word for *cherub* mean "holding something in safe keeping."

We stopped before two large cherubim that flanked the entryway. Each cherub had two faces. One cherub had the face of a man in front and of a lion in back. The other had the face of an eagle in front and of an ox in back. Each cherub had two wings and hands under the wings. Their legs were straight like a man's but ended in hooves. Taupe-colored feathers covered their bodies like fish-scale mail. They were full of eyes around their bodies and within their wings. They were fearsome-looking creatures.[4]

The cherubim bowed to Elijah. The face of the man asked, "How are you this blessed day in the kingdom of our God?" Then the four faces of the two cherubim burst into song, "Bless His name forever and ever!" They were a quartet.

Elijah spoke to them, "I am accompanying Anna into the garden."

"Welcome," said the face of the eagle. Then the quartet sang, "Praise Him, praise Him, all His handiwork."

Elijah turned to me. "Shall we go, Anna?"

"Yes, please," I answered.

"Splendor and majesty, glory and honor are Yours, O God," sang the cherubim. Their wings were raised and touching over the entrance.[5] The eyes of all four faces were lifted in praise as we passed beneath their wings.

Eden

My longing eased somewhat as we entered the garden. The Lord's presence was there. We started down the path. The sound of praise from the cherubim grew fainter the deeper we went into the garden.

The area was bountiful. It looked as though every variety of tree, shrub, flower, and herb grew within its circumference. The fruit-bearing trees had flowers and leaves and were also heavy with fruit. I was in awe. "I am walking in the original of the garden that graced Earth at the dawn of Creation," I said to myself. "And this is the way it smelled," I added, because of the deliciously intoxicating aromas.[6]

The Septuagint, the Hebrew Old Testament in Greek, translates the word *Eden* as "paradise." Eden is a word related to another Hebrew word meaning "a delight."

"Is the garden still on Earth?" I asked Elijah.

"No," he answered. "It was carried away with the flood."

"Why are the cherubim at the entrance?" I asked.

"To join in the hymn of praise rising from this place to your Father," he said. "Listen."

It was as though everything within the garden was given a voice with which to sing in unison.[7] The sound was not loud. I needed to still myself to hear it. It blended like music coming from all that made up the garden—all that reflected Christ.

"Sweet music," I said.

2. The marriage of two people on Earth whom God has joined together is a sign of Christ's union with the bridal church that the Father has given Him (Eph. 5:31–33; John 6:37–39).

3. "God our Savior... desires all men to be saved and to come to the knowledge of the truth. For there is one God, and one mediator also between God and men, the man, Christ Jesus, who gave Himself as a ransom for all" (1 Tim. 2:3–6).

4. Two cherubim also are positioned beneath the armrests on either side of God's throne in heaven as an honor guard of His awesome glory (Ezek. 10:1, 18–21).

Some cherubim have two faces, while others have four faces, and others only one (Ezek. 41:18–19; 1:10; Rev. 4:7).

5. The figures of the two golden cherubim above the ark of the covenant in the holy of holies represent heaven in honoring the presence of the holy God on earth. They faced each other and extended their wings toward the center to cover the mercy seat (Exod. 25:18–20; Heb. 9:5).

In the same way the wings of two live cherubim covered the entrance to Christ's garden in heaven. It signified the honoring of the life and glory of the Father's only begotten One (Heb. 2:9).

6. The exquisite odors in this garden of Christ's heart testify to the fragrance of His sacrificial love unto His Father (2 Cor. 2:14–15). His obedience is as "a burnt offering, an offering by fire of a soothing aroma to the Lord" (Lev. 1:9; Eph. 5:2).

7. All that is good and perfect originates in God the Father (James 1:17). This is true of holy singing. There are examples of the things of Earth singing or rejoicing before God (Ps. 98:8; 96:12). In Psalm 148, all of creation that is good praises the Lord.

8. All things were created to manifest and to glorify the Son (Col. 1:16, 18). The Father sings of His love for His Son (Ps. 42:8; John 17:26). The heart of Jesus sings back to the Father through His garden. The saints in heaven sing the song of the Lamb (Rev. 15:3).

9. The tree of life in the Garden of Eden on Earth was a physical representation of the tree of God's life in Christ's garden in heaven (Gen. 2:9; Rev. 2:7). The earthly tree was washed away by

"Sweeter still because it comes from the heart of Him who is beyond compare. It comes from the heart of Jesus," he added.[8]

The flowering plants that God originally created are in the garden of God the Son. They all reflect the loveliness and aroma of His heart character. The thornless rose of Sharon has a prominent place there as it beautifully mirrors His tender love (Song of Sol. 2:1).

The garden was cool, not sticky as I would have imagined with so much foliage. We passed small waterfalls and hidden pools. The rose of Sharon grew near the water.

"Does Jesus walk here?" I asked Elijah.

"Yes," he smiled. "This is His garden. He walks here."

"It is very beautiful," I said.

"Yes," he agreed, "the life breath of God, the garden of Jesus."

We came to a clearing in what I supposed to be the center of the garden. The rose of Sharon grew around its perimeter. In the center of this meadow grew a large, bright tree. It was the shape of a many-branched oak tree or a very large apple tree. The branches were heavy with fruit. It shone with so much light that it was not the color of a tree on Earth. Elijah gestured toward it as we moved into the clearing: "The tree of life," he proclaimed.[9] "I will take my leave of you now, Anna."

"Oh, Elijah," I exclaimed.

He turned to face me. "Remember, Anna, in that which is to come, remember that you are loved," he said.

In the past I had found that such statements did more to stand my hair on end than to comfort me. This time was no exception.

"Remember," he said again, kissing my hand. He vanished.

Seemingly I was alone in the garden. I looked around the clearing. A slight breeze stirred the flowers and grasses in the meadow. I began to walk toward the tree of life.

The Suffering Christ

When halfway to the tree, the Lord materialized before my eyes. He stood before me beaten, bruised, His garments stuck to His wounds that were still open, gouges in His skull, swollen fingers, and swollen face.

The suffering Christ materialized in His garden in heaven because this garden represents His heart where the deepest pain is felt.

I cried out in alarm. I did not know what to do or how to help. I was in shock. I sank to my knees, for all the strength left me. My hands covered my face.

"Anna," He said, "this is your Husband, too. I still bear wounds from the faithless in the world."[10]

I could not look at Him.

"It is all right, Anna," He said. "It is all right." He took both of my hands into His and helped me to rise. "Look at Me, Anna," He continued. He had changed and now looked as I usually see Him. "I am both—what you see and what you saw. You need to know that you are marrying into both, one but both."

"I do not know what to say," I whispered.

"Say nothing," He said. "What is there to say? But you need to know Me as both so that you do not wed blindly."[11]

"What does this mean?" I asked.

"Those who are one share all," He said. "You wish to drink deeply, to share fully, to know even as you are known. This too is part of the knowing, the sharing, the being one. There are not many who turn from their own interests to seek the interests of God.[12] But those who are called and chosen to live in God desire to share the sufferings of the Godhead."[13]

It was as though I was struck dumb.

He continued, "I realize that you are in shock. Therefore I will not ask you now if you are willing to share My sufferings, My sorrows."

"Lord," I said, trying to face the reality of what I had seen, "make me willing. I want to be one with You. I would deny You nothing, nor would I turn away from You because there are sorrows to bear—as long as we are together."

the flood (Gen. 7:4, 23). But the true tree of life in heaven will be available forever. This applies even to the peoples of the nations who will live outside of the walls of the New Jerusalem. They may visit the city and the tree during the daytime (Rev. 21:24–26; 22:1–2, 14).

10. There are at least five categories of causes for the Lord Jesus' continuing anguish and grief:

(1) Christians who become part of Him and then deny or disregard Him (Heb. 6:4–6; 10:26–29; 1 Tim. 5:11–12).

(2) Christians in His body on Earth who cause suffering to one another (Matt. 25:40; 1 Cor. 12:26).

(3) His own earthly race, the Jews, together with the Gentiles, who will not receive Him and so come under judgment (Hos. 11:8; John 3:18).

(4) Those of His disciples who are persecuted for their faith and the gospel (Acts 9:4–5, 15–16; 2 Tim. 3:12).

(5) His disciples who learn obedience through the things that they must suffer, as Jesus had to learn on Earth (Heb. 2:10; 5:8–9; 1 Pet. 4:1–2).

11. In becoming a disciple of the Lord Jesus, as in being His bride, the Christian must know what the decision involves (Luke 14:28–33). The issue is the intimacy of one life shared (John 17:21). One life together with Christ includes His continued suffering caused by the sins of mankind (Col. 1:24; Rom. 8:17).

12. Paul said of his son in the spirit, Timothy, "I have no one else of kindred spirit who will genuinely be concerned for your welfare. For they all seek after their own interests, not those of Christ Jesus" (Phil. 2:20–21; Matt. 16:23).

13. To truly know the Lord Jesus in His resurrected life, one must know "the fellowship of His sufferings" (Phil. 3:10). Christians have the Spirit of glory rest upon them when they are reviled for His name's sake (1 Pet. 4:12–14).

We rejoice, "for just as the sufferings of Christ are ours in abundance, so also our comfort is abundant through Christ" (2 Cor. 1:5).

14. The heavenly host adores God for His mercy, praises Him for His goodness, and worships Him for His holiness as the "wholly Other" of all beings. None of the heavenly ones are more glorious in the burning holiness of worship than the seraphim stationed

"Do you mean this?" He asked.

"Yes, Lord," I said.

"Behold," He exclaimed, turning to face the tree of life and gesturing in its direction.

The Wheel of Fire

A huge, gold ring began to spin before us. It was as tall as the Ferris wheels that are part of the world's fair exhibitions on Earth. It spun rapidly, bursting into flames.

I realized that the flames were fiery seraphim, hundreds, no thousands, of them. Their flames were as intense as blowtorches. But a figure similar to a man's was at the core of each torch. Each seraph had six wings. With two they covered their eyes, with two they covered their feet, and with two they flew. A unique and pure music came from their midst.[14]

"Who will ride the wheel of fire?" the seraphim called. Their voices had a strange sound, as if their words were passing through some medium to which we are not accustomed on Earth.[15]

I realized I would need a greater spiritual maturity than I now possessed if I would desire to share the burdens of God. I did not know what this would mean. But evidently this fire was a first step if I wished such maturity. I turned to Jesus, "I want to ride the wheel, my Lord."

He smiled. "We will ride it together."

I called to the seraphim, "We will ride."

Jesus took my right hand, and we started forward. The closer we came to the wheel, the hotter grew the flames with which it burned. The sound of thousands of blowtorches was formidable. But through the flames I could hear an adoration of God that was of such purity that it startled my senses.

The *ring of gold* represents being wed to Christ. The *ring of fire* is a symbol of the process of sanctification that includes sharing Christ's sufferings (Phil. 3:10). Not all Christians want to participate in this aspect of union with Him.

As we arrived at the fiery wheel, a seraph beckoned for us to enter the flames. The seraph spoke to me. "Few wish to ride the ring of fire. They want the ring of gold but not the ring of fire."

I looked at Jesus. Then holding tightly to His hand, we both entered the fire. It was extremely hot among these flaming seraphim.

A seraph gestured for us to sit down. We did. The wheel began to turn. We went up as if the fiery ring was actually a huge Ferris wheel.

The Ministry of Seraphs

Jesus said, "The seraphim will train you in a holiness that will bring forth pure worship, holiness burning like a torch, intense in its focus. If you will yield to the ministry of these servants, you too will be like a flame and burn like a torch of love and purity for your God."[16]

He continued, "The fire is for all. Learn to live in the fire by allowing it to burn away all that will not pass through as purely of Me. Learn to love the fire of God."[17]

The Flaming Coal

As the wheel climbed, it seemed as though I could see the entire universe—the beyond of beyond.

A seraph flew to me with a live coal and placed it on my lips and tongue. The fire burned across my face and down my throat into my heart.

The seraph said, "Let your words be fewer and only those that come from the throne."[18]

above the throne (Isa. 6:1–3). They are clothed with awesome fire as witnesses to the absolute purity of the holiness of God that is His alone. Only holiness can exist in such consuming flame. Therefore, the singing of these seraphim is the sweetest and purest known outside of God.

15. Voices from heaven that are heard on Earth, especially God's, may at times sound different from earthly voices (Ezek. 43:2; Rev. 1:10, 15).

16. Divine love is "the very flame of the Lord." It is unquenchable and imparted only by grace. The Lord's disciples are to set the intense flame of Jesus's love as a seal over their hearts (Song of Sol. 8:6–7). His love sustains each one while undergoing the burning away of all fleshly idolatry in body and soul (Song of Sol. 8:6; Matt. 3:11–12).

17. The divine fire is for all disciples who will count their old self dead in order to fully embrace God's purposes. They seek the reality of abiding in spirit "with Christ in God [the Father]" where they were placed by the new birth (Col. 3:1–3). The baptism with the Holy Spirit and fire that Jesus gives will burn away the chaff that is not of Christ in them (Matt. 3:11–12; Dan. 12:10). One is then drawn closer to the heart of the Father and learns to live in the consuming fire of His love (Deut. 4:24, 36; Ps. 50:3; Dan. 7:9–10).

18. A seraph touched the prophet Isaiah's lips with a burning coal (Isa. 6:6–7). God chose his mouth to be purified because control by the Spirit of one's tongue is the key to God's control of the whole body (James 3:2, 6). "No one [human being] can tame the tongue" (James 3:8). Christ Jesus alone has the authority (the right) and the power "to subject all things to Himself" (including the tongue) (Matt. 28:18; Phil. 3:21).

19. The Hebrew word for the spice *calamus* means "a stalk or reed." It is translated "right or upright" in Scripture. Christ Jesus alone is upright or righteous in His Father's eyes (2 Cor. 5:21; Rom. 10:3–4).

20. The primary root of the word *cinnamon* means "emitting an odor." The new heart of each Christian is a fragrant garden, enclosed and set apart for Christ alone. It is to be formed in the image of the heart of the Lord Jesus that is undivided in His consecration unto the Father (2 Chron. 16:9; Luke 10:22).

21. God spoke this message through an angel: "Jerusalem will be inhabited without walls . . . For I," declares the Lord, "will be a wall of fire around her, and I will be the glory in her midst" (Zech. 2:4–5).

The *fire of God* is a manifestation of the purity of His holiness (Lev. 10:1–3). The seraphim's song proclaimed that God would be a wall of fire to those being trained in holiness. The Holy Spirit would be the separation and protection for them around their

The first biblical example of *calamus* to mean moral uprightness was God saying, "Do what is right in His [God's] sight" (Exod. 15:26).

In the Song of Solomon, cinnamon grows in the locked garden that Jesus calls "my sister, my bride" (Song of Sol. 4:12–14).

Calamus and Cinnamon

The smell of calamus and cinnamon was intense within the flames. I knew that calamus means upright in God's sight.[19] Cinnamon bespeaks the smell of holiness that comes from a heart pure before God, holiness of heart.[20]

Song of the Seraphim

The thousands of seraphs sang:

Let all in heaven,
Let all on earth
Proclaim His holy name.

Let all in heaven,
Let all on earth
Speak of His glory and fame.

A wall is used to separate and protect that which it encloses.

A wall of fire around our hearts,
A wall of fire around our minds,
A wall of fire around our feet,
Holy is His name.[21]

I looked at Jesus. The more they sang, the more light poured through His skin. "Your skin," I said, "it is so…different. It is as though light comes from it."

Those Who Draw Near

The skin of Moses's face also shone from being in the presence of God and His glory (Exod. 34:29–30, 35).

"Light does pass through My skin," He said. "But Anna, light can pass through your skin, for those who draw near to Me are light bearers. The nearer they come, the more light passes through their skin to others."[22]

"Like Moses?" I asked. I thought to myself of how separated his life became. Moses would go alone to the tent of meeting, alone to the mountaintop, alone with a veil eventually over his face because of the glory of God upon his countenance. The Lord read my thoughts.

"There is a separation that occurs, Anna. As one draws closer to God, there is a burning away of the dimness over the eyes of the mind and the eyes of the heart. For these the world loses its luster. The ingenuity of mankind becomes a passing spectacle that only causes the person to turn with a sigh back to God."[23]

He continued, "When the True comes, that which is but a copy, but a reworked speck of a magnificent whole, cannot hold that person's interest. God alone can capture their spirits, hearts, souls and bodies."

Adoration

As the fiery wheel reached its zenith, Jesus began to praise the Father. The seraphim burned more brightly in response to His adoration. "O incomparable Father, who or what is like You? The vast universe is held in existence by the might of Your power. Each hair is numbered because of Your tender compassion. Who is like You, Father? How awesome in majesty! How faithful in covenant! Unsurpassed in beauty! Blessed are those who draw near to You. Blessed are those who dwell in You. They will forever praise You and minister to You the desires of Your heart—love undivided, burning in the zeal of holiness, suitable for God alone. And those who draw near, those who enter, they will never go out again."[24]

Christ Transformed

He was transformed into pure worship before me. It was as though He could not help Himself. Once begun, He could only enter in more deeply, express His love more passionately, burn more intensely. The passion of His ardor came from complete understanding. It was love

hearts, their minds and their feet (their conduct or walk) (Phil. 4:6–7; Gal. 5:25).

22. "Jesus took with Him Peter and James and John his brother, and brought them up on a high mountain by themselves. And He was transfigured before them; and His face shone like the sun, and His garments became as white as light" (Matt. 17:1–2; Rev. 1:16; 10:1).

A heavenly messenger prophesied to the prophet Daniel about the last days: "Those who have insight will shine brightly like the brightness of the expanse of heaven, and those who lead the many to righteousness, like the stars forever and ever" (Dan. 12:3).

Jesus said that at the end of the age, "The righteous will shine forth as the sun in the kingdom of their Father" (Matt. 13:43).

23. Christians "see" (perceive) the true reality of the deceptive world system with the eyes of their new hearts first (Col. 2:8). Paul prayed for the Ephesians that "the eyes of your heart may be enlightened, so that you will know what is the hope of His calling, what are the riches of the glory of His inheritance in the saints, and what is the surpassing greatness of His power toward us who believe" (Eph. 1:18–19).

24. Jesus promised the overcoming Christians of the church in Philadelphia to be made pillars (given permanent places) in the temple of God. For He said, they "will not go out from it any more" (Rev. 3:12).

25. The zeal of Christ's love for His Father ("Your house") consumed Him (John 2:17). Such love "surpasses [human] knowledge." It is beyond comprehension (Eph. 3:19).

26. Pure *nard* is a very costly spice (John 12:3). The word *nard* (spikenard in the King James Version) is from the Hebrew root meaning "light."

The figure of the Father is visible in heaven by the pure, uncreated light of His nature (1 John 1:5).

27. Eternal life is offered freely to any who will receive and grow up into Christ (John 3:16). Many may accept the invitation (Matt. 22:10). But "the worries and riches and pleasures of this life" hinder the forming of Christ in some of them (Luke 8:14).

and praise that sprang from knowledge such that only complete union can bring forth.

As I watched, He had passed into an ecstasy of love and passion that was incomprehensible to me. The intensity and purity of His expression—His all-consuming zeal for His Father—was so far beyond my understanding that it was wholly "other."[25]

The divine light was made visible in Jesus when He was transfigured. His whiteness was beyond any earthly whiteness (Mark 9:3).

God invites all people to draw near to Him (Matt. 11:28).

He burned with a laser-white light. By being with Him, I was carried further in my own passion and zeal for God. It was as though the alabaster vial had been broken, for the smell of costly spikenard accompanied this spiraling upward. He became pure, uncreated light.[26]

Eventually, the white flame of His ardor for His Father subsided, like the intensity of a powerful light being reduced. He became the Lord I could comprehend. "Love God, Anna," He said. "He has invited you into His heart. Do not treat this as a trivial invitation."[27]

Leaving the Garden

The wheel of fire stopped at the apex of its rotation. Suddenly Jesus became the white Eagle. "Climb onto My back," He said.

I did so, lying down and putting my arms around His neck as I had done many times. Then from the top of the wheel, He began to fly.

"The time has come," He said.

Chapter Seven

The Valley of the Shadow of Death[1]

The great white Eagle plunged through the darkness. I held on to Him with all of my might, burying my face in His feathers and keeping my eyes tightly shut. With all that was within me, I concentrated on clinging to Him.

Although the dive was as harrowing as dropping miles in a vertical, greased chute, the white Eagle landed gently in the sheepfold within the second heaven. This dark, dank, spiritual realm is populated with demons of great grotesqueness. It is Satan's headquarters.

The Sheepfold

Within this corrupted spiritual territory, our Lord retains an outpost—His sheepfold.[2] It is a safe haven for His own.

The *sheepfold* is a manifestation of His lordship in the middle of the base of Satan's worldwide operation (Eph. 1:20–22; Col. 2:15).

A stone wall encloses the protected area. The wall is topped with thorns, as it might be if it were actually a desert sheepfold. A covered, though open, shelter and one wooden bench are within the wall. There is one gate only into this protected area. Although surrounded by defiling contamination, the sheepfold remains inviolate.

The Preparation

The white Eagle became Jesus. Strangely, He said nothing. Instead, He handed me a pair of porpoise shoes dyed red.[3] I had worn these shoes before when the Lord had taken me into this territory. Now I sat down on the bench near the gate and began to put them on my bare feet. I was puzzled.

Porpoise skin is water repellent. It was the outer covering on the tabernacle (tent) in the wilderness (Exod. 26:14).

1. "Even though I walk through the valley of the shadow of death, I fear no evil [harm]" (Ps. 23:4).

2. Everything must bow the knee before Christ Jesus (Phil. 2:10). Like sheep, Christians are utterly dependent upon the Lord Jesus, the Good Shepherd (Ps. 61:3; 2 Cor. 3:5). This truth is seen dramatically when for God's purposes the Lord brings one of His flock into and out of the devil's headquarters (Ps. 23:5; John 10:9, 28).

3. Nothing of the corruption and death in the devil's domain, not even the watery slime on the ground, is to touch the believer (2 Cor. 6:17; 7:1). The shoes are red. They signify the shed blood of Christ on the cross by which Satan was defeated (Rev. 12:10–11; Col. 2:15).

He too sat down and began putting on a pair. As He put on the shoes, He spoke. "I asked you once before, Anna, and now I ask you again: Do you trust Me?"

"Yes, Lord," I answered. My reply was given with less assurance than the first time He had asked. I realized that before I had not lived up to my own expectations. Now, at least a grain of humility had been refined in me from the greater knowledge of my own frailty.

The *shepherd's staff* was an emblem of God's authority and power in the hand of Moses (Exod. 4:2–5, 17; 17:8–11).

"I have need of you," He said as He rose to His feet. His shepherd's staff appeared in His right hand.[4] With His left hand, He reached down to help me rise. He looked solemn. "When you were here before, I warned you to touch nothing. Now I tell you to speak nothing. Walk straight ahead of you, and when requested, do only that which I indicate to you." He searched my face. "Anna," He said, "carefully follow My instructions."[5] He spoke with a quiet intensity that suggested great, perhaps fatal, danger.

I nodded. The gravity of His words made an audible reply impossible. As He opened the gate, He exhaled a breath as if centering Himself before a trial. We went out. The gate closed behind us. I was nervous. I followed in His footsteps, holding on to the back of His garment.

The Descent

I expected to see what I had seen before when we visited this diabolical place. I did not. Instead we began a dark descent.

I could feel something sliding past my feet on the path. Primitive revulsion made me try to get my feet out of the way. After my eyes adjusted to the darkness, I could see by the light emanating from Jesus that vipers were slithering all over the wet incline.

I momentarily froze, losing my grip on the Lord's garment. I could not call to Him. All I could do was move forward. By His light I could see that the snakes fled from Jesus. But would they flee from me?

Everything within me was becoming fragmented. I knew that I had to center my focus. I stopped looking down. Instead I fixed my eyes on the Lord.

Now I could not see the snakes, but still I could feel them slither past me. I walked haltingly. Every part of my body was tense, almost rigid.

Test of the Soul—the Emotions[6]

Satan tries to shock, startle, or frighten a Christian to gain access to that one's soul (mind, emotions, and will).

Suddenly I heard a familiar sound. It was our dog barking with excitement, as if he had heard me coming. We had raised this dog from the time he was a puppy. He was greatly loved.

Instinctively I turned my head in the direction of the welcoming bark. Just as quickly, however, I snapped it back to fix my eyes on Jesus. I knew that the darkness and the slippery incline had disoriented me. I was trying to keep my attention centered.

Then I heard the sound of a speeding vehicle coming toward the sound of the dog's welcoming barks. The wheels of the vehicle squealed, as if to make an emergency stop. There was a bump, a sickening thud, and then the sound of the dog yelping as if he had been hit.

I stopped again, catching my breath in short gasps, my ears straining to hear the location of the sound. It sounded as though the dog was crying in pain. But because of his love for me, he was still trying to drag himself to me. It tore my heart out.

Then I heard my mother cry out. Her voice sounded near the dog's yelps. "Help!" she cried.

My breath almost stopped as I strained to hear. I could not call the Lord.

"Help the dog, Anna!" my mother's voice cried out.

4. David said of the Lord, the Good Shepherd: "Your rod and Your staff, they comfort me. You prepare a table before me in the presence of my enemies" (Ps. 23:4–5; John 10:11).

5. As long as Christians obey the present word of the Lord Jesus to them, the enemy does not have ground (legal right) to accuse them and possibly obtain permission to afflict them (Rev. 12:10; Luke 22:31; Job 2:4–6). The devil can only tempt an obedient Christian (1 Thess. 3:5; Heb. 2:18).

6. He uses these means and others to open the soul. Once the soul has been destabilized, he proceeds with his main objective. Often the emotions are the first objective because they are the most difficult to regulate since they bypass the mind. Therefore, the human soul life must be tested (tempted and tried) time after time until Christians have confidence only in the soul life of Christ in them.

The devil seeks to gain the legal right to afflict a Christian by tricking that one to accept a lie. In unending variations, he uses the same method that he used with Eve in the garden. Thus, he leads the disciple to sin.

7. Soulish affection is the hardest area of a Christian's emotional life to yield to the cross. Peter confessed Jesus as the Christ by revelation from God. Then immediately he let his unsanctified devotion for the Lord Jesus allow the devil to speak through him (Matt. 16:16–17, 21–23). God requires that we love Him always by the Spirit with all our being and for His sake (Matt. 22:37; 2 Thess. 3:5). Then the Spirit can govern our giving love to people so that it is of Jesus and for His sake (Col. 1:8; John 13:34).

8. Satan cannot speak the truth—only half-truths or lies (John 8:44). The truth of His Father's words enabled Jesus to expose the deceit of the devil in the wilderness testing (Matt. 4:4, 7, 10–11). Truth is the first piece of the armor of God given to the Christian to withstand the evil one and his demons (Eph. 6:13–14).

9. The present, proceeding word from Scripture is the defense that Jesus used against the enemy in the wilderness temptations (Heb. 4:12; Matt. 4:4). Satan also uses the Word of God, but it is not Spirit inspired.

God's Word for this present test was, "If anyone comes to Me, and does not hate his own father and mother and wife and children and brothers and sisters, yes, and even his own [soul] life, he cannot be My disciple" (Luke 14:26). We must always choose obedience to God's Word instead of fleshly (natural) affection (Matt. 10: 37–39; John 12:25).

Suddenly my emotions, which had been as scattered as a frightened bird loosed from a cage, snapped into a steely lucidity. Satan had overplayed his hand. The voice that had sounded like my mother's had called me "Anna." My real mother would not have called me that because on Earth my father and mother had named me Ann.

Everything had happened so quickly that I did not have time to think. Satan had bypassed my mind and engaged my emotions. But it was a lie…a lie![7]

Recovery

When a believer knows the truth in a particular matter and holds to it, the deception of the enemy is dispelled (John 8:31–32; 2 Thess. 2:9–12).

I began to move forward again with tiny, frozen steps. With recognition of the deception, the sounds ceased.[8] But I was shaken from having my emotions shredded. Jesus was ahead of me, but the distance between us was widening. I needed to move more quickly to catch up with Him.

Inwardly, I began to quote Scripture. "Unless you hate father and mother…,"[9] I said, seeking to move more swiftly.

Test of the Soul—the Mind

The Greek word for divination is *python*. It is the name of the mythical serpent that guarded the Delphic oracle in ancient Greece. People thought that secret truths were revealed at the oracle.

Satan primarily tries to disorient people through sudden, dreadful thoughts of pain and tragedy.

Suddenly the small snakes became huge ones. I shuddered within myself, "O Lord!" I hoped that Jesus would turn around. These pythons had lettering on them, symbols or formulas.[10]

One gigantic snake reared up to fling itself at me, to knock me down. I knew that if it knocked the breath out of me, it could wrap itself around me and squeeze the life out of me.

"Divination," I said within myself. "Witchcraft, sorcery, the powerful black arts."[11]

Shock and fear scrambled my mind. I dared not scream or dodge its lunge. The incline had become steeper and slicker. I did not know if I could keep my footing. The snake lunged, barely missing me. Then three or four huge snakes reared up at the same time to lunge. I was frozen on the path, terrified.

Suddenly, horrible mutilations flashed into my mind in rapid succession. It was as though I was being dismembered and disemboweled. Pictures of horrible tortures assailed me, mixed with visions of being buried alive or falling from a plane.

Angels of Light[12]

Swiftly the horrific pictures fled from before my eyes. In their place the huge snakes became giant, demonic beings, richly attired.

They spoke to me, "There is greater power than you ever dreamed of having. Power," they said together. "You can have anything you want. You can take it with this power."[13]

"They must have showed me the mutilations that will occur if I refuse their offer of demonic power," I said within myself. "They want to terrify me, paralyze my mind." I steeled myself. "I will not be afraid of them." I continued to inch forward. "I will not be intimated." Within myself I began to repeat, "'Not by might, nor by power, but by My Spirit,' says the Lord."[14] They were right in the steep path. I was getting closer to them. "'Not by might, nor by power, but by My Spirit,' says the Lord."

The large demons were right ahead of me. I braced myself and kept moving ahead. Incredibly, I passed right through them. I was perplexed.

Recovery

"They are phantoms," I said within myself. "Not real at all. They are a trick of the mind."

I did not want to lose this clear understanding, for Satan had managed to take clarity and perspective away from me in this place. Since I was seeing more clearly, I began to repeat the Word of God within myself again. I moved ahead more rapidly now that presence of mind had been restored. I dared not call to Jesus. I needed to remember that.

10. Often magic formulas, omens, curses, spells, and such things are used to gain power and knowledge from the enemy (Acts 16:16). God strictly forbids all such practices (Deut. 18:9–12).

Serpents, dragons, and scorpions are major symbols of the satanic in Scripture (Rev. 12:9; Luke 10:19). The huge pythons represent the black arts directed against the mind of disciples to cause them to lose some control of their thinking. A Christian need accept only one lie from the devil. This gives him ground (legal right) to coerce part of that person's mind (Gen. 3:4–7, 13).

11. The mind also may become partially paralyzed by fear (or by other causes like passivity or a blank mind). Evil spirits are then able to insert flashing thoughts and pictures into our brains. God does not break into our normal ways of thinking like this.

Though the enemy usually attacks our emotions first, the real battleground is in the thought life of the disciple (2 Cor. 11:3). It is the weakest part of our being, especially for Christians whose minds have not been fully renewed (Rom. 12:2; Eph. 4:23). All of the devil's strongholds, such as pride, deception, unbelief, and disobedience that result from human speculations, must be torn down (2 Cor. 10:5).

12. Sometimes "Satan disguises himself as an angel of light" (2 Cor. 11:14). In his former life in heaven, he was called "star of the morning," a Hebrew word meaning "shining one" (Isa. 14:12). In his present state, his light is not real but a deception (Rev. 12:9). True light is of God (John 1:9; 1 John 1:5).

13. The devil made the offer of the power and glory of his world system to Jesus in the wilderness (Matt. 4:8–9). But all power belongs to God (Rev. 19:1; Job 1:12; 2:6).

14. The Spirit brings Scripture to mind to help us recognize deception. "'Not by might, nor by power, but by My Spirit,' says the Lord of hosts" (Zech. 4:6).

However, Jesus began to move ahead more quickly than I could keep up. He was disappearing into the darkness of the valley ahead of me. I wanted to cry out and run to Him. But I remembered His admonition.

"Surely He will sense that I have fallen behind," I said within myself. "Surely…," I repeated frantically within.

The will is meant by God to be the most effective part of the disciple's soul.

Test of the Soul—the Will[15]

I continued to place one foot ahead of another. Now, however, I was in total darkness—black, no light, no sound, nothing—nothing.

Blackness is terrifying. It is the kind of terror that makes you want to scream just to relieve the tension you are experiencing. I felt that I was suffocating with no escape. Evil pressed in on me.

I began to talk to myself within, trying to cling to a measure of sanity. "Any minute I will see His light ahead of me," I thought.

No, nothing. I was groping with my feet on the dangerous incline. I had to remain upright. I was alone. I could not sense His presence at all. I prayed within myself. The prayers were as heavy as stone. I quoted the Word within myself. But it seemed to have no power.

"O God," I thought, "don't leave me!" Suddenly I caught myself. "No," I said within. "I will not accuse Him of leaving me. I will not feel abandoned."

Nothingness

For the child of God who loves the light, darkness is torturous. For those accustomed to His presence, His absence is excruciating.

I thought, "In my Lord's agony on the cross, He must have experienced this blackness.[16] Only He had all the sins of the world upon Him.[17] Cruel demons must have been released to torture Him."

An overcoming Christian is one in whom Jesus the Lord shares His overcoming of all the enemies of God. They are sin, self, the devil, the world, the flesh, and death (Matt. 16:24; Col. 2:15; John 8:29; 16:33; Rom. 8:3, 8–9).

"They Overcame"

I began to confess within myself the benefits of the blood of Jesus and the victories He had won through His broken body. I testified within myself—to myself—of the attributes found within Him and of the victories won by Him.[18]

Somehow, dishonoring God became more heinous than perishing. I did not want to put the Lord to open shame. I did not want to crucify Him to myself again.[19] I did not want to cry out and disobey in this place where the enemy could win a victory and laugh Him to scorn again.

"No," I said within, "no accusations. No bitterness. No more 'whys.' No more a need to be pampered. By His grace I will walk the course He needs me to walk. Him...not me. His honor...not my safety. His glory, not mine. Him. Him. He alone is worthy. He alone is worthy.

"O my God," I sobbed within. "I love You so much. What does this matter? Though You slay me, yet will I trust You.[20] What does it

15. The enemy's final objective is to recapture some part of the will of the Christian. God continually preserves in us the freedom of the will to choose Christ or to reject Him in every situation (Philem. 14; Rev. 22:17). The light of Christ can penetrate any darkness, and the darkness cannot overpower it (John 1:5). That is why Jesus is the true light within every human being, waiting to be chosen (John 1:9).

Satan's third test was of the will, the capacity to choose. Under the authority of the Holy Spirit, the sanctified will is to regulate the whole person.

16. "Now from the sixth hour darkness fell upon all the land until the ninth hour. About the ninth hour Jesus cried out with a loud voice, saying, *'Eli, Eli, lama sabachthani?'* that is, 'My God, My God, why hast Thou forsaken Me?'" (Matt. 27:45–46).

17. "He Himself bore our sins in His body on the cross, so that we might die to sin and live to righteousness" (1 Pet. 2:24; Isa. 53:5).

18. "And they [the overcomers] overcame him [Satan] because of the blood of the Lamb and because of the word of their testimony, and they did not love their life even when faced with death" (Rev. 12:11).

19. Christians "who have once been enlightened and have tasted of the heavenly gift and have been made partakers of the Holy Spirit, and have tasted the good word of God and the powers of the age to come, and then have fallen away, it is impossible to renew them again to repentance since [or while] they again crucify to themselves the Son of God and put Him to open shame [before His enemies]" (Heb. 6:4–6).

To be a friend of God is to be an enemy of the world system of self-love (James 4:4).

20. The Spirit brought to mind the words of Job 13:15: "Though He slay me, yet will I trust Him" (NKJV). Others besides Job in Scripture have come to the point of possible death and realized that they loved God more than their earthly lives (Esther in Esther 4:16; Paul in Acts 21:13).

21. "For if we live, we live for the Lord; or if we die, we die for the Lord; therefore whether we live or die, we are the Lord's" (Rom. 14:8).

22. When we love the Father, the love of the things of the world is not in us. "Do not love the world [system controlled by Satan] nor the things in the world. If anyone loves the world, the love of the Father is not in him. For all that is in the world, the lust of the flesh and the lust of the eyes and the boastful pride of life, is not from the Father, but is from the world" (1 John 2:15–16). When the Holy Spirit fills our hearts with the love of God, the power of the love of the flesh is overcome. For there is no room for loving our fleshly self when we hope for the glory of God that satisfies every need (Rom. 5:2–5; Phil. 4:19).

23. The Lord said, "If anyone wishes to come after Me, he must deny himself [the unsanctified expression of the soul through the body], and take up his cross daily and follow Me. For whoever wishes to save his [soul] life [of his own mind, emotions, and will] shall lose it, but whoever loses his [soul] life for My sake, he is the one who will save it" (Luke 9:23–24). The crux of sanctification—the eye of the needle for disciples—is to come to the place of hating one's own thoughts, desires, will, words, and actions apart from God (John 12:25).

The Spirit then begins to pour the Father's love for the Son into our hearts (John 17:26; Rom. 5:5). A point can be reached where we no longer worry about what happens to us on Earth as long as Christ is exalted (Phil. 1:20–21).

24. "The law of the Spirit of life in Christ Jesus has set you free from the law of sin and of death" (Rom. 8:2). Christians know that this is true of us in Christ in heaven. It also must become true in our experience of Christ in us on earth.

25. The first aspect of our growing mature (complete) in Christ is for Him to share His overcoming of all of God's enemies with us (Rev. 3:21). Then we are able to receive more and more of the Father's love for the Lord Jesus (John 17:26). This love for Christ controls us, "holding [us] to one end and prohibiting [us] from considering any other" (2 Cor. 5:14, Wuest). The capacity of our new, spiritual heart is boundless because it is created in the image and likeness of Jesus's heart (Col. 3:10; Eph. 4:24). No distress can separate us from the Father's love for us in Christ, but in all these things we triumph through His unconquerable love (Rom. 8:35–37).

We cannot remove the inborn love for ourselves, nor can we of ourselves love Christ. But the Holy Spirit can contain the first one and impart the second to us (Gal. 5:17; 2 Thess. 3:5).

matter? If I live or die, I am Yours.[21] That is all that matters. I love You beyond danger or mayhem or darkness or death."

Love

Suddenly, my heart cracked open. I was unable to contain the love that I now felt. I burst free, from what I did not know. It was as though love for the Lord had loosed me from a prison, as though I had pulled away from the gravity of the flesh.[22] I loved Him. I loved Him more than I wanted to preserve myself.

The natural self cannot be obliterated, but it can be kept confined and powerless by the Spirit of God (Gal. 5:16–17; 1 Pet. 4:1–2). This is the meaning of carrying your own cross continually as Jesus does His.

It was a strange, exhilarating experience. It was as though I was loosed from self.[23] Not that I did not realize, even then, that the cross would need to be applied to my flesh nature daily to hold it in the place of death. But something had happened. I had broken free.

No longer would it be as easy to embrace the flesh. I would need to work deliberately at employing the flesh now, whereas before it had seemed inevitable. Now I was being drawn into the orbit of the Son of God. I could already feel myself moving toward Him more rapidly. The law of the Spirit of life in Christ Jesus was the new gravity that was drawing me into God Himself.[24]

Love like a river began to rush through my heart—love unhindered, unstoppable, unimaginable.

A Speck of Light

Quickly a tiny speck of light appeared in the path ahead of me. I made the calculation that if that light had been a little to the right or left, the darkness would have hindered me from seeing it. I continued to move forward. Within the light emanating from Him stood Jesus.

He was waiting for me in the valley. As I drew nearer, He smiled and opened both of His arms. I seemed to cover the distance between us supernaturally and was in His embrace. Even within His arms I dared not speak, for He had requested this. He likewise said nothing. His embrace said it all.

All Christians are tested in the area of the three components of the human soul—our own thoughts, desires, and choices.

He within me, by the power of the Holy Spirit, had demonstrated His victory. The enemy did not entangle my emotions, corkscrew my mind, or pervert my will. Love, His love, was triumphant within me.[25]

There was little time to rejoice, however, for past His shoulder I saw a very large black building brooding in the wet darkness.

Chapter Eight

Satan's Trophy Room

Jesus held me at arm's length, studying my face. He smiled, turned, and led the way toward the building.

The atmosphere in the valley was red as though the building was catching the light from a distant forest fire. It was eerie. It cast long shadows across the valley.

The shadows traveled up the building until they reached two enormous black marble dragons on top.[1] These dragons were facing each other with their wings uplifted and touching like the cherubim over the mercy seat.

White marble stone (or alabaster) represents permanence and beauty (Esther 1:6). The color *black* is a perversion of the symbolism that God uses with the color white.

The building was a mockery of the ark of the covenant.[2] It was deathly dark as if it were made from antimatter. The black marble exterior was wet, and the overbearing humidity made it difficult to breathe.[3]

Shadow Warriors

Thousands of soldiers were standing shoulder to shoulder on all four sides of the building. They wore an ancient style of armor whose design I had never seen. These warriors were camped around the building,

1. Satan uses for this building a black imitation of the marble that was used to build Solomon's temple (1 Chron. 29:2). The dragons are demons that seemed to be encased in a coating of simulated marble. Fear so pervades everything in Satan's realm that nothing is merely decorative but must be useful in repelling any invader.

2. The two black marbleized dragons were a derisive mimicking of the two golden cherubim whose wings touched above the ark of the covenant (Exod. 25:18–20).

3. There are bodies of water in Satan's domain in the *second heaven* (this term explained in note 5 of chapter 2). All the ground is wet because the devil and his horde hate dry places. Parched ground reminds them of their coming end in the lake of fire (Matt. 12:43; Rev. 20:10).

4. "But the Levites [tribe of Levi] shall camp around the tabernacle of testimony, that there may be no wrath [of God] on the congregation of the sons of Israel" (Num. 1:53). Only the Levites attended to the obligations of the tabernacle, the sanctuary of God, on behalf of the rest of the Israelites (Num. 18:2,4).

5. "Now the two angels came to Sodom in the evening as Lot was sitting in the gate of Sodom... They turned aside to him and entered his house... and they struck the [evil] men who were at the doorway of the house with blindness" (Gen. 19:1, 3–4, 11; Deut. 28:28–29). The men of Sodom were rendered incapable of doing the wickedness that they intended.

The Lord Jesus has placed the soldiers and other creatures in Satan's domain in a state of temporary, suspended animation or immobility.

6. As the sun set each day, the ancient Egyptians believed that the sun god began his daily travel through the black underworld. They observed that monkeys chattered effusively at sunset. They assumed that these animals were paying homage to the sun god as he entered the darkness. Consequently, some of the first demons the god met in the underworld were pictured as monkeys who praised and adored him.

7. Satan undoubtedly helped to formulate this language to foster rebellion against God (Gen. 11:1, 4, 6–9).

8. There are two biblical accounts of the rebellion of a magnificent cherub in heaven (Isa. 14:12–14; Ezek. 28:12–18). He was called in Hebrew *Helel,* meaning "shining one" and translated as "star of the morning" (Isa. 14:12).

The Levites were a buffer between the judgment of God going out upon the other tribes who were always rebellious (Deut. 9:7). In Satan's domain the soldiers guard against the reverse—anything of God coming in.

just as the Levites were instructed to camp around the desert tabernacle.[4] None of them moved when we passed through their numbers, however.

"Why?" I wondered. I glanced down their ranks to see if I could discern the reason for their inaction. The faces within the helmets were shadow. But their eyes tracked us.

I suddenly remembered how the two angels that were sent to rescue Lot had temporarily blinded the men of Sodom.[5] Jesus, I thought, must have rendered these demons inert. They were alert. But they were incapable of action. They held their ranks like clay soldiers buried with early Chinese emperors.

The Approach

Satan has these marbleized monkey demons outside of his trophy room because he desires above all to be worshiped (Matt. 4:9).

After passing through most of the ranks of the soldiers, Jesus approached the building. The structure had the appearance of a gigantic mausoleum. As we drew near, I could see that the black marble dragons were breathing. So were the black marble monkeys that formed a decoration around the top of the building.[6] These leered down at us.

The massive double doors unlatched as we approached. They opened slowly. Each door was of great weight. They pictured Satan's supposed conquests. They were executed in bronze relief and were similar to the doors of European cathedrals that often depict the life of Christ.

Within

Cuneiform writing dates as far back as the ancient Sumerians and Babylonians. It is the world's oldest written language in existence.

The doors opened outwardly to give us entry to a large, windowless room. The smell within the room was odious. The room, like the valley, seemed lit by distant fires. My eyes traveled up to a heavy, raised cornice. It formed a crown around the top of the room. A text was written upon it in an ancient language of wedges and triangles.[7]

Jesus waved His hand, and the lettering changed so that I was able to read the inscription. The text proclaimed Satan's five "I wills" with which he intended to vault himself above the throne of God and crown himself king of the universe.[8] I shuddered.

The phrase "the terror by night" in Psalm 91:5 may refer to this vampire bat that was thought to suck blood from humans in the darkness.

Hanging upside down from this cornice were half-female, half-batlike demons—the Lilith, the vampire demons that hunt at night.[9] They were repugnant. I dropped my gaze and saw the reason for the stench in the room. Bat guano.

On Display

Display tables flanked either side of the room. These were covered with what seemed to be black velvet. The objects on display were shining with light from within. The objects were beautiful, not because of exquisite workmanship nor because they were encrusted with jewels. Instead, they seemed to have some beauty bestowed upon them by God. They were His, for His people had used them. Now they sat on display like war mementos. I quickly glanced over the tables in astonishment. This was a trophy room.

Stolen From God

Each article was labeled with a clay marker. The same wedges and triangular-shaped writing was on these markers as was on the cornice. Again, Jesus waved His hand. The language changed so that I could read the labels.

On display were the just measure, Miriam's tambourine, Bezalel's renderings for the workers (of the patterns given to Moses on the mount), the widow's bowl, various musical instruments of ancient design, and on and on.[10] We passed article after article that had been used by God in some extraordinary way and then stolen from Him. I could only suppose that these had been taken into the enemy camp because of the sins of God's people.

Musical instruments in the Bible are mainly associated with the reign of King David (1 Chron. 16:5). They were preserved at least until the time of Nehemiah some five hundred years later (Neh. 12:36).

Five times he spoke assertions in his heart beginning with the words "I will . . ."—"I will ascend to heaven; I will raise my throne above the stars of God [the angels]; and I will sit on the mount of assembly in the recesses of the north. I will ascend above the heights of the clouds; I will make myself like the Most High" (Isa. 14:13–14).

9. The Hebrew word for this female vampire demon is *Lilith*. The word is translated "night monster" in Isaiah 34:14.

10. God commanded the Israelites: "You shall have a full and just measure [*ephah*, in Hebrew]." An *ephah* was a measure of grain.

The prophetess Miriam, Moses's sister, with the other women celebrated God's victory over the Egyptians at the Red Sea by singing and dancing with tambourines (timbrels) (Exod. 15:20–21).

God appointed Bezalel of the tribe of Judah to supervise all the craftsmanship in building the tabernacle in the desert (Exod. 31:1–5). He probably drew the plans on sheepskins.

In a terrible drought, the widow of Zarephath had only a handful of flour and a little oil. But she was willing to use this to prepare a small bread cake for the prophet Elijah. God promised her that she would eat from the flour bowl and the oil jar until the day that He sent rain (1 Kings 17:9–16).

11. Abimelech the priest kept Goliath's sword at the city of Nob. He gave it to David, who asked for it when he had to flee from Saul (1 Sam. 21:8–9).

12. David was a God-anointed harpist (1 Sam. 16:21–23). His worship of the Lord upon the harp led to his composing many of the psalms (Ps. 144:9).

13. A *fresco* is a painting applied on a moist, plaster surface with the colors ground up in water or in a limewater mixture.

14. True light comes from God (John 1:9). Those in sin love darkness rather than the light (John 3:19). Satan uses candles so that there is as little light as possible.

15. A *hologram* is a three-dimensional image made by means of a laser beam on a photographic plate. The picture seems to have progressive action to someone moving in front of it.

16. From the beginning of the human race, people have been aware of hostile demons or spirits. These supernatural creatures

I was heartened, however, by the empty spaces on the tables. The labels showed articles that apparently had been rescued to be used by God's people again. Goliath's sword that was used by David was missing.[11] David's harp had been retrieved.[12] There was an empty space where once a banner had been displayed. As we neared the rear of the trophy room, I saw a white embroidered robe on a black clothes stand. It was luminescent. Satan had displayed it by itself, as if it were a prized acquisition.

The Fresco

It is well documented that human followers of Satan on Earth today use black candles.

Beyond this article on the rear wall was a vivid fresco.[13] Before the fresco burned black candles.[14] The flickering lights from the candles seemed to give the fresco a life of its own.

The fresco began at its base with recounting after recounting of brutal tortures of some of God's people. Those being tortured still seemed alive. The fresco was like none I had ever seen. It was similar to a hologram.[15] Light from the candles caused the pictures to have progressive action, so that those suffering suffered again, with Satan supposedly gaining the victory again and again. Barbarous.

The Throne of Skulls

The image of a satyr is an appropriate one for Satan. The domestic goat serves man's needs. The wild goat seeks high places to dwell, placing itself above others, serving no one, submitting to none (Ps. 104:18; Isa. 14:13–14).

My eyes traveled up this mountain of slaughter to about one-third of the way to the ceiling. Here the fresco began to depict a mound of skulls. This mound rose to a throne of skulls upon which sat the goat-like legs of a satyr.[16]

The enthroned creature had the torso and arms of a human but the head and horns of a goat. In this goat/man's left hand was held a picture of the world.[17] In his other hand was the location for two keys. The outline of the keys was still there, but the keys of death and of Hades had been removed from his hand.[18]

The fresco vaulted up until it covered the first half of the ceiling like a frightful canopy. It was Satan, goatlike, enthroned upon a mountainous pile of human skulls. He was gloating in sinister splendor. As God the Father is enthroned upon the praises of His people, Satan is enthroned upon his murderous savageries and sadistic cruelties.

A chill ran through me. Flickering light from the black candles caused Satan's face to move, seemingly to change before my eyes. His snake-like eyes glared at me.

The Embroidered Robe

Jesus touched my shoulder. I flinched. We began to walk toward the acquisition at the very back—the embroidered robe.

It was full length with long sleeves. The design of the garment was simple. A man or woman could have worn it. Its richness lay in the embroidered work that was executed in white gold of exceptional purity. The embroidery arose from the robe. The pattern was intricate and exceptionally beautiful. As I moved a little before the garment, all the colors within the radiance of the Father seemed to play across its surface.[19]

The weight and thickness of the various gold threads seemed to symbolize attributes of the Lord. The robe reflected these as if they had been woven into the garment.

The Embroidery

I had no idea a garment could communicate that which was of the character of Christ. Still, I wanted to move slightly before the embroidery to ascertain what was woven into the fabric.

were considered more like beasts, for they were ordinarily represented as hairy and frequenting desolate places (Isa. 34:13–14).

Part man and part goat, *satyrs* are mentioned in 2 Chronicles 11:15. In Leviticus 17:7, the word is translated "goat demons," to which some Israelites offered sacrifices.

17. "The whole world [Godless system of mankind] lies in the power of the evil one" (1 John 5:19; John 12:31).

18. Christ Jesus, after He was resurrected, descended as "a life-giving spirit" to *Hades,* or *Sheol* (the place of the departed spirits of people up to that time) (1 Cor. 15:45; Ps. 16:10). He recovered the keys of death and of Hades from Satan (Rev. 1:18). He then preached the gospel to the spirits there (1 Pet. 4:6). All authority and power had been given to Him (Phil. 2:9–10).

19. The radiance of the Father upon His throne is compared to the colors in a magnificent rainbow (Ezek. 1:28). The range of colors begins with dazzling white and moves through the full light spectrum (Rev. 4:3).

20. "So, as those who have been chosen of God, holy and beloved, put on a heart of compassion, kindness, humility, gentleness, and patience" (Col. 3:12).

21. "Bearing with one another, and forgiving each other, whoever has a complaint against anyone, just as the Lord forgave you, so also should you" (Col. 3:13).

22. "Beyond all these things put on [divine] love, which is the perfect bond of unity" (which binds everything together in complete harmony) (Col. 3:14).

23. Satan, an expert legalist, primarily accuses believers before God of disobedience to the greatest commandment: to love God (Rev. 12:10; Job 1:9–11; Matt. 22:37). The devil can detect this sin by observing the lack of love between the brethren. God's Word says, "The one who does not love his brother whom he has seen, cannot love God whom he has not seen" (1 John 4:20).

The lack of love in the body of Christ had reached a point where there were few Christians who manifested Christ's love for all the saints (Col. 1:4).

24. The garment is intended by the words, "That Christ may dwell in your hearts through faith" (Eph. 3:17). His love is to fill our hearts and overflow into the soul capacity of our will. The will is to steadfastly choose to love others in His name—"to preserve the unity of the Spirit in the bond of peace" (Eph. 4:2–3).

The garment was lost through disobedience to the Lord in His church. It could only be recovered through obedience. Christ Jesus does not act on Earth by the Holy Spirit apart from some obedient member of His body. And the Lord Jesus gives the Holy Spirit to those who obey Him (Acts 5:32).

25. "You shall love the Lord your God with all your heart, and with all your soul, and with all your mind" (Matt. 22:37). It is not possible for human beings of themselves to love God

I received the impression of "a heart of compassion, kindness, humility, gentleness, and patience."[20] The garment also reflected "bearing with one another" and "forgiving each other."[21] The thread that had the greatest weight and was the most frequently used was "love."[22]

In time past, the enemy must have argued successfully before God that he had legal right to have the garment of brotherly love.

These were part of the character of Christ that Paul enumerated in Colossians 3:12–14. He had told the body of Christ alive at that time to "put on" this garment. If he had told them to put it on, they must have had it in their possession but were not wearing it. I gathered that sin had eventually allowed the garment to be taken from God's children.[23] Sad. We had great need of it.

Jesus spoke to me quietly. "The garment is for the soul and heart. It is an inner garment that becomes visible through actions, through decisions that effect unity [oneness in Christ]."[24]

To be clothed in the Lord Jesus is to be beautiful in the eyes of the Father (Isa. 62:3; Zech. 9:16–17).

He continued, "I am the new, inner garment—others rather than self. The supreme Other is God [the Father] Himself—His rights, His needs, and His desires before all.[25] I have purchased you for our Father. I have washed you and clothed you with garments of holiness and beauty, garments of salvation and righteousness.[26] Anna, clothe yourself in Me—garments of salvation for the whole person [body, soul, heart, and spirit]. Clothe yourself in Me—attributes of righteousness that are beautiful to God [the Father]."[27]

I turned back to look at the robe. It was exquisite. The Lord's virtues woven into the garment had brought the body of Christ into "the perfect bond of unity." Paul had said this. How we needed it now.

He continued, "The embroidered garment is to be worn by those who are the bride. It was handed down in our family. Those who were entering into fuller union with Me wore it. There is none like it. It belongs to our household."

As I looked at the robe, I realized that to enter into a deeper relationship with Christ meant to enter into a deeper covenant with His body. The two are inseparable.[28]

The Recovery

"Carefully listen to Me," Jesus said softly. "I want you to remove the garment, then quickly climb onto My back." Without hesitation He placed His hand on the top of the velvet clothes rack.

I did not have time to think. Instantly I obeyed and began to remove the robe. The more I disengaged the garment, the harder He pressed on the top of the rack. I supposed He was compensating for some weight of glory in it. He continued to press on the top of the rack as I folded the embroidered robe so that it could be carried.

When the garment had been secured, I looked at Jesus. He gave the flicker of a smile, winked at me, and then removed His hand from the rack.

The Escape

Screams, sirens, and alarms of all kinds immediately arose together. All restraints were removed from everything within this realm.

Quickly the Lord became the white Eagle. Nervously I scrambled onto His back.

The vampire bat demons unfolded their huge wings. Their eyes were bloodred. They hissed through their fanged mouths. They were deranged with fury.

The doors to the front of the trophy room began to close. The white Eagle had to fly with His wings perpendicular to the floor to pass through the narrow opening. I tightened my arms and legs around Him, pressing the robe between my flattened body and His back. We passed through the opening like a single unit. With searing screams everything—bats, monkeys, dragons, soldiers—wrenched awake.

(Rom. 3:11, 13–15). However, when a Christian embraces Christ Jesus as one's only life, He becomes the new inner garment of ever-increasing love for God and for others (Col. 3:4; Phil. 1:9; Eph. 1:15).

26. "Shepherd the church of God which He [Christ] purchased with His own blood" (Acts 20:28; Rev. 5:9).

"Then I [God] bathed you with water" (Ezek. 16:9–10; Eph. 5:26).

"You shall make holy garments for Aaron your brother, for glory and for beauty" (Exod. 28:2; Ps. 29:2, NKJV).

"My soul will exult in my God; for He has clothed me with garments of salvation, He has wrapped me with a robe of righteousness" (Isa. 61:10).

27. Jesus says here that the whole of our being is to be saved—body, soul, heart, and spirit. "For the word of God is living and active and sharper than any two-edged sword, and piercing as far as the division of soul and spirit, of both joints and marrow [the body], and able to judge the thoughts and intentions of the heart" (Heb. 4:12; 1 Thess. 5:23).

God alone is righteous. This means that the divine nature is perfectly just (fair and impartial) and right (true and upright).

Human beings were created "that we might become the righteousness of God in Christ Jesus" (2 Cor. 5:21). Christians put on the new inner self (heart and spirit) that God created and that is becoming like Christ "in righteousness and holiness of the truth" (Eph. 4:24; Col. 3:10).

28. Christ Jesus is the head (Eph. 4:15). Christians are members of His body. We are part of Him and of each other (1 Cor. 12:27; Rom. 12:5). This means that a person who is in covenant with the Lord Jesus is also in covenant with all other believers. All Christians "are members [of Christ's body] belonging to one another" (Eph. 4:25, WUEST).

29. "Thanks be to God, who always leads us in triumph in Christ, and manifests through us the sweet aroma of the knowledge of Him in every place. For we are a fragrance of Christ to God" (2 Cor. 2:14–15).

30. The resurrected, ascended Lord Jesus has overcome and has been given all authority and power (Matt. 28:18; Phil. 3:21). He is the conquering Lion from the tribe of Judah (Rev. 5:5). The Hebrew word for the spice *onycha* comes from the root meaning "to roar" or "a lion." The release of this fragrance in Satan's domain is a reminder to its inhabitants that their leader has been defeated and that Christ's disciples share His authority "to tread upon serpents and scorpions, and over all the power of the enemy" in His name (Luke 10:19).

The word *cacophony* means a ghastly discordance of sounds.

It seemed as though everything in the corrupted stratum breathed down upon us in the chase—screeching, squalling, shrieking, a cacophony of blood-curdling sounds raised behind us. They were a frenzied juggernaut.

The marble dragons wrenched free from the top of the building with all the cracking and tearing that accompany a structure being torn apart. The black marble monkeys violently ripped free to join in the hunt. The Lilith and shadow warriors rabidly pursued. Whether hoofed, winged, clawed, flightless, or airborne, they pressed us. They were a murderous horde of frenzy and rage.

Quickly demons from elsewhere in the second heaven joined these in the chase. The whole second heaven sounded like one dangerous, wounded animal. The bone-chilling cries that went up from that place made my blood run cold. Horrific.

I clung to the white Eagle. It was a wild ride. Wild!...but exhilarating. I threw back my head, gulping air and laughing silently. Let them roar. That was all that it was, a roar. A show. I was with Jesus, and Jesus had won the victory! Let them roar!

Saffron and Onycha

The triumph of the cross and resurrection of the Lord Jesus over all the enemies of God is the victory of His faith in the Father (1 John 5:4; Heb. 2:13). It was a very costly victory and so is represented by *saffron*, a most expensive spice.

Suddenly there was a release of the fragrances of saffron and onycha. More costly than pure gold is the fragrance of saffron coming from the Lord's betrothed, for it symbolizes faith.[29] Onycha means "roar," but it is the authoritative roar of the Lion of the tribe of Judah.[30] These priceless fragrances released in the midheaven exhibited the Lord's overcoming victory.

The Flight

The white Eagle flew to the sheepfold. My porpoise shoes dropped from my feet as He swooped through the single gate and began to climb upward. The demons outside of the wall wailed in fury. They would be punished for allowing the garment to be taken. Both they and we knew this. The Lord continued to fly upward. There was great strength in the beat of His wings. The caterwauling became less distinct as we pulled away toward the third heaven.

While flying He spoke loudly to me so that I could hear Him. "You will wear this robe, Anna. It has been restored to the household of our Father. Now many will wear it."

With great power He continued to climb upward. Almost laughing He shouted to me, "Something old."

Chapter Nine

Something Borrowed, Something Blue

Swiftly, the white Eagle flew to the throne room in the third heaven. As He descended to the sea of glass, I noticed that there was no one in sight except my heavenly Father. I knew that others had to be there, but I could not see them.

I climbed from the white Eagle's back. Instantly, He became Jesus. He grabbed me around the waist, picking me up and swinging me around several times. He was laughing. I too was laughing. We were breathless from excitement when He set me down.

Presenting the Robe

"Come," He smiled, gesturing toward my Father. He put His left hand at the back of my waist to escort me forward.

I was still hugging the robe when we approached the throne. Jesus indicated that I should hand it to Him, and I did. The Lord held it up, letting it unfold to its full length in all its lustrous beauty. Then He laid it on the sea of glass before our Father.

"The covenant garment has been returned, Father," He said. We both prostrated ourselves before Him.

"I am pleased," my Father said. "Place it in My hands."

We rose. Jesus lifted the garment to our Father's hands of light. God the Father received it, cupping it in both hands as you would a baby chick. His hands became laser bright. I diverted my gaze. When I looked again, the garment had disappeared.

"Thank you," my Father said to me.

1. "He who overcomes... I [Jesus] will write on him... My new name" (Rev. 3:12). When Jesus writes His name on the forehead of an overcoming Christian, it signifies His open acknowledgment of that one's relationship as His betrothed and priest (Rev. 14:1). That person belongs to Him (1 Cor. 3:23).

2. An example of sealing the bondservants of God on their foreheads is Revelation 7:2–4. There the sealing insures the Lord's protection of these godly ones. (See also Revelation 9:4.)

Something New

"Now My sister, My bride," Jesus said, stepping between my Father and me. He turned to face me. "Look at Me," He said.

I did. My Father placed His hands of light on Jesus's shoulders. Then Jesus raised His right hand to my forehead. Light shot from His finger as He wrote upon me. It was a strange feeling.

"I write upon you My new name," He said.[1]

Sealing by the Holy Spirit authenticates and records the work of the Lord Jesus and His Father in the annals of heaven (Luke 10:20; Rev. 20:12).

"Sealed," said the Holy Spirit, who must have been present all along.[2] I felt a stamped pressure over the area where Jesus had just placed His name.

Now I had two names on my forehead. My Father had placed His name there when He asked me to be His chancellor (secretary to a king).

Jesus smiled at me. "Something new," He said.[3] "Now you have something new that you will wear forever. You are marked and sealed, My sister, My bride." My Father removed His hands from the Lord's shoulders.

Departure

Jesus took my right hand in His. "I must go," He said. "When I return, I will give you your heart's desire. This, My love, will seal your heart." He continued looking deeply into my eyes. He was so remarkably handsome, so beautiful in holiness, that at times He took my breath away. "Anna, I am coming soon," He said. He kissed my hand and looked into my eyes again. "Soon," He said—then disappeared.

With My Father

There was a pause as my Father allowed me to savor all that the Lord had said to me.

Eventually, God the Father said, "My child, come up here." He picked me up and placed me on the armrest of the throne.

"Anna, who is beloved of My Son," He said, "I would not only feed you from My hand, but also I would feed you from My very heart. Purity and holiness are not words that describe My qualities. They are tangible in the person of My Son. He is not a shadow or a reflection—but My heart manifested."

He continued, "The spirit alone can understand this. For the spirit comes from Me and understands its own. The spirit transcends all boundaries necessitated on Earth. Its knowing is a pure knowing because, as in the giving of all such gifts, pure knowing comes from above."

From His Hand

He held out His hand. "Here, Anna, eat this. Not manna from above, I feed you from My very heart."

His hand of light held in its palm something that looked like—nothing. I could see nothing in His hand. I looked toward His face area, then back to His hand.

Suddenly, the center of His hand burst into flame. The blaze shot up very high, then reduced to a small fire. Then the flame disappeared entirely. In the center of His hand of light were tiny, smoldering nuggets. They were coals or smoldering light (if light could burn).[4]

"Eat from My hand," He said.[5]

I leaned over and ate from His hand. My Father seemed pleased. I wondered why this gave Him such joy.

Scriptures repeatedly speak of God the Father's hands of light that are in the form of human hands (Jer. 1:9; Rev. 5:1, 6–7).

The Father's Desire

He spoke, "It is My desire to raise up many white eagles, Anna, to raise up a bride who will love My Son more than his or her own soul life. I desire to raise up a priesthood that will be incense in My nostrils, breathed in as a sacrifice and breathed out carrying life to others.[6]

God calls disciples to take three positions—His white eagles, the bride of His Son, and His priests.

3. In the last words of chapter 8, Jesus said that the recovered robe was "something old." He gives something new with His name on one's forehead. Jesus said, "Every scribe [teacher of sacred writings] who has become a disciple of the kingdom of heaven is like a head of a household, who brings forth out of his treasure things new [as to quality] and old [by reason of use]" (Matt. 13:52).

4. Within God the Father are the fiery coals of His nature of love (Deut. 4:24; 1 John 4:8). "Its flashes [of love] are flashes of fire, the very flame of the Lord" (Song of Sol. 8:6). The prophet Ezekiel saw coals of fire in the midst of the four living creatures that surround God's throne (Ezek. 1:13). Ezekiel then saw fire within the upper part of the figure of God on His throne (Ezek. 1:26–28). The outward radiance of the glory of God issues from His burning love within (Exod. 33:18–19).

5. God told Ezekiel the prophet to eat a scroll with words of woe written upon it. "So I [Ezekiel] opened my mouth, and He [God] fed me this scroll" (Ezek. 2:9–10; 3:1–2). Elsewhere in Scripture, God said, "And I bent down and fed them [the children of Israel]" (Hos. 11:4).

6. Disciples share in the ministry of Christ Jesus as the great white Eagle, the Bridegroom, and the great High Priest. Each of these three offices involves serving the Father through the Son.

Spiritual eagles represent the mantle of a prophet. *Eagle Christians* share in the prophetic ministry of Christ Jesus. Please see notes 19 and 20 of chapter 2.

The bride participates in the Bridegroom's oneness of love with the Father. That person manifests the glory of the divine love to others (John 17:22–23; 1 John 1:3). That one will share the reign of Christ the King beginning with His thousand-year kingdom on this earth (Rev. 20:6).

"I am your Father. A father's greatest desire is to have children to whom he can give all. I have such a child in My only begotten Son. But I long to raise up those of My adopted children who will draw near to Me and will not be satisfied with less. When such a one longs to eat from My hand, I am given much joy."

My Father's House

"Anna," He said, "life in this household is a simple life—meals around the family table, concern over family members, joy over births into the family, the celebration of anniversaries, the sharing of labors side by side. Simple."

I thought of the Lord's words, "Unless you are converted and become like children, you shall not enter the kingdom of heaven."[7] It was as though we needed to reach some saturation point in complexity before we were ready to turn and simply seek Him.

He continued, "The splendor of My majesty lies in the depth of My love."[8]

To Nest Above

"Your feathers are white now, My eagle," He said. "You are ready to nest above."

The first area that one enters in heaven is a vast park called *Paradise* (Rev. 2:7). Then there is Mount Zion on which the heavenly city of God is built. The center is the throne of God (Heb. 12:22–24).

He waved His hand to allow me to see an ivory palace on a high mountain.[9]

"This is yours, if you want it," He said.

"It is very beautiful, Father," I said slowly, not wishing to seem ungrateful. "But," I smiled wistfully, "I would never be there. I would always be away from home because I would want to be near You. You are my home, Daddy, just as You are my Beloved's home.[10] It has taken me a great deal of time to realize this. But now I know that there is nothing on Earth or in heaven that I desire. I want only my Father. I want Jesus. I want my friend, the Holy Spirit. If I may live where I would be the happiest, allow me to live amid the coals of fire within You.[11] Let me be a pillar in the temple of my God, never to go out again."[12]

My Father gave a small cry of pure joy. "You have chosen," He said.

Aloes

Suddenly, there was a release of the fragrance of aloes.[13] I knew that aloes meant "little tents" (so named for the intimacy of the bridal tent/ chamber). I too had chosen intimacy. I had chosen nearness to my God.

The meaning of the Arabic word *aloes* is "little tents." That definition derives from the triangular shape of the capsules from the *lignaloes* tree. Its resin provides this fragrant spice (Song of Sol. 4:14).

I breathed in the fragrance. So did my Father. It was satisfying.

The Crown

My Father continued, "Anna, My child, you will need to borrow your crown for the ceremony. You will wear it for this special occasion. But it will not be placed into your hands until your service on Earth is completed."[14]

A crown of gold came from my heavenly Father. He held it higher than my eye level. The crown had two gems. The large emerald that my Father had given me was in the center. The slightly smaller emerald given to me by Jesus was on the side. There were golden sockets for other jewels. No other gemstones were present at this time, however.

He continued, "I have added to your crown twenty-four sapphires."[15] These immediately appeared, encircling the large emerald on the front.

The number *twenty-four* signifies delegated authority in the heavenly realm (Rev. 4:4).

"Thank You, Daddy," I said. I wondered how I merited these gems.

The priest ministers Christ to the Father in prayer, fellowship, and worship, and manifests the life of God to those on earth (Eph. 6:18; 1 John 1:3; Phil. 3:3).

7. The Lord Jesus spoke these words in Matthew 18:3. He said that the proud must humble themselves (Matt. 18:4). We are to receive the kingdom in the simple faith of a child (Mark 10:15). Compared to God our Father, we are as very little children.

8. The awesome brilliance of the glory of God comes from the deepest part of who He is—Love (1 John 4:8; Exod. 33:18–19; 34:6–7).

9. In the city there are beautiful houses for all the redeemed who want to live in them (Luke 16:9; Heb. 11:16).

10. Christ Jesus lives at all times within the heart of His Father (John 1:18; Heb. 12:22–24). Yet He is able to appear elsewhere in heaven or on Earth (Acts 7:55; 9:5, 17).

When a person is born again into Christ, the new spirit is thereby also in the Father in heaven (Col. 3:3). Jesus desires that all those whom the Father has given Him might dwell with Him within the Father eternally (John 17:24). It will depend upon each believer's response over the years to this spiritual position in God.

11. Please see note 4 of this chapter.

12. Jesus said, "He who overcomes, I will make him a pillar in the temple of My God, and he will not go out from it anymore" (Rev. 3:12).

There is a temple in the present heaven (Rev. 11:19). But there will be no temple in the new heaven. The Lord God and the Lamb will be its temple (Rev. 21:22). We can begin to live in spirit within God while still walking on Earth (Col. 3:1–3; Phil. 3:20).

13. The small tent signified here is the tent on the housetop, a place of intimacy, sometimes called a bridal tent (2 Sam. 16:22).

14. The Father promises the crown of eternal life to those who persevere under trials and hold fast their love for God and His children to the end (Rev. 2:10; James 1:12). Also in Revelation 3:10–11, Jesus appears to refer to the crown of life for the same reasons.

15. The *blue color of sapphires* represents heaven in the Bible. (See note 22 of chapter 4.)

There is an old saying about brides: "Something old, something new; something borrowed, something blue."

My Father answered my thoughts. "You cannot earn the uncreated," He said. "But you can grow up [into Christ] to manifest the uncreated.[16] Something borrowed," He added, "something blue."[17]

The Attendants

My Father continued, "Twenty-four stars attend this crown.[18] They will bring to you the covenant garment, your crown, and your veil. These will dress you and attend you at the ceremony."

I saw that the crown had twenty-four points around the top. I wondered if there was some connection between the points of the crown and the angelic attendants. But He did not give an explanation.

"Is there something that I need to do, Daddy?" I asked.

The Hebrew word for the spice *henna* is translated "camphire" in the New King James Version. It is the same Hebrew word for "ransom" (Song of Sol. 4:13; Isa. 43:3). A bride in the Middle East applies the spice as a paste to her hands and feet on the night before her wedding.

He answered, "Sleep with henna on the palms of your hands and the soles of your feet as an outward sign [of an inner grace].[19] My Son is coming," He said. "Be ready."

Twenty-four angels that looked like young women appeared on the sea of glass. They were dressed in white. My Father handed to them the crown, the covenant garment, and the veil. The gown and veil also came from His own person.

"My child," the Father continued, "you have My blessing." His glory came from Him and kissed my forehead.[20]

"Thank You, Daddy," I said.

He picked me up and placed me in front of the twenty-four angels. "Go with your attendants," He said.

We all bowed. Then the angels parted to allow me to pass through their number. They escorted me from the throne room.

Instantly we were walking across the meadow in the Garden of God.

Henna

We walked to the tree of life. I was silent. I did not feel like talking. The angels were silent also. A very important event lay before me. But I did not know what it was or even how it would look.

Once we reached the trunk of the tree, the attendants busied themselves applying henna paste to the palms of my hands and the soles of my feet. The air hung heavy with the smell of the spice.

I held on to the tree that was strangely warm. I did not watch the angels because I was nervous, distracted.

Wishing to encourage me, one of the angels said, "Henna is the last of the spices." It faintly registered with me that I had been carried through Esther's preparations.[21]

When the statement did break through to my consciousness, I thought, "How right that I should enter the kingdom through the shed blood of Jesus, and now before this important event, an outward sign should be placed upon me." Within myself, I thanked the Lord for forgiving me. Then I continued aloud, "I ask for forgiveness for any sin that I have committed, and I forgive everyone for sins committed against me." I looked at the angels, "It says in the Word to confess your sins to one another."[22] The angels looked bewildered. Then I realized that angels do not confess to one another. I changed the subject. "Does anyone know what I am to do here at the tree of life?"

There is no sin to confess to one another in heaven.

Rest

"Rest," one angel said. "You have experienced much."

I laughed wearily. "Yes," I affirmed. "But I am very excited and nervous."

"Resting in the tree of life will strengthen you," another added. "We will lift you into its branches," said another. Before I could think about it, they lifted me. They began carrying me upward. It seemed as though the tree accommodated us, for we struck no branches.

High in the tree, they lay me in a juncture that cradled me. It was very comforting to rest in its branches.

"We will return when you have rested," an attendant said.

"Thank you," I smiled at them.

They were gone.

16. "Speaking the truth in love, we are to grow up in all aspects into Him who is the head, even Christ" (Eph. 4:15). The manifestation of Christ involves "always carrying about in the body the dying of Jesus, that the life of Jesus also may be manifested in our body. For we who live are constantly being delivered over to death for Jesus' sake, so that the life of Jesus also may be manifested in our mortal flesh" (2 Cor. 4:10–11).

17. At the end of chapter 8, Jesus provided something *old* in the recovered covenant garment. Later He wrote His *new* name on her forehead. Now the Father allows her to *borrow* the crown of life for the coming ceremony. He adds to it twenty-four *blue* sapphires.

18. The Bible calls angels in the third heaven "stars" (Rev. 1:20; 12:4). The Father designates twenty-four angels to accompany this wearer of the crown of life in heaven.

19. For Christians the hands (work) and the feet (conduct) are to give forth the sweet fragrance of Christ's sacrifice on the cross as our ransom for sin (Eph. 5:2; 1 Tim. 2:6).

20. Please refer to note 33 of chapter 2.

21. Please see note 14 of the Preface and note 26 of chapter 2.

22. "Therefore, confess your sins to one another, and pray for one another so that you may be healed" (James 5:16).

I lay there looking up into the branches of the tree, thinking of my Lover, my Friend. The soft lights of the leaves and fruit soothed me. I did not think I could rest. But I did.

Before falling asleep, I lifted my hands to look at them again. I spoke quietly, "O my Beloved, what is going to happen?"

Chapter Ten

Consecration[1]

Slowly my mind inched toward consciousness. I opened my eyes. Intense balls of light were hovering before my face. Within these lights were the outlines of spirits the size of hummingbirds.

I was too mellow from slumber to be startled. Instead, I was bemused watching them. While I was looking at these spirits, angels below me in the garden began to sing. Amazingly, they were addressing the rocks, hills, trees, and streams of the Garden of God.

A good *spirit* is a heavenly being with a body more ethereal and transparent than that of an angel (1 Kings 22:19–23). Angels also are called "spirits" (Heb. 1:13–14). But they are usually larger and can be touched and seen more definitely.

Song of the Twenty-four Attendants

O, let us hear you sing of God,
The great Almighty One,
Whose fire of burning holiness
Is seen within His Son.

Come now, ancient hills, proclaim
And streams re-echoing,
And rocks and grass and trees burst forth.
Together let them sing.

1. The verb *to consecrate* means to set someone or something apart as holy (sacred) unto God for His use (Exod. 19:22–23). God is the one who consecrates (Exod. 29:44). He also may use a human being to act for Him, as He did Moses (Exod. 29:1). God also may ask individuals to consecrate themselves (Lev. 11:44).

2. Everything, except in Satan's domain, has its own way of sounding or moving to give glory to God (Ps. 148; Ps. 69:34). A few examples from the earth are the skipping hills (Ps. 114:46), the singing mountains and trees (Ps. 98:8; 96:12), and the clapping rivers (Ps. 98:8).

3. There is a temple in the present heaven of God (Rev. 14:15, 17; 15:5; 16:1).

4. God commanded Moses to consecrate the Israelites by bathing themselves and washing their clothes before they went to meet with Him at Mount Sinai (Exod. 19:10–11).

Part of the Jewish bridal process involves a *mikvah*.

5. Moses began the ritual of consecrating Aaron and his sons to the priesthood by washing them with water publicly (Exod. 29:1, 4).

6. The phrase "who cleanses us with the water of the Word" refers to Christ cleansing the church (Eph. 5:26).

In Scripture, the Israelites often would introduce their words of thanksgiving for some particular blessing from God with the phrase, "Blessed be the Lord God of Israel, who . . ." (1 Sam. 25:32; 1 Kings 1:48; 8:15).

7. God showed Moses the altar of burnt offering in the tabernacle in heaven (Exod. 25:8–9). It was the first article of furniture that the Israelites encountered when they entered the court of the desert tabernacle (Exod. 40:6).

8. Christ said, "[Animal] sacrifice and [burnt] offering You [Father] have not desired" in comparison to knowing God and obeying His will (Heb. 10:5–7; Hos. 6:6).

His grandeur more than these can tell,
Ancient though they be.
While spanning time as if a day,
He, eternity.

But let them sing and let them tell
For they too would proclaim.
They too would clap; they too would dance;
They too would bless His name.

O ancient hills, what do you know?
And trees, what will you sing?
And rocks, what virtues you extol?
And streams, what wisdom bring?

O, let us hear you worship God.
Enlighten through your praise.
Through your instruction, may we too
Behold with steadfast gaze

His splendor borne of purity,
His beatific grace.
Passed all created, 'til like you,
We gaze upon His face.[2]

The song ended. I reached up with my right hand toward the spirits within the balls of light. They scattered. I sat up.

"Anna," an angel called to me from beneath the tree. I peered down at her upturned face. It was one of the attendants. "We have come to take you to your consecration."

All twenty-four of the white-clad angels began to rise through the branches. They were standing on the air near the juncture in the tree where I had rested. They were smiling.

"Hello," I smiled back at them, thinking how odd it was that anything could stand on air.

"Hello," they answered, trying to contain their excitement. "Are you ready to go?"

"Yes," I answered. Suddenly my hands went to my face. Realization had rushed in on me. This was the time for which I had been waiting. But waiting for what? And how would it be accomplished? "Yes, I am ready," I reiterated aloud. I did not want to ask questions. I did not want to prattle. This was much too serious and my love for Jesus much too intense.

The angels helped me to rise. For a moment I was standing high in the tree of life with all of its shimmering leaves and fruit around me.

Instantly we were in a temple complex.[3]

The Temple

I received only an overall impression of the temple, for I was intent upon that which lay before me. I saw neither side walls nor ceiling. That I do remember. I wondered where the temple stood, but I did not ask.

The Immersion Pool[4]

For observant Jews—men and women—there is a rite called *mikvah*. It involves an individual, spiritual cleansing and dedication to God by immersion in a small pool of flowing water. It symbolizes renewal or a new level of relationship with God.

The angels escorted me to a sunken pool that contained moving water. The water flowed into the pool from an invisible source beneath the floor and flowed out again just as mysteriously. It was accessed by stairs that extended beneath the water's surface.

The angels led me to the top of these stairs. Then they circled the pool holding above their heads a long sheeting of white linen. This portable curtain extended from their upraised hands to their feet, effectively providing privacy.

"I wonder what this might mean?" I asked within. I had already been baptized after accepting Christ. "I do not need to show again that I have passed from death into life, do I?"

"By... [the Father's] will we have been sanctified through the offering [on the cross] of the body of Jesus Christ once for all" (Heb. 10:10). "He [Christ] offered one sacrifice for sins for all time"(Heb. 10:12).

9. Christians move beyond the animal sacrifices on the altar of burnt offering of the old covenant. They come to Christ Jesus, the one true sacrifice, and His "sprinkled blood" within the Father (Heb. 12:22–24). The Lord Jesus "is able also to save to the uttermost [completely, perfectly, finally, and for all time and eternity] those who come to God [the Father] through Him" (Heb. 7:25, AMP).

10. To be *unclothed* has the spiritual meaning of allowing one's sinful nature to be exposed (Gen. 3:10). Mankind "is flesh" in its meaning of utter corruption (Gen. 6:3, 5). For Christians, the *breeches* mean to "put on the Lord Jesus Christ, and make no provision for the flesh in regard to its lusts" (Rom. 13:14). Our flesh nature is under the curse of God (Jer. 17:5).

11. God the Father asked the betrothed one, "Are you willing... to stand rightly before Me?" This phrase is a true definition of righteousness. The white linen tunic was the basic garment of the priestly sons of Aaron (Exod. 39:27).

The *white tunic* for the Melchizedek priesthood represents the "robe of [Christ's] righteousness" in which we stand before God (Isa. 61:10; Rev. 19:8). The only righteousness that the Father honors is His Son (Rom. 10:3–4; 2 Cor. 5:21).

12. Elisha told his servant to "gird up your loins" and quickly go on an urgent errand for him (2 Kings 4:29). The physical meaning of the phrase was to fold his long robe under his belt or sash so that he could move quickly. The spiritual dimension was that his servant should be faithful in obeying his master.

The sash worn by priests of Christ was like a belt around the tunic (Lev. 8:13). Scripture calls "faithfulness the belt around His [Christ's] waist" (Isa. 11:5). He alone is faithful (Rev. 1:5).

13. The Father asks the betrothed one to consecrate all the functions of the head to be those of His Son.

God communicates with seers through all five of the bodily senses and the mind. The seers of God's people are therefore called "your heads" (Isa. 29:10).

Before Major Events

To consecrate Christians according to the order of Melchizedek, God follows the same sequence of events that He used for instituting the Aaronic priesthood.

Then I remembered that those being consecrated (before embarking upon priestly duties) passed through a washing.[5] "Perhaps," I thought, "a cleansing precedes all major events in one's life, whether we know it or not."

Even though I did not understand completely, I wanted to respond out of obedience to all that I believed the Lord was asking of me. I determined to enter the pool.

As I started to take my first step in faith, my robe disappeared. Carefully I descended the stairs, entering the pool. The water was about chest high.

The cool, clear liquid flowed passed me. It was soothing. I lowered myself completely beneath the water.

The Blessing

The beginning of the blessing spoken here are words used by Jews today to offer thanks to God for new or unusual experiences.

When I surfaced, I felt urged to bless the Lord aloud. I said, "Blessed be the Lord God, who cleanses us with the water of the Word."[6]

"Yes," I said to myself, absolutely amazed by the revelation given by that act of obedience, that cleansing is continual.

I turned around and ascended the stairs. The angels remained holding the white fabric above their heads. They gathered around me closely. Together we walked toward the large altar of burnt offering.[7] I was still hidden within the linen enclosure—dripping wet.

The Altar of Burnt Offering

The angels circled the bronze altar, holding the linen enclosure above their heads. I looked at the coals burning beneath the grate. They were hot.

Nothing was being offered upon this altar because our Lord was the sacrifice of the whole burnt offering on the cross.[8] I looked at the burning coals. No one said what I should do. "It must be a puzzle whose answer I already know," I said within myself. I began to think. "If Jesus has paid the full price already, then the altar of burnt offering is not something you go around. You must go through it."[9]

As strange as it was to me, I began to walk forward. I passed right through the bronze altar, coals, heat, and all. Incredible!

The Examination

On the other side of the altar my Father's voice spoke audibly within the temple. "Are you willing to live a life of purity, sanctified to Me alone?"

"Yes," I answered aloud, "the Lord being my helper."

"The linen breeches," He said.

Linen breeches appeared. I stepped into them. I supposed that they were a sign of the salvation that had been won for me on Earth. The priests had worn these to cover their nakedness.[10]

The linen breeches to cover the Aaronic priest's nakedness as he approached the altar was a matter of life or death before God (Exod. 28:42–43).

Again my Father spoke, "Are you willing to be teachable, tender, pliable—to stand rightly before Me?"

"I will, Christ being these through me," I said.

"The tunic," He said.

A linen tunic dropped over my head from above.[11]

14. Jesus is the head covering of His betrothed ones (Eph. 4:15). They walk under His favor, protection, and authority. This is necessary so that their senses and "minds should [not] be led astray from the simplicity and purity of devotion to Christ" (2 Cor. 11:2–3).

15. *Oil* is a symbol of the Holy Spirit. The Father anointed Jesus with the Holy Spirit (Acts 10:38). The ascended Christ pours out His anointing upon obedient disciples who seek the full gift of the Spirit (Acts 10:44–47; Acts 5:32).

16. The anointing oil of the Holy Spirit through Christ our High Priest "is like the precious oil upon the head, coming down upon the beard, even Aaron's beard, coming down upon the edge of his robes" (Ps. 133:2). Part of this priestly anointing is the precious "unity of the Spirit in the bond of peace" among the brethren (Eph. 4:3).

17. God told Moses, "You shall slaughter the ram [of ordination] and take some of its blood and put it on the lobe of Aaron's right ear and on the lobes of his sons' right ears and on the thumbs of their right hands and on the big toes of their right feet" (Exod. 29:20).

The *blood* represents the cleansing from the unrighteous use of not only the ears, hands, and feet but also of the whole body (Heb. 9:22; 1 John 1:9). Priests of Christ are to present their bodily "members as instruments of righteousness to God," as "a living and holy sacrifice" (Rom. 6:13; 12:1).

18. The center of all creation is the sprinkled blood of Christ within the Father. Christians "have come to... God [the Father]... and to the spirits of righteous [saints]... and to Jesus... and to [His] sprinkled blood" (of the new covenant) (Heb. 12:23–24; Col. 3:3).

19. Animal flesh and bread (to be offered on the altar) were placed on their hands to invest them with the functions of the priestly order (Exod. 29:22–24). Their main duty in the court was to present sacrifices on the altar.

Christians also are born into the priestly family of God by their spiritual birth (Rev. 5:9–10). They are to manifest the victorious life of the Lord Jesus, their High Priest, over every enemy—sin, Satan, the flesh, the world, and death. They are to be ordained into the eternal priesthood according to the order of Melchizedek (Heb. 7:15–17).

20. The Aaronic priests lifted their hands that were filled with elements for the sacrifices on the altar. They moved them from side to side before God as a wave offering (Lev. 8:25–27). In a wave offering by the officiating priest (in this case, Moses, by God's appointment), he receives it later as his portion of the altar sacrifices (Lev. 8:29).

The Christian priesthood presents to the Father the *wave offering* that is Christ by His cross and resurrection. Because He died and rose again, they die and rise again with Him (Rom. 6:8, 13). They are "always carrying about in [their] body the dying of Jesus, that the [resurrection] life of Jesus also may be manifested in [their] body" (2 Cor. 4:10).

21. "The four living creatures and the twenty-four elders fell down before the Lamb... and they sang a new song" (Rev. 5:8–9). Scripture records that the heavenly council of the living creatures and the elders sing together.

Again my Father spoke aloud, "Are you willing to be made faithful?"

"Yes, Lord," I answered.

"The sash," He said.

A sash encircled me.[12]

A *seer* in Scripture is a servant of God who not only hears words from Him (prophecy) but also sees messages from Him pictured in visions (Amos 7:1–13).

My Father continued, "Are you willing that the whole head [representing the seer] be for Me alone: the mind of Christ, the sight of Christ, the hearing of Christ, the smelling and the tasting of Christ and the response to touch?[13] Are you willing to be holy unto Me alone, with the covering of My Son upon your head?"[14]

"Yes, Lord," I answered.

"The cap," He said.

The white linen cap enfolded my head.

The anointing oil was poured over the heads of the Aaronic priests as the first stage of their consecration to God (Lev. 8:12; Exod. 40:14–15).

Anointing oil was poured over my head.[15] It ran down the garment to the hem.[16] Suddenly blood appeared on my right earlobe, right thumb, and right toe.[17] It had to be the blood of Jesus, for His is the only blood in heaven.[18]

The angels dropped the linen enclosure. It disappeared from their hands. The twenty-four attendants indicated that I should move forward. They did not go with me.

The Hebrew word for *ordination* to the Aaronic priesthood means, "filling the hands."

As I moved forward, the weight of that which was won by Christ on the altar of the cross came onto my upturned hands.[19] I could see nothing. But I felt this and lifted my hands to wave His sacrifice before the Father.[20]

As I walked toward the entrance to the holy place, I heard the twenty-four elders and the four living creatures begin to sing.[21]

Song of the Heavenly Council

Bring forth the priests unto our God,
He who sits as King.
Loose Your great power o'er the earth,
That Earth like heaven may sing.[22]

Holy God, our great delight,
Swallow sin in darkest night.
Begin, for mercy's sake, the fight.
O God, begin the end.[23]

Praise to the King who reigns on high,
Zion above will sing.
We hold before You bowls of prayer;
Their tribute too we bring.

Release the seal that they may stand
Firstfruits here above,
Bloodwashed in the blood of the Lamb,
Gifts of His infinite love.[24]

Our crowns we throw beneath Your feet,
Eternal God of might.[25]
All power, love, and majesty
Are Yours, great God of Light.

Though standing still upon the earth,
Let them live above
To join us in continual praise,
Consumed, at last, by love.[26]

Let them walk 'mid coals of fire;
Hear, great Yah, our prayer.
Let the circle be complete,
O King, beyond compare.[27]

Let them hear and let them speak
To hallow Your great name.
Let Your glory be visibly seen.
Set their hearts aflame.[28]

The heavenly council "fell down before the Lamb, having each one a harp and golden bowls full of incense, which are the prayers of the saints" (Rev. 5:8).

To *walk 'mid coals* of fire means to have access to the heart of the Father with the Son.

22. The heavenly council begins their song of praise and of prayer for God to call forth the eternal priests of Christ—both men and women on earth (Rev. 5:9–10). These priests will join them in songs of worship and thanksgiving to God.

23. *The end* means the final days of Planet Earth as we know it (1 Pet. 4:7). After a very dark time of tribulation on Earth, Christ will return to establish His kingdom here (Rev. 11:15–17). The Father is merciful to thereby overthrow satanic rule on earth.

24. The Father will release Jesus to break the seal that will begin the calling forth of the firstfruits priests (Rev. 5:5). Scripture describes what it will be like when they stand in spirit with their High Priest, Christ Jesus, before the Father in heaven (Rev. 14:1, 4). There are firstfruits priests in every generation.

25. The twenty-four elders wear *golden crowns* representing their heavenly authority (Rev. 4:4). Upon occasion they "will cast their crowns before the throne" to signify their complete and loving submission to the Father's supreme authority (Rev. 4:10).

26. The bodies of these priests will be on the earth, but their spirits will live with Christ in the Father in heaven (Col. 3:3). They will bless the Father with a life of prayer and praise as Christ Jesus their High Priest does out of a heart of love (Heb. 7:25; 2:12).

27. Lucifer, the magnificent cherub before he rebelled, had such a place in the heart of God (Ezek. 28:14). The Father and His Son are the eternal temple in the new heaven (Heb. 12:22–24; Rev. 21:22).

The circle is complete when the full complement of firstfruits priests of every age are sharing in the worship of God.

28. God will call firstfruits priests from every generation. Those who still live on the earth will reveal the divine glory on this planet. Their hearts manifest Christ's heart as a flame of love for the Father (Song of Sol. 8:6; John 17:26).

Release the Lamb to open above
The seal that seals the end,
That righteousness with purest love
Might dwell on Earth again.[29]

Holy God, our great delight,
Swallow sin in darkest night.
Begin, for mercy's sake, the fight.
O God, begin the end.

Their song ended as I crossed the threshold to the holy place. The weight of the wave offering was lifted from my hands.[30]

The pure *frankincense* was placed on the loaves of bread to symbolize the purity and fragrance of Christ, the true bread of God (Lev. 24:5–7; John 6:32–33). The word *frankincense* is from a Hebrew word meaning "pure" or "white."

The Holy Place

As I passed into the holy place, I appropriated that which symbolized Christ there—the light of the golden lampstand, as well as the bread, wine, and frankincense on the table of shewbread.[31]

All prayers of Christians arise to the Father through the Son (Col. 3:17; Rom. 8:34).

The Altar of Incense[32]

I came to the altar of incense before the holy of holies. Because I had passed through the bronze altar, I felt that I must pass through this altar also. It symbolized Christ's ministry of intercession.[33]

As I began to move through the altar, the aromas of the smoking incense clung to me.[34] I continued to move forward, lifting my hands.

The Holy of Holies[35]

The Aaronic high priest burned incense once a year, which made a cloud of smoke that covered the mercy seat, "lest he die" when entering the holy of holies (Lev. 16:12–13).

I passed the veil, which had been rent at the time of our Lord's death, and entered the holy of holies.[36] The sprinkled blood of Christ's sacrifice was already on the mercy seat.[37] The smoke of His fragrant intercession filled that chamber. The unburned spices of the incense that is most holy to the Lord were also present.[38]

Since Christ had paid the full price to gain our access to the Father, I passed through the ark of the covenant.[39]

Consecration

On the other side of the ark of the covenant, the blood of Christ as well as the holy anointing oil was sprinkled upon me and upon the priestly garments.[40]

My heavenly Father spoke to me again: "You are ordained and consecrated unto Me this day, Anna, a priest forever.[41] There is a time of being shut away, however, before you assume your duties."[42]

The angelic attendants appeared after my Father's admonition.

It is the same with those in the Melchizedek priesthood of Christ, all of whom need to mature by growing up into Christ (Eph. 4:13, 15).

Dressing for the Ceremony

As my Father had said, the twenty-four attendants brought to me the covenant robe, the veil, and the crown.

29. One of the twenty-four elders said, "The Lion that is from the tribe of Judah, the Root of David, has overcome so as to open the book and its seven seals" (Rev. 5:5). Jesus "the Lamb broke one of the seven seals" later and so began the series of God's judgments that led to the end (Rev. 6:1).

"Righteousness with purest love" will "dwell on earth again" when the kingdom of the Lord Jesus is established here (Rev. 11:15).

30. Aaronic priests before the altar of burnt offering would lift their hands that were filled with the elements of the sacrifice there. They would move their hands from side to side as a wave offering to God (Lev. 8:25–27).

The Christian's wave offering of Christ's sacrifice on the altar of the cross is left in the outer court. When one enters the holy place, other aspects of Jesus's ministry are to be presented as an offering.

31. The golden lampstand

Jesus said, "I am the light of the world" (John 8:12; Gen. 1:3). He also said of believers, "You are the light of the world" (Matt. 5:14). As we abide in Him and His words abide in us, He becomes the light of God shining through us (John 15:7).

The table of shewbread

"The bread of the Presence" (literal Hebrew is "Face") (called "shewbread" in the King James Version) is a prototype of the body of Christ in the Lord's Supper (Exod. 25:30). Likewise the wine foreshadows His sacramental blood (1 Cor. 10:16). The wine is implied in Exodus 25:29 when "bowls, with which to pour [out] libations" were set on the table. Libations were drink offerings of wine poured out to God (Lev. 23:13).

32. God placed the "most holy" altar of incense directly in front of the veil that separated off the holy of holies (Exod. 30:1–10). It represented perpetual prayers to God (Exod. 30:8; Eph. 6:18).

The original altar of incense continues to be used before the throne of God in heaven (Rev. 8:3–4).

33. "Another angel came and stood at the altar [of incense], holding a golden censer; and much incense was given to him, so that he might add it to the prayers of all the saints on the golden altar which was before the throne. And the smoke of the incense, with the prayers of the saints, went up before God out of the angel's hand" (Rev. 8:3–4).

34. Those who are the firstfruits priests apprehend the fragrance of the smoking incense. All prayers of Christians are through Christ Jesus, and smoking incense represents His fragrance rising to the Father (2 Cor. 2:14–15).

35. A veil separates the holy of holies from the holy place in the desert tabernacle. The holy of holies contained the mercy seat on the ark of the testimony (tablets of God's laws) (Exod. 26:33–34).

36. "And Jesus uttered a loud cry, and breathed His last. And the veil of the temple was torn in two from top to bottom" (Mark 15:37–38).

37. Once a year the Aaronic high priest sprinkled the blood of animal sacrifices on the mercy seat in the holy of holies in the desert tabernacle (Lev. 16:14–15).

Since Christ's death and resurrection, His blood is on the mercy seat of the ark of the covenant in heaven (Heb. 9:11–12).

38. Moses placed some of the "most holy" incense before the ark of the covenant to remain there unburned, a symbol of the sweet fragrance of Christ's intercession to the Father directly (Exod. 30:35–36). The burned incense rising in smoke represented prayers of believers on Earth ascending through Christ to the Father (Rev. 8:3–4).

39. "Therefore, brethren, since we have confidence to enter the holy place by the blood of Jesus, by a new and living way which He inaugurated for us through the veil, that is, His flesh [on the cross], and since we have a great priest over the house of God, let us draw near with a sincere heart in full assurance of faith" (Heb. 10:19–22).

40. Moses sprinkled Aaron, his sons, and their garments with the anointing oil and with blood from the bronze altar to consecrate them (Lev. 8:30).

Priests of Christ share in the anointing of the oil of the Holy Spirit that Christ received (Acts 10:38). His blood sanctifies (consecrates) them unto God (Heb. 13:12).

41. Christians are to be ordained priests forever by filling them with the victorious death and resurrection life of Christ Jesus to be manifested by the Spirit (2 Cor. 4:10–11). (See notes 18 and 19.)

The final stage of their consecration is the sprinkling with Christ's blood and the anointing oil of the Holy Spirit. They are set apart as holy unto God forever. (See sidebar on page 228 regarding the first stage, and note 40 regarding the final stage of consecration.)

The headgear of a priest became internal. The breeches, tunic, and sash remained on me. As the angels prepared to dress me, one attendant said, "You come to this union with nothing but the Son of God's cleansing, His sacrifice, His blood, His aromas, and His anointing."[43]

In ancient Israel, the bride-groom would often come for the bride late at night. Her attendants always were to be watchful for his arrival and to alert the bride so that she might be ready (Matt. 25:1–6).

Suddenly, we heard the blast of a distant shofar.[44] "He comes!" the angels said with much excitement.

The horn blew again.

Quickly they slipped the covenant robe over my head. The garment had the fragrance of myrrh, aloes, and cassia. Mingled with these aromas were those of the spices of the holy anointing oil, of the holy incense, and of the garden. Each aroma was intensified when the embroidered robe was worn.[45] The fragrance was everywhere.

I noticed that the palms of my hands were still stained red from the henna. I supposed that the soles of my feet were still stained also.

It was a custom in ancient Israel for the family of the bride to veil her.

The angels placed the borrowed crown of life upon my head. Together they raised the circular, full-length veil. I thought that they would release it to float down upon me. Instead, I realized that my heavenly Father was veiling me by the power of the Holy Spirit.[46]

As it descended, He spoke a blessing over me: "Become thousands of ten thousands, My child."[47]

Suddenly, we heard a shout.[48] Then Jesus called to me from a distance, "Anna!" I turned to look for Him.

"He comes!" the angels said excitedly.

In early Christian weddings, the bride and groom wore crowns for the same reason. As Christians they have been "advanced to royalty" with Him forever (Ezek. 16:13; Rev. 22:5).

Immediately He burst into view. He was riding the most beautiful white steed I had ever seen.[49] The horse was galloping at top speed. The sight of Jesus knocked the breath out of me. He was wearing white, with a gold crown on His head.[50] He was every inch a king and every inch the desire of all nations.

The Catching Away

Without allowing the horse to break stride, He scooped me up and pulled me onto the horse to sit in front of Him. With His left arm He held me securely to Himself.

The angelic attendants clapped and jumped, spinning around with joy.[51]

The white stallion began to climb, up and up over the terrain of Paradise. He galloped on the wings of the wind. It was glorious!

When we reached the sea of glass, the white horse began his descent. He came to a halt at the back of the throne room. All assembled raised a great shout of joy.[52]

Then cutting through the shout, one lone angel near the throne began to sing:

> Blessed is He who comes.
> Blessed is He who comes.[53]

42. After their ordination and consecration, the Aaronic priests remained shut away with God in the holy place for seven days (Lev. 8:33). God ratified their priesthood through illumination of His Word (the golden lampstand), communion with Him (the bread of the Presence), and prayer and praise to Him (the altar of incense).

43. "What do you have that you did not receive [through Christ Jesus]? But if you did receive it, why do you boast as if you had not received it?" (1 Cor. 4:7). "Christ is all things and in all things" (Col. 3:11, Wuest).

44. The first instance of a *shofar* or ram's horn being blown in Scripture announced God's coming down on Mount Sinai to meet the Israelites (Exod. 19:13, 16).

Christ will return for His betrothed ones "with a shout... and with the trumpet of God" (1 Thess. 4:16).

45. The author of Hebrews affirms that Psalm 45 refers to the marriage of King Jesus (Heb. 1:8–9). His garments are said to be scented with myrrh, aloes, and cassia (Ps. 45:8). There are nine other spices that form the combined "fragrance of Christ to God [the Father]" (2 Cor. 2:15). All the spices are intensified when the betrothed one wears the covenant robe, because it reveals the deepest, sweetest mystery—Christ's love for the Father and others (Col. 2:2–3; 3:12–14; Eph. 3:19).

46. When Rebekah, the betrothed of Isaac, saw him for the first time, "she took her veil and covered herself" (Gen. 24:65). The *veil* represents divine favor (grace) that encircles those whose hearts are set apart unto the Lord (Ps. 5:12).

47. The first five words of this blessing of fruitfulness were spoken by Rebekah's family to her (Gen. 24:60). She was departing from their home to travel to a strange land to marry Isaac (Gen. 24:58–59).

God blessed Adam and Eve before their joining with these beginning words: "Be fruitful and multiply" (Gen. 1:28).

48. The bridegroom in biblical times gave a shout upon his arrival at the bride's house: "Behold, the bridegroom! Come out to meet him" (Matt. 25:6).

49. The Holy Spirit is taking part in the ceremony. The power and righteousness represented by a *white horse* in Scripture is a symbol of the Holy Spirit (Rev. 19:11, 14).

50. Jesus wears a gold crown in Revelation 14:14. In ancient Jewish betrothal ceremonies, both the bride and the groom wore crowns. They were treated as a king and a queen that day.

51. The twenty-four attendants share in the joy of the bride and Bridegroom and the whole heavenly family (Isa. 62:5).

52. All of heaven will rejoice in the future day when "the marriage of the Lamb has come and His [corporate] bride has made herself ready" (Rev. 19:7). "Shout to God with the voice of joy" (Ps. 47:1).

53. These are the first five words of the jubilant greeting that the great multitude gave Jesus as He rode into Jerusalem on a young donkey: "Blessed is He who comes in the name of the Lord, even the King of Israel" (John 12:12–13). Now He comes riding in heaven as the King of creation, as "Lord of all" (Acts 10:36). Jesus said that He would not return for His bride until the words, "Blessed is He who comes in the name of the Lord!" were said (Matt. 23:39).

Chapter Eleven

Ceremony of Formal Betrothal

Jesus dismounted from the white horse. Immediately, He turned to help me dismount. Holding me around the waist, He lowered me onto the sea of glass.

As I passed in front of Him, He breathed in the fragrance released from the covenant robe. He said, "You have made My heart beat faster, My sister, My bride."[1]

For a moment we stood looking at each other. Then both He and the white stallion disappeared.

Angelic Attendants

The twenty-four angelic attendants appeared near me on the sea of glass. They busied themselves preparing me for the ceremony. They smoothed the covenant garment and straightened the veil. As they worked, they smiled up into my face at times to reassure me.

Suddenly I realized that I was facing the entire assembly of heaven. The collective splendor before me was overwhelming.

The Throne Room

The sea of glass was packed with angels and the redeemed. Angels also filled the atmosphere above. Everyone wore white. There were

1. This sentence is from the Song of Solomon 4:9. The Lord Jesus calls His betrothed ones "My sister" because they "are all from one Father; for which reason He is not ashamed to call them brethren [male and female]" (Heb. 2:11).

2. The throne of the Father is a magnificent chair of light upon which He sits (Rev. 4:2–3; 5:7; Matt. 23:22). His form is of incomparable whiteness. The glorious light that Jesus manifested on one occasion on Earth was similar to this brightness (Matt. 17:2). The Father is true light (1 John 1:5). Divine light is the illumination in heaven (Rev. 21:23).

Scripture compares the upper half of the radiant sphere of incomparable colors surrounding the Father to a splendid rainbow (Ezek. 1:28; Rev. 4:3).

3. The twenty-four elders around the Father's throne are those with governmental authority and faithful seniority. Their delegated rule is seen in the crowns they wear that at times they cast before the Father, falling down in worship (Rev. 4:4, 10). They also praise God in song and speech, play musical instruments, and present some of the prayers of the saints to the Father (Rev. 5:8–9).

thousands upon thousands gathered. They shone like icicles on a sunny winter's day. They glistened.

Brighter than them all was the glory of my Father. His piercing white light at the center of the throne radiated out into a rainbow of vibrant colors.[2]

Many scholars believe that the elders are the eldest angels who have oversight in the administration of other angels and of the universe for God.

The twenty-four stately elders flanked Him.[3] Angels of His presence stood near the altar of incense before the throne.[4] The four living creatures that are full of eyes were watching.[5] The huge cherubim on either side of the throne peered through the intense light.[6] The seven torches that symbolize the attributes of the Holy Spirit burned even brighter in front of my Father.

The *seven great flames* of fire or torches are manifestations of the sevenfold ministry of the Holy Spirit that are seen in fullness in Christ Jesus (Rev. 3:1; 5:6; 4:5; Isa. 11:2).

Planets and Stars

Amid this breathtaking splendor, images of the planets and stars were passing in review before their Creator. Creation itself was "trooping the colors," paying homage to its King.[7]

Again, the one lone angel sang:

> Blessed is He who comes.
> Blessed is He who comes.

Canopy of Light

The Hebrew word for a canopy or chamber is *chuppah*. At Jewish betrothal ceremonies, the *chuppah* is a large, square piece of cloth held up by four poles.

My heavenly Father laced together the fingers of His hands of light. Slowly He stretched out His arms over the sea of glass. His hands cupped into a dome, a canopy.[8]

Then Jesus, more beautiful than all creation, stepped beneath this canopy. He was dressed in white with a gold crown on His head.[9]

The images of the stars and planets halted in place. The seven flames of fire swung around to circle the canopied area. Now Father, Son, and Holy Spirit were manifested together for the ceremony.[10]

At betrothal ceremonies, God is blessed before the bride and groom are blessed. This custom derives from the fact that Melchizedek, priest of God Most High, blessed God as he blessed Abraham (Gen. 14:19–20).

So extraordinarily thrilling was the sight that the mighty assembly erupted into praise:

> Glory to the Lamb.
> Glory to the King.
> Glory to the Three in One.
> Let exaltations ring![11]

The Procession

The twenty-four attendants began to move forward by twos.[12] There was awe in their reverence. I remembered the words of Psalm 2:11: "Worship the Lord with reverence, and rejoice with trembling."

The nearer these angels drew to the canopy of my Father's hands, the brighter they shone. I could understand why my Father called them stars. They were like brilliant lamps or torches.[13]

Torches symbolized the fire of God on Mount Sinai where the giving of the Law is seen by Jews as representing their betrothal to God (Deut. 5:23; Exod. 19:18).

4. The angels of His presence stand in close proximity to the Father to serve Him (Luke 1:19; Rev. 8:2). Some of them offer prayers of the saints on Earth to Him from the altar of incense (Rev. 8:3–4). (Please see note 2 of chapter 1.)

5. Surrounding the throne are the *four living creatures* who are one form of the several kinds of cherubim (Rev. 4:6–8; Ezek. 10:14–15; 1:5, 10). They "give glory and honor and thanks" to the Father on behalf of all of His creation (Rev. 4:9). They represent four major divisions of living creatures—the lion, the wild beasts; the calf, the domesticated animals; the man, humanity; and the flying eagle, the birds (Gen. 9:8–10). Their many eyes indicate completeness of spiritual perception, understanding, and appreciation of God the Father as far as creatures are concerned (1 Cor. 2:9–10, 14–15).

6. The Hebrew root for the word *cherub* means "holding something in safe keeping." Two cherubim are stationed beneath the armrests of the Father's throne (Ps. 99:1; Ezek. 10:1). They serve as an honor guard to uphold the glory of Almighty God (Ezek. 10:18–19). Both cherubim are a composite of the four main categories of living creatures because God created them to live in harmony together (Gen. 2:19–20). Each cherub has the face of a man, the wings of an eagle, one portion of the body that of a lion, and the other portion that of an ox.

7. The planets and stars are part of the whole "creation [that] waits eagerly for the revealing of the sons [heirs] of God." All creation, including the heavenly bodies, "will be set free from its slavery to corruption" to share in "the freedom of the glory of the children of God" (Rom. 8:19, 21).

God "summons the heavens above" (Ps. 50:4). When "He calls an assembly, who can restrain Him?" (Job 11:10). The images of the planets and stars, with the "sun and moon [that] stood in their places," pay homage to God who made, placed, counted, named, leads forth, and sustains each one (Gen. 1:14–18; Ps. 147:4; Isa. 40:26).

8. The *chuppah* can represent the place in his father's house that the bridegroom in ancient Israel had prepared for the couple to begin life together.

For Christians, our Father God fashions a canopy with His hands to signify what the Lord Jesus called "My Father's house." There Christ lives within His Father and prepares a place for His disciples (John 1:18; 14:2–3; 17:24). Christians are meant to abide in spirit there even though they walk and work on the earth (John 15:4; Col. 3:3).

At Jewish betrothals, the words "Blessed is he who comes" are chanted as the bridegroom approaches the *chuppah*. These same five words were shouted by the multitude of disciples who welcomed Jesus into Jerusalem (Matt. 21:9).

9. In Scripture, *white garments* represent purity (Rev. 3:5). During the ancient betrothal of the Jewish bride and groom, they wore white robes.

Christ Jesus promises those betrothed to Him in purity, those "who have not soiled their garments," that "they will walk with Me in white" (Rev. 3:4).

The apostle John saw Jesus in heaven wearing a gold crown on His head (Rev. 14:14). The Greek word used here for *crown* means honor and blessing rather than authority. It is like a wreath awarded to those who triumph.

The Lord Jesus enters the *chuppah* first to welcome His betrothed one. This custom began at the very first wedding. God fashioned Eve and brought her to Adam who was already in the garden (Gen. 2:22).

10. The biblical law of requiring two or three witnesses for establishing a matter is applied in the case of the ancient betrothal of a bride and groom (Deut. 19:15). The two essential elements that constitute a valid Jewish betrothal are 1) the giving of a ring (or some article of recognizable value) to the bride who accepts it, and 2) this act is witnessed by two reputable persons.

Jesus's Father (God) and the Holy Spirit, the Friend of the Bridegroom, are the two official witnesses, as well as the two customary attendants of the Bridegroom.

11. Great praise erupted in heaven at this betrothal where all three persons of the Trinity now are manifested at the canopy.

12. The custom of having attendants for the bride is found in Scripture (1 Sam. 25:42; Ps. 45:14; Matt. 25:1). These bridesmaids in the Bible were virgins.

13. The twenty-four attendants also serve the purpose of the ancient use of torches or lamps to escort the bride to the groom.

Torches to accompany the bride also indicate joy. The joy of the twenty-four attendants increased as they drew near to the Trinity of God at the *chuppah*, causing the light in them to shine brighter (Ps. 45:14–15).

Two of these angels remained with me to help me move forward at the right time. When the other attendants had stationed themselves outside of the seven flames of fire, the angels with me indicated that now I should move toward the canopy.

I swallowed hard.

I began to walk toward Jesus, feeling very small among this stunning assembly. I marveled that the stars and planets would be witnesses to the ceremony also. Then the entire gathering began to sing. As they extolled our God, I lost my nervousness; instead, my heart raced with expectancy.

Exaltation

Brighter than a thousand suns
Is the Son of Righteousness,
Through whom all things were begun,
In whom all things blessed.

Bow before His majesty,
Th' created of the sod.
Glory to the One, yet Three,
Glory to our God.

Countless, countless thousands
Bow before His throne.
Countless, countless thousands
Worship God alone.

He created heavens and Earth,
Eternity's vast plan.
By His Word, He brought to birth
Blessings from His hand.

Power hides He in His hand,[14]
Light within His Son.[15]
Unfolding mercies like a span,
Hail, great Three in One!

God "has rays flashing from His hand, and there is the hiding of His power" (Hab. 3:4). The hand of the Father is represented by the power of the Holy Spirit silently and unobtrusively extended throughout creation to accomplish the will of God (Ezek. 37:1; 2 Chron. 20:6; Luke 1:64–66).

My Earthly Father's House

As I continued forward, I saw many whom I knew within the crowd. Some were relatives who had died in years past. My earthly father was among them. But my eyes and attention were upon Him to whom

I was going. I thought of Psalm 45:10–11: "Forget your people and your father's house; then the King will desire your beauty." I did feel that I was being transferred from my earthly father's house to the abode of my Husband.

Also among those gathered were the angels assigned to me. Some I knew. Some I did not know. But I could tell that these were angels assigned to help me because they were smiling broadly.

My Father's House

As I neared the little house of light created by my Father's hands, I wanted to share my consent. I wanted to say, "Yes, yes, I agree," to all three members of the Trinity.[16] I felt as light as a wisp of air. I was a cornucopia of joy.

Biblical law required the prospective bride to freely give her consent.

Jesus smiled at me as I passed one of the manifestations of the Holy Spirit stationed around the perimeter of my Father's canopy.

My Assent

As I stepped beneath the canopy, I could contain my joy no longer. I began to walk through an acceptance. The movements were like a stately dance.

I circled Jesus three times, one encircling for each member of the Trinity.[17] As I weaved gently between the mighty torches of the Holy Spirit, I overflowed with love for all Three.

The Jewish bride began the ceremony of betrothal under the *chuppah* by circling the groom three (or more) times.

Like Rebekah, I wanted to say, "I will go with this Man."[18] I began to sing a new song.

14. This verse is part of the song to accompany the procession to the *chuppah*. In Jewish ceremonies it is a custom to play music that is chosen with great care as the bride is led to the canopy. The music is to exalt God.

15. There is a difference between light and the Light. The Light is the true Light of God (John 1:5, 9). Christ Jesus said, "I am the Light of the world," and anyone "who follows Me will not be walking in the dark [of sin and death] but will have the Light which is Life" (John 8:12, AMP; Rom. 8:2).

Christ Jesus is also the light of the revelation of His Father (John 14:9).

16. Rebekah's family asked her if she was willing to accompany the caravan of Abraham's servant to the land of Canaan to become Isaac's wife. And Rebekah replied, "I will go" (Gen. 24:57–58).

The Trinity is the eternal family in God. They wait for each Christian to give full consent to the betrothal to the Lord Jesus.

17. One biblical rationale for three times is found in Hosea 2:19–20 where God promises that He will betroth His people to Himself in three ways.

The betrothed here circles the Lord Jesus three times in recognition of the three persons of the Trinity. These motions convey consent to each of Them.

18. Please see note 16 of this chapter.

Song of the Bride

By the Spirit and the water of the Word of Christ, one is born again and at the same time given to the Lord Jesus as His betrothed one by the Father (John 3:5; 17:2).

Hear, Thou great Redeemer blessed,
Deep within my heart find rest;
You who birthed me from Your side,
Then called me forth to be Your bride.[19]

I exult in You alone,
And take Your heart to be my home.
Lover, Friend, Redeemer, Son,
Eternal Husband, make us one.

A Private Moment

According to Jewish custom, the bride stands to the right of the groom under the canopy.

When the third circuit had been completed, I took my place at the right of Jesus.[20] I had publicly given my consent before a multitude of witnesses.

He looked deeply into my eyes and spoke privately to me:

Set Me as a seal upon your heart,
As a signet ring upon your finger.[21]

Under His Covering

In some Jewish betrothal ceremonies, a *tallith* is draped over the couple to indicate that the man will assume the protection and provision for his future wife.

Gently a tallith settled over our heads.[22] Jesus spoke again, this time in a manner that would bear public witness to all:

I betroth you to Me forever.
I betroth you to Me in righteousness and in justice,
In lovingkindness and in compassion,
I betroth you to Me in faithfulness—and you will know God.[23]

A Ring More Precious Than Gold

Then lifting my veil slightly, He took my right hand into both of His. He held my right index finger encased within His right hand as He spoke:

The giving and the receiving of a ring (or something of known value) change the status of both to that of married persons.

Behold, you are consecrated to Me.[24]

A golden light encompassed my right index finger. From my finger the light spread over my whole being.[25]

My Father's hands of light became a brilliant cocoon. Besides Jesus, the only other one I could see was the Holy Spirit manifested in flaming towers. The light became more and more intense. I saw two white eagles cartwheeling.

Mahanaim[26]

Mahanaim means "two companies" or camps. The spiritual meaning of the two companies is heaven and Earth coming together.

Then slowly, as in a ritual dance of birds, I felt suspended within the dazzling light and fire. It was as though Jesus and I began a stylized, courtship dance. I felt that I was vapor that could be inhaled, vapor that could be carried into fire and light.

19. After Christ had died on the cross, a soldier thrust a spear into His heart. Blood and water miraculously poured forth (John 19:32–35). Blood and water are present at a birth. Spiritually the event signified the bringing forth of the bride of the Lord Jesus as God formed Eve (a type of the bride) from the opened side of Adam (a type of Christ) (Gen. 2:21–22; Rom. 5:14).

Jesus said, "Truly, truly I say to you, an hour is coming and now is, when the dead [in their sins] will hear the voice of the Son of God [to come unto Him], and those who hear will live" (John 5:25; Eph. 2:1).

20. In Psalm 45, a song about King Jesus and His bride, verse 9 says, "At Your right hand stands the queen in gold from Ophir."

21. The spiritual heart is the seat of faith and love (Rom. 10:10; 5:5). To set Christ as a seal upon the betrothed one's heart is to mark off that faculty as reserved for Him alone (Song of Sol. 4:12; 1 Pet. 3:15).

Here Jesus quotes from the literal Hebrew of Song of Solomon 8:6. In ancient times people had signet rings engraved with each one's unique seal (an emblem, word, letter, figure, or symbol). They used the rings to make an impression in wax or clay to certify to one's identity or to authenticate a transaction (Gen. 38:17–18, 25).

To have Christ as the signet ring upon the betrothed's finger means that all one does is to bear the mark that identifies the work with the Lord Jesus, not with oneself (Gal. 2:20). The betrothed disciple is chosen and precious to God like a signet ring (Hag. 2:23; Jer. 22:24).

22. Numbers 15:38 is thought by Jews to refer to their prayer shawl, called a *tallith*. In this scripture God told Moses to tell the sons of Israel to "make for themselves tassels on the corners of their garments" and to "put on the tassel of each corner a cord of blue." *Blue* is the color of revelation from God in heaven in this case. The tassels were to remind the Israelites of God's revealed commandments and of His calling to be holy (vv. 39–40).

In betrothal to Christ Jesus, the *tallith* represents the covering of the Lord as the redeemer to protect and provide for the betrothed one as part of His family (Ruth 3:9).

23. In the Old Testament, God said that He would betroth His people to Himself with the same covenant promises here spoken by the Lord Jesus (Hos. 2:19–20; Ezek. 16:8). The goal of the betrothal vows spoken by Christ here and of the new covenant in His blood is the same—to know God (Hos. 2:20; Heb. 8:11). Both sets of promises are entirely by grace through Christ Jesus.

24. In the ancient betrothal ceremony, the groom places a ring on the index finger of the right hand of the bride. It is the finger most easily extended and visible. He recites the traditional formula—"Behold, you are consecrated [set apart] to me with this ring according to the Law of Moses and Israel."

25. In Jewish betrothals the bridegroom must own the ring.

Christians are to become partakers of the divine nature (2 Pet. 1:4–5). Jesus gives something of His nature more valuable than gold to the betrothed one. Christ is the true Light (John 1:9). This ring of His Light is His Life (John 8:12, AMP).

26. *Mahanaim* is a Hebrew word first used in Genesis 32:2. It is the name Jacob gave to the place where a company of angels met the company of his household and their goods.

27. From eternity the Son of God emptied Himself of the use of His own soul faculties (His mind, emotions, and will) in order to live by the mind, emotions, and will of the Father (Phil. 2:7; Matt. 10:38–39). Jesus said, "I do nothing on My own initiative" (John 8:28).

The Christian is also to be emptied of the natural soul life in order to live by the mind, emotions, and will of the Lord Jesus. The vacuum created by this emptying is filled by the Spirit of Christ (Matt. 16:24–25). Deeper union with the Father, Son, and Holy Spirit is realized thereby in the betrothed one. "I in them, and Thou [Father] in Me, that they may be perfected in unity [with Us]" (John 17:23).

28. The Jews believe that God betrothed Israel to Himself at Mount Sinai in His appearing and giving the Law. There God descended with lightning, in fire, and in a thick cloud (Exod. 19:16–18; 20:21; Deut. 5:22).

The literal Hebrew of the Song of Solomon 6:13 has been translated "the sword dance of the two companies." (For the meaning of "the two companies," or *Mahanaim*, please see note 26.) The ancient sword dance around a large campfire was spectacular with the blades flashing in the firelight. This is an earthly example of the appearance of the glorious dance of the Spirit of Jesus with the spirit of the betrothed one.

This was light that could be breathed. It was light that was alive. It went through me as if I was not there at all. I became one with the light—in a dance with it. It was as though within the light and fire, I too became light and fire.

This "dance" involves the spirits of Jesus and the betrothed one. The deeper union takes place after the Christian matures in the process of sanctification.

We were vaporous—blending, circling, homogenized yet distinct, fused but separate. The two became entirely one, then separate again.[27]

Although this dance began slowly, it accelerated to a lightning speed. The dance was lightning—lightning, fire, and light, glorious in the extreme.[28]

Lullaby to Creation

The Father through Christ "upholds all things by the word of His power" (Heb. 1:3). In Christ "all things hold together" (Col. 1:17).

Then, as if in some suspended silence, I began to hear my Father sing.[29] It was creative sound, a lullaby from the heart of Him who sings to His creation, from Him who holds all things together by the word of His power.

He had given the universe its sounds so that all might sing back to Him. In this rare, suspended silence, I could hear that singular sound released from all creation. From deep within Himself, our God, like a father rocking his child, sang lovingly to His universe.

I sensed the perfect unity within the Godhead, their harmony.[30] By being brought into the Godhead, I began to experience their unity.[31] I shared in their oneness. Jesus was giving me the desires of my heart. As He had sworn, in greater measure I began to "know God."

Return to the Ceremony

From this suspended place, I became conscious again of the ceremony. My Father's canopied hands, the seven torches of fire, Jesus, the attendants, the angels, and the redeemed all came back into focus. I was once again under the canopy with Jesus.

A jubilant shout came from those assembled. Together they proclaimed:

The whole service of betrothal is called in Hebrew *kiddushin*, a word meaning "consecration." The bride and groom are set apart to each other before God.

> Consecrated![32]

Celebration

The throne room erupted into celebration. Dancers began careening past us, reaching out to wish us well. Jesus touched hand after hand. I was smiling but somewhat dazed.

Jesus looked over at me.

Then speaking with affection to those who were reaching toward us, He said, "Please excuse us."

Smiling, He took my hand and said, "Come."

29. In Hebrews 2:11–12, the author of the Book of Hebrews says that it was Jesus Christ speaking in Psalm 22:22. This verse says "I will proclaim Thy [the Father's] name to My brethren, in the midst of the congregation [of worshiping disciples] I will sing Thy [the Father's] praise."

We know from Scripture that Jesus said, "I do nothing on My own initiative, but I speak these things as the Father taught Me" (John 8:28). He also said, "Whatever the Father does, these things the Son also does in like manner" (John 5:19). Therefore we know that if Jesus is singing praise to the Father, the Father has first been singing to Him and to all creation through Him (1 Cor. 8:6).

30. In the only God there are three persons—the Father, the Son, and the Holy Spirit—and They are one (Isa. 45:21; Matt. 28:18–20; Deut. 6:4). An example of the Three working together occurred when Jesus came out of the water at His baptism and was praying (Luke 3:21). The Holy Spirit descended upon Him "in bodily form like a dove." And the Father spoke from heaven to acknowledge Him as His beloved Son (Luke 3:22).

There is but one God. There are three persons but one God. The Father, the Son, and the Spirit are each a distinct person.

31. One of the promises spoken by God to His people is found in Hosea 2:20: "Then you will know the Lord." This knowing is through intimate experience in the betrothed one's inner person of heart and spirit. It is a knowing by the spiritual infusion of God. Illumination and revelation can only take the Christian so far. To "know" God in greater measure requires an infusion of God Himself. Infusion is described as a "dance."

32. After the groom places the ring on the bride's finger, the Jewish ceremony of betrothal is complete. It is customary for all the people present to proclaim with joy a Hebrew word, *mekudesheth,* meaning "consecrated."

Chapter Twelve

The Spirit and the Bride

Instantly Jesus and I were walking on a path in Paradise.

"I was a little overwhelmed," I sighed wistfully. Then, rallying with unexpected speed, I smiled, "People come and go so quickly here."

Jesus laughed. He put His arm around my waist. "I wanted to be with you privately before your return," He said. "They will understand."

"I want to be with You, too," I said. His answer made me feel very loved. I leaned my head on His shoulder.

Separated Unto Christ

I noticed that the covenant robe and the golden crown I had worn were gone. Again I was wearing the plain, white robe. Although I could barely see the veil, it remained. It was more of an indication than a noticeable presence. I felt that it was a sign of being separated unto Christ. I supposed that I would be seen after we were fully married.[1]

The words *married* and *wedded* may have broader meanings of blending together or uniting inseparably. For example, God promises that the land of Israel will be married to Him (Isa. 62:4).

The Rose of Sharon

The path we were walking topped a hill. From there, other hills lay before us. Each was covered with the rose of Sharon. The rolling terrain was a vivid red.

We walked in silence. I could sense that something was on His heart.

1. Scripture calls the final stage of union of the priestly bride with the Lord Jesus "the marriage of the Lamb" (Rev. 19:7). At that time the members of the hidden, corporate bride in resurrected bodies will be seen fully in their likeness to Christ (Col. 3:4). "It has not appeared as yet what we shall be. We know that, when He appears, we shall be like Him, because we shall see Him just as He is" (1 John 3:2).

2. "So you will again distinguish between the righteous and the wicked, between one who serves God and one who does not serve Him" (Mal. 3:18). The Lord says that they who fear Him will be made His "special treasure" (Mal. 3:16–17, MARGIN).

3. Jesus spoke about those people to whom the Holy Spirit had revealed Christ and His kingdom and who had responded in reverential fear of sinning against God by ingratitude. He said that more revelation would be given to them.

But those people who had not perceived the meaning of Christ and His kingdom and acknowledged His lordship, even the little they did understand would be taken from them (Matt. 13:11–12, 19).

4. Pharaoh told Joseph to bring his father and all their households and come to Egypt. Pharaoh promised that he would give them "the best of the land of Egypt and you will eat the fat of the land" (Gen. 45:18).

Sharing His Heart

God has already dropped a *plumb line* from heaven to Earth. It is used figuratively in Scripture of God measuring the vertical dimension or uprighteousness of His people (Amos 7:7–8).

"Anna," He said finally, "divisions are coming."[2] He looked out over the hills. "For those who embrace the fear of the Lord and follow His precepts, His golden goodness will pour upon them.

"But for those who do not embrace the fear of the Lord," He continued, "who scorn His precepts and His ways, that which they already have will be taken from them.[3] God is not mocked, Anna, and the ways of the flesh are not condoned."

The Sunshine of His Face

Here, *fat* is a symbol of abundance, that is, over and above that which is strictly necessary.

He continued, "But the sunshine of His face will shine upon the righteous. He will set the captives free. He will nurture them with lovingkindness, and they will eat the fat of the land.[4] For He is a Father who has mercy upon His children, and He will not hide His eyes from their distress.

"He is from everlasting to everlasting, My love, and His goodness stretches as far as His never-ending presence."

Fellowship With God

"For those who embrace His precepts," He continued, "He will open every door to His storehouses. No good thing will He withhold. They will swim; they will float on the fat of the land. They will stride from mountaintop to mountaintop measuring off their inheritance and celebrating His ever-present nearness."

The Holy Spirit brings together those who reverence the Lord God so they may encourage one another in Christ (Heb. 3:13).

He continued, "He will take these aloft.[5] They will sit with His Son and sup with Abraham, Isaac, and Jacob.[6] He will bring together those who fear His name, and they will have fellowship in Him."[7]

The Unrepentant

"Those who are swindlers and liars also will find each other," He said, "and their fellowship will be with their father.[8]

"Those who love themselves more than they fear the Lord will have their old nature as their companion. Fretting and self-righteousness will be their reward. They will face closed doors to God's glory at every turn. Grace will slam its door in their faces. The wall between them and God's goodness will be too high to climb, and they will spend their days searching for God as a blind man gropes in a foreign land."[9]

A Canopy of Glory

He continued, "But for those who hold to His ways and fear His name, a canopy of goodness will be their shelter; a canopy of glory will be their home.[10] Not even a toe will poke its way from beneath the mercy and lovingkindness of the Lord."

God's glory will cover the people of Zion and meet every need (Phil. 4:19).

He tilted His head back as if to proclaim over the hills.

5. "If then you have been raised up [resurrected in your inner person] with Christ, keep seeking the things above, where Christ is, seated at the right hand of God. Set your mind on the things above, not on the things that are on earth. For you have died [to sin] and your life [in spirit] is hidden with Christ in God [the Father]" (Col. 3:1–3).

Jesus asked that those whom the Father had given to Him in betrothal be with Him where He is in heaven (John 17:24; 14:3; Phil. 3:20).

6. Paul said God had "raised us up with Him [Jesus], and seated us with Him in the heavenly places, in Christ Jesus" (Eph. 2:6). This could be paraphrased to say that God had resurrected the born-again believers in their new inner person of heart and spirit and seated them with Christ Jesus in heaven now though their outer person of body and soul still walked on the earth (1 Pet. 3:4; Col. 3:1).

Jesus said, "Many shall come from east and west, and recline at the table with Abraham, Isaac, and Jacob in the kingdom of heaven" (Matt. 8:11). "Blessed are those who are invited to the marriage supper of the Lamb" (Rev. 19:9).

7. "Then those who feared the Lord [with awe and veneration] spoke to one another, and the Lord gave attention and heard it, and a book of remembrance was written before Him for those who fear [to dishonor or profane the name of] the Lord and who esteem His name" (Mal. 3:16).

8. Jesus told the people, "You belong to your father, the devil, and you want to carry out your father's desire" (John 8:44, NIV). Those who do not do what is right or love one another are "the children of the devil" (1 John 3:10).

9. The Lord said, "I will build a wall against her [unfaithful Israel] so that she cannot find her paths" (Hos. 2:6).

Moses told the people of the grave consequences of disobedience to God: "The Lord will scatter you among all the peoples... Among those nations you shall find no rest... but there the Lord will give you... failing of eyes and despair of soul" (Deut. 28:64–65). They would search futilely for the Lord among heathen people, like a blind man seeking his way in an unknown land.

10. "The Lord will create over the whole area of Mount Zion and over her assemblies a cloud by day, even smoke, and the brightness of a flaming fire by night; for over all the glory [of God] will be a canopy. There will be a shelter... and refuge and protection" (Isa. 4:5–6).

Zion is a symbol of God's people who obey Him out of reverential love. This prophecy about the reign of Christ promises full provision for those of spiritual Zion. It will be like His care during the wilderness journey in Moses' day (Ps. 132:13–14).

11. Christ strolled in fellowship with Adam and Eve before they sinned. They knew the sound of His walking (Gen. 3:8).

God calls Abraham "My friend" (Isa. 41:8). The Lord shared His heart with Abraham, saying, "Shall I hide from Abraham what I am about to do?" (Gen. 18:17).

12. Jesus said to His first disciples, "You shall see the heavens opened" (John 1:51).

The Bible calls the angels of God "stars" (Rev. 1:20; 12:4). The Lord Jesus calls Himself "the bright morning star" that arises to herald the dawn of His kingdom (Rev. 22:16). Daniel 12:3 speaks of certain saints who will shine as stars in heaven.

Paul said, "Our citizenship is in heaven, from which also we [in spirit] eagerly wait for a Savior, the Lord Jesus Christ" (Phil. 3:20).

13. The Lord Jesus promises the overcoming Christians of the church in Philadelphia (meaning brotherly love) a permanent place—"a pillar in the temple of My God." They "will not go out from it anymore" (Rev. 3:12). That eternal temple is the Father and the Son (Rev. 21:22). These saints will make their home within God forever.

14. The life of the inner person of every born-again believer has been resurrected with the risen Lord and "is hidden with Christ in God [the Father]" (Rom. 6:13; Eph. 2:5–6; Col. 3:3). One's response to this fact is to "keep seeking the things above, where Christ is" and to "set your mind on the things above, not on the things that are on earth" (Col. 3:1–2).

15. Jesus said, "In My Father's house are many dwelling places... for I go to prepare a place for you... that where I am, there you may be also" (John 14:2–3). Christ Jesus lives within the heart of His Father, though He also may appear elsewhere at times (John 1:18; Acts 7:56). Christians are destined to share the oneness between the Father and the Son (John 17:21–23; 2 Pet. 1:4).

16. In the Song of Solomon the betrothed one says to her beloved shepherd, representing Christ Jesus, "Come, my beloved, let us go out in the field... Let us rise early and go to the vineyards. Let us see whether the vine has budded and its blossoms have opened" (7:11–12). The Lord Jesus and His future bride are now together in all things on Earth. They are attentive to the signs of new spiritual growth and fruit bearing in others wherever they go.

Proclamation

"To walk among the stars" here means to fellowship [in spirit] with Christ Jesus and all of heaven.

"Rejoice, O righteous ones, your God is coming down to you. You will walk with Him as at the dawn of creation, and He will share with you as a man shares with his dearest friend.[11] He will reveal mysteries to you and fling open the portals of heaven, allowing you to walk among the stars.[12] From forever to forever, He is. From forever to forever, His goodness will be savored by those who love the Lord. Rejoice, you people of God. He is coming down to you, the light of His glory shining from His face, and you too will share His goodness with others to the glory of His name."

He continued, "Prepare, for He comes, and all eyes will see Him in you [His people], and you will be hidden, enfolded in the wings of His love—never to come out again.[13] Let the righteous rejoice!"

Living Above

To live above means that the inner person (the heart and the spirit) of the Christian is abiding in fellowship within the Father and the Son (1 Pet. 3:4; John 15:4; 1 John 1:3, 5–7).

He turned to me, "As for you, Anna, you have begun to live above.[14] You will no longer call Earth your home. When each day ends, you will return to your Father's house.[15] There you will rest.

"We will be together, My love. We will go into the fields that are white for harvest and into the vineyards to inspect the vines."[16] His hand reached out to me. "My beautiful bride, My chosen one," He said.

I took His hand, kissed it, and held it to my cheek.

He continued, "There is much to see, know, and understand. You have only begun, Anna. We will go higher, My love, ever higher.

"Right now," He said, "your work on Earth awaits." He bent down and gathered an armful of the rose of Sharon. "For you, My bride," placing them into my left arm.

"Thank You," I whispered, pressing the flowers to me.

The Holy Spirit

The Holy Spirit appeared on the path. He was turning gently, as an upward spiral of smoke might rise.

"The Holy Spirit has come to escort you, My love," He said. "Are you ready to return?"

"I am ready," I said to Jesus. I still was holding His hand. Reluctantly, I released it.

However, He held on to my hand. Looking deeply into my eyes, He said, "You have ravished My heart, My sister, My bride. You have ravished My heart."[17] Both of our eyes filled with tears. He released my hand. I took a step backward to show that I was ready to leave.

The circling wind of the Holy Spirit enveloped me. Instinctively, I closed my eyes. Through the whirling sound, I heard Jesus call, "You are My beloved!"

I responded, "And You are my Friend!"[18] I was choking back tears.

The Holy Spirit picked me up. Suddenly, He went "swish" down through the turf of Paradise. I did not want to look.

On Earth

When I opened my eyes, I was standing in the living room of our apartment in Florida. The flowers were gone. But the hope chests were piled up to, and then through, the ceiling as before.

The Holy Spirit swirled around me. His whirlwind left circles of supernatural fire on the floor. I held out my hands to feel the tiny, brilliant lights that whirled within the funnel. They tickled like sparks from sparklers.

"Oh, my Friend," I said to the Holy Spirit, "we will work together, will we not?" The light within the funnel brightened immensely in response. "I already miss Him," I confided. I reflected a moment. "It says that the

17. In the Song of Solomon, the shepherd lover (representing the Lord Jesus) says to the maiden, "You have made my heart beat faster, my sister, my bride; You have made my heart beat faster with a single glance of your eyes" (4:9).

18. In the Song of Solomon the maiden witnesses to other women about her dear shepherd (a type of Christ). She says, "This is my beloved and this is my friend" (5:16).

19. In Scripture, this is the prayer of the Holy Spirit and the church: "The Spirit and the bride say, 'Come.' And let the one who hears say 'Come.' And let the one who is thirsty come; let the one who wishes take the water of life without cost" (Rev. 22:17; cf. Isa. 55:1).

20. A flame of fire rested upon the head of every Christian gathered in the upper room on the Day of Pentecost (Acts 2:3, NKJV). This represented a share in the anointing of the Holy Spirit that fully rested upon the Lord Jesus (Acts 2:33; John 3:34).

21. Every true anointing includes "the fear of the Lord" (Isa. 11:1–3).

22. The Father answers the prayers of His Son, who is present when two or three members of His body on Earth agree together that His will alone be done in all matters (Matt. 18:19–20).

Who is closer to the heart of Jesus than the members of His bride who cry out for His coming to lift them up to heaven in their new bodies for the wedding (1 Thess. 4:16–17; Rev. 19:7)?

23. Please see note 23 of chapter 10.

24. "Christ was faithful as a Son over His [the Father's] house whose house we are" (Heb. 3:6).

God prophesied through Isaiah that Eliakim would become a faithful steward over the king's household to replace the unworthy Shebna. God said, "Then I will set the key of the house of David on his [Eliakim's] shoulder. When he opens, no one will shut. When he shuts, no one will open" (Isa. 22:15, 19–20, 22). Eliakim is a type of the Lord Jesus who said the same words about His authority (Rev. 3:7).

25. Isaiah prophesied of a coming day when the glory of the divine love will be seen under a *chuppah* or betrothal canopy. "For over all the glory will be a canopy" (Isa. 4:5). This verse points to the time when the Lord Jesus is present to betroth His own to Himself (Hos. 2:19–20).

26. Now the bride prays for a second coming down to Earth of Christ His Son with manifest glory and hosts of angels (Matt. 16:27).

27. The last book of the Bible closes with Christ Jesus saying, "Yes, I am coming quickly." John then prays, "Come, Lord Jesus" (Rev. 22:20).

Spirit and the bride say, 'Come.'"[19] He joined me in saying, "Come [to Christ]."

This seemed to please Him greatly. The sparklers plumed into a fiery whirlwind of God. He began to ascend through the ceiling. As He rose, He burned through the roof, opening the entire apartment to heaven.

I watched Him rise. He was spectacular. I thought of the children of Israel and the pillar of fire by night.

A *flame of fire on the shoulders* stands for the authority of the Holy Spirit in prayer that is upon the Lord Jesus to open or to shut (Rom. 8:26–27; Isa. 22:22; Rev. 3:7). He exercises that authority through His church (Matt. 16:19).

Then I realized that the Holy Spirit had left behind Him flames of fire on my head and on both of my shoulders.[20] They formed a canopy. Jesus had spoken of a covering of goodness and of glory. Was this canopy of fire an anointing that would rest upon those who fear the Lord?[21] Had the time come for His bride to call Him down?[22] As the heavenly council had prayed, was it time for the Lord to begin the end?[23]

I exploded with hope and joyous anticipation. Looking into the open heavens, I affirmed:

Declaration

The weight of glory of our God
Rests upon His head.
And keys of the greater David
Are on His shoulders spread.[24]
Fire is burning up above
And fire on either side.
Beneath this canopy of Love
His presence does abide.[25]

The glory of God the Father is the awesome splendor of the goodness of His love as manifested in Christ Jesus (Exod. 33:18–19; John 15:9).

Call of the Bride

Come down, our glorious Majesty!
Come down, our righteous King!
Descend in holy fire once more
With hosts past numbering.[26]

God descended the first time to Earth in His glory on Mount Sinai (Exod. 19:11, 16). Verse 18 says that He "descended upon it in fire."

I raised my arms toward the open heavens and with great yearning, called again:

Come down, our glorious Majesty!
Come down, our righteous King!
Descend in holy fire once more
With hosts past numbering!

"Come, Lord Jesus."[27]

Appendix A

Glossary of Principal Words

The meaning of certain key words as they are used in the Scripture notes are as follows:

Believer (a Christian). Every person who has been born again spiritually through the Holy Spirit and the water of the Word concerning Christ (John 3:3, 5; Eph. 5:26; Rom. 10:17).

Born again (new birth). Every person who believes the good news concerning Christ Jesus and confesses Him as Lord receives His eternal life to live by as a new creation of God (Rom. 10:9–10; 2 Cor. 5:17; 1 John 5:11–12).

Bride of Christ. At the moment every person receives Christ, the Father gives that one to be betrothed to His Son (John 6:37–39). The eventual bridal joining is the highest possible spiritual bond for eternity (John 17:24; Rev. 19:7).

Christ in us. The degree of the Lord Jesus being formed within the believer on Earth is dependent upon the degree that one's heart and spirit abides in Him in heaven (Gal. 4:19; John 15:4–5; Col. 3:3).

Crosses of Christ. There are two crosses of Christ in Scripture:

At Calvary He died once to obtain forgiveness for sins and release from the power of the sin nature (Rom. 6:5–7; 2 Cor. 5:14–15).

From eternity, Christ has voluntarily denied His own self-expression in order that He might reveal His Father's heart and soul (Phil. 2:5–7; John 12:44–45). Every disciple of the Lord must carry the same kind of cross in denying one's outer self-expression so that Jesus's mind, emotions, and will may be manifested in one's soul (Matt. 16:24–25).

Death. The spiritual state of a person being separated from the eternal life in Christ that God created that one to live (Eph. 2:1, 5).

Disciple (of Christ). A believer who denies his own soul life that Jesus may live His soul life in that one (Matt. 16:24–25). The disciple has laid aside all that is of oneself in order to have Christ Jesus as one's all (Luke 14:33; Col. 3:11).

Eagle Christians. These believers are given revelations from God to communicate to people on Earth for their "edification and exhortation [encouragement] and consolation" (1 Cor. 14:3). Divinely inspired utterance or writing through a human being is called prophecy (2 Pet. 1:21).

Eternal life. God's own life that is given to the Christian through Christ Jesus (1 John 5:11).

Flesh. The corrupt human nature with which all persons are born (Ps. 51:5; Rom. 7:18). God said that the human race "is flesh" (Gen. 6:3). That nature will be present in our bodies as long as we live on Earth.

Glory of God. The splendor of the goodness of His inestimable love (Exod. 33:18–19).

Grace. The favor of God's goodwill freely given through Christ to those who are utterly undeserving (Eph. 2:8–9; John 1:17).

Heart. The spiritual faculty with our strongest motivation, the seat of character and the things we treasure, and the place where the gifts of faith, hope, and love operate (1 Chron. 16:9; Matt. 12:34–35).

In Christ. The Holy Spirit puts the human spirit of the believer into union with Christ's resurrected human spirit within that one. The bond is meant to grow so that the two spirits become one (1 Cor. 6:17).

Living above. The Holy Spirit makes it possible for the believer's heart and spirit (the inner person) to abide with Christ in the Father, though one's body and soul (the outer person) are on the earth (Col. 3:1–3; John 17:24).

Nature (human). All of us are born with the law of sin that operates in the members of the physical body and also affects the soul (mind, emotions, and will) (Eph. 2:3; Rom. 7:23). Only the Spirit of life in Christ Jesus sets a person free from the functioning of this fixed principle of evil (Rom. 8:2).

Oneness (deeper union). The Father and the Son share one life (John 10:30). They desire all born-again believers to be perfected in the same union with them (John 17:21–23).

Overcomer. A Christian who overcomes is one whose union with Christ Jesus results in sharing in the Lord's victory over all the enemies of God (1 John 4:3–4; Rev. 2:7, 11, 17, 26–28; 3:5, 12, 21).

Redeemed (the). Christians who are now living in heaven (Eph. 4:30; Heb. 9:12).

Second heaven. The territory below God's heaven where Satan and his host have their headquarters for a time until they are cast down to the earth (Rev. 12:7–9).

Self (new). The inner spiritual person (heart and spirit) that is being formed in the image and likeness of Christ (Col. 3:10; Eph. 4:24).

Sin. To sin is to fall short of the glory of God in Christ Jesus that the Father created us to reflect (Rom. 3:23; 2 Cor. 3:18).

Soul. The human soul is comprised mainly of the mind, emotions, and will. The natural soul expresses itself through the body as the old psychological self or individuality of the person that is to be laid aside (Prov. 2:10; Ps. 84:2; Matt. 22:37; 1 Cor. 15:45; Eph. 4:22).

Spirit (human). The spirit is the faculty that the Holy Spirit enables to know the things of God through worship, fellowship, conscience, and intuition or revelation (direct sensing of truth independently of outside influence) (John 4:23; 1 John 1:3; Heb. 10:23; 1 Cor. 2:9–13).

World (the). Human society that is masterminded by Satan (1 John 5:19; Eph. 2:2–3). His kingdom involves all fields of human endeavor where God is not honored and obeyed (Eph. 6:12; John 14:30). The basic deception of this satanic system is that people can live independently of God (Ps. 10:4).

Appendix B

Mountains of Spices

Below are a list of spices and their descriptions used in the preparation of the bride.

Myrrh: Obedience Unto Death

The spice myrrh comes from a thick gum that flows from the pierced bark of a knotted, thorny tree. The gum hardens into red drops called "tears." The word myrrh comes from a primary root in Hebrew meaning "bitter suffering." It represents the bitter sufferings of Jesus as a man on Earth.

The Greek word denotes a spice used in burial. In the New Testament, the Magi brought gifts to the Christ child, including myrrh, a foreshadowing of His suffering and bitter death on the cross (Matt. 2:11).

The original sense of the word is that of "distilling in drops"—a slow process of purification. Christ lived a life of distillation, for "although He was a Son, He learned obedience from the things which He suffered" (Heb. 5:8). Jesus emptied Himself of His own will, and this culminated in obedience to the point of death on a cross (Phil. 2:7–8). Likewise, each child of God is called to smell of the myrrh of distillation day after day by denying his or her own self life and walking in obedience to the will of Christ alone (Matt. 16:24–25; 6:10).

Cinnamon: Holiness of Heart

The primary root of the word *cinnamon* means "emitting an odor." The spice is harvested in quills of the fragrant, inner bark of a tree of the laurel family.

In the Song of Solomon, cinnamon grows in the locked garden that Jesus says is "my sister, my bride" (Song of Sol. 4:12–14). The new heart of each believer is a garden with fragrant spices—a heart enclosed and set apart for the Lord Jesus alone—as the heart of Jesus is undivided in His consecration unto the Father alone (2 Chron. 16:9; Luke 10:22).

In Proverbs 7:10, the adulterous woman, "dressed as a harlot and cunning of heart," has sprinkled her bed with fragrant spices that also include cinnamon (Prov. 7:17), a counterfeit of the heart of the bride. She flings her heart open to embrace every sort of spiritual adultery.

In both instances, cinnamon emits an odor: either of consecration in holiness unto the Lord (Lev. 8:12), which is sweet in the nostrils of God, or the corrupted odor of deception and seduction (Prov. 7:17–19), which is a stench to Him.

Cinnamon is one of the spices in the holy anointing oil that was used to set apart people and things as holy for God's use alone (Exod. 30:23–25, 30). Jesus and those in Him are priests who are "holy to the LORD" (Exod. 28:36).

Cassia: Homage to God Alone

Cassia is also from the laurel family, smelling and tasting somewhat like cinnamon but considered inferior to it, a humbler plant. God exalts this lowly tree to provide one of the four spices used in the holy anointing oil (Exod. 30:23–25). Its name, representative of its properties, comes from a root word meaning "to bow down," "to stoop," "to pay homage," depicting the humility of Christ before His Father. Jesus said, "I honor My Father...I do not seek My glory" (John 8:49–50). Although as believers we are to show ourselves humble before others (1 Pet. 2:17; 5:5), we are to bow down in worship to God alone (2 Kings 17:35–36; Matt. 4:10).

The word *homage* means "to show a reverential fidelity and respect" (Exod. 34:8). We, like Jesus, are to reverence our Father with holy fear and veneration, treating Him as sacred in the sight of others (Num. 20:10–12; Ezek. 36:22–23) and in the depths of our hearts (1 Pet. 3:15).

Calamus: Uprightness

Calamus is a fragrant oil derived from a marsh plant known as sweet flag. The Hebrew word for this spice means "a stalk or a reed (as erect)," or upright. We see a biblical meaning of *upright* in the first instance of that Hebrew word in Scripture, being translated "right in [God's] sight" (Exod. 15:26). God's poetic name for His people Israel was "Jeshurun," a word meaning "upright one" (Isa. 44:2). In His Father's eyes the Lord Jesus was upright in Himself (Ps. 25:8), in His words (Ps. 33:4), and in His ways (Isa. 11:4).

The second biblical meaning of *upright* includes also that of being smooth and straight, that is, without deviation, a true and direct course. Everything about Jesus Christ is in true alignment with who the Father is. There is no obstruction or unevenness in Him to hinder the clear revelation of God (John 5:30; 14:9). Christians, like John the Baptist, are to "make straight the way of the Lord" (John 1:23), so that God's

Son may be seen and heard through them without any obstacle of their "flesh" (Rom. 7:25; Gal. 6:8). Isaiah cried, "O Upright One, make the path of the righteous level" (Isa. 26:7), so that their walk is straight toward God. Christ alone is upright or righteous in the Father's eyes, and we in Him (2 Cor. 5:21; Rom. 10:3–4).

Henna: Forgiveness

Henna, translated "camphire" in the King James Version, comes from a tree whose leaves yield a stain used as a red dye. The Hebrew word means "to cover, a redemption price, a ransom." The primary root of the word means "to forgive" (Song of Sol. 4:13; Isa. 43:3). Therefore this fragrant spice signifies the shed blood of Christ on Calvary as our ransom from sin and death (1 Tim. 2:6).

In the Middle East on the night before a wedding, the bride has henna paste bound to the palms of her hands and soles of her feet. In Christian symbolism her hands (works) and feet (walk) are to exude the sweet smell of forgiveness and show forth the red stain of His shed blood on the cross. Christ calls His bride to walk continually cleansed through the forgiveness won for her by her Bridegroom (1 John 1:9) and to pass that forgiveness on to others (Matt. 6:14–15).

Aloes: Intimacy

The word *aloes* is from an Arabic word meaning "little tents," descriptive of the three-cornered shape of the capsules of the lignaloes tree whose resin is fragrant.

The small, pointed tent is the type spoken of in 2 Samuel 16:22, meaning a "pleasure tent on the housetop" or a "bridal tent": a place of intimacy. Outside the camp Moses pitched a private tent of meeting where God spoke to him face to face (Exod. 33:7, 9, 11). David also erected such a tent on Mount Zion for the ark of the covenant, where he could be as close as possible to the presence of the Lord (2 Sam. 6:17). Jesus has perfect intimacy with His Father, an intimacy for which the Holy Spirit is preparing us and into which we are being perfected: "As Thou, Father, art in Me, and I in Thou, that they also may be in Us" (John 17:21, 23). Our constant heart's cry should be to go with Him into the intimacy of the bridal tent that He might know us and we Him (John 10:14–15). Only through intimacy in spirit with Jesus do we bring forth spiritual children for His kingdom (1 John 1:3; Gal. 4:19; 1 Cor. 4:15).

Nard: Light

Pure nard is a very costly and precious spice (John 12:3). It is produced from the hairy, dried stems of a plant grown at heights up to thirteen thousand feet in the Himalayas in the purer, stronger light of the sun. The word *nard* (*spikenard* in the King James Version) is from the Hebrew root meaning "light."

God's reality in heaven is visible by the pure, uncreated light of His nature. He is light, and there is no darkness in Him (1 John 1:5). His Son, Christ Jesus, is the true light from the Father (John 1:9)—the reality of God made visible in a human being (John 1:14). There is no darkness of sin in Him, for He walks in the light of His Father (John 8:29; 1 John 1:7).

Christians are to become partakers of the divine nature and manifest the light of Christ (2 Pet. 1:4; Matt. 5:16), living their lives before God and man truthfully, being the same person outwardly as they are within their hearts. We are to be the transparent lamps through which the heavenly light of Christ shines (Rom. 13:12). As bearers of His light, we are to cooperate with the Holy Spirit as He takes His stand against all darkness within us (Eph. 5:8). Eventually even our shadows are to be so infused with the light of God that as we pass, the sick are healed (Acts 5:15).

Saffron: Faith

Saffron is a very expensive spice. It is collected from the three tiny, orange-red stigmas of the flowers of the crocus sativus. About two hundred twenty-five thousand of these stigmas must be picked out by hand to produce one pound of saffron. This extremely valuable spice is yellow-gold in color when dried, and it is literally worth its weight in gold. Medicinally it strengthens the heart. For these reasons, saffron is symbolic of the faith Jesus Christ held in His heart toward His heavenly Father (Heb. 2:13). His faith in His Father's words to Him was tested and perfected (Heb. 12:2) throughout His ministry years on Earth, beginning with the first temptation in the wilderness (Matt. 4:3–4).

The Son imparts His faith to His disciples, and it is by grace through faith we are saved (Eph. 2:8). By faith we live (Hab. 2:4), and it is perfected faith that Christ is seeking when He returns. "However, when the Son of man comes, will He find (persistence in) the faith on the earth?" (Luke 18:8, AMP). Therefore we rejoice in trials so "that the proof of [our] faith, being more precious than gold which is perishable, even though tested by fire, may be found to result in praise and glory and honor at the revelation of Jesus Christ" (1 Pet. 1:7).

Frankincense: Purity

Frankincense is a gum resin that flows from the inner wood of a tree resembling the mountain ash. The word in Hebrew comes from a root meaning "pure" or "white" because of the glittering, milk-white, resin "tears." These tears, when burned, give off a strong, balsam odor. The finest incense contains pure frankincense, rising in white smoke to symbolize the prayers that ascend to the throne of God (Rev. 8:3–4). Frankincense was part of the holy incense used in the desert tabernacle (Exod. 30:34–35). It represents the purity of the consecration of the resurrected Christ in His ministry on our behalf before the Father (Rom. 8:34). Our Lord Jesus has sanctified or set Himself apart (John 17:19) unto the Father as the "holy, innocent, undefiled" high priest (Heb. 7:25–26) in order to "redeem us from every lawless deed and to purify for Himself a people for His own possession" (Titus 2:14).

When Christ appears in glory, "we shall be like Him, because we shall see Him just as He is. And everyone who has this hope fixed on Him purifies himself, just as He is pure" (1 John 3:2–3).

Onycha: Authority

The Hebrew word for the rockrose, *onycha*, comes from the root meaning "to roar" or "a lion." The resurrected Lord is the Lion of the tribe of Judah, who has been given all authority in heaven and on Earth (Rev. 5:5; Matt. 28:18), with power "to subject all things to Himself" (Phil. 3:21). The Father's authority through Christ is symbolized in the roar of the lion in Hosea 11:10–11: "They will follow behind Yahweh; He will be roaring like a lion—how he will roar!...and his sons will come speeding from Egypt like a bird, speeding from the land of Assyria like a dove" (JB).

The smell emitted by onycha in the holy incense not only testifies to Christ's authority, His lordship here on earth, but as it rises through the mid-heaven, daily it reminds Satan that he is a defeated foe. Christians share in Christ's authority "to tread upon...all the power of the enemy" in His name (Luke 10:19).

Galbanum: Worship, Praise, Adoration, and Thanksgiving

The Hebrew for the word *galbanum* is from a primary root meaning "fat" or "the richest or choicest part" or "the best." The spice is a gum resin collected by slicing the stems of the plants of the ferula family. Fat was one of the two parts of the animal sacrifice that was entirely reserved for God (Gen. 4:4; Lev. 3:16–17). It signified the finest offering that could be given to Him, that which was beyond all else in pleasing Him: joyful worship "in spirit and truth" (Deut. 28:47; John 4:23) and joyful praise and thanksgiving to honor the Father by His Son and by His disciples (Ps. 50:23; Heb. 2:12; 13:15).

Satan promised "the kingdoms of the world and their glory" to Christ in exchange for His worship (Matt. 4:8–9). The enemy drives unbelievers to seek "the fat" of this age—to receive praise, worship, gratitude, and adoration for themselves (John 5:44). In direct opposition to the Word of God (Isa. 42:8), many in the body of Christ are spiritually overweight from taking to themselves that which belongs to God alone: the fat.

Stacte: Truth With Mercy

Stacte is from the root meaning "to fall in drops" gently or "to prophesy" words from God. Since "the testimony of Jesus is the spirit of prophecy" (Rev. 19:10), the holy incense (of which this spice is a part [Exod. 30:34–35]) prophesied of Christ to God, but it also struck terror into those who were enemies of Christ (Josh. 2:9–11). The aroma of the incense rising from the tabernacle ascended to the throne in heaven and went throughout the camp. It also could be smelled for miles, even across the Jordan by the Canaanites (2 Cor. 2:15–16). It testified to the truth of salvation in Christ alone (John 14:6), for our Father wishes all men to be saved (1 Tim. 2:3–4). The truth of Christ, of which stacte prophesied, "fell in drops" or softly, mercifully. Proverbs 16:6 says, "By mercy and truth iniquity is purged: and by the fear of the LORD men depart from evil" (KJV). Rahab the harlot must have been among those who smelled this prophetic testimony of Jesus—the Way, the Truth, and the Life—and who feared God and believed into the salvation He provided (Josh. 2:11–13).